System and Story

Princeton Theological Monograph Series

K. C. Hanson, Charles M. Collier, and
D. Christopher Spinks, Series Editors

System and Story

Narrative Critique and Construction in Theology

GALE HEIDE

PICKWICK Publications · Eugene, Oregon

SYSTEM AND STORY
Narrative Critique and Construction in Theology

Princeton Theological Monograph Series 87

www.wipfandstock.com

Pickwick Publications
A Division of Wipf and Stock Publishers
199 West 8th Avenue, Suite 3
Eugene, Oregon 97401

ISBN 13: 978-1-55635-498-4

Cataloging-in-Publication data:

Heide, Gale.

System and story: narrative critique and construction in theology / Gale Heide.

xxviii + 306 p. ; 23 cm. — Includes bibliographical reference.

Princeton Theological Monograph Series 87

ISBN 13: 978-1-55635-498-4

1. Storytelling—Religious aspects—Christianity. 2. Hauerwas, Stanley, 1940– 3. Luther, Martin, 1483–1546. I. Title. II. Series.

BT83.78 H40 2009

Manufactured in the U.S.A.

For Mary

Waiting

Expectation is patience in lengthened silence;
Endurance compels belief;
Years hold the promise of completion;
Yet, years are lived every hour.

Contents

Acknowledgements

How does one thank his friends for teaching him to read and think, and even more, to become like the ones he imitates? To thank them often implies attainment, which is to say, gratitude is sometimes a lie. I do not wish to claim any sense of accomplishment, since my best is still but mere imitation. Thankfully, such is the lot of every Christian. Every testimony of progress must always be qualified by the standard of perfection, Jesus himself. They are further qualified by the knowledge that everything we know, or claim to know, is learned. We stand as a community of learners, awaiting the final revelation of knowledge that is always beyond our reach. Yet, we continue to pursue knowing. From one generation to the next, teachers do what they can to help those of us who pretend to understand and only begin to gain a glimpse of knowing when we admit ignorance. My teachers, Stanley Hauerwas, Bruce Ware, Gerry Breashears, and others whose names are found in the footnotes of the following pages, did a marvelous work in presenting their best understanding for me to observe and grasp. Instead of offering thanks for all I have gained, I humbly request forbearance for all I have missed. My hope is that the pages I've pored over will be sufficiently understandable for critique and correction. Perhaps that is the greatest gift I can offer in return to those who have invested in my mind and life: a continued craving to learn.

My time has never been my own. As I have discovered the joy of marriage and having children, I find that the time to write is truly a gift from many people. I owe my greatest debt to Mary and our girls, Trina and Alethia. They have spent hours looking at the back of my head and wondering what it was all finally going to accomplish. Pages of words hardly seem like a triumph and certainly cannot substitute for a listening ear or eyes that understand. Their gift of time and encouragement to me has made finishing this project an urgent privilege. Further, it has trained me to work and play better. Playing with my children is a skill of which I need constant reminding. They have afforded me great kind-

x   *Acknowledgements*

ness through their patience as I have occasionally needed retraining. My wife's patience has run much deeper, as she has waited years for me to give her my attention in more than passing glances. I fear with more learning comes less time, and she has borne such a realization with such a grace as can only be described as saintly. Perhaps, time is best equated with the meaning of our lives. Our lives are owned by the friends with whom we invest our worship. This is the gift we offer a Lord who has everything. Humility has never seemed so inadequate a description!

Abbreviations

AsTJ	Asbury Theological Journal
ETL	Ephemerides theologicae lovanienses
EvQ	Evangelical Quarterly
ICC	International Critical Commentary
JAAR	Journal of the American Academy of Religion
NICNT	New International Commentary on the New Testament
NIGTC	New International Greek Testament Commentary
SJT	Scottish Journal of Theology
TDNT	Theological Dictionary of the New Testament. Edited by G. Kittel and G. Fredrick. Translated by G. W. Bromiley. 10 vols.
ThTo	Theology Today
TNTC	Tyndale New Testament Commentaries
WBC	Word Biblical Commentary

Introduction

ONE OF THE MORE INTERESTING CONTEMPORARY DEBATES IN THEOLOGY centers on the epistemological appropriateness of using system as a hermeneutical device for theological investigation and construction. Much of this debate centers on the perceived reliance of systematicians on the epistemological assumptions of modernity, which may include such things as rationalism,[1] foundationalism,[2] and a correspondence theory of truth.[3] The modern theological enterprise, including these

---

1. Rationalism is here understood as a confidence in "a priori reason to grasp substantial truths about the world" (Williams, "Rationalism," 69–75). Included in such a description of rationalism would be a preference for natural science and a more scientific metaphysic in discovering truth and knowledge of theological realities. Likewise, theological truths may be limited to the natural, denying any sense of the supernatural. Many theologians would agree that a rationalistic approach to the truths of God is a limited approach, denying the value of revelation, or even the reality of revelation. For example, see Nicholas Lash's critique of Enlightenment thought, where his concern centers primarily on the issue of priority being granted in the church and theology to rationality over faith and practice. Cf. Lash, *Beginning and End of 'Religion,'* 24.

2. Foundationalism may be best described as "[A] theory about knowledge. More specifically, it is a theory about how claims to know can be justified. When we seek to justify a belief, we do so by relating it to (basing it upon, deriving it from) other beliefs. If these other beliefs are called into question, then they too must be justified. Foundationalists insist that this chain of justifications must stop somewhere: neither must it be circular nor must it constitute an infinite regress. Thus, the regress must end in a 'foundation' of beliefs that cannot themselves be called into question." Hauerwas et al., *Theology Without Foundations*, 9. While Murphy traces this back, at least, to Descartes' rejection of his education and the rebuilding of his epistemology on what he believed could be known at a more purely subjective level—"I think," this is fleshed out in modern theology in the attempt to justify all theological knowledge on a grounding that is acceptable to all, or self-evident. As will be seen below, Hauerwas is particularly critical of such attempts because they tend to compromise the nature of the knowledge in question. In other words, foundationalism reduces the life and history of Jesus to mere principles or a body of information. Cf. Kirkham, *Theories of Truth*, 213–15.

3. The correspondence theory of truth is the belief that "'truth consists in some form of correspondence between belief and fact' against the theory of the absolute idealists that 'truth consists in coherence' that is, that the more our beliefs hang together in a system, the truer they are." See Prior, "Correspondence Theory of Truth," 223–32.

metaphysical issues of modernism, is variably called into question by
narrative theologians. These theologians have been identified as (or
can be accurately considered) postmodern or postliberal because of
their self-professed attempts to avoid designated modern and liberal
governing assumptions in theology. This is the case in spite of the fact
that some of these working assumptions (e.g., a correspondence theory
of truth) may also have been held in other periods in history, e.g., the
ancient, medieval, renaissance, and reformation periods. Many of these
postliberal and postmodern theologians propose that theology is more
appropriately pursued in a manner similar to the recounting of a story,
with emphasis placed upon the continuity of the Christian community
with tradition rather than on the veracity of statements purported to
represent the universal reality of some object. Some even make the case
that story, or narrative, is the best avenue for theology, since "the structure of human consciousness is necessarily narrative."[4] For postliberals,
doctrine may continue to have a function as a linguistic guide to the
Christian community,[5] or it may serve as a partner with action in a dialectic of metaphysics and narrative.[6] It may also simply be an outmoded

---

The rejection of a correspondence theory and the embracing of coherence are made
somewhat explicit by Hauerwas in *Theology Without Foundations*, 12–15. Though the
Introduction there is written by Nancey Murphy, Hauerwas was one of the editors of
this work, and would seemingly be included in her occasional "we." It is interesting to
note that though Hauerwas objects strenuously to the theologian's capacity to know
anything in a purely factual or corresponding manner, he is by no means an idealist.
In other words, though Hauerwas and the idealists, such as Kant or Hegel, may share a
critical stance toward correspondence, they do not seem to share as strong an embrace
for coherence as one might expect. In fact, as will be seen below, Hauerwas' strongest
critique of systematics in its theological or philosophical form is against Kant. Nicholas
Lash seems a bit more willing to embrace coherence with his notion of theology still
needing to "hang together" in some sense; however, he is, on the other hand, critical of
the tendency in theology to remain aloof of factual accountability. See Lash, *Theology
on the Way to Emmaus*, x.

4. Lauritzen, "Is 'Narrative' Really a Panacea?" 329. Lauritzen is here summarizing the beliefs of Metz with regard to the necessity of narrative. He makes the further
case that both Hauerwas and Metz have, at least, an implicit anthropology/psychology
grounding such necessity.

5. Lindbeck, *Nature of Doctrine*.

6. Nicholas Lash is perhaps the most articulate proponent of such a view. For a
summary of his dialectic and its function, see my "The Nascent Noeticism of Narrative
Theology," 466–71.

vestige of Enlightenment rationalism.[7] Whatever the case, postliberals have been distinctly critical of the pursuits of systematicians.

While the discussion regarding the historicity of system may provide some helpful inroads into how system, or some variation of system (logical structure, order, pedagogy, or the like) is best understood and contextualized as a theological tool in its various appearances throughout history, resolving the historical question does little to answer the debate of recent years regarding the appropriateness of system in theology.[8] This debate is the subject to which the attention of this study will be devoted.

The recent issue centers specifically on epistemological issues, but the import of the debate is far reaching in its effect on the church. The larger concern centers on the value of theology for the church, particularly for the laity of the church who participate in the activities of worship and Christian life. If theology remains an academic discipline, as critics of system accuse systematicians of advocating, then its value is more purely for the theological elite and assists the church only in obtaining appropriate limitations for reflection, or in providing information, with the epistemological expectation that information constitutes knowledge. The epistemology associated with such a project construes knowledge as discovered primarily in cognitive recognition or apprehension. The activities or practices associated with living the Christian life (e.g., moral theology) are but a consequence of prior thought. Appropriate thinking will lead, perhaps even naturally, to appropriate action; but cognitive apprehension remains the primary focus. Within such a scenario, theology then becomes merely a mental discipline, opening itself to the criticism of bearing gnostic tendencies.[9]

The intriguing answer offered in contrast to systematic theology's transformation of theology into a body of knowledge is found in the critique and constructive work of narrative theology. Here, an attempt is being made to relate theology more closely to the church by epistemologically redefining theology as action. Since narrative theologians

7. Stanley Hauerwas is one of the better-known critics of Kant and of all those who exemplify the rationalistic tendencies of Enlightenment thought. Due attention will be given below to Hauerwas' critique of Kant.

8. For a discussion of the historical issues surrounding the use of system, see my *Timeless Truth in the Hands of History*.

9. E.g., see Hauerwas, *Wilderness Wanderings*, 42.

are attempting a paradigm shift, of sorts, in theology, it is incumbent upon them to demonstrate what this means epistemologically. As will be seen in the chapters below, some have taken up this challenge; others have merely given it a "sidelong glance."[10] However, in most cases of narrative theology, the epistemology of modernism is reversed so that action is primary and thought is secondary for "knowing" or "doing" theology. This allows the life of the church to become the locus of theology. The everyday activities of being church are understood as the primary substance of theology, while dogmatic or doctrinal theology takes on a more regulatory role for guiding and correcting action. Thus, the life of the people who constitute the church becomes primary, or in theological terms, ecclesiology takes precedence as the paradigm through which theology is rightly constructed and understood. Action, then, becomes epistemologically prior to thought.[11]

Many narrative theologians believe the modern/liberal enterprise remains largely encapsulated in the systematic pursuits of theology. As a consequence, they have aimed their critical efforts at system, defined according to a more philosophical/rationalistic description. System seems to represent best for them the manner in which modern epistemology (i.e., thought is prior to action) has been integrated into theology. Therefore, much of the debate centers on system as an appropriate method for theology.

Since the alternative to system typically offered is narrative theology, there is the further question of the systematic nature of story, or alternately, the narrative nature of systematics. Perhaps one could even pursue the way in which system and story function together in most theologies. Harry Huebner asserts that "story does not exclude system. It requires it."[12] On the other hand, Stanley Hauerwas proposes that we must "learn to write theology in a way that denies that theology can be systematic."[13] While it may be beyond the scope of this study to theoretically propose an answer to the question of interdependence be-

10. Hauerwas, "Why the Truth demands Truthfulness," 141.

11. As will be seen below, narrative theology's preference for action seems overstated. Instead, this study proposes a reciprocity between thought and action, in which each has opportunity to inform the other. This allows for a more circular relationship of thought to action, rather than a linear relationship in one direction or the other.

12. Huebner, "Within the Limits of Story Alone?" 161.

13. Hauerwas, *After Christendom?* 182.

tween story and system, time will be devoted to demonstrating the ways
in which the subjects of this study, especially Hauerwas, seem to make
heavy use of narrative without ever truly leaving certain systematic tendencies behind. This seems to open the door for the possible inclusion
of more systematic elements, even in a narrative theology intended to
avoid or replace a more rigid system. In the end, it seems as though
a certain amount of system, perhaps as merely a coherentist effort at
maintaining consistency with Scripture, is inescapable in theology.

Because of the similarities in their critique of modernism, postmodernists are often lumped together as singular in their voice against
the various attributes of Enlightenment modernism. Thus, some voices
in Emergent theology are sometimes associated with postliberal thinkers like Hauerwas.[14] This especially becomes the case when the critique
is more narrowly focused on system. Leaning on the narrative critique
of system, Emergent thinker Brian McLaren draws us into his anthropology by way of a conversation in his novel *A New Kind of Christian:
A Tale of Two Friends on a Spiritual Journey*, "According to the Bible,
humans shall not live by systems and abstractions alone but also by stories and poetry and proverbs and mystery."[15] Don Carson has helpfully
differentiated amongst the critiques of modernism by various scholars,
pointing out that the critics of modernism cannot paint with quite such
a broad brush, as Emergent thinkers seem prone to do.[16] Carson demonstrates that the Emergent reaction against Enlightenment thought
centers primarily on a rejection of absolutism, or against the universal
"metanarrative" of those who would boast depicting universal truth.[17]

14. E.g., see R. S. Smith's *Truth and The New Kind of Christian*, esp. chs. 2–3, and
esp. 64–65, 70, 137, 151. Smith creates a direct link between Hauerwas and Emergent
voices like Brian McLaren and Tony Jones. Though certainly some similarities may
exist, I remain unconvinced that having the same enemy qualifies as friendship. As will
be seen below, Hauerwas wishes to remain true to a theological enterprise and is hardly
relativistic. Unless, of course, Smith is ready to call the permeating Christian commitment to the lordship of Jesus found in Scripture (i.e., the absolute truth of revelation)
something akin to relativism. In actuality, it is those who are leaving revelation behind
in favor of a contextless "objective" truth who have relativised the truth of revelation to
the Enlightenment culture.

15. McLaren, *A New Kind of Christian*, 159. Of course, little development is made of
the reference to systems and abstractions, which seem summarily dismissed in many
Emergent approaches.

16. Carson, *Becoming Conversant with the Emergent Church*, 71.

17. Ibid., 71–86.

Further, the Emergent critique seems to stem from a preference for history. While such a preference is somewhat inevitable, given that human existence is necessarily historical, the difficulty arises when such a critique lapses into relativism.

It is on this point of relativism that the difference between someone like Hauerwas and the Emergent movement becomes important. The Emergent movement has consistently moved ahead as a voice critical of Enlightenment modernism, offering its own version of narrative theology in place of any constructive effort. However, very little careful thought girds up the narrative appeal to aesthetics (e.g., language or story) as epistemology. Instead, stories are simply offered up *as* the best theological option. While I grant that this seems consistent with the more rigid narrative approach, even Hauerwas remains committed to certain theological presuppositions that he regards as critical for the story to remain true to the Christian tradition. Like Barth, Hauerwas depends on a strong sense of revelation, particularly in the incarnation. Though a careful critique of Hauerwas will show that he has not sufficiently developed his display of revelational support, nevertheless, his high regard for revelation as an epistemological category seems distinct from many of the Emergent voices. Some major Emergent thinkers seem to substitute anthropology in place of revelation, allowing their ecclesiology to become mere anthropology (i.e., community for community's sake). Hauerwas is also guilty of this, but he makes many attempts to overcome it. Indeed, while Emergent theology seems at this point irrecoverable from its preference for anthropology, it seems Hauerwas's work can easily escape such a criticism, when grounded in the absolutism of the revelation he seems to prefer. Certain doctrinal notions (like sin) still loom rather large for him. Hauerwas is not opposed to absolutism or universalism *per se*. Instead, as will be seen below, he is simply opposed to the ahistorical absolutism visible in various bastions of Enlightenment liberalism.[18] His critique of Enlightenment

18. Interestingly, it is in the snare of liberalism that some defenders of Enlightenment modernism become entrapped. For instance, despite claims to understand and appreciate the historical nature of epistemology, D. A. Carson still "trumps" other claims to truth by appealing to "objective truth," which seems for him to be a larger category than revelation. See Carson, *Becoming Conversant*, 192–93. More will be said below on the problematic nature of depicting truth according to external verification that takes precedence over revelation. Truth that is removed from context ignores (destroys?) the universality of the Incarnation. Smith (*Truth and the New Kind of Christian*, 145–55)

modernism is distinct from that of many Emergent voices. Thus, his answer is also crafted in terms allowing for an approach more aligned with historical theology's preference for Scripture.

For the sake of producing a formative study that may be used in circles larger than just a discussion of Emergent theology, the focus of this study will center on a more philosophical narrative critique of system, and on the development of the narrative epistemology offered in place of system. The bulk of the study will be an examination of Hauerwas's rejection of the modernist epistemology associated with system. While some narrative theologians may be prone to providing a philosophical grounding for their theological method, Hauerwas more explicitly rejects foundationalism.[19] This makes a critique of Hauerwas rather difficult.

> Because Hauerwas' argument is so consistent, criticizing it tends to become a circular business. To criticize usually means to step out of a tradition to a supposedly neutral standpoint—which is the very habit Hauerwas doubts so much.[20]

Many narrative theologians are highly critical of a correspondence theory of truth as it is represented in representative, or referential, language. The narrative alternative of doctrine as regulative will be examined as to its systematic tendencies and its ability to support the theological claims offered. Hauerwas embraces a mild form of coherence theory, though the coherence is found in the community and practices as they align with tradition, rather than amongst statements of doctrine.[21] Thus ecclesiology becomes central in his theology. However, what Hauerwas lacks is firm substantiation in the tradition for his primacy of ecclesiology, at least in the manner in which he af-

---

seems to recognize this but resorts to conceiving of the incarnation, amongst other doctrines, as facts outside of history. The historical nature of God's work is once again dismissed, causing his revelation in history to be reduced to statements of information, i.e., liberalism.

19. For an example of a narrative theologian who provides a modest foundationalism for his narrative method, see again my discussion of Nicholas Lash, "Nascent Noeticism of Narrative Theology," esp. 460.

20. Wells, *Transforming Fate into Destiny*, 116.

21. As will be seen below, Hauerwas is careful not to give a theory of truth apart from a theological depiction of Jesus. Hauerwas believes it more important to ask "Who is the truth?" rather than "What is true?"

firms it. He can, and does, appeal to the tradition of ecclesial authority, but the kind of narrative formation he advocates does not seem intact in the tradition. Part of this may be due to the fact that his theology is primarily a critique of modernity and only secondarily constructive. In fact, because of Hauerwas's epistemological stance, he remains unable to engage in construction in any significant manner.[22] This leaves him in a precariously immanentist position.[23] He finally lacks the means to claim a narrative preference for ecclesiology from the tradition (e.g., Scripture), causing his ecclesiology to be left at the level of a mere anthropology. Wolfhart Pannenberg is introduced into the discussion with Hauerwas to provide some of the constructive elements necessary for an ecclesiological primacy in theology. His is a much more systematic enterprise, which is relatively unavailable to Hauerwas. At the same time, Pannenberg's claims regarding doctrinal realism are tempered with a recognition of the tentative nature of human knowledge in his-

22. One may object to the manner in which this study treats Hauerwas, since he is best described as a moral theologian. To place on him the burden of doing systematics may be deemed either overly generous or unfair. However, I wish to treat him fairly and remain cognizant of his own understanding of the theology in which he perceives himself to be engaging. As will be evidenced below, throughout Hauerwas' critique of systematics, he wishes to redefine the parameters of what is rightly understood as theology, placing the qualification of what is theological in the context of the life and activities of the church. This blurring of distinctions in Hauerwas' thought allows him to regard what he is doing as more generally theological in nature than technically oriented to one specific branch of theological investigation. Thus, to require of him a certain comprehensiveness and consistency in his enterprise seems legitimate.

23. Immanentism is here understood as the move in modern theology away from the medieval primacy granted to transcendence in discussions of God's existence and activity toward a more immanentist understanding. Immanentism, beginning particularly with Descartes, is the attempt to do theology from below, presuming this as the only realm of sure knowledge. The irony associated with attributing immanentism to Hauerwas is seen specifically in the contradiction between his critique of immanentist sources, e.g., Descartes and Kant, and his pursuit of a theology from below discovered in the narrative community. Though he may object to such a depiction of his theology as "from below," given his theological centrality for the Eucharist and its supernatural effect, nevertheless, he remains immanentist in his ecclesiology. For Hauerwas, the connection between the divine and the human in his ecclesiology remains too weak to support the primacy he wishes to grant to the practices of the church (practice includes more than just the Eucharist). Thus his ecclesiology amounts to little more than an anthropology, leaving him vulnerable to one aspect of the very critique he has leveled at immanentist sources. For an interesting discussion of the history of immanentism in pneumatology from Descartes and Spinoza through Kant to Schleiermacher and Hegel, see Clayton, "In Whom We Have Our Being," 216–27.

tory. His doctrinal realism is finally only affirmed through a proleptic affirmation of history by God in the eschaton. This allows Pannenberg to develop the framework for a strong ecclesiology. However, he stops short of a primacy of ecclesiology, I believe rightly offered by Hauerwas, since Pannenberg observes a distinction between the theoretical nature of the church and the historical reality. Pannenberg lacks the justification for granting such a central position for the church in his theology, remaining as it is primarily reflection. To fill what is lacking in both theologians, this study finally offers a thoroughgoing pneumatology placed in the context of ecclesiology. The argument for such a development is as much a linguistic argument as it is a substantive argument.[24] This final portion of the study gives Hauerwas the scriptural language to fill in what has not been developed extensively in the tradition, though perhaps it has been implicit in the life of the church. At the same time, it offers systematic theologians a helpful corrective in bringing their theology to bear in a more appropriate context and under a more appropriate epistemological paradigm. The life of the church is not primarily discovered in reflective theology but in the activity of being church. This is finally the definition of what constitutes theology—a combination of both approaches.

Having stated the purpose of our study, I find it appropriate next to spell out a bit more of the detail of the specific chapters. In flesh-

24. As will be seen below, Hauerwas seems critical of a representative, or referential, use of language. Language can still function as a guide for him, but it cannot describe reality, at least not in any theologically significant way with regard to God. However, he seems to use language referentially when it comes to descriptions of the human community. On the other hand, Pannenberg does use language referentially when speaking of God. He recognizes that his language must be somewhat tentative, given that we live in a historical reality. Through a kind of proleptic confirmation, Pannenberg asserts that his descriptions will finally be demonstrated as true, or at least reflective of the true reality, in the eschaton. Chapter 7 below attempts to draw out the strengths and weaknesses of each author by proposing a pneumatology based in a multifaceted use of scriptural language, including the referential. Hauerwas' use of theological language leaves him finally able to speak about merely human reality, voiding, or at best presupposing, any referential affirmation of the transcendent nature of God. Pannenberg affirms God's transcendent nature and work through the Holy Spirit; however, he leaves God's work in a more traditionally modern context, causing the Spirit to be understood in modern terms somewhat antithetical to the emphasis of Scripture on character and action. Chapter 7 will affirm the realism of scriptural language based on the nature of Scripture as revelation, but at the same time will recognize that the relationship between Scripture and the interpretive life of the church is historically conditioned.

ing out the purpose of this study, the initial chapters that follow will offer an examination of the critique of system developed by Hauerwas, and will explore his alternative to such a systematic enterprise. He pursues what may best be described as an *ad hoc* approach to theology, focusing on the identifying narrative and the formative practices of the Christian community. He does not object specifically to logic and order as appropriate measures of the veracity of theology but does call into question any movement from construction to claims of finality. The thrust of the postmodern/liberal critique of system centers more on the issue of theology's use of modern epistemological categories to arrive at final conclusions regarding theological knowledge.[25] Some of the specific contentions regarding the appropriateness of system typically equate the systematic effort in theology with the philosophical enterprise of modern thought.[26] This critique of system would include in its purview the endeavor to secure universal knowledge—knowledge that is ahistorical in the sense that it is overarching, beyond circumstance and context.[27] It would also include efforts toward comprehensiveness. Citing the thought of Levinas, David Tracy affirms that "[Levinas], like [the postmoderns], knows that a desire for totality is the concealed wish and death-dealing fate of modern reason."[28] What postmoderns/liberals oppose most vehemently is the notion that theology can and should be conducted in a manner similar to what could be classified

25. Though Hauerwas may object to the nomenclature of postmodernism or post-liberalism, he seems best described by these categories, given his disdain for certain modern and liberal presumptions within the theology of the last two centuries.

26. For instance, see Hauerwas' discussion of the manner in which theological ethics has, by and large, simply restated the ethical reflections of modern philosophy. Hauerwas, "On Keeping Theological Ethics Theological," 16–42.

27. E.g., see Pannenberg, *Introduction to Systematic Theology*, esp. ch. 1. Though certainly more extreme examples than Pannenberg exist in systematics, he provides a good illustration in that even given his tremendous emphasis on history in his theology, he still explicates the need for overarching knowledge in very clear terms. "The task of the theologian . . . is a critical one as well as a systematic one . . . because the distinction has to be made between what is historically relative in the traditional teaching and what is its *abiding core*" (7, emphasis mine).

28. Tracy, *On Naming the Present*, 17. Tracy knows well that Levinas is no friend of postmodern thought but nevertheless shares their critique of modernity. Tracy himself shares the same critique of modernity. However, he seems yet entrenched in liberalism to the extent that he embraces certain veridical categories as foundational for his thought.

as modern science, treating God as an object awaiting discovery.[29] As a consequence of their critical rejection of modernity's methodology, this study must distinguish the characteristics of the critique of systematics by Hauerwas, as well as examine the ways in which he and other critics have actually escaped, or been ensnared by, modernity in their own proposed alternatives.

I believe Hauerwas is, in certain respects, correct in his criticism of systematic theology, insofar as the characteristics he identifies are true of systematics. Specifically, his rejection of the requirement to demonstrate the veracity of theology according to external criteria seems theologically appropriate. In other words, his efforts to save faith from the plight of rationalism are historically, Biblically, and logically warranted. Further, his disdain for the turn to the subject associated with Enlightenment autonomy is a needed correction in theology.[30] Such disdain specifically stems from Hauerwas's rejection of the Enlightenment pursuit of ethics, including moral theology, according to universal principles exclusive of historical or ecclesiological circumstance.

However, Hauerwas fails to recognize that in spite of his critical posture toward a more philosophical systematic theology, he remains somewhat systematic in his own approach to theology by modestly embracing a coherence theory of truth. For Hauerwas, the use of system is rather implicit, in that neither does he attempt to lay out his method for theology, nor does he give explicit criteria for measuring its veracity. Nevertheless, he is by no means a relativist. He does have criteria for evaluating the truthfulness of the church's living of theology. While avoiding a direct correspondence between the church and propositional qualifications, Hauerwas employs a form of coherence between the practices found in tradition, and the life of the contemporary church. He is highly critical of theology's connection to foundationalism, and more moderately critical of a correspondence theory of truth as it is represented in referential language. In place of a correspondence theory of truth, he seems to embrace a form of the performative nature of truth, affirming the truth of doctrine as it aligns, or becomes coherent, with the *a priori* practices of the church already in place in the

29 Hodge, *Systematic Theology*, 18.

30. It is somewhat ironic, given his objections to the Enlightenment turn to subject, that Hauerwas, as will be seen below, should finally fall prey to a form of immanentism himself.

tradition. Doctrine then serves in a regulatory capacity, rather than in a foundational role. However, he appears to recognize that though foundationalism may be escapable, the philosophical voices of coherence and realism are somewhat necessary for his purposes. Thus, he remains somewhat entrenched in a philosophical systematic approach.

On a more positive note, I am compelled by Hauerwas's emphasis on the community of the church as the primary locus for theological formation, including for both thought and action. His use of Aristotle and Thomas seems to align fairly well with the scriptural teachings regarding a primacy of ecclesiology for epistemological and moral formation. Aristotle and especially Thomas serve as his primary sources in the tradition.

What is lacking in Hauerwas is the theological support for his ecclesiology. While his emphasis on a stronger ecclesiology is appropriate, and his critique of its loss due to Enlightenment rationality seems rightly constructed from both an internal and an external perspective, he has yet to provide the stronger theological alternative necessary to support his claims for ecclesiology's primacy. His conclusions are, for the most part, developed and defended primarily on the basis of his critique of the Enlightenment and from more purely philosophical/ sociological sources. Either he presumes that premodern theology is relatively self-explanatory (i.e., the narrative connection between pre- and postmodern will naturally come through the means of tradition rather than through proposition), or his narrative epistemology, with a primacy of action, will not allow him to engage in construction.[31] Whatever the case, his development of the tradition in either theological or scriptural terms seems somewhat tenuous, leaving the connection of tradition to his narrative formulations remote. Further, the question looms as to whether the narrative he prescribes can actually be found in the biblical or theological tradition.

Though Hauerwas would agree the Trinity is the focal point for his theological and doctrinal reflections, however such reflections may be used, he has done little to ground his ecclesiology in Trinitarian theology. While sociological developments of ecclesiological themes are

---

31. One difference between Hauerwas and other narrative theologians is that others seem willing to engage in construction, but Hauerwas finds it impossible. He seems more compelled to borrow the construction of other theologians when it suits his purposes.

quite helpful, if left without doctrinal positioning or placement, they amount to little more than a secularization of theology.[32] At worst, one could even conclude that Hauerwas is more purely immanentistic, in that he props up his ecclesiology on the sociological human community without a clear divine connection, while at the same time calling it a divine community. This leaves his theology more at the level of a mere anthropology. Certainly, as will be seen, he is a strong proponent of Trinitarian reflection and worship. What is lacking is the biblical/ doctrinal connection between the community of the church and the Triune Godhead. Hauerwas relies heavily on the supernatural effects of the Eucharist to accomplish this union, but this connection seems somewhat tenuous.

To a certain extent, Hauerwas is forced into a position of emphasizing sociology over doctrine because of his perception in Thomas and Aristotle of a primacy of action. Hauerwas seems to see action as primary almost to the extent of excluding reflection in any significant manner. This means that reflection, at least so far as it is represented in systematic endeavors, can exercise little influence in his theology, if any at all. Though he nowhere affirms such a conclusion, by implication, the tradition of doctrine seems, in Hauerwas, to be complete, in that reflection is rather limited.

I believe a more thoroughgoing understanding of the Holy Spirit in the context of ecclesiology would better support and allow for more complete biblical and theological development of Hauerwas's position. Thus, the alternative I propose to his sociology is a modestly systematic approach to ecclesiology and pneumatology by means of scriptural reflections on ecclesiological themes within Hauerwas. In order to accomplish this, the systematic efforts of Wolfhart Pannenberg are introduced (though not significantly developed), to provide Hauerwas with some theological description of themes critical to his efforts. Though Hauerwas would likely be reticent to accommodate such a systematic endeavor, Pannenberg does demonstrate some parallel concerns and similar conclusions in regard to Trinitarian theology and its relation-

---

32. I use the term "sociological" throughout the study simply to indicate that Hauerwas is quite dependent on the relationship of humans in community qua human relatedness for his understanding of ecclesiology. Sociology is therefore used in the somewhat loose sense of referring to humans relating to one another, with all the incumbent implications addressed in a more technical definition of sociology left aside.

ship to ecclesiology. Likewise, Pannenberg qualifies his efforts by means of an appeal to a proleptic confirmation of his doctrinal realism. This allows Pannenberg to make bold claims about the Trinity and the manner in which ecclesiology may be subsumed into a social Trinitarianism, while at the same time to recognize that such claims remain somewhat tentative, based on the continued openness of history prior to the eschaton. On the other hand, it seems apparent from his discussions of methodological order and foundations that Pannenberg's ecclesiology is lacking the connection between theoretical development and the real community of the church. Pannenberg has constructed his ecclesiology by carefully including a central place for pneumatology. However, he does not make the connection between the human and the divine in pneumatology as clear as seems necessary for an ecclesiology that may be found in material existence. He draws the human and divine together with his notion of human participation in the Triune Godhead through the Holy Spirit. But even here, the reality of a material community that may be seen as an enfleshment of his ecclesiology and pneumatology is lacking. He is certainly right to construct an ecclesiology that relies upon a dynamic pneumatology, incorporating human action as participation in the Triune God. However, whereas Hauerwas lacks the scriptural or doctrinal support and development to ground his more purely sociological understanding of ecclesiology in the Christian tradition, Pannenberg lacks the materialization of his ecclesiology in a local church. This is primarily due to the fact that Pannenberg grants primacy to reflection over, or prior to, action. His is a more traditionally modern moral epistemology in that he believes right thinking will lead to right action. Hauerwas reversed this notion, a reversal allowing him to focus specifically on the actions or practices of the church as the locus of theology. Pannenberg cannot grant such a primacy for action, since he still believes in the necessity of a theoretical foundation for doctrinal knowledge. Combining Pannenberg's theoretical developments in pneumatology with Hauerwas's material ecclesiology seems to arrive at a theology for the church with doctrinal development sufficient to support the ecclesiological connection to the tradition that Hauerwas's ecclesiology requires and to warrant the epistemological value of the church's practices. However, a primary testing ground in the tradition for the veracity of any theology for the church is its "fit" with the primary language of the church: Scripture.

The final chapters in this study culminate in a scriptural explication of the humanity of the Holy Spirit discovered in the local church, demonstrating pneumatology to be the focal point where the divine and human meet in ecclesiology. Immanentism is avoided by developing the kenotic nature of the Spirit's activity in a manner paralleling the kenosis of Jesus. Scripture is the primary language used, and forms the substantive narration for doctrinal discussion of pneumatology in the context of ecclesiology. This gives Hauerwas the scriptural and theological language to avoid a more anthropological rendering of his narrative construction. At the same time, it grounds Pannenberg's more theoretical theology in the reality of the material existence of the church. The doctrine of ecclesiology is primarily discovered in the activity of being church and is then amplified through theological reflection by those who are skilled at being church. Thus, a reciprocity, of sorts, exists in the scriptural language regarding thought and action. While at times the Aristotelian primacy of action seems clearly emphasized in Scripture, the occasional primacy of thought can also be discovered in Scripture in the authority of reflective wisdom. Action and reflection are, therefore, seen to be reciprocating influences in the life of the church for those who are mature. This reciprocity of reflection and action grants significant, if not even foundational, value to the practices in the church, while at the same time appealing to doctrinal reflection as another formative influence in guiding the church toward fulfillment of its telos. Therefore, the modest defense of system offered here is not a defense of modern epistemology (i.e., individual thought as prior to action), nor is it a defense of system *per se*. Instead, it is a focused effort to provide footing for doctrine on the same plane as action in a reciprocating epistemological effort. Since modern epistemology has ruled the day for at least two centuries in theology, the bulk of our discussion in these chapters will be spent on discovering the manner in which action is, at least, epistemologically equivalent to thought in ecclesiology. Neither thought nor action can be granted priority at the expense of the other, and at the same time, neither can be isolated from the other. However, interestingly, action seems to take a modest precedence in many passages of Scripture. This discussion in later chapters will be set in the context of both scriptural development and response to objections. Anticipated criticism could come from various quarters, including scriptural, philosophical, and historical. Therefore some specific attention will be given to the interrelationship of Scripture, Aristotle, and Luther, specifically from the context of the relationship of the Holy Spirit to the dynamics of communal action in the church.

Several themes developed by Hauerwas, including the metaphor of body as not so metaphorical, and Aristotelian apprenticeship as discipleship, are examined from a more thoroughly biblical standpoint. What has seemed lacking in Hauerwas is any serious engagement with the scriptural teachings on pneumatology and ecclesiology. While he may wish to defer to scriptural experts, he has failed to see the scope of his studies in the fullest sense of theological reflection. Thus, he has not significantly engaged the very tradition to which he would appeal. Scripture must be more than simply an element in the study. For a theology to become a part of the Christian ecclesiological tradition, particularly along the lines of a shift in theological thinking such as Hauerwas's, it must finally be measured by scriptural teaching, whether traditionally interpreted or otherwise. To his credit, he does, on occasion, quote Scripture or give deference to its authority in theological studies, but he rarely engages the text in more than a cursory fashion. Chapter 7 attempts to shore up this tendency.

The final conclusion reached in this study is that an ecclesiologically molded doctrine of the Holy Spirit accomplishes in doctrinal terms what Hauerwas is attempting to do in more philosophical terms. Though his discussions are at times more or less philosophical, he never moves his epistemology into the language of historical theology, relying instead on the sociological formation of a community guided by tradition. At the same time, the scriptural discussion offered below brings the doctrine more fully into the language and reality of the church, something lacking in the theoretical development found in a representative systematician like Pannenberg. Such a biblical/doctrinal discussion of the issue decidedly moves the discussion from the context of modernism into a realm more reflective of the history of theology, and, more important, into the tradition and life of the church.

1

A Narrative in the Making

In Conversation with Stanley Hauerwas

THE THEOLOGY OF STANLEY HAUERWAS PRESENTS A CRITICAL CHAL-
lenge to systematic theology in the contemporary context. He believes
that the Christian narrative theology provided by the community of
faith is the most appropriate context in which to "do" theology. The
"doing" of theology, in such a context is not the academic reflection
and thematic construction often associated with systematic theology.
Instead, theology is best discovered and discussed as the living of the
Christian life. Thus, theology is a discipline of the church, rather than
of scholarly pursuit, though certainly scholarship may be included.
Ecclesiology, then, becomes central for Hauerwas.

Of course, Hauerwas cannot escape saying something theological. He must still attempt to convey the usefulness of theology for the
church. He believes that theology is best conceived as a story, rather
than as the logically coherent system of doctrines displayed in modern
theology. He further believes that this story is grounded in the practices
of the Christian community, especially baptism and the Eucharist. As
the Christian community exhibits the life of Christ in its own life, it
displays the story that is uniquely Christ's. Hauerwas wishes for theology to be discovered and depicted primarily in action, rather than in
theoretical reflection, allowing it to encompass the lives of those who
live the reality of the church in everyday life. He rightly recognizes the
theological necessity to ground any discussion of theological import
in the reality of the church. Theoretical discussions of doctrine are of
little value to the church in themselves, since, Hauerwas believes, as will

be seen below, that action takes priority over theory, or in his words, practice takes priority over system.

It seems wise at the outset to explain a bit about how our study of Hauerwas is going to proceed, before delving into direct interaction with his work. This chapter will attempt a more extensive introduction to major themes in Hauerwas's thought. He can be difficult to "pin down," so we will give an overview of the study with some critical interaction regarding what subjects seem to stand out as requiring further development. It is in the following chapters that these major themes will be discussed in detail.

What is unique about Hauerwas is that he represents, in the typological language of Gary Comstock, a "pure narrativist."[1] As a pure narrativist, Hauerwas sees little use in developing a "theoretical justification of narrative hermeneutics."[2] What this means for Hauerwas is not simply that he doesn't spell out in detail what his theoretical commitments are, but, in fact, he cannot, according to his own schema of rationality provide a theory of rationality qua rationality, nor can he give an "account" of his epistemology.[3] Hauerwas does his best to skirt traditional metaphysical formulations (i.e., *a priori* categories à la Kantianism), giving them, at most, only a "sidelong glance."[4] Accordingly, Hauerwas is opposed to providing a methodology prior to outlining his own theology.

Developing a study on the theology of Hauerwas is, consequently, somewhat difficult, given his disdain for providing any theoretical delineation of his thought or justification for his beliefs. The fact that Hauerwas is prone to avoid theorizing does not mean that he has no theological beliefs or provides no warrant for holding such beliefs. On the contrary, he is quick to advocate the belief of the church as it is represented in its traditional teachings through history. He regards appeals to theoretical justifications for belief (i.e., foundationalism) as aberrations in theology, due to the influence of Enlightenment presuppositions regarding epistemology.[5] Consequently, instead of establish-

1. Comstock, "Truth or Meaning," 119.

2. Ibid., 121.

3. Hauerwas, *Wilderness Wanderings*, 232–33.

4. Hauerwas, "Why the Truth Demands Truthfulness," 141. This article was also reprinted in Hauerwas and Jones, *Why Narrative?* 303–10.

5. I recognize the danger of assuming something called the Enlightenment rep-

ing his thought on theoretical grounds, Hauerwas wishes to ground all beliefs of the church in what has been taught through the ages in the community we call church.

Hauerwas may be difficult to understand or read at times, due to his avoidance of the theoretical, but he does not wish to be illogical or subjective. He provides readers with a clear understanding of the impetus for the death of liberalism. When he turns to provide his own (although he would prefer to call it the church's) alternative, he does not wish to lapse back into what he deems the mistakes of liberalism. Therefore, he cannot provide the rational account of his thought one might expect, i.e., in terms justified more purely in what is reasonable to any mind. Indeed, such expectations are a telling part of the problem. Hauerwas believes theologians must avoid attempting to justify their theology on grounds other than those that are specifically Christian, i.e., Christians should not appeal to the rationality of the faith according to some external standard of truth or verification. Consequently, he is opposed to the tendency he finds in systematics to qualify theological assertions according to a rationality that is demonstrable qua rationality, or to finding warrant for theological assertions only in what is verifiable via the reason of any rational creature. For Hauerwas, such a project is theologically suicidal, since Christian theology cannot be reduced to what is common to all humanity, Christian and non-Christian alike. What is needed is both a rejection of the systematic (i.e., modernistic) tendencies and an affirmation of the true "foundation" for Christian truth—Christ and his body, the church.[6] As will be seen, the

---

resents a single historical position or influence. Certainly, there is no such thing as *the* Enlightenment. Many figures represent varying positions over the course of a few centuries. However, certain tendencies amongst some of the figures influential during the period loosely bounded as the Enlightenment seem connected enough to warrant such a generalization. As will be seen below, Hauerwas and others treat Enlightenment thought as fairly cohesive. Thus, we will continue to refer to the Enlightenment as a unified philosophical movement, with special attention given to specific figures when warranted.

6. I have placed "foundation" in quotes here because, as will be seen below, Hauerwas calls himself an antifoundationalist. In the traditional Enlightenment sense of the term, that is, that foundational propositions are basic and rely on no other propositions for their justification, he is right. However, he does still seem to use Jesus in a somewhat foundationalistic sense, though by no means does this resemble the philosophical notion of foundation as an unassailable beginning point. Indeed, Scripture would seem to lead him to this—Jesus is "the chief cornerstone" of the foundation of the church (Eph 2:20).

systematic tendencies Hauerwas especially disdains include rationality as the ground for theological assertions, autonomy of the individual (systems of doctrine are inherently individualistic in that they can be derived from and appeal to the individual's rationality, rather than from communal effort), the ahistorical nature of doctrinal claims, and the presumed universalism or finality of the products of systematic theology. All these things he finds most explicitly expressed and developed in Enlightenment thought, and as he is hesitant to categorize his critique, he generally gathers these systematic tendencies together under the somewhat broad term *liberalism*.[7]

This portion of our study is intended to demonstrate that Hauerwas's critique of system, as a response to the influence of liberalism in theology, rightly elevates the narrative of the church over theory in epistemology; that is, practices become constitutive of knowledge, rather than knowledge's being based on foundational beliefs discovered in the abstract nature of pure reason. However, as will be seen, Hauerwas's approach to narrative maintains certain elements of system (e.g., an understanding of the Eucharist as the human connection to the divine) and avoids or assumes others (e.g., a development of Trinitarian theology that would account for human participation), leaving his narrative of the church unsupported by certain doctrines necessary to avoid the accusation of the church's being a mere human community. The study finally moves to establish for Hauerwas, from scriptural sources, a thoroughgoing doctrine of the Holy Spirit, to provide him with sufficient connection between the human and the divine for his ecclesiology. This allows his narrative to avoid the criticism of remaining at the level of anthropology, that is, only at the level of human interaction qua human.

Chapters 2 and 3 will attempt to examine Hauerwas's rejection of Enlightenment rationality and the liberalism spawned by it. The following two chapters will then move to draw together, as much as is possible, the direction Hauerwas believes the church should go in "discovering" or "recovering" an appropriate context for theology. Here we will see the extent to which Hauerwas has escaped certain systematic or liberal tendencies, specifically an appeal toward a universal anthropology (à la the Enlightenment turn to the subject), and the direction he needs

---

7. The neo-orthodox context for the development of Hauerwas's thought will be quite evident in the paragraphs below.

to pursue to remain consistently Christian in his narrative epistemology.[8] The final chapters will then move to provide Hauerwas with some scriptural/theological language to avoid the criticism of reverting to a universal anthropology.

Chapter 2 demonstrates ways in which Hauerwas has been mentored in his critique of liberalism. The direct influence of Paul Holmer and other of Hauerwas's professors is made clear, alongside the influence of such distant figures as Aristotle, Aquinas, Kierkegaard, Wittgenstein, and Barth. These all give Hauerwas the ammunition he needs in chapter three to attack the liberalism he believes is rampant in contemporary theology, and this he does poignantly. His stripping away of the modernistic/systematic tendencies in theology mentioned above is a needed step in correcting the embrace between theology and Enlightenment thought as it is represented in systematic theology. Hauerwas makes clear that systematics has become the means by which liberalism has infiltrated and marginalized the church. He views Kantian rationalism and autonomy as primary sources for establishing the context in which system could become the definitive expression of Christian theology. Though Kant may not always be the best subject of such a critique, given that he was not the progenitor of Enlightenment thinking, I am, nevertheless, compelled by Hauerwas's objections to the Kantian interpretation given. In spite of his intentions toward bolstering Christian doctrine and the Christian community, Kant can fairly be judged to represent the full flowering of certain Enlightenment themes that Hauerwas finds objectionable. In our discussion of Kant, we will focus primarily on the universalizing nature of his ethics. As will be seen clearly in Hauerwas's primacy of ecclesiology, focusing on ethics

---

8. The term "narrative epistemology," though never used by Hauerwas, is meant to indicate his belief that knowledge is based primarily in the contextualized practices of the church. In other words, Christian knowledge is discovered in the specific Christian context of the actions that constitute what qualifies as a Christian community. Tradition becomes integral to such a learning of knowledge due to the necessity of an uninterrupted connection between the human community and the type of actions advocated (i.e., those found in revelation) and practiced by that human community throughout history. Thus, a Christian narrative epistemology is one that defines the truth of knowledge according to the correspondence between habitual action in the human community and traditional accounts of practices in both revelation and tradition.

is equivalent to focusing on theology, since theology, for Hauerwas, is ethics, and ethics is theology.[9]

Chapter 4 attempts to demonstrate the way in which Hauerwas moves away from liberalism toward a narrative theology that he finds expressed in the tradition of the church. Since Hauerwas believes that liberalism is a narrative tradition alongside Christianity, he does not engage it at the level of the theoretical. Instead, he engages various members of the tradition as they are situated in their specific context. When he comes to offer his own alternative to these other traditions, he is then able to argue for the tradition qua tradition, albeit in the context of historical figures, rather than to appeal to some external criteria for justification. In other words, Hauerwas appears to be attempting to outnarrate liberalism by providing a more Christian narrative of the church. Such a move means that Hauerwas need not develop his thought in a more systematic fashion (i.e., with justification and warrants for acceptance based on sources outside of the theological tradition—in other words, based on rationality). However, this does not mean that his thought is without affirmations of what he believes to be the truth of theology. Hauerwas consistently relies on the reality of theological claims affirmed throughout the centuries, even claims with universal import. Thus, he escapes the criticism of being sectarian in his approach to theology by undercutting the supposed neutrality of those accusing him of sectarianism, since a sectarian critique itself presupposes a specific narrative of what may be regarded as universal or relativistic. On the other hand, Hauerwas does not seem to recognize that such a move still lands him in a position of having, at least an implicit system to his theology. I'm not sure that Hauerwas would wish to argue the matter since the system he criticizes does not bear many similarities to the systematic tendencies that seem to be at work in his theological claims. Hauerwas believes a certain amount of orderliness is a necessary element of theological conversation. He would be quite reticent to accept that such a logic makes him systematic; he is simply unwilling to engage in the theological prolegomena endemic to theology since the Enlightenment. Nevertheless, his retention of certain elements of sys-

---

9. E.g., see Hauerwas's discussion of the relationship between theology and ethics historically in his "On Keeping Theological Ethics Theological," 16–42. Also with regard to demonstrating this as a primary emphasis of his Gifford Lectures, see Hauerwas, *With the Grain of the Universe*, 16–17.

tematic theology, in the broader or softer sense of the term (i.e., logical ordering, coherence, and embracing certain fundamental doctrines), does place his critique of systematics in need of some qualification.

Such a qualification is best found by contrasting elements of Hauerwas's theology, for the sake of clarification and complementary critical interaction, with certain theological themes in the work of Wolfhart Pannenberg. Though by no means an exhaustive reflection on Pannenberg's work, the brief comparisons will aid Hauerwas by establishing both the connections for certain extant themes in Hauerwas, as well as provide a context in which traditional language (i.e., Scripture) can be used to put "flesh" on the bones of Hauerwas's framework. Substantively, Pannenberg provides Hauerwas with Trinitarian language and a further development of Christology in eschatological perspective. Each point will help Hauerwas support his notions of human participation in God's Triunity and the eschatological teleology of the church as a body that proclaims the lordship of Jesus. The modest nature of Pannenberg's claims regarding knowledge parallels some of the concerns over systematics raised by Hauerwas.

Hauerwas believes that action is primary in epistemology; thus the living narrative community of the church becomes the route for learning to "do" theology through the practices. As will be seen below, he explicitly acknowledges his indebtedness to Aristotle, and Aquinas's transformation of Aristotle, for the primacy of practice and the devotion to community prior to the individual. Hauerwas, following Barth, also develops his narrative along themes primarily christocentric. This makes it impossible for him to engage in a theoretical conversation about the merits of such an epistemology. However, it does not stop him from making some universal claims as his ecclesiology is displayed in chapter 4, since the universe is finally God's universe. Chapter 5 provides the reader with a fuller discussion of what Hauerwas's ecclesiology finally looks like as he has attempted to give it form in his theology. Obviously, this is by no means an adequate representation of his theology, since he believes theology must be a living reality. Hauerwas never gives an overarching view of how it all "fits together." Nevertheless, this chapter serves as a fairly comprehensive summary of Hauerwas's conception of the connection between ecclesiology and Christology—his primary themes. Further, the connection between Hauerwas's primacy of ecclesiology and the Trinity is outlined in this chapter, with specific attention to how Hauerwas maintains this connection. Hauerwas's attempt to provide the theological support for investing the human community of the church with divine significance is finally found to be too weak to support the comprehensiveness of his epistemology. In other words, the practices Hauerwas finds constitutive of the connection of the human community of the church to the Triune God is too limited to support the breadth he grants to narrative formation. Hauerwas finally appears to lapse back into a merely modified form of the universal anthropology he is criticizing.[10]

The values of Hauerwas's theological conversation, as alluded to above, are found primarily in his critique of the modernistic infestation of Christian epistemology and the alternative he offers as an appropriate mode of theology. I agree that the rationalistic tendencies in some "systems" must be excised from theology. Likewise, I find the ahistorical nature of systems to be not merely immodest, but even, on occasion, idolatrous. In this regard, Hauerwas's critique is much needed. The alternative theological approach he offers is also, I believe, rightly aimed. His emphasis on christocentric ecclesiology aligns well with both a traditional theological and a scriptural analysis. His understanding and use of Aristotle seems, at least, complementary to Scripture, and certainly seems a better context than modernity from which to understand scriptural teaching and *do* theology.

From an external perspective, what is lacking in Hauerwas is more theological development of appropriate theological and biblical themes that could demonstrate the further tradition that seems supportive of his endeavors. Hauerwas needs fuller ecclesiological development to support his strong use of the narrative community. He lacks, in a Wittgensteinian sense, the language to complete his goal of resting theology on an epistemology solely grounded in the narrative community of the church. In other words, because he rests on more philosophical language specific to narrative, rather than on language invested with biblical/theological (i.e., more traditioned) import, Hauerwas still

10. As will be seen below, Hauerwas is highly critical of the nontheological nature of modern theology, based as it is in a mere study of humanity, as though the human is all there is. In contrast, he wishes for the church to proclaim the reality of its own doctrinal affirmations of who God is and what he is about in the story of Jesus. The issue I am raising as a critique of Hauerwas is how consistently he maintains a commitment to such doctrinal affirmations. I will argue that he needs fuller development of pneumatology in order to maintain his high commitment to ecclesiology.

seems entrenched in a universal anthropology. His response would be to point to Aquinas and Barth, but Hauerwas has developed little of the language himself. Aquinas doesn't seem to address Hauerwas's concerns specifically, and Barth is finally without the resources to provide a solid alternative language for the divine connection to the human.

A further critique of Hauerwas offered in this study centers around his presumption that theological explanation, specifically in a biblical context, is necessarily to be associated with foundationalism. Hauerwas seems to believe that to provide theological explanation for his program means that he is engaging in a form of justification deriving from the rationalization required by Enlightenment thought. Therefore, he will give no method and supports his claims with little doctrinal warrant. However, he fails to give credence to the fact that explanation and justification in both theological and Biblical terms has been the mode of theological investigation for centuries prior to the Enlightenment. Explanation need not be taken as the provision of rational warrant required by foundationalism. It can just as easily be the careful consideration of the right interpretation of Scripture and appropriate interaction between the intellect and action, even in a narrative scheme.[11] Hauerwas seems to recognize that this is the case with Barth.

> Barth was well aware that, in a time like ours, his theology could not help but be read by Christian and non-Christian alike as one assertion after another. It should now be clear, however, that he could not attempt to "explain" what he was doing without ceasing to do the very thing that begged explanation. But that does not mean that he did not seek ways to show that theology was not simply "confessional" or, worse, subjective. Indeed, as I read it, the *Church Dogmatics* is Barth's attempt not only to train his readers in the proper use of Christian speech but also, and at

11. It should be noted that I am not here presupposing that doctrinal justification is needed before Hauerwas's theology can be accepted. This would be to slip back into a modernistic requirement of rational foundations prior to belief. Instead, I am simply saying that Hauerwas provides too little theology as either foundation or explanation. (As will be discussed below, Hauerwas seems to understand explanation as a form of foundationalism.) Hauerwas needs to provide a niblical and theological language for what he currently accomplishes in more anthropological terms. Though I would agree with Hauerwas that such language may not be *a priori* to action, it is still an essential part of the Christian life and a necessary connection to the tradition.

the same time, to develop a theological metaphysics, that is, an account of all that is.[12]

Though Hauerwas would wish to pursue a course similar to Barth's, as will be seen below, he still suffers from some of the same theological difficulties that faced Barth, such as how to connect ecclesiology with Trinitarian theology. Hauerwas, in his attempt to escape the Enlightenment through a more pure narrativism, has recounted admirably the centuries of explanation provided by theologians who wished to bolster the tradition with belief that could engage both mind and action, but he has done only little constructive work himself. This has left him in a context where he must presume doctrinal discussion without engaging it seriously. What this means for our study is that we cannot engage Hauerwas directly on truth claims regarding the divine-human connection, though he does at times seem to make or imply such claims. Rather, we must tease such claims from his suggestive arguments. Therefore, the critique of his thought throughout this study will attempt to provide an overall "narrative" of his theology so that we may engage it at certain points of inconsistency, while at the same time demonstrating where his lack of explanation leaves his claims hollow. This means that the primary critique of Hauerwas given in this study, particularly in chapter 5, will finally be external, with certain elements of internal inconsistency pointed out. I will attempt to demonstrate, through brief systematic and more extensive biblical consideration, the doctrinal discussion that is lacking in Hauerwas.

The chapters that remain following our discussion of Hauerwas attempt to develop specific Hauerwasian themes from the language regarded as more traditional for the church: Scripture. The language Hauerwas lacks for the divine-human connection is best found in a biblically based doctrine of the Holy Spirit. Others have noted such a lack. As Samuel Wells makes clear,

> Most of the criticisms of Haueras have clustered around the issues of sectarianism and fideism. Perhaps because of this, he has not been pushed to clarify some of the more doctrinal features of his position. I believe he could and should do this by developing his description of the role of the Holy Spirit.[13]

12. Hauerwas, *With the Grain of the Universe*, 184.
13. Wells, *Transforming Fate into Destiny*, 97. Wells identifies this need in Hauerwas,

Ecclesiology and the human connection to Christology must finally be rooted in a thoroughgoing pneumatology. This is where much of our critical interaction is finally aiming. As Joseph Mangina notes with regard to Hauerwas,

> Critics [of Hauerwas] tend to ignore the messianic Christology, centered on Jesus' identity as the inaugurator of the kingdom of God, that frames his account of the virtues and the narrative character of the moral life. In a striking juxtaposition, Hauerwas thus situates a 'catholic' account of the church as a public within an 'evangelical' eschatology. Here a promising space begins to open up for reflection on the activity of the Spirit—a task to which Hauerwas's theological program points us, even though he does not develop the theme himself.[14]

Hauerwas makes the need for the narrative community apparent, and rightly fills that need with the church. However, he fails to access the theological and biblical resources necessary for his position to fit well with the theological tradition he wishes to accommodate. In other words, his ecclesiology is left perilously close to becoming a mere anthropology, i.e., immanentism. Hauerwas may believe that scriptural development of his ecclesiological themes smacks too much of the rationalistic tendency to provide a foundation for belief (though I believe that a case could be made that such a revelational foundation is warranted). However, I believe that such scriptural development is better understood as an attempt to teach Christians—theologians and lay alike—to read Scripture well on the subject of ecclesiology, something that Hauerwas would likely find more appealing.[15] This seems a legiti-

---

but does not proceed to offer any development of what such a doctrine might look like.

14. Mangina, "Bearing the Marks of Jesus," 271. Mangina rightly goes on to claim, "An authentic theology of discipleship or imitation—'bearing the marks of Jesus,' as I have put it—depends on situating the church within the larger context of the Spirit's work" (292). Unfortunately, he does not then proceed to do any of the theological work to accomplish such a necessity.

15. Hauerwas occasionally interacts with the text of Scripture; however, his interaction is infrequent in his theological studies. He recently dedicated substantial time to a commentary on the Gospel of Matthew that demonstrates his affinity for the text and his belief that the text is formative in its own right (Hauerwas, *Matthew*). This commentary was an exciting development, in that Hauerwas writes, as he is prone to do, from his "no-nonsense" perspective. Accordingly, he defies many presuppositions of the historico-critical method. His intention is to interact theologically with the text, and he

mate way, indeed the only legitimate way, to make clear the connection between Hauerwas's thought and the tradition of theology as it is used by and in the church. In language that would likely be more appealing to Hauerwas, scriptural development seems best understood as an attempt to draw theologians into the primary formative narrative.

Before moving into the chapters themselves, I should point out at the outset that this study is finally engaging in a conversation with Hauerwas rather than a detailed analysis. A few studies have been done in the last decade, interacting with Hauerwas in a substantive manner. Unfortunately, none of these works attempted to give any comprehensive overview of Hauerwas's project. Instead, they either took a specific point or aspect of Hauerwas's thought and developed it more broadly than he has done himself,[16] or they used Hauerwas as a springboard for reflecting on or interacting with ideas already existent in their own work.[17] Further, critiques of specific aspects of Hauerwas's thought are abundant.[18] This study will attempt to put as much of Hauerwas's

---

does this with great breadth and insight. As one might expect, Hauerwas understands that "Matthew's gospel is about the "politics of Jesus" ([29] Hauerwas acknowledges he is borrowing this phrase from John Howard Yoder), which permeates Hauerwas's comments. Perhaps that is why Hauerwas was chosen to write on Matthew, since Matthew is quite clearly a political treatise. Unfortunately, as will be discussed further below, Hauerwas does not use this occasion to develop his understanding of epistemology or ecclesiology in the biblical context of the Holy Spirit.

16. Two studies that may fit this category are Rasmusson, *Church as Polis*; and Hütter, *Evangelische Ethic als Kirchliches Zeugnis*. Several similarities exist between the study below and Rasmusson's work. Rasmusson was well aware of the evolving nature of Hauerwas's thought, and attempts to distinguish how Hauerwas's later work is different from the earlier (177–79). Rasmusson does not attempt to summarize Hauerwas yet still believes certain themes are overarching. The primary disadvantage of Rasmusson's study is simply the continued proliferation of material that comes from the pen of Hauerwas. Hauerwas has continued to demonstrate his preferences in varying ways, allowing for more development of the overarching themes. This study seems to arrive at conclusions similar to those in Rasmusson; however, we will develop themes from other sources and perhaps provide a slightly differing perspective, given Hauerwas's own continued evolution.

17. Mark Thiessen Nation and Samuel Wells (*Faithfulness and Fortitude*) have compiled a collection of articles by British theologians interacting with various themes discussed by Hauerwas over the years.

18. E.g., critiques that will be discussed in some detail in the chapters below include Gustafson, "Sectarian Temptation"; Holland, "The Problems and Prospects of a 'Sectarian Ethic;" and Mangina, "Bearing the Marks of Jesus." Gustafson's critique of Hauerwas as sectarian is refuted by Hauerwas himself as the latter rightly sees such a

thought together as is possible, while remaining sympathetic to his intentions. Hauerwas avoids writing in such a way as to be easily summarized or viewed from a more comprehensive perspective. He never gives a summary of the conversation.

> Indeed one of the frustrations for anyone willing to undergo the regime of reading me [Hauerwas] is that when you are finished, you will not be able to neatly summarise what you have learned. If I cannot neatly summarise 'my position', why should anyone else be able to do so. . . . I have, like Barth and Wittgenstein, tried to write in a manner that defies summary.[19]

If Hauerwas does not provide any summary to his thought and believes such a task to be difficult, then the intentions of this study, including the attempt to be comprehensive, may seem rather daunting. However, as will be seen below, Hauerwas is hardly inconsistent or obtuse in his writings, opening himself to certain comprehensive themes. Further, this study's goal to provide Hauerwas with a more substantive grounding in pneumatology, though as we noted above with Mangina, this study will move forward the conversation about how to remove the Enlightenment tendency toward anthropology as primary.

Hauerwas may appear, at times, to be rather eclectic, even "cannibalistic,"[20] never demonstrating his own position on grounds that

---

critique as self-refuting. Holland's critique of Hauerwas as lacking development of and sufficient connection to human experience merely serves to display Holland's precommitment to anthropology as primary. As the only study to engage Hauerwas from a more internal perspective, Mangina clarifies why pneumatology is the missing piece of Hauerwas's thought; however, he does little to develop how such a pneumatology might be conceived. The first two critiques mentioned come to Hauerwas with Enlightenment presuppositions still intact and attempt to evaluate him based on such presuppositions. This study, in parallel to Mangina's study, will attempt to critically assume many of the presuppositions Hauerwas holds in order to expose, evaluate, and, if necessary, correct them in a manner consistent with what Hauerwas would agree is the church's traditional/historical position.

19. Hauerwas, "Where Would I Be Without Friends?" 316.

20. Given that Hauerwas is a theologian for the traditioned church catholic, it would be dangerous for him to claim any sense of novelty in his theology. The best that he seems ready to claim is that his theology lives off communities that bear the marks of the true church in ways that not every church can or does. The fact that his own Methodism has a distinct paucity of such communities means that he must graze over traditions, finding ones most suitable to demonstrate his theology (dare I say "system"?). This gives Hauerwas the freedom to use the theological notions of people from varying traditions without actually joining their tradition, which is convenient given

could be claimed as his own.[21] Though he is quite unique in his style and, consequently, in his substance, he tries to avoid making statements that claim any novelty or independence.[22] Hauerwas always seems to understand himself to be in the midst of the conversation.[23] Therefore,

---

that many of them belonged to traditions long since past. For this reason, Hauerwas willingly describes himself as cannibalistic. See Hauerwas, *In Good Company*, 67.

I would like to suggest that another way exists in which Hauerwas is cannibalistic. He relies quite heavily on traditional theology in order to avoid developing or "explaining" his own project. Surely he doesn't expect Christians to readily identify traditional doctrine as an "obvious" thing, as though it were somehow untaught knowledge. For instance, as will be discussed below, Hauerwas faces a very real danger of being accused of anthropological reductionism due to his strong emphasis on the community as the primary, if not sole, location of divine activity. The way in which he attempts to avoid such reductionism is through an appeal to the supernatural effects of the sacraments. In other words, the sacraments raise the human community beyond itself through the infusion of grace into what is, without the sacrament, merely human. However, the sporadic nature of the sacraments seems inconsistent with his desire to see the supernatural as permeating the community in a constant manner. He is finally left with only an occasional connection between the human community and God. As will be argued below, Hauerwas needs to develop his ecclesiology in the context of pneumatology.

21. The search for independence seems to be the impetus for his work *The Peaceable Kingdom*. As he notes in the preface (xii), the question of the difference his thought made in how he taught Christian ethics caused him to begin to formulate his own thought, somewhat independent of other thinkers. However, such independence is not so much independence of ideas as it is independence in pedagogy. Hauerwas continues to believe that he has not really said anything particularly new.

22. Indeed, such independence would be suicidal for Hauerwas. See Hauerwas, *Dispatches from the Front*, 24–25.

23. Indeed, an interesting way of conceiving Hauerwas's method is suggested by Hauerwas himself in his description of the theological style of Walter Rauschenbusch and Reinhold Niebuhr (Hauerwas, *Better Hope*, 96–99). Here Hauerwas depicts Rauschenbusch's ethics as "essentially theologically and morally informed journalism. He narrated the social realities of his day by redescribing them Christianly . . . In an interesting way Reinhold Niebuhr worked much in the same fashion, even though Niebuhr appears to be clearer about the nature of 'ethics' in distinction from theology" (96).

Hauerwas could be accused at times of engaging in journalism himself in that he is constantly working in a descriptive mode, using and analyzing the thought of others to make his own case. He attempts to do theology as a sort of reporting of the advances and failures of the theology of others. Thus, his theologizing and narrative ethics in general, if such a thing exists in Hauerwas, becomes rather unassailable in that it cannot be submitted for critique. It must be judged merely as good or bad journalism. Instead of asking whether the story "got the facts straight," one must ask, "How well does the story read?" In this, certain criteria are still available to the reader for the sake of evaluation, such as the accuracy of description, the value of description, and, perhaps more important for our discussion, the appropriateness of the language of description.

this study will proceed more along the lines of description rather than of analytical outlining (i.e., system). Indeed, it would be difficult to perform a detailed internal analysis of Hauerwas's method, since he attempts to avoid any explicit statements regarding method. It is not possible to say that Hauerwas contradicts his own method, since he attempts to disown any pretext of methodology. As has been mentioned above, it is difficult to gain a comprehensive vantage point on Hauerwas's thought. We cannot "lay out" the argument concisely or clearly from Hauerwas's own texts. Nevertheless, Hauerwas does wish to be consistent within his own thought and to the tradition of the church. This being the case, it may be better to state our critical purpose as one of discovering remnants of Enlightenment thought in Hauerwas's theology, rather than attempting to measure his "system" against some standards that he recognizes as external to his theology. On the other hand, his positive contributions to the conversation need merely to be emphasized, while at the same time it must be demonstrated that he has not provided sufficient theological (i.e., doctrinal/scriptural) thought on the subject for it to become part of the tradition. This demonstration will finally be offered in the form of scriptural reflections on themes discovered in Hauerwas.

With this notion of the conversational, even argumentative, nature of Hauerwas's theology in mind, I should indicate that it is the aim of this study to deal with the mature (though I am certain he would not like such an adjective) thought of Hauerwas. As he states, "[T]heology, if it is to reflect truthfully on God, must remain forever unfinished."[24] He frequently acknowledges progression within his own thought. Since the evolution of his thought is beyond the scope of this study, and since he believes his thought can never actually be finalized or complete, the

---

Description becomes much more of a theological art form for both the author and the reader. Therefore, it can take the nuances and shape of art in its intentions and impact. But such an art must be more than simply "interesting"—the curse of liberals gone deconstructionist. Such an art must be good in order to be regarded as true. By *good* I mean it must be an embodiment of Jesus coordinate with the depiction found in Scripture. Thus, the language of Scripture and its enactment, or performance, become a "measure" of truth. The question is finally, then, how does Hauerwas do in this medium? Hauerwas is not trying to obscure the truth, as a deconstructionist might. Instead, he wishes to redefine the criteria for recognizing or identifying it.

24. Hauerwas, *Wilderness Wanderings*, 14.

primary focus will be on what he has said in approximately the last twenty years.[25]

Certainly Hauerwas has undergone what may be called a progressive conversion in his thought over the years. In his earliest writings, such as his dissertation at Yale University (Hauerwas graduated in 1968; his dissertation was originally published in 1975 as *Character and the Christian Life*), we see the seeds of narrative already developing in his concern for character and the primacy of the human community for moral formation. Here we see Hauerwas concerned with justifying his notions by providing an explicit epistemology of action from Aristotle. Over the next ten to fifteen years, Hauerwas continues to develop his concern for narrative, and does so with an eye to continued theoretical development of the anthropological justification for narrative formation, e.g., see his discussions of narrative in *Truthfulness and Tragedy: Further Investigations in Christian Ethics* (1977), and discussions of Aristotle and Aquinas as foundational for his thought in *The Peaceable Kingdom* (1983). It is in his continued contact with narrative theologians and philosophers at the University of Notre Dame (he taught at Notre Dame from 1970–1984), specifically John Howard Yoder, Alasdair MacIntyre, and David Burrell, that Hauerwas begins to develop a concern for a narrative in ecclesiology that is explicitly and solely reliant on the Christian tradition for its justification. Shortly after Hauerwas arrived at Duke University (1984–present) he stopped making statements regarding the epistemological warrant for narrative. Instead, he recognized that his primary focus must be to become a theologian for the church, as opposed to a theologian for the academy (e.g. *Resident Aliens* [1989]). Though he does not entirely abandon his former epistemological presuppositions, he makes clear that making them explicit

---

25. The division of Hauerwas's work into early and later developments is rather arbitrary. However, he does seem to have a concern for providing theoretical warrant for his thought in his early works that is not found in his later writings. The early works to which I'm referring include *Character and the Christian Life*, *Vision and Virtue*, *The Peaceable Kingdom*, and *Christian Existence Today*. His later works include *Resident Aliens*, with William Willimon; *God, Medicine, and Suffering*; *After Christendom*; *Unleashing the Scripture*; *Dispatches from the Front*; *In Good Company*; *Christians Among the Virtues*; *Wilderness Wanderings*; *Sanctify Them in the Truth*; *The Truth about God* (with William Willamon); *A Better Hope: Resources for a Church Confronting Capitalism, Democracy, and Postmodernity*; and *With the Grain of the Universe: The Church's Witness and Natural Theology*.

is not a prerequisite for their rationality. Instead, Hauerwas wishes to demonstrate the rationality of faith in opposition to Enlightenment rationality. Even when he is asked to engage in a discussion of justification, e.g., the limitation by the Lord Gifford's will of Hauerwas's Gifford Lectures in 2001 to natural theology from a more theistic perspective (see Hauerwas's discussion of the limitations in *With the Grain of the Universe* [2001]), he grows more entrenched in his belief that what humans wish to demonstrate cannot finally be demonstrated in human rationality, or reason. Indeed, to put it in terms that Hauerwas may appreciate, perhaps the evolution of his thought could best be read as a rational soul attempting to finally find peace in undertaking unending theological revision made certain only in the irrationality of friendship with God through Jesus. And such a certainty can only be realized in the friendship we find with one another when we are faced with the terrifying reality of living lives before each other in the crucible of his body—the church.

2

Flight from Modernity

Hauerwas's Critique of System as a Deconstruction of Modernity's Narrative

Introduction

STANLEY HAUERWAS REPRESENTS, IN GARY COMSTOCK'S WORDS, A "PURE narrativist."[1] Hauerwas makes little attempt to philosophically support his emphasis on a narrative epistemology. Instead, he simply pushes ahead, using a narrative approach and defending it in a somewhat *ad hoc* fashion. As will be seen below, Hauerwas believes he is recovering theology for the church. Theology, in his estimation, has become enchanted with redeeming itself as knowledge that can be verified according to Enlightenment principles of rationality. Hauerwas wishes for us to return to a more premodern model of theology. Indeed, as will be argued in a later chapter, Hauerwas's insight seems correct, if only a bit theologically shortsighted. As will be argued later, his argument remains somewhat entrenched in modernism and would be better made from the text of Scripture itself. By way of introduction, we will first survey his understanding of system, then turn to a survey of influences contributing to Hauerwas's current position. The next three chapters will continue our conversation with Hauerwas, detailing his project by outlining some of its sources and displaying his intentions against the backdrop of implicit doctrinal and philosophical considerations.

---

1. Comstock, "Truth or Meaning," 120–21.

A Brief Synopsis of Hauerwas's Critique: System as an Extension of Liberalism

Stanley Hauerwas's career has been marked by a consistent and thoroughgoing critique of liberalism. As will be discussed in detail below, his academic career began as, more or less, an attempt to engage the tools of liberalism in the development of a moral theory of character. As he began to study the impacts of liberalism on the church, and particularly as he was introduced to various figures critical of the liberal project, he discovered the vacuous nature of liberalism's claims regarding knowledge and the means for moral transformation. As he began to realize what liberalism was doing to the church, he experienced a sort of "conversion" from liberalism.[2] It is against such a backdrop of

---

2. Hauerwas readily identifies himself as a "postmodernist" or "postliberal" in whatever way the terms may be helpful. (Recently, however, he has taken fairly strong objection to being qualified as "postmodern." See Hauerwas, *Better Hope*, 35–39.) However, prone as he is to objecting to "definitions," he is not well "nailed-down" by such appellations. A question that seems ripe for Hauerwas, as well as for other postliberals/postmodernists is, does not the belief that we are *post*modern, with the implication that modernism is dying (or, rather, that postmodernists are killing it) indicate that postmodernists are somewhat metatraditional? In other words, does not the fact that postmodernists can reject modernism, and subsequently "choose" to either forge ahead in a new tradition or return to pre-Enlightenment traditions, imply that they are somehow outside tradition, if only perhaps for the fleeting moment (or for decades, since length of time is not at issue) in which their "conversion" (as Alasdair MacIntyre would have it [MacIntyre, *Whose Justice? Which Rationality?* 396–97]) takes place?

This sense of switching traditions seems to imply the ability to judge between traditions, to decide which is a more appropriate rendering of the overarching narrative. (Inhabiting multiple traditions does not seem to be a huge problem for Hauerwas, since, as he is fond of saying, he is both a theologian and a Texan. The problem arises when the traditions are antithetical to one another. Then, in order to leave one tradition for another, one must have the ability to choose which one is preferable.) The ability to judge between traditions seems to imply a neutrality associated with Enlightenment rationality. Even if this neutrality is qualified, it is still a "standing back" to get a glimpse of the larger picture. Thus arises some of Hauerwas's dilemma about the nature of conversion, and its necessarily violent nature in squashing one tradition in favor of another, specifically in the case of crushing modernity to learn a Thomistic sense of community.

Hauerwas would likely wish to say that some type of choice from a neutral position is not what is at issue. Rather, conversion is about training someone to *do* what is right, not to choose what is right. Such training removes the neutrality of volitional and voluntaristic aspects associated with conversion in a modernistic context. But how can a person stand in one tradition and be able to recognize the good and bad of other traditions, or even to recognize the good and the bad within his or her own tradition?

Hauerwas's critical engagement with liberalism that any interpretation or discussion of his work must take place.

It is in the context of his critique of liberalism that Hauerwas places his discussions of method. He will claim to avoid methodology and any attempt to make method *a priori* to actually doing theology.[3] Indeed, he believes one of the problems of modern theology is its need to have a method that is unassailable before it is able to make claims regarding the substance of its knowledge. As will be discussed further in the next chapters, Hauerwas responds to such a foundationalistic approach with a sort of revelational realism. Believing as he does in the created nature of the world, Hauerwas sees little necessity for such a justification of knowledge.

Systematic theology, in Hauerwas's thinking, is a relatively new conception of doing theology. He never offers a full-blown critique of systematic theory, prone as he is to avoid engaging in more purely theoretical, that is, noncontextualized, discussions. Nor does he engage a particular theologian on the subject of method. No one figure is representative of system. Further, in order to critique system as a theory, Hauerwas would necessarily have to compare it to narrative, specifically narrative *as* a theory. Hauerwas believes narrative cannot be so conceived. As will be demonstrated later, narrative is, quite simply, a given for theology, or in Hauerwas's language, a "gift."[4] Since Hauerwas provides no systematic critique of system, it will be necessary to identify the characteristics of system he finds particularly objectionable and attempt to place them in relationship with one another in such a way as to gain a clearer picture of the story Hauerwas would wish to tell of system. I do not mean to attempt to develop Hauerwas's systematic treatment of

---

Have we a history of such training that is reliable, i.e., uninterrupted?

I am here making a point given in a somewhat different frame of reference by Robert Jenson. See his short but poignant, "Review of Stanley Hauerwas's *After Christendom?*" Also cf. Holland's discussion of Hauerwas's creation of a "positivism of communal peoplehood" in Holland's "Problems and Prospects of a 'Sectarian Ethic'," 166.

3. Hauerwas, *Dispatches from the Front*, 22. Hauerwas here uses Yoder (*Priestly Kingdom*, 7) to demonstrate that what comes first is not the demonstration of the reliability of knowledge. Instead, what comes first is the demonstration of the life (i.e., narrative) of the church as the primary reality.

4. Hauerwas, *In Good Company*, 29. Hauerwas discusses Milbank's conception of the work of the Spirit as a gifting of unity through the Eucharist (See Milbank, "Enclaves, or Where Is the Church?" 342).

system for him, since he would obviously find such an attempt illegitimate. Instead, I merely wish to place his critical comments and remarks concerning system in closer proximity to gain a clearer understanding of the exact nature of his critique of system. I recognize the dangers of such an attempt, since it will undoubtedly be somewhat destructive to the context in which he has placed his critical remarks. The remainder of the chapter should help alleviate some of those dangers by placing the critique back into the narratives from which the following brief discussion is taken. While any discussion of method remains derivative of Hauerwas's larger discussion of the church and liberalism's destructive forces, our treatment of system seems to provide a specific inroad to his theology unavailable from other approaches. Likewise, it bears on one of the primary points of confrontation between Hauerwas and modern theology.

The connection Hauerwas posits between liberalism and systematics centers on the attempt by systematics to bolster the liberal project by providing the kind of knowledge necessary for theology to proceed as primarily knowledge. Stemming as it did from Enlightenment roots, liberalism was bound to a rationalistic approach to securing knowledge. Rationalism depended upon having a theory of knowledge that was foundational in such a way that the theory provided justification for the reasonability of the knowledge. Hauerwas has worked hard to overcome this tendency in rationalism.

> I have tried very hard to forget that I once thought I had to have a theory of knowledge to know what I know. That is, I have learned that it is an epistemological mistake and, even more important, a theological mistake, to think a "ground" must be secured to begin theological reflection. In a similar fashion, I do not think you can or should try to develop a rational theory about rationality. You can always learn something from such theories, but what you learn is not necessarily dependent on the theory.[5]

---

5. Hauerwas, *Wilderness Wanderings*, 232–33. Hauerwas doesn't appear opposed to the notion of grounding, as long as one understands this to mean describing the link between a present context and tradition in such a way that the description becomes a form of biographical habituation, i.e., narrative. As will be discussed below, one of Hauerwas's problems lies in describing tradition. In other words, Hauerwas speaks of tradition in a somewhat unified sense, as though one single tradition may be identifiable. Of course, he knows that even within a tradition as unified as Roman Catholicism

The influence of the Enlightenment caused the modern church to justify itself based on the reasonability of its beliefs, rather than standing more firmly in the tradition of beliefs it affirmed as real for centuries. In other words, the Enlightenment caused the church to search for justification and warrant in places external to itself and its faith. Knowledge needed to be verified according to its relationship to the discursive nature of human reason. This move in theological knowledge parallels the impulse in all fields of knowledge since the Enlightenment, including moral knowledge, toward self-evident foundationalism.

> It has been the hallmark of ethical theory since the Enlightenment to ground morality in rationality qua rationality; in other words, morality only has meaning when considered as a schema of laws or principles self-evident to any reasonable person. But such accounts of morality, by their own admission can give only extremely thin material content to their standards of right and wrong; they can proclaim that certain kinds of behavior are wrong "in principle." But when forced to consider added parts of a person's history, the circumstances of a situation, the role of the community in an individual's life—these material conditions of morality are set aside in favor of a simple assertion of what "in principle" must be true anytime and anyplace. The loss of material content is a small price to pay for this assumed universality. The issue, then, for such systems of ethics becomes how such universally derived principles are to be applied in concrete cases.[6]

The drive to ground knowledge in reason meant that knowledge should be ordered in a fashion so as to demonstrate its reasonableness from the standpoint of any rational creature, i.e., from the standpoint of "anyone."[7] Thus, the compulsion for system became coupled with the need to make knowledge "democratic," or in more technical terms, universal. The product of such constructions could then be claimed

---

some divergence occurs. The question then becomes, which tradition? As will be seen in the next chapter, Hauerwas seems somewhat eclectic in choosing historical figures who have influenced him. He does not seem to answer explicitly the question as to why he has chosen these and not others. Indeed, to provide such an answer would require an appeal to theoretical considerations that Hauerwas deems distracting to theology. Of course, ignoring, or even rejecting such considerations does not mean they don't exist. Hauerwas is simply unwilling to acknowledge them in any theoretical sense.

6. Hauerwas, *Dispatches from the Front*, 138–39.

7. Ibid., 139.

as a universal representation of knowledge, since it corresponded to what was finally provable according to human reason qua reason. René Descartes's dictum regarding the grounding of theological knowledge in human reason became the mode of theological investigation.

> I have always thought that two issues—namely, God and the soul—are chief among those that ought to be demonstrated with the aid of philosophy rather than theology. For although it suffices for us believers to believe by faith that the human soul does not die with the body, and that God exists, certainly no unbelievers seem capable of being persuaded of any religion or even of almost any moral virtue, until these two are first proven to them by natural reason. ... And in *Romans*, Chapter 1, ... it appears ... that everything that can be known about God can be shown by reasons drawn exclusively from our own mind.[8]

With this as the primary theory of influence on the discovery of theological knowledge, system quickly became the tool for extending the reach of such discovery according to human reason. The nature of system itself is not to proceed according to reason qua reason. This is the philosophical presupposition displayed by modernity's use of system. Instead, system is grounded in a specific philosophical perspective and becomes the *method* of grounding and justifying the claims of that philosophy. In other words, system is a tool used by the theologian or philosopher in the discovery and display of knowledge. Hauerwas learned such an understanding of system from Karl Barth.

> A "system" is an edifice of thought, constructed on certain fundamental conceptions which are selected in accordance with a certain philosophy by a method which corresponds to these conceptions. Theology cannot be carried on in confinement or under the pressure of such a construction.[9]

8. Descartes, *Meditations on First Philosophy*, para. 2. One can easily see Descartes's emphasis on theism in this statement, since the passage in Romans that he has in mind addresses only the "invisible attributes, eternal power, and divine nature" of God (1:20). Nothing is said about Christ or the work of God in redemption. Thus Descartes is here clearly leaving specifically Christian theology behind in favor of the theism of philosophy. Cf. Buckley, *At the Origins of Modern Atheism*, 68–99.

9. Barth, *Dogmatics in Outline*, 5. Hauerwas quotes this "definition" of system in his *With the Grain of the Universe*, 178–79. Though Hauerwas does not engage Barth on this subject, I wonder if perhaps he would take issue with the way in which Barth so easily separates system from its philosophical foundations. In other words, I'm not sure Hauerwas would see system as something that could exist apart from specific philosophical convictions. They seem to be of the same vein.

Thus, system became the means by which the reach of Enlightenment rationalism was extended through theological knowledge. Hauerwas makes no attempt to separate system from its Enlightenment philosophical foundations, though he is quick to point out the perilous nature of such foundations.[10]

One of the more devastating implications of extending Enlightenment rationalism into theology has been the effect it has had on the connection of the church's knowledge with its history. Systematizing knowledge according to the principles that could be extracted from any historical situation divorces knowledge from its historical context. Specifically, rationality's claims to universalism have made the church's parallel claims to universalism illegitimate based on their lack of warrant. In other words, because the universals claimed by the church are encumbered with historical claims and are not open to rational demonstration according to accepted principles of epistemological inquiry (i.e., an epistemology grounded in human reason), their veracity is, at best, questionable. Hauerwas will rightly demonstrate the permeating nature of narrative and the way in which history functions in judging truthfulness (we will discuss this further in the chapters below); however, before doing so, he must deconstruct the narrative of Enlightenment claims to be beyond history. His reason for attempting such a critique are intertwined with his theological goal to call the church toward faithfulness.

The Enlightenment compulsion toward arriving at universal knowledge has crippled the church in its attempt to remain faithful to its calling. Claims to universal knowledge based in reason alone are, by necessity, ahistorical. The Enlightenment's preference for autonomous reason divorced the language of the church from its connection to the person of Jesus and the witness of the early church to his life and message. Theological language, to be universal, needed to be translated into language for any rational creature. Thus, the particularity of Jesus's life

10. As will be discussed below, Hauerwas does single out such things as foundationalism and referential language as convictions behind certain systematic tendencies. However, he does not engage them as theoretical "alternatives." Instead, he focuses on the way in which they are devastating to the life of the church. One could almost say Hauerwas's ecclesiology is his own foundation underlying his system of narrative, but obviously such a theoretical description of Hauerwas's work would be rather superficial and not rightly "aimed" in that it already presupposes theory is the best manner in which to depict theology.

and history needed to be removed from theology in a manner quite similar to the way in which the historical needed to be removed from theories of morality.

> [Universal] theories of morality attempt to free moral convic-
> tions from their history and, in particular, from their Jewish
> and Christian roots. From this perspective, for a principle to be
> moral it must be capable of being held and applied by anyone,
> whether they be Christian, Muslim, or American.[11]

Such universalism destroys precisely the element that makes the church what it is: its memory. If the church is forced to give up its connection to the past, it is left without any means to fulfill its function as church. This causes it to search elsewhere for its convictions. This loss of memory overcame the church as its historical nature became a merely academic concern. History simply "contained" the universals in such a way that they needed to be extricated by discovering what was timeless and rationally defensible. The task of systematics was precisely this discovery and extrication.[12] The church's historical context and circumstances, including the life and message of Jesus, became part of the larger question of what is merely past. "Inherent to liberalism is the attempt to create societies and people without memory. 'History' becomes an 'academic' subject that serves no moral purpose."[13]

System represents the rational epistemological framework on which liberalism was able to build its dehistoricized knowledge. By removing the historical context (i.e., action and the practices of being church) from the knowledge of theology, systematicians believed they were arriving at knowledge that was universal or final. Discovering truth was then merely a matter of corresponding the principles extracted from a historical context with the overarching principles of universal knowledge already organized in a rational system (thus correspondence and coherence work hand-in-hand in systematics). Because such a move

---

11. Hauerwas, *Dispatches from the Front*, 139. One can begin to see here that Hauerwas makes little distinction between ethics and theology as disciplines. Indeed, as will be shown briefly later, he believes that they are equivalent.

12. Hauerwas paints with a rather broad brush at times, providing little substantiation for the claim I have outlined here. However, he is not without examples of such an approach to systematic theology and history. E.g., see Hodge, *Systematic Theology*, 1–4.

13. Hauerwas, *Dispatches from the Front*, 228 n. 9.

places theological knowledge under the authority of the rational mind, Hauerwas rightly sees that the church is relegated to, at best, a collective of like-minded individuals, and, at worst, an encumbrance to the spiritual progress of the individual. Even more troublesome is the way in which systematic knowledge is inherently docetic in that it makes the life and death of Jesus unnecessary.[14]

In the following sections we will attempt to understand further how Hauerwas came to such a critique of system. In order to gain an inroad into his critique, we will begin with a brief analysis of the influence of certain figures on his relationship to liberalism. Hauerwas was reminded by Paul Holmer early in his education at Yale that theology was more than constructing theories of knowledge. It was more specifically concerned with the creation of character in the self, in such a way that the life of a person became the measure of truth. Theology was primarily about the life of the Christian as it could be seen and shaped in certain practices.

The Roots of Hauerwas's Critique in the Work of Paul Holmer and Studies at Yale University

Hauerwas's own testimony with regard to his objections to liberalistic tendencies within theology begins in a somewhat biographical fashion. It is as if he is telling us his own story of how he was "converted" from modernism. The story begins in his days as a student at Yale University. Though many figures have had a deep influence on Hauerwas as his thought has changed over the years, the initial influence is to be found in Paul Holmer, one of his professors at Yale. Holmer had occasion to teach Hauerwas lessons in reading Søren Kierkegaard and Ludwig Wittgenstein—lessons that helped Hauerwas begin his flight from modernity.

Hauerwas went to Yale, by his own admission,

14. Hauerwas, *Wilderness Wanderings*, 41–42. Hauerwas uses Reinhold Niebuhr to illustrate this point. Though Niebuhr, more than most, stresses the importance of history, he understands the cross in symbolic terms that finally make it, ironically, ahistorical: "It sounds like orthodoxy to claim, as Niebuhr does, that the cross is the 'solution' to history, but the strength of such a claim is undercut by Niebuhr's insistence that the cross is first and last a 'symbol'—namely, the name for the eternal possibility that transcends the ambiguities of history" (42).

> [T]o investigate whether Christianity could be made to con-
> form to the challenges of modernity. . . . Accordingly, I thought
> my task was to determine how religious claims could be made
> true by finding a better theory. Such theories, I assumed, would
> be supplied by philosophy.[15]

As Holmer introduced Hauerwas to Kierkegaard, Hauerwas discovered
that the emphasis in Christian belief was not so much on the *what* as
on the *how*. In Hauerwas's early search for the final criteria by which to
measure the truth of Christianity, he had not expected the answer to be
found in devotion. But that was where Holmer pointed him.[16] The lives
of the faithful were the locus for discovery of the truth, even the prayers
by which they spoke their devotion. Hauerwas sees the contrast now in
the way theology has been traditionally done over the last few centuries
and the devotion it has finally abandoned.

> I do not think theologians, particularly in our day, can or should
> write "big books" that "pull it all together." Any theology that
> threatens to become a position more determinative than the
> Christian practice of prayer betrays its subject. At best, theology
> is but a set of reminders to help Christians pray faithfully.[17]

It is not accidental that Holmer's influence leads Hauerwas toward an
attraction to the work of Wittgenstein.[18]

---

15. Ibid., 144.

16. Ibid., 144–45.

17. Hauerwas, *With the Grain of the Universe*, 10.

18. Though Hauerwas does not frequently engage Wittgenstein directly in his discussions of theology, it is apparent that Wittgenstein's discussions regarding the "use"
of language and the way in which language must be placed into a context in order
to have meaning have impacted him immensely. Hauerwas uses the notion that the
truthfulness of language has more to do with the speaker than the words, in order to
underwrite his concern that theology is first concerned with the moral character of the
church. Thus, theological language is not intended to represent reality. Rather, its "use"
is primarily found in the way in which it helps to shape and mold the reality in which
it is placed. Wittgenstein is helpful in this regard, since he believed that in order to engage in the various aspects of description in context (i.e., naming in a language game),
one must first have mastered the language game itself. In other words, for Hauerwas's
purposes, in order to rightly name the Triune God of Christian theology, one must
first have engaged upon, and even mastered, a life of holiness. Speaking rightly of God
requires the prior necessity of living rightly. For development of how Wittgenstein is
here understanding the relationship of language to meaning and the "use" of language,
see Wittgenstein, *Philosophical Investigations*.

Holmer "sav[ed Hauerwas] from the presumption that Wittgenstein had any theory about meaning, or anything else for that matter."[19] Instead, Hauerwas began to understand that truth was found in the person making truth claims, not in the claims independent of the person.[20] Hauerwas was learning the "new language" of belief.[21] This new language entailed learning a new life. As Holmer claims, "the use of religious language requires participation in the religious life and this involves exposure to the community of believers."[22] Hauerwas believes, likely with Holmer, that "exposure" is now considerably too weak a term to describe what is required.[23]

The influence of Wittgenstein on Hauerwas extends beyond this point of exposure to or interaction with the life of belief. For life begins, in Hauerwas's understanding of Wittgenstein, at the level of language.

> [Wittgenstein] slowly cured me of the notion that philosophy was primarily a matter of positions, ideas and/or theories. From Wittgenstein, and later David Burrell, I learned to understand and also to do philosophy in a therapeutic mode. But there were also substantive matters to be learned from Wittgenstein. Originally sparked by my interest in history, I had begun to work on issues in the philosophy of mind such as the relation of "mind-body problem," "intentionality," and "motivation." Wittgenstein (and Ryle and Austin) helped me to see that "mind" did not relate to body as a cause to effect, for "mind" was not a singular thing or function. Moreover, Wittgenstein ended forever any attempt on my part to try to anchor theology in some general account of "human experience," for his writings taught me that the object of the theologians' work was best located in terms of the grammar of the language used by believers.[24]

19. Hauerwas, *Wilderness Wanderings*, 144.

20. Ibid., 145.

21. It should further be noted that Hauerwas seems to be critical of referential or representative language, which purports to somehow represent reality. See Hauerwas, Murphy, and Nation, *Theology Without Foundations*, 14–15. Hauerwas pays little attention to the linguistic debate per se. However, he does employ referential language when he needs to ground a premise in doctrinal realism (e.g., the miraculous nature of the Eucharist).

22. Holmer, *Theology and the Scientific Study of Religion*, 109.

23. Hauerwas, *Wilderness Wanderings*, 146.

24. Hauerwas, *Peaceable Kingdom*, xxi. One can begin to see here why Hauerrwas has such a preference for the language of tradition, though Hauerwas seems, at times,

The connection between the language one uses and that same person's reality is not a connection of mere coincidence, nor is it simply representative of reality. The interplay between language and reality is fundamental for Hauerwas's narrative. For Hauerwas, language, particularly theological language, serves to shape and mold the reality of the community of belief as it learns to name the tradition through shared practice.[25] "I think of theology as an attempt to assemble the grammatical reminders that point to the significance of what we say for helping us live truthful lives, that is, lives that witness to the fact that all that is is God's good creation."[26] Though language may also at times be used to represent what the community affirms as real, its primary function is pedagogical. It is an integral part of the context in which the believer learns and is trained to participate in the life of the community of belief. As will be seen in the subsequent chapters, Hauerwas employs such an understanding of language by constantly making his argument from the context of ecclesiology. His argument for what constitutes an appropriate narrative and the identifying qualities of that narrative is saturated with language contingent on the theological reality of the church as Christ's body. While I think Hauerwas is right to couch his argument in such language, indeed, he would say that as a Christian he can do no other, I am not convinced the language of church in the tradition to which he is bound can support his claims of church as a divinely representative community, at least not to the extent he wishes. As will be seen especially with regard to discussion of the Eucharist in chapter 5, he does not seem to have a sufficiently theological language in which to frame his narrative community. This means that, at times, he appears to be engaging merely in anthropology or sociology, i.e., in human interactions in community qua human. In other words, he needs to "do" a little more theology in his language.

reticent to make fuller use of the language of revelation, i.e., of Scripture.

25. Wittgenstein was not particularly original in his language games and in the incumbent practices necessary to engage the game. As will be discussed below, Barth also did this in the *Church Dogmatics* through his "method" of repetition, though with a more theological/biblical intention. Hauerwas does not make extensive reference to a comparison of Wittgenstein to Barth, though he is certainly aware of the similarities. See Hauerwas, *With the Grain of the Universe*, 173 n. 1.

26. Hauerwas, "Where Would I Be Without Friends?" 315.

Entrenching his theology in the life of the community means that everything Hauerwas says and does must somehow be Christianly construed. This creates what is called by Hauerwas's critics a "sectarian" problem when it comes to making claims to truth. Hauerwas seems unable to engage in any significant discussion about reality for anyone other than the Christian. In other words, doesn't such an interactive rationality between community and theory, or between life and language, offered by Wittgenstein, and subsequently limited specifically to the church by Holmer and Hauerwas, necessarily imply relativism?

As will be seen in the discussion of Barth in the next chapter, and church and world in chapter 5, Hauerwas believes that the subjective-objective distinction so often paraded before everyone wishing to enter in discussions of truth is no longer valid. Ultimately, Christian truth is truth for the world as well, though the world may be unlikely to accept it. God's truth of his revelation in his Son, Jesus, is universal truth. Hauerwas believes Christians have been too embarrassed or too mired in the world themselves to make this claim boldly.[27] On the other hand, what Christians have said has largely been an engagement with the intent to convince, rather than an engagement with the intent to witness. Any discussion of truth that can be undertaken without regard for the truthfulness of the lives of those involved is simply not "good theology."[28]

Far from being a fideistic retreat from rationality, claims about participation in the community, and the metaphysical implications of a strong commitment to narrative formation (that is, that narrative is prior to theoretical justification and may even replace justification) are hardly relativistic. Hauerwas cannot allow that Holmer's, and his own, views be dismissed as merely sectarian. Instead, becoming a part of the community requires training in the historical beliefs that are implicit in every specific community's historical particulars, at least insofar as the community in question can plausibly be called the church. Those beliefs must become a living reality in those who hold them, which is a matter of formation.

27. As Hauerwas exclaims (Hauerwas et al., *Theology Without Foundations*, 326 n. 3) with regard to the possibility of sounding imperialistic, "I confess I find the 'humility' of much of current Christian theology and practice humiliating. In a time like ours the Church's task is to celebrate the triumph of our Lord."

28. See Hauerwas's discussion of Holmer in *Wilderness Wanderings*, 144–47.

Indeed, [Holmer] would not know what [a sectarian, relativistic] description of Christian practices would mean, since to be a Christian requires training in a very definite set of "beliefs." Furthermore, part of the problem is the very language of belief itself; too often beliefs sound like "things" toward which I can assume an attitude. That is why, following McClendon, I resorted to the language of convictions as a reminder that any belief that matters is never something different from who I am.[29]

However, Holmer, and Hauerwas with him, have not been able to escape the accusation of being sectarian.[30] Though this accusation does not seem to worry Hauerwas a great deal, he does nonetheless wish to challenge the presuppositions which seem to make the accusation of fideism so forceful. As he states in defense of Holmer,

Yet the presumption persists that Holmer is one of the sources of what is frequently called "Yale fideism." Such a position, it is alleged, attempts to insulate Christian convictions from philosophical and scientific challenge. Not only that, but the Christian convictions so protected are of the most conservative brand. That nothing Holmer has said would entail such characterizations only seems to invite, from those intent on espousing the virtues of "theory," the idea that he must be trying to protect Christian practice from external challenge. That such accusations persist raises the question of how one is to go on in the face of such persistent misunderstanding.

One of the ways I think Holmer has tried to go on is by helping us forget certain kinds of questions—questions like "How can we determine the meaning of God language?" To be sure, such questions are assumed fundamental if theology is to be a

29. Hauerwas, *Wilderness Wanderings*, 146. For his understanding of convictions, Hauerwas is here relying on McClendon and Smith, *Convictions*.

30. Perhaps the most poignant, and certainly the most personal for Hauerwas, critique of his work as sectarian came from Hauerwas's teacher James Gustafson in Gustafson's "Sectarian Temptation." For Hauerwas's response, see the Introduction to his *Christian Existence Today*, 1–21. Also cf. Roberts, "Theology and the Ascetic Imperative," esp. 188–89. Another interesting way of phrasing this critique is found in Keen, "Human Person as Intercessory Prayer," 44. Writing of the sanctification espoused by Hauerwas in the context of ecclesiological body life, Keen surmises "although the perfection Hauerwas describes may well be perfect friendship, it is not perfect agape." Keen sees Hauerwas's community as restrictive of God's activity in such a way that church can no longer maintain its universal implications for witness. It is finally a guarded community or life for the individual and the church in that the contact between church and world remains a bit too formal for Keen.

respectable academic subject matter. Yet he refuses to privilege such questions, particularly in the abstract, because to try to answer such questions abstractly can only distort the character of theology.

In contrast, I think Holmer has tried to remind us that theology is the attempt to display the kind of lives necessary if we are to speak well of God.[31]

Being called a sectarian seems to imply that Hauerwas is part of some enclave of Christian belief specific to one time and place. In other words, perhaps Hauerwas can be dismissed as a poignant voice for twentieth-century American Methodists, but he has little to say that could be interesting to the universal church. Calling Hauerwas sectarian makes him historical in a sense that finally makes him irrelevant. However, Hauerwas does not see himself as a theologian for a specific community (such as the Methodists, Catholics, or Mennonites). He wishes to be a theologian for "the church catholic."[32] He is tremendously influenced by John Howard Yoder (who was, of course, a Mennonite). Nevertheless, he does not believe that this qualifies him, or Yoder for that matter, as necessarily a radical sectarian. Hauerwas does belong to a specific community and consequently believes it is that community that will shape him and mold him into what he is and shall be. Nevertheless, he wishes his voice to be heard beyond the walls of his home church, classroom, or university.[33] Sectarianism is only a threat if you believe the presupposition that in order for one to speak broadly or generally one must first have common ground with the audience. In other words, Hauerwas believes he is speaking universal truth; he is simply unwilling to translate it into language for anyone, i.e., he is

31. Hauerwas, *Wilderness Wanderings*, 146.

32. Hauerwas, *Dispatches from the Front*, 22. Hauerwas is here citing Yoder, *Priestly Kingdom*, 3–4.

33. I am not sure what to make of Hauerwas's desire to be a "theologian of the church catholic." Such aspirations could be understood as a will to power, or as a desire to have the ability to speak universally, i.e., to what is true for all people in the church everywhere. Each of these would obviously be suicidal for Hauerwas's theology of narrative. Perhaps a better explanation is simply that Hauerwas believes his theology is, and should be, everyone's theology. If you like it, welcome to the family. If you don't, then don't read it. It is, for him, a form of witness, and in that respect does speak to the church catholic.

unwilling to engage in what he believes has entrapped the church in is current liberal state.[34] Perhaps this can best be displayed by returning to Hauerwas's own history.

Convinced of the lessons that Holmer taught him, Hauerwas pursued the relationship of the *what* and the *how*. Holmer had shown him that the *what* could never be abstracted from the *how*, or as Hauerwas states with regard to Holmer's lessons in Kierkegaard,

> I had decided to become an ethicist, ugly as the word is, because Holmer had convinced me that Kierkegaard had rediscovered "the pragmatic significance of the person of Jesus Christ" (*TSSR*, 203). I thought that "doing ethics" was a way to explicate the practical significance of learning to talk well as a Christian. I assumed, moreover, that ethics was a way to explore the truthful character of Christian speech, or better, how Christian speech requires us to develop the skills to be truthful.[35]

The implication of Kierkegaard's rediscovery is, of course, that this aspect of ethics was at one point lost. Hauerwas, like Kierkegaard, blames Enlightenment rationality for leaving behind this 'pragmatic significance'. As Kierkegaard points out,

> The medium for being a Christian has been shifted from existence and the ethical to the intellectual, the metaphysical, the imaginary; a more or less theatrical relationship has been introduced between thinking Christianity and being Christian—and thus being a Christian has been abolished.[36]

If Hauerwas is to pursue what he believes to be the appropriate context in which to "do" ethics, he must first separate himself from those

34. Hauerwas, "On Keeping Theological Ethics Theological," 17. Hauerwas believes the issue of translation to be a problem for both conservatives and liberals alike. As he states (Hauerwas, *Better Hope*, 119), "For many Christians, *ethics* names the attempt to develop natural law accounts or draw on other nontheological sources of moral wisdom to make it possible for Christians to responsibly participate in, as well as be of service to, the American democratic experiment. Conservative and liberal Christian ethicists, who often disagree about everything else, agree that some 'third language' must be developed if Christians are to act in public."

35. Hauerwas, *Wilderness Wanderings*, 147–48. Hauerwas is here citing Holmer's *Theology and the Scientific Study of Religion*, 203.

36. Kierkegaard, "Armed Neutrality" cited by Hauerwas and Willimon as an epigraph to *Where Resident Aliens Live*, 10.

he considers responsible for "forgetting" the context of the life of Jesus in the story of Christian ethics.

> In order to pursue [the appropriate context for Christian ethics], I was forced to provide a different account of "ethics" than that supplied by the prevailing Kantian (and liberal) paradigms. I had the good luck to be at Yale, where the influence of H. Richard Niebuhr persisted. I was not particularly taken with Niebuhr's "radical monotheism," impressed as I was by Barth, but I did learn from Niebuhr (and Gustafson) that history and the communities that constituted memory matter morally. So focused, I discovered the significance of Aristotle's account of virtue, believing as I did that the virtues named those habits (qualities) necessary for us to be agents of memory.[37]

The "prevailing Kantian (and liberal) paradigms" were responsible for modernity's forgetfulness of historicity (the context of real historical communities) in ethics. Hauerwas believes that it is in the presence of the rationality of Immanuel Kant that Christianity finally loses its memory. But how does Hauerwas understand this to have taken place, and why is Kant to blame for this? Thus far, we have only been introduced to some of the issues behind Hauerwas's rejection of modernity. In order to gain a "thicker" understanding of Hauerwas's reasoning, we must first attend to his critique of liberalism, specifically as it relates to systematic theology, and subsequently must address his reading of Kant.

Conclusion

Hauerwas understands himself to be part of a story (narrative) begun for him at Yale, but stretching well beyond the confines of one university or even the short years he spent there. His professors trained him well in the vein of what may be called postliberalism. He came to recognize the hollow claims of liberalism, but even more, he came to see the vacuous nature of the Enlightenment presuppositions upon which liberalism rested. With this brief introduction to some of Hauerwas's history, our next chapter explores Hauerwas's critique of liberalism, demonstrating his keen awareness of the destructive nature of liberalism to the substance of the church. He learned very well his lessons at Yale. His resources for a response and his own "constructive" suggestions are the subjects of the following chapters.

37. Hauerwas, *Wilderness Wanderings*, 148.

$$3$$

System as Liberalism

Hauerwas's Critique of Immanuel Kant

Introduction

THE SHORT INTRODUCTION IN THE LAST CHAPTER TO HAUERWAS'S CRITICAL analysis of liberalism and its effects hardly does justice to the depth of his understanding of certain permeating philosophical notions that have penetrated theology. The church, particularly Protestant liberalism, has adopted many of these notions and has tailored its epistemology to the Enlightenment to such an extent it no longer looks like the church Hauerwas imagines in light of Scripture. Hauerwas's critique of system is an intentional attack on the modernism that has crept into theology. On the other hand, Hauerwas's concerns are not limited merely to narrative theology's critique of systematics, as though his designs were merely academic. Other theologians, including systematicians, also recognize the immodesty of claims in theology stemming from modernism. Such notions as comprehensiveness of knowledge seen in universal doctrinal claims seem to go beyond the limits of appropriate theological language, even revelational language. In this chapter, we will explore further Hauerwas's critique of liberalism by outlining his argument against what he considers the sources of liberalism, as well as by engaging the arguments in which he finds himself when confronted by the liberal commitments of his contemporaries in theology. We will finally conclude with a detailed discussion of Hauerwas's critique of Kant as an ultimate, though certainly not as the only or original, source of liberalism. Alongside the discussion of Hauerwas's critique of liberalism, a clearer picture of his own alternative will begin to emerge. As will be seen in the development of his critique, much of his negative response toward liberalism stems from a fairly developed conception of narrative. Indeed, as Hauerwas would argue, he cannot critique liberalism from a totally objective standpoint, since no such thing exists. Instead his own biases will be displayed as the alternative to liberalism. His own historicism, or context, is no arbitrary matter when it comes to his critique of liberalism and the alternative he offers. In true narrative (i.e., Aristotelian) fashion, it makes all the difference.

Hauerwas's understanding of Modern Liberalism

Hauerwas identifies several liberal tendencies in modernity that he finds problematic. However, he does not give a definition of liberalism, as some have supposed him to do.[1] Early in his career, Hauerwas was willing to qualify liberalism as follows:

> In the most general terms, I understand liberalism to be that impulse deriving from the Enlightenment project to free all people from the chains of their historical particularity in the name of freedom. As an epistemological position, liberalism is the attempt to defend foundationalism in order to free reason from being determined by any particularistic tradition. Politically, liberalism makes the individual the supreme unit of society, thus making the political task the securing of cooperation between arbitrary units of desire. While there is no strict logical entailment between these forms of liberalism, I think it can be said they are often interrelated.[2]

In more recent years, he has tended to avoid definitions. Indeed, as Hauerwas states, "I have strong philosophical doubts about the very idea of definition."[3] Accordingly, it would be difficult to find in Hauerwas a list or systematic analysis of the deficiencies he has identified in liberalism.[4] Nevertheless, he does attack certain aspects of liberalism, making it possible to identify some of the issues he regards as

---

1. Christopher Beem attributes a rather "thin" definition of liberalism to Hauerwas in Beem, "American Liberalism and the Christian Church," 119–33.

2. Hauerwas, *Against the Nations*, 18.

3. Hauerwas, *Wilderness Wanderings*, 229.

4. Certainly, attempts have been made to provide a list of Hauerwas's problems with liberalism. For a concise and modest attempt, see Brennan, "Stanley Hauerwas and the Critique of Secular Liberalism," 2–4.

important. Among these, one, which is related to the epistemological liberalism cited above, seems to stand out as particularly objectionable: the compulsion to establish a universalism by which all particulars can be explained or objectified. Though certainly other tendencies of liberalism are distasteful to Hauerwas, this one is central enough to warrant specific attention. Hauerwas sees this compulsion infiltrating theology in the form of systematics, in that theology is transformed into a body of knowledge or information unrelated in a direct manner to history or context, even to the originating biblical context. The consequence of systematics is seen in the turn of theology from being church to having a verifiable list of beliefs.

Hauerwas is quite ready to implicate modernity in the loss of a sense of community within the contemporary church—i.e., modernity has reduced being church to having knowledge about the church.[5] Of course, the focal point of modernity for Hauerwas is its inception: the Enlightenment. With the Enlightenment came the desire to pursue universal theories of knowledge that produced rationally verifiable statements or principles, and consequently the moral theories implied by such principles of knowledge.[6] Ethical theories, in the spirit of Enlightenment thought, are driven to excise any remnant of the particular from their midst. To be truly universal, they must be ahistorical. This is especially the case with regard to morality, since prior to the Enlightenment, ethics was the domain of the church, a very historical institution. This is the predicament of the modern person, or as Hauerwas would rather characterize it, of the liberal self. Universalism, or the forgetting of history, is precisely the conundrum in which liberal-

---

5. Although Hauerwas is certain that the Enlightenment destroyed any real appreciation for the particulars of history, he is unclear as to whether he actually believes such an appreciation existed prior to the Enlightenment. (Though relatively early in his career, he does mention, at least once, that he believes pre-Enlightenment thought made no distinction between theology and morality: Hauerwas "On Keeping Theological Ethics Theological," 19–20.) Though he does not seem to have a repristinatory project toward the Middle Ages in mind, his discussions of the Enlightenment and his preference for Aquinas seem at times to imply such a project. Perhaps he sees in Aquinas a sense of community from which the Constantinian elements can be excised. Of course, such a primitivist notion has the connotations of sounding terribly theoretical and abstract, even supratraditional. Nevertheless, as will be seen below, Hauerwas is unrelenting in his appeals to Aquinas and Aristotle. Cf. Hauerwas, *With the Grain of the Universe*, 32.

6. Hauerwas, *Dispatches from the Front*, 138–39.

ism has placed the church. It is against such a project of "forgetting" that Hauerwas has aimed his critique. Though other aspects of liberalism (enlightened self-interest, individualism) may still matter, Hauerwas's problem is with the ahistorical nature of liberal thought, implied by its universality. His primary concern "has always been what liberalism does to remembering as a political task."[7] As Hauerwas makes clear, "Inherent to liberalism is the attempt to create societies and people without memory. 'History' becomes an 'academic' subject that serves no moral purpose."[8] By "academic," he means that history becomes morally benign. History is conceived in such a manner that it has no relevance for a contemporary context. Liberals may find history "interesting," but they dare not let it make a difference.

> History, from a liberal perspective, is the study of the past in order to render the past impotent for the ongoing determinations of our lives. In short, history becomes the way to put the wrongs of the past truly and irrevocably in the past through a kind of forgetfulness.[9]

Of course, what this means for the liberal church is that Christianity dare not make any specific historical claims, since to do so would be suicidal. Instead, theology must become another disinterested subject available for academic consideration.

> In order for Christianity to gain intellectual and political intelligibility within the world of political liberalism, it must first be transformed into (i.e., reduced to) "beliefs." The way this transformation is accomplished is to focus on the "problem of history." History becomes the shorthand term for maintaining a causal account of human behavior to which God can only be an "externality." Such an account then produces the question "How,

---

7. Hauerwas, *Wilderness Wanderings*, 230. As an illustration of such forgetting, Hauerwas displays the way in which liberalism has skewed the memory of Martin Luther King Jr. "I think there no better example of the deficiencies of liberal remembering than what is happening to the memory of Martin Luther King Jr. . . . Liberal memory makes King the great hero of the liberal ideals of 'freedom of the individual' and 'equality,' but King did not represent 'individuals.' He did not seek individual freedom for African-Americans. King sought freedom for African-Americans as a people to remember slavery and the triumph over slavery offered by the black church" (230).

8. Hauerwas, *Dispatches from the Front*, 228 n. 9.

9. Hauerwas, *Wilderness Wanderings*, 10.

if at all, can God act in history?" That question presupposes that history names a world that is not God's creation.[10]

Stating the problem in such a way makes clear that Christians are not merely subject to ethical floundering; it also demonstrates the political incapacitation of the church. Christianity has little to say concerning the ongoing function of the world, since it is no longer God's world. The church becomes a spectator in the grand scheme of ever-evolving processes in the activities of the world. Accordingly, the "overriding issue becomes: 'How can hope be sustained in a world that is not created?' In such a world, history is but another name for resignation, the stoic acceptance of our fate."[11]

The response by the liberal church to such a dilemma has been to attempt to make theology into a moral language for anyone, regardless of their religious conviction.[12] But such an effort to make Christianity palatable (i.e., translatable) to the rest of society has destroyed any capacity the church may have had for speaking morally to believers. Liberalism, in particular Protestant liberalism, attempted to give the church a place at the table by bringing its voice "in tune" with the wider voices of society.

10. Ibid., 7. Hauerwas makes it clear that such a compulsion was not limited to Protestant Christians: "Spinoza, of course, wrote the script for this account of the world. It was not just Protestants that accepted this narrative of the world, however, but also Jews. David Novak, in *The Election of Israel*, observes that even if many Jewish thinkers did not accept Spinoza's particular religio-political conclusions, they did accept his general premises—which meant they were lead to alter radically 'the classical Jewish doctrines of creation, election, revelation and redemption into the ideas of origin, destiny, insight and progress. Creation was changed from the founding cosmic event into the perpetual origin of cosmic process; election was changed from external choice into an intuition of one's own destiny; revelation was changed from the voice of God to man into the insight of man about God; and redemption was changed from an apocalyptic event into culmination of historical progress' (47). No better description could be given of the project of Protestant liberal theology exemplified by [Reinhold] Niebuhr, [John] Cobb, and [Peter] Hodgson" (18 n. 11).

It is somewhat ironic that, in light of Hauerwas's concern for history, he should fail to provide a fuller account of God's activity as history. Though he does attempt to do this through a Barthian Christology, the connection between the narrative human community and Jesus is left rather weak. This is where I believe a thicker account of the Holy Spirit would provide the theological and scriptural narrative needed for such a connection.

11. Hauerwas, *Wilderness Wanderings*, 7.

12. Hauerwas, "On Keeping Theological Ethics Theological," 17.

> Protestant liberalism bequeaths to Christians a misguided
> sense that they actually know where they are. Liberals are con-
> vinced that particular knowledges are certain in a manner that
> Christian orthodoxy cannot be. By representing the faith in a
> manner that will appear both intellectually respectable and po-
> litically responsible, liberal Protestants try to help the rest of us
> "fit in."[13]

Thus was Protestant liberalism led to use a language with little resemblance to Christianity. Even further, it was led to a largely non-Christian
theology. Theology was easily transformed into a science through the
conversion of theological knowledge to rational knowledge available to
any rational mind. As will be further depicted in the next section, this
is what Hauerwas describes, somewhat broadly, as systematic theology.
In Hauerwasian language, Protestant liberalism attempted to transform
the church into the world, albeit a better (i.e., nicer) version.

Wolfhart Pannenberg's System and Claims to Knowledge

Of course, other versions of the appeal for universal knowledge exist to
which Hauerwas pays little attention. As mentioned in the introduction,
it may be useful to compare Hauerwas's understanding of epistemology
and the verification of knowledge with a more systematic thinker such
as Wolfhart Pannenberg. By no means is this intended as a systematic
correction of Hauerwas, since Hauerwas cannot be so easily dismissed.
Instead, introducing the work of Pannenberg serves as an attempt to
see in what ways Hauerwas may be complemented and challenged by
interacting with systematicians. At the same time, it may become apparent that Hauerwas has not left systematics entirely behind. Indeed,
the contrast between Pannenberg and Hauerwas will finally be seen as
not nearly so sharp as one might expect. Pannenberg and Hauerwas
share many of the same concerns regarding knowledge and, at times,
even seem to pursue the same course. Though I don't believe this is
due to Hauerwas's relying on Pannenberg, it may be the result of both
having to do theology in the wake of Barth's influence on the twentieth
century.

It would be hard to lump Pannenberg's claims regarding universal knowledge into the same categories just depicted by Hauerwas.

---

13. Hauerwas, *Wilderness Wanderings*, 6.

Pannenberg's claims to knowledge seem based on a firm understanding of revelation, while at the same time they make far-reaching claims about the import of theological knowledge. One wonders at this point if systematics is as monolithic as Hauerwas seems to believe. Hauerwas may wish to qualify his critique, depending on the particular systematic theologian in mind. An illustration of Pannenberg's conception of verifying the universal nature of theological knowledge may serve to demonstrate the need for such a qualification.

Pannenberg applies comprehensiveness to his definition of knowledge in a way that incorporates any and all disciplines into the whole. In fact, he gives some indication that such a holistic approach must accompany theology. Such aspirations may indicate that Pannenberg is rather immodest, believing as he does that systematic theology is a part of the "public discourse"[14] and "must be concerned to integrate into its own synthesis the wealth of insight gained by the secular disciplines into the mysteries of nature, of human life and history."[15] One could easily presume from such statements that Pannenberg is attempting to discover public knowledge that is final and universal in its scope. In fact, just the opposite appears to be the case with Pannenberg.

Pannenberg acknowledges that we have claims to truth inherent in affirmations of specific doctrines, such as the doctrine of revelation. However, he believes that in spite of such seeming security, "our knowledge is imperfect . . . We are called to accept this situation and not to demand a final guarantee of truth before we even start to think."[16] Pannenberg ascribes such an imperfection in our knowledge to the nature of our existence as historical creatures. Systematic theology, then, is not as concerned with discovering the final or universal truth as it is with discovering the truth as it can best be restated in a specific context.

> [T]he task of distinguishing in a particular traditional assertion the core of truth from the passing forms of language and thought arises again and again. In each historical epoch, systematic theology has to be done all over again.[17]

14. Pannenberg, *Introduction to Systematic Theology*, 14.
15. Ibid., 18.
16. Ibid., 17.
17. Ibid., 7.

There is, for Pannenberg, no finality in the systematic endeavor. Knowledge is always subject to rediscovery due to the relativity of human existence. Further, Pannenberg asserts that our knowledge is conditioned due to the continued outworking of salvation history.

> The results [of systematics] will remain provisional, but that is in keeping not only with the spirit of modern science but also with Paul's understanding of the provisional form of our knowledge, due to the incompleteness of salvation history itself.[18]

The compulsion for Pannenberg's modesty in theological affirmation stems from his recognition that history is not yet complete. Only when God, in the eschaton, confirms or denies the final veracity of any theological claims or constructions will we be able to state unequivocally that our theology is true.

> In the discussion of systematic theology, then, in the sequence of its argumentation, in its construction of coherent models of the world as determined by God's action, the question of truth should be regarded as open. Of course, if it turns out to be true that there is a God, that Jesus is risen, and that everything is in his hand, then this has been true all along.[19]

A proleptic affirmation of truth is Pannenberg's means to positing theological claims in the present historical context. He works diligently to offer a theology that purports to represent (here even in the technical sense of the use of language[20]) theological reality. At the same time, he also recognizes that whatever he says is historically contingent. Therefore, the truth of theology is always going to be provisionally affirmed. Pannenberg wishes to stress the historical veracity of such doctrines as the incarnation and resurrection.[21] At the same time, such historicity is precisely what compels him to remain modest in his claims. Likely, Pannenberg would finally see Hauerwas as a sort of theological fundamentalist. However, I'm not sure that Hauerwas would be both-

18. Ibid., 18.

19. Ibid., 17.

20. See Pannenberg, *Anthropology in Theological Perspective*, 384–96. Here Pannenberg affirms the multifaceted use of language in theology, including a representative or referential use, while at the same time concluding that even our language is still subject to a proleptic confirmation of its truth in the eschaton.

21. Pannenberg, *Jesus—God and Man*.

ered by such a critique. Having seen that Hauerwas's claims regarding systematics may be in need of some qualification, we must next turn to some of the specifics regarding how, in his view, systematics and liberalism are connected.

System as an Extension of Liberalism

It is on this point of certain knowledge that Hauerwas finds the "systematic" endeavor within theology especially objectionable. By translating theology into a system of beliefs (i.e., rational knowledge), theologians and philosophers alike ripped theology from its traditional ecclesial context. By attempting to make theology a knowledge that could somehow be impervious to historical contingencies, liberal theologians rendered theology harmless.

> Christian beliefs about God, Jesus, sin, the nature of human existence, and salvation are intelligible only if they are seen against the background of the church —i.e., a body of people who stand apart from the "world" because of the peculiar task of worshiping a God whom the world knows not. This is a point as much forgotten by Christian theologians as by secular philosophers, since the temptation is to make Christianity another "system of belief."[22]

The kind of system to which Hauerwas is opposed is not the orderedness or logic of theology.[23] His objections are directed toward the attempt to make theology a knowledge unto itself, to make theology subject to a construction external to the subject of theology itself. Hauerwas was led to this conviction, again, through one of his professors.

> [U]nder the tutelage of Julian Hartt I became increasingly skeptical about the very idea of "systematic" theology. Indeed, the more I pondered not so much what Barth said about how to do theology, but how he did it, I became convinced that the idea of "system," at least in the nineteenth-century sense of system, distorted the ad-hoc character of theology as a discipline of the church.[24]

22. Hauerwas, "On Keeping Theological Ethics Theological," 34.

23. Hauerwas, "Storytelling," 173; Hauerwas, "Where Would I Be Without Friends?" 319.

24. Hauerwas, *Peaceable Kingdom*, xx. For a useful discussion of the influence of Julian Hartt on Hauerwas's thought, see Wilson, "From Theology of Culture to

As mentioned earlier, it was from Barth that Hauerwas learned

> A "system" is an edifice of thought, constructed on certain fundamental conceptions which are selected in accordance with a certain philosophy by a method which corresponds to these conceptions. Theology cannot be carried on in confinement or under the pressure of such a construction.[25]

Hauerwas is dissatisfied with the nature of belief in the modernist context. Faith has evolved into a more rationalistic sense of belief, rather than belief's being predicated on the epistemology of habituation, i.e., on the living of the Christian life. In contrast, Hauerwas believes

> ... Christianity is not a set of beliefs or doctrines one believes in order to be a Christian, but rather Christianity is to have one's body shaped, one's habits determined, in such a manner that the worship of God is unavoidable.[26]

Hauerwas is particularly opposed to the notion, characteristic of nineteenth (and twentieth)-century positivism, that we can arrive at some kind of finality in our knowledge of God.[27] Often systematic theology has implied, by claiming universality, that the knowledge gained in the system was complete or final. This finality removed theological knowledge from the context of belief, that is, from the life of the worshiping church. With regard to Thomas Aquinas, Hauerwas observes

> The *Summa* is from beginning to end a work of instruction designed to develop in the reader the moral and intellectual virtues correlative to a proper understanding of God. Central to such understanding is the recognition that given the material

Theological Ethics," 149–64.

25. Barth, *Dogmatics in Outline*, 5. Hauerwas quotes this "definition" of system in *With the Grain of the Universe*, 178–79.

26. Hauerwas, "Sanctified Body," 22.

27. By finality I mean the belief that since theology is discovering universal truths, which are ahistorical in nature, they are absolute for any historical context. Though they may be subject to further clarification in other times or cultures, they are discovered with sufficient clarity to be considered unchanging and unchangeable. As an example of this, see Hodge, *Systematic Theology*, 1–17. See especially his discussion of the uniformity and permanence of causes and effects in the discovery of scientific knowledge, in which theological knowledge is included.

content of the Christian faith, any attempt to display the rationality of this faith must be unending.[28]

Hauerwas does not believe such finality is possible, nor is it profitable for theologians to abandon the context of the church by seeking
after a system that is somehow beyond history. As Hauerwas states with
regard to a recent work of his,

> On finishing this book the reader will not discover "who did it."
> For one thing, I do not know how the story will end. For anoth-
> er, I do not have a finished theological system nor do I believe in
> such a thing. I do not know what a finished theological system
> would look like, and even if I knew, I am pretty sure that I would
> not want it. My suspicion is that the desire to have such a system
> may indicate the theologian's lack of faith in the church. Indeed,
> the church across the centuries and through the communion
> of saints believes more than any theologian could possibly say.
> The theologian is therefore free to wander and wonder, knowing
> that the truth of what the church believes is not threatened by
> the theologians' [desire] to "put it all together."[29]

But it would be a mistake to think that Hauerwas is so unsystematic
as to oppose coherence and order in his theological discussions. Indeed,
he remains quite rigid in his concern for consistency. However, it is a
consistency of a different sort, compelling the church to remain faithful
to its calling to be church. The kind of system Hauerwas opposes is
the ahistorical universality common to the rationality of knowledge in
Enlightenment thought, that is knowledge based more purely in human
reason. Hauerwas seems to embrace a kind of logic or order that can be
discovered in right living. The convergence of such living and knowledge is best found in the telling of the story, rather than the provision of
a rational justification. This concern for consistency may perhaps best
be called a "narrative coherence," of sorts.[30] But in this, he has not left

---

28. Hauerwas, *With the Grain of the Universe*, 175. Hauerwas here also draws attention to his belief that Barth's project was similar to Aquinas's in the way each attempted to make their work instructional for all who would wish to witness truthfully
of the God revealed in Scripture. In other words, both the *Summa* and Barth's *Church
Dogmatics* were designed to train the reader, rather than merely to inform. Thus, disputation (Aquinas) and repetition (Barth) caused the process of learning how to faithfully
witness to be an unending task. Formation, not information, was the goal.

29. Hauerwas, *Wilderness Wanderings*, 5.

30. Hauerwas seems to embrace, with other nonfoundationalists, a coherence

system behind entirely. Indeed, as he makes clear with regard to ethics, which for Hauerwas is theology,

> The standard account's project to supply a theory of basic moral principles from which all other principles and actions can be justified or derived represents an attempt to make the moral life take on the characteristics of a system. But it is profoundly misleading to think that a rational explanation needs to be given for holding rational beliefs, for to attempt to provide such an account assumes that rationality itself does not depend on narrative. What must be faced, however, is that our lives are not and cannot be subject to such an account, for the consistency necessary for governing our lives is more a matter of integrity than one of principle. The narratives that provide the pattern of integrity cannot be based on principle, nor are they engaging ways of talking about principles. Rather, such narratives are the ones which allow us to determine how our behavior "fits" within our ongoing pattern. To be sure, fittingness cannot have the necessitating form desired by those who want the moral life to have the "firmness" of some sciences, but it can exhibit the rationality of a good story.[31]

It should be noted that Hauerwas first said this in 1977. He may wish to back away from this statement a bit today, given the somewhat implicit theoretical nature of what is a good story. Hauerwas fleshes out a bit what constitutes a good story and what the orderedness of such a story might look like. But he is caught in the dilemma of providing a theoretical picture of what is a good story or simply falling

theory of truth. See Hauerwas, et al., *Theology Without Foundations*, 12–15. He seems to make such an embrace explicit in his discussion of how the Spirit brings about our assent to belief. See Hauerwas, *With the Grain of the Universe*, 213–15.

> The work of the Spirit is not to create evidence for the truth of what Christians believe, because there can be no "evidence" for beliefs beyond the totality of beliefs to which any contested claims might be brought. Thus, the Spirit does not, as Marshall (Bruce Marshall, *Trinity and Truth* [Cambridge: Cambridge University Press, 2000], 204) puts it, "persuade by adding something to the totality of belief, by giving us reasons or evidence we do not already have, but by eliciting our assent to a way of structuring the whole" (214).

31. Hauerwas and Burrell, "From System to Story," 170–71. This article originally appeared in Hauerwas, *Truthfulness and Tragedy*, 15–39. What may also be seen in the first sentence of this quote is the way in which Hauerwas implies a parallel between system and foundationalism.

back on some universal understanding or sense of what constitutes a good story.[32] It is Hauerwas's concern for orderedness in the narrative that makes Hartt appear to understand Hauerwas's narrative to be compatible with a strong sense of comprehensiveness and coherence, finding comprehensiveness and coherence relevant to an appropriate understanding of a good story.[33] Underlying Hauerwas's affinity for story seems to be an implicit anthropology or psychology. Hauerwas seems to hold that the story constitutes the best pedagogical tool for the church in theology. Thus, he has not distanced himself completely from a certain systematic, or universal, understanding of humanity. Further, Hauerwas also holds that God's nature is a nature best understood as "storied." "The God of Israel and Jesus, the God we find in Scripture, is a storied God. That we learn of God, or more exactly, that we learn who God is through a narrative is not accidental but rather indicative of God's nature."[34]

This leads to a distinct systematic tendency that becomes apparent from the discussion about the universal nature of narrative reality. Hauerwas seems to have a lingering commitment to foundationalism through his development of a universal anthropology. He believes that all reality is, in one way or another, whether realized or not, narratively constructed. Of course, Hauerwas is quick to point out the way that some other defenders of narrative move from the telling of the story into claims regarding all humanity.[35] He understands the tendency among systematicians toward a desire for certainty to be due to a universality implicit within their own narrative.

32. Hauerwas and Burrell, "From System to Story," 179–80.

33. Hartt, "Reply to Crites and Hauerwas," 153–55. This article was also reprinted in Hauerwas and Jones, *Why Narrative?* 311–19. The point discussed above can be found on 316–18.

34. Hauerwas, *Better Hope*, 121.

35. See Hauerwas, *Why Narrative?* 7–8. Here Hauerwas accuses Stephen Crites of moving beyond Niebuhr's claims regarding religious language into making "anthropological claims" (8). Further, one could read my discussion of pneumatological support for Hauerwas's ecclesiology in the final chapter below to be subject to this critique as well. My only response is that a Biblically grounded discussion is necessary for Hauerwas's ecclesiology to avoid becoming a mere anthropology. Though he will attempt to avoid this through specific practices, e.g., the Eucharist and baptism, the mystical nature of such practices expresses a pneumatology I believe to be only sporadically effective against rationality, as well as Scripturally displaced in emphasis.

> But it is difficult to identify any one narrative that sets the con-
> text for the standard account [systematics]. For it is not one but
> many narratives that sustain its plausibility. The form of some
> of these stories is of recent origin, but we suspect that the ba-
> sic story underlying the standard account is of more ancient
> lineage, namely, humankind's quest for certainty in a world of
> contingency.[36]

One could perhaps dismiss this statement as simply a tendency that
reigned supreme among those who were a part of the "standard account," but even Hauerwas himself seems here to be relying on some
universal notion of anthropology. He lends further credence to accusations of foundationalist tendencies in his theology with occasional
appeals to human nature as narratively construed.[37] While it may be the
case that Hauerwas explicitly attempts to avoid appeals to universals,
his theology nonetheless seems to implicitly employ a universal understanding of reality as narratively formed.[38]

A further point on this critique must be made with regard to
Hauerwas's commitment to the primacy of action in his epistemology.
Though Hauerwas claims no theory of epistemology, he employs a preference for practices in such a way that they are formative for "knowing"
the truth of doctrine. With this in mind, one could well ask if Hauerwas
has actually abandoned foundationalism or merely moved from a rational foundationalism to a practical foundationalism. Todd Whitmore
picks up on Hauerwas's tendency toward universalism in his practical
reason, claiming that Hauerwas displays a "hunger for absolutes" that
parallels that of the foundationalist.[39] Whitmore demonstrates such a
conviction toward universals in Hauerwas through what Whitmore
calls the "problem of change and revisability."[40] This is seen explicitly
in the way Hauerwas demands pacifism as a mark of the Christian
community.

> [Foundationalism] locates the starting point in a neutral first
> principle and emphasizes deduction, while [Hauerwas] begins

36. Hauerwas and Burrell, "From System to Story," 173–74.
37. Ibid., 177.
38. See especially Hauerwas's comments below with regard to the narrative/tradi-
tion of rationality, spawned by Kantianism.
39. Whitmore, "Beyond Liberalism and Communitarianism in Christian Ethics," 211
40. Ibid., 208.

with a particular narrative and stresses how the community must align its practices with its story. Nonetheless, both alike manifest the hunger for absolutes in the apparent unrevisability of their final casuistry, however understood, both in its generalities (in Hauerwas's work, the interpretation of the kingdom of God in terms of the narrative of Jesus) and its particulars (in Hauerwas's work the requirement of pacifism).[41]

In essence, Whitmore is claiming that Hauerwas has a rather rigid set of practices that establish the veracity of Christian community. This parallels the foundationalists' claim that truth must be measured by principles both rational and universal. In other words, an external that is overarching, i.e., pacifism, still exists for Hauerwas's community, against which the community must be measured in order to account for its veracity.

From a rather different perspective, Gloria Albrecht accuses Hauerwas of remaining rather foundationalistic in his desire that the church remain somewhat uniform throughout history, i.e., ahistorical. Hauerwas "replaces rational man and ahistorical reason with Christian man and a master narrative."[42] She accuses Hauerwas of attempting to maintain a "timeless story of what Christians are, always have been, and always will be, regardless of specific conditions of history or human condition."[43] Though I am reticent to agree with Albrecht that the corrective to Hauerwas's traditioned universalism is to turn to a more radical historicism (relativism?), her critique of Hauerwas seems to be accurate. He does seek a Christian community that is "true" to its heritage as represented in the traditions of past Christian communities, even the first communities; and in that sense he may be regarded as searching for overarching tendencies regarded as timeless. However, as

---

41. Ibid., 211. I suspect that Hauerwas would admit that the veracity of the Christian church is dependent on or at least intertwined with its practice of pacifism. However, Hauerwas would also make a distinction that Whitmore seems to ignore. Whitmore presumes that pacifism names something external to church. In other words, Whitmore believes pacifism can be defined in itself or *per se*. Hauerwas would rather see pacifism as bound up not only in the identity of the church but also in the identity of God. Thus, pacifism cannot be understood as a foundation external to church by which church may be measured. See Hauerwas, *With the Grain of the Universe*, 218–25.

42. Albrecht, "Myself and Other Characters," 111.

43. Ibid., 110.

Paul Lauritzen recognizes, such seems to be Hauerwas's lot if he wishes to be a part of a community that can be called truly Christian.[44]

Hauerwas seems to recognize that he does still have a foundation functioning within his theology. However, he wishes to transform or redefine what this foundation is and how it functions within the context of the formative nature of the church. Aligning himself with James McClendon's Baptist tradition, Hauerwas believes that "there is no foundation other than Jesus Christ."[45] Hauerwas does not engage in the foundationalist/antifoundationalist debate in any theoretical way, though if he were forced to choose, he would cautiously side with antifoundationalism.[46] In this, he seems to be following a path made for him by Barth. As John Webster observes,

> [T]he Barth of the early *Dogmatics* is no foundationalist: he is entirely reluctant to sever the identity between 'the absolute' or 'that which is of ultimate significance' and the content of the Christian faith, above all its Trinitarian and Christological content. Underlying all this is Barth's theological *realism*. His rejection of non-theological prolegomena to dogmatics, his 'maximization of the difference between *Wissenschaftslehre* and theology', is much more than an attempt to secure cognitive privileges for the theologian by separating theology from the 'non-theological' disciplines. It is grounded in an assertion of the *ontological* supremacy of God in his self-manifestation.[47]

Hauerwas is not attempting to devise a better theoretical grounding for doing metaphysics; he wishes to redefine how the church does metaphysics, that is how the church grasps identification of who and what it is. His foundation is the reality of the lives of believers. As such, there is really no beginning point from which to establish how

44. Lauritzen, "Is Narrative Really a Panacea?" 324–26. Lauritzen, following Stout's *Flight from Authority*, sees that Hauerwas, indeed all Christians, must walk the line between falling into the temptation to either "attempt to revise their beliefs in an effort to meet the new criteria of truthfulness [indistinctness], or they cling to traditional beliefs, however improbable these beliefs may appear [irrelevance]" (324). Lauritzen attempts to shed such an either/or by pursuing a different tack. However, it appears as though he merely arrives at another revisionistic model, rather than truly providing a distinct alternative.

45. Hauerwas, "Church's One Foundation is Jesus Christ Her Lord," 143.

46. Hauerwas, *Wilderness Wanderings*, 94 n.2.

47. Webster, *Barth's Ethics of Reconciliation*, 26. Hauerwas makes note of Barth's place as a nonfoundationalist in *With the Grain of the Universe*, 180–81 n. 15.

to go about laying a foundation. The foundation has already been laid in the person of Jesus and the lives of saints throughout history who display His life and serve as the practical foundation for the church to learn how likewise to live the life. In reference to the lives of past saints like Martin Luther King Jr., Sarah and Jonathan Edwards, Dietrich Bonhoeffer, Dorothy Day, and his own father, Hauerwas claims, "God has forced us to see that there is no 'foundation' more sure than the existence of such lives. Moreover, just as these lives are witnesses . . . our theology is futile unless it too is governed by the witness of such lives."[48] Finally then, Hauerwas's foundation, though it may not stand up to the scrutiny of a more clearly rationalistic foundationalism (i.e., what is reasonable to any rational creature), is consistent with his concern that the church learn once again to be church, even at the level of metaphysics.[49] Further, as will be seen more clearly in chapter 5, such a foundation allows the church to unashamedly claim her theology as not merely truthful, but as Truth.

Naming Hauerwas's work foundationalist in the sense of relying on practices as determinative for human epistemology and ontology would likely seem anachronistic to Hauerwas. Indeed, he would regard the notion that foundationalism and epistemology are prolegomenal to theology as conventions of modernism.[50] Thus, he would argue that theologians prior to the Enlightenment, such as Aquinas, did not "have" a grounding for knowledge that could somehow be evidenced prior to knowing the truth of theology, since rationality was not prior to, that is, authoritative over, revelation in Aquinas.[51] Hauerwas is here making the argument that modern metaphysical categories are conventions of modern philosophy and theology to the relatively new requirement of justification for belief. In Aquinas's world, though it was by no means pristine, justification for the affirmation of revelational knowledge was unnecessary. Any description other than the theological description of reality was mythological, or at least subject to further judgment by theology. Hauerwas believes this is the way in which the church should regard the world when it comes to the justification of Christian belief.

48. Hauerwas, "Church's One Foundation is Jesus Christ Her Lord," 162.
49. Ibid.
50. See Hauerwas, *With the Grain of the Universe*, 25–31.
51. Ibid., 29–30.

Rather than assuming the defensive posture of always feeling compelled to justify belief, the church should recognize its conception of reality as determinative for the world.[52] Thus, accusing Hauerwas of being foundationalistic is to place him in categories both unfamiliar and unfriendly to the church. Nevertheless, we will continue to use them for the sake of maintaining a fairly consistent conversation between Hauerwas and his critics, and to provide those unfamiliar with Hauerwas a better glimpse into his thought.

As is clear from this discussion, Hauerwas's opposition to system does not mean that he is somehow incoherent with regard to certain realities that the church has affirmed throughout the centuries. It would be not merely illogical but also heretical for him, in his rejection of referential language and of measuring veracity by appealing to foundational external facts, to attempt to remove all affirmations of doctrinal realism from the church's theology. Indeed, such a removal of theology from claims of reality would entail subsequently denying historical realities as well, something Hauerwas could not do. The implications of specific doctrines press Hauerwas to affirm the value of metaphysics, that is, to identify the nature of doctrinal affirmations as they relate to reality, but only insofar as such identification can help the church be church. As Hauerwas makes clear, metaphysics does not ground the church, in the sense that one must have an appropriate metaphysic in order to establish the rationality of the church.

> My reticence about metaphysics is a correlate of my attempt to resist reductionistic accounts of theological claims so common in modern theology. Obviously, Christian conviction entails metaphysical claims—such as all that is, is finite—but one does not first get one's metaphysics straight and then go to theology. Rather, metaphysical claims are best exhibited as embedded in, not as the "background" of, our behaviors. This applies not only in Christian theology but also in any endeavor.[53]

Hauerwas does not deny the value of claims regarding reality and how doctrinal statements may be construed as real; he simply wants such metaphysical issues to be contextualized appropriately (i.e., he is unwilling to grant an *a priori* status to metaphysical claims). Similarly,

52. Ibid., 31–37.
53. Hauerwas, *Wilderness Wanderings*, 168 n. 8.

he does not deny that theoretical display can have tremendous value, if used appropriately. He cannot allow that it be the "foundation" for theological veracity, but it can have an *ad hoc* value in the church. Commenting about the work of Oliver O'Donovan, Hauerwas, along with James Fodor, is quick to point out that "Although we do appreciate the relative value of theory, we are more convinced of its *ad hoc* employment than of the need, as asserted in O'Donovan's work, for its systematic display before any important work in political theology can be done."[54] Thus, Hauerwas finds liberal theology, which he quickly associates with any systematic (i.e., universal) endeavor, to be a tool of Enlightenment rationality rather than a tool of the church. Liberal theology worked toward the betterment of all society. Put in theological terms, liberalism attempted to make society into the Kingdom of God. As a consequence, it rendered theology vacuous of its social meaning in the context of the church. The church could not act as a social institution since its social impact had been reduced to mere "beliefs" to be applied to the society at large.

Reinhold Niebuhr is especially interesting for Hauerwas in this regard, since he was quite critical of the liberal project and of the typically American defense of the self but nevertheless remained entrenched in liberal thought.[55] Niebuhr was never able to escape the liberal tendency to seek universals, particularly in his discussion of history. This is an unusual critique of Niebuhr, given his stress on the importance of history for the church. But as Hauerwas points out, "Niebuhr's account of the cross is finally but another variation of the Gnostic temptation to turn the cross into a knowledge that is meaningful separate from the actual death of a man called Jesus."[56] Niebuhr believes that the cross is finally the answer to the "problem of history." However, in Niebuhr's understanding, the cross must remain, first and last, a symbol that transcends

---

54. Ibid., 209.

55. Hauerwas (*With the Grain of the Universe*, 87) even goes so far as to state that "Niebuhr's Gifford Lectures are but a Christianized version of [William] James's account of religious experience." This is another way of saying that Niebuhr's theology was simply James's humanism in Christian language. On James's humanism, see Hauerwas, *With the Grain of the Universe*, 65–86.

56. Hauerwas, *Wilderness Wanderings*, 41–42. The cross was a useful symbol for Niebuhr, but only to the extent it could serve to persuade or illumine humans of their condition and of the necessity for pursuing a self-sacrificial form of love.

the "ambiguities of history."[57] Niebuhr was never able to lose sight of
the temptation to uncover the universal in history. His was a history
that remained dedicated to the liberal project of understanding the
overall picture, of stepping back for a more objective view, particularly
of the human condition. As Hauerwas states, "Niebuhr cannot be satisfied with history understood as a particular community's remembered
past, but history must be that which 'comprehends the whole.'"[58] Thus,
Hauerwas's understanding of Niebuhr fits Niebuhr quite nicely into the
program of liberalism.[59]

57. Ibid.

58. Ibid., 43. Hauerwas is here making a distinction characteristic of Niebuhr's view
of history—a distinction that Hauerwas finds inconsistent with how Christianity has
viewed history. The distinction is not that Niebuhr is attempting to be universal while
Hauerwas believes the church should not be. Instead, Niebuhr's embrace of universals is one that removes historical contingencies, whereas Hauerwas believes that the
church's embrace of history should be one that finds universals explicitly bound to history. Hauerwas seems to be saying that this is the difference between an academic and a
theological rendering of history. The academic merely uses history to search for preex-
isting universal principles. The theologian sees the universal nature of God revealed in
history in such a way that it cannot be understood without the historical context.

59. Hauerwas believes Niebuhr's liberalism is especially apparent in his conception
of sin. As Hauerwas states, "Niebuhr's account of our sinfulness is a Protestant form of
natural law that attempts to make intelligible, on grounds of general human knowledge,
what can only be known in the light of the kingdom established in Jesus' cross and
resurrection." (Hauerwas, *Wilderness Wanderings*, 44). Hauerwas is here building on
Karl Löwith's critique of Niebuhr's understanding of history (see Löwith, "History and
Christianity," 281–90). In this short article, Löwith criticizes Niebuhr for addressing
history as a problem to be solved, that is, as an ever-progressing process. Löwith asserts
that the eschatological nature of classical Christian theology would see history as a
realm in need of redemption by a Savior, leaving humanity without recourse in itself
(282–83). In other words, a history of humanity is a "hopeless history," grounded as it is
in the expectations of human progress; whereas, the history of the kingdom, through an
eschatological expectation of Jesus's final redemption, is a history that is full of promise
due to its foundation in a Redeemer who can reclaim the history of humanity, marked
as it is by its own inability to fulfill its end.

Hauerwas sees Niebuhr's understanding of sin as conforming to the "hopeless"
nature of human history by addressing human sinfulness as a qualification of social
progress, rather than as a theological qualification of human nature. Both may require
universal claims regarding anthropology, but one is a decidedly Christian construal of
humanity, while the other is attempting to address humanity without recourse to the
necessity of revelation (*Wilderness Wanderings*, 43–45). Thus, Hauerwas sees Niebuhr
as entrapped in the very liberal presuppositions that he wishes to overcome.

Niebuhr's liberalism is especially evident in the way in which he remains committed to devising and understanding theology as primarily anthropology. As Hauerwas concludes,

> For Niebuhr, theology was tested—or, to use his language, validated—by its ability to provide provocative accounts of the human condition. Accordingly, Niebuhr's theology seems to be a perfect exemplification of Ludwig Feuerbach's argument that theology, in spite of its pretentious presumption that its subject matter is God, is in fact but a disguised way to talk about humanity.[60]

What is at stake in the question of liberalism's redefinition of historicity (i.e., history is what *contains* the universal) is precisely its ability to maintain some universal point of view when faced with the particulars of its own history or goals. In other words, "Can liberalism survive the acknowledgment that it is a tradition when its epistemological commitments are based on the denial of tradition?"[61] When a person is released from all constraints to tradition, he or she is set adrift in the sea of belief, never able to drop anchor in a specific port of tradition. What is left is simply to reject all traditions and the beliefs they spawn in favor of the presumption of remaining neutral. Borrowing from Alasdair MacIntyre, Hauerwas seems ready to identify the neutral liberal self as

> . . . the person who finds him or herself an alien to every tradition of enquiry which he or she encounters and who does so because he or she brings to the encounter with such tradition standards of rational justification which the beliefs of no tradition could satisfy. This is the kind of post-Enlightenment person who responds to the failure of the Enlightenment to provide neutral, impersonal tradition-independent standards of ratio-

---

60. Hauerwas, *With the Grain of the Universe*, 115. The parallel that Hauerwas makes between William James and Niebuhr seems doubly justified on these grounds. Not only may Niebuhr be understood as a humanist in theological guise (i.e., theology is synonymous with anthropology); he is also a pragmatist to the extent that theology, finally, only makes a difference to the extent that it rightly reflects, or perhaps better resonates with, the "human condition." The final test for theology is the difference it makes in the social interactions of humans.

61. Hauerwas, *Wilderness Wanderings*, 84. Hauerwas is here using MacIntyre's language to press Martha Nussbaum on her recovery of Aristotle in what Hauerwas perceives as a more liberal context.

nal judgment by concluding that no set of beliefs proposed for acceptance is therefore justifiable.[62]

Of course this also means that a person must, at least insofar as they are consistent, reject the tradition of Enlightenment rationality. The neutrality it purports to offer is but a sham.

> The political arrangements of liberalism seek to free us from history by creating social orders in which "we can be what we want to be." Yet the means necessary to secure such "freedom" in an egalitarian manner creates societies that make our lives all the more determined by powers we do not recognize as powers.[63]

In such a context of freedom, we are given the illusion that we know "where we are." But freedom remains just that—an illusion. We are part of a tradition already, even while we are being deceptively informed that no traditions exist. This is the great apparition Hauerwas perceives in modernity.

> By modernity, I mean the project to create social orders that would make it possible for each person living in such orders "to have no story except the story they choose when they have no story." That is to say, modernity is the attempt to so dis-embed and estrange peoples from the peculiarities, distinctiveness, and contingencies of their respective traditions as to form the illusion that the only story now worth telling is one entirely of their own devising. For on modernity's terms the past as such does not truly exist, nor can it have any bearing on our present choices. Hence, the only story countenanced by modernity is one that is predicated on the false belief that since we are unencumbered by any received story, we are truly free to fashion *de novo* any narrative we wish and thus make (and remake) of ourselves whatever we will.[64]

---

62. MacIntyre, *Whose Justice? Which Rationality?* 395. Hauerwas uses this quotation in the context of a discussion of conversion in *Dispatches from the Front*, 188 n. 4.

63. Hauerwas, *Wilderness Wanderings*, 10.

64. Ibid., 26. Leslie Muray ("Confessional Postmodernism and the Process-Relational Vision,") believes Hauerwas has not completely escaped the modernist conception of the self as self-determined and self-contained. He points out that Hauerwas's scheme of character virtue ethics still retains a self as "being" that is prior to the self as "action." However, in Hauerwas's defense, I note that Muray supports such a criticism from Hauerwas's early writings. Such an account does not seem applicable to Hauerwas's more mature thought.

Of course, Hauerwas cannot allow such critiques of liberalism to remain in abstract or theoretical terms. He must set his own critique of liberalism against the backdrop of the tradition of Enlightenment rationality. This he does through the work of Immanuel Kant. Though Kant is certainly not the only figure deserving attention as a progenitor of the universalism that gave rise to liberalism, and could plausibly be defended as sharing a concern for Christian pragmatics similar to that of Kierkegaard, mentioned above, Hauerwas considers Kant's work singular enough to warrant individual attention. Obviously, Kant is not a tradition unto himself, but his work is substantially formative for subsequent thought. Therefore, let us turn our attention to Hauerwas's reading of Kant.

Immanuel Kant's Influence on the Modern Liberal Project: Hauerwas's Critique of Kant as a Primary Source for Liberalism

In Hauerwas's understanding, the modern church is faced with danger from many sides. The most menacing threat of all has been slowly assimilating itself into the church for at least 200 years. Liberalism has crept into every aspect of the church, causing the latter to succumb to the temptation of being reduced to an arm of the state. In other words, the church has come to the realization that it exists simply to support democratic liberalism. This reduction occurred when the church embraced a universal understanding of human teleology (i.e., anthropology) expressed as support of a specific political ideology (i.e., Enlightenment autonomy). Bringing the church around to this perspective, whether or not the church realized that it was being brought around, took a good deal of time, and was necessarily based on teachings that were attractive and popular to theologian and layperson alike. It took a great deal to get the church to "give up" its commitment to the historicity of the cross and of the man called the Christ, and subsequently, to pursue the systematizing efforts of universalistic rationality. The emphasis on ahistorical reason transformed theology into a rationality instead of a living reality. Such was the wizardry of the Enlightenment.[65]

65. It is interesting to note that though Hauerwas may be an astute critic of the Enlightenment influence, he never addresses Scholastic humanism and the confidence of Scholastic thought in reason as inherently good due to God's goodness and due to

Though, as mentioned above, no one person's thought can justly be accused or celebrated as the foundation for the Enlightenment, one person's thought does seem to summarize it fairly well, at least for Hauerwas. Immanuel Kant was the herald trumpet sounding forth the climactic march of Enlightenment thought, and at the same time, sounding "taps" for the church. Hauerwas believes that Kant is responsible for much of the liberalism now infesting the church. Hauerwas does not believe that Kant was intending to lead the church into liberalism. However, his work to defend a place for Christian knowledge finally led Christianity to be reduced to a universal anthropology.

> Under Kant's influence, Christian theologians simply left the natural world to science and turned to the only place left in which language about God might make sense, that is, to the human—and not just to the human, but to what makes the human "moral." . . . In the words of George Hendry, "When Kant gave priority to the ethical over the natural as the gateway to God, he provided a city of refuge to which harassed theologians fled from their philosophical and scientific pursuers in increasing numbers in the nineteenth century."[66]

Given this subjugation of theology to anthropology, Hauerwas believes Kant's influence must be identified, and removed or countered. Our discussion of Kant in this section is primarily directed toward Hauerwas's interpretation of Kant's influence. Here we will display the beliefs held by Kant and assimilated into the church—beliefs that Hauerwas considers detrimental to the existence of the church as church.[67] Hauerwas's

---

his creation of human reason. Hauerwas has an obvious affinity, as will be explored further below, for Aquinas and his assimilation of Aristotle. However, Hauerwas does not distance himself from the presupposition of universal reason in Scholastic theology as far back as Anselm. One is led to wonder if Hauerwas has merely traded one universal reason (Enlightenment) for another (Scholastic). This is one of the points leading to the critique below of Hauerwas's remaining entrapped in a universal anthropology. Perhaps this anthropology stems not from Enlightenment sources but from Scholasticism, e.g., Scholastic humanism. For a brief discussion of the relationship of Scholastic reason to the postmodern context of theology, see Dabney, "Starting with the Spirit," 21–22.

66. Hauerwas, *With the Grain of the Universe*, 37–38.

67. It should be acknowledged at the outset of this section that Hauerwas's critique of Kant is by no means the only way in which Kant is understood today. Though Hauerwas's position may be the predominant understanding of Kant, another school of thought maintains that considering Kant to be ahistorical in his ethics misses much of the point of his ethics, as well as his understanding of politics. See Wood, *Kant's Ethical*

own alternative, of tradition and the formative narrating community of the church, though mentioned briefly, will be developed more fully later.

In Hauerwas's understanding, Kant, among others, was concerned with deriving an ethic from the innate sensibilities available to all humans—ethics based on a universal anthropology. The formation believed necessary by the church for character transformation was unnecessary in Kant's scheme, since even the common citizen, whether Christian or not, could rely on ethical tools available to all who were willing to use reason to discover their social and moral duty.[68]

While Hauerwas certainly realizes that an anthropology independent of any theological influence may not have been Kant's intention, Hauerwas nevertheless holds Kant responsible for substantiating this new tradition; a tradition formed on the autonomy of the individual and on the universality of rationality. Hauerwas counters that "All rationality, more than Kant realized, depends on tradition, is based upon a view of the world, a story and way of looking at things."[69] The effects of Kant's work for the church have been, and still are, devastating. As Hauerwas makes clear, Kant's new community grounded in the self would quickly replace the community of the church.

> Although he does not seem to have realized it, Kant also devised an ethic out of a new community, the community engendered by the European Enlightenment, a community that sought to rally people around a modern invention called reason. The Enlightenment devised its own tradition of scientific investigation, individualism, and rights with attendant institutions built upon its values. . . . Enlightenment thinking, breaking us away from our tradition in order to make us reasonable and to enable each of us to think and act for himself or herself, fostered its own tradition, which accounts for the modern world.[70]

Thought, 207–15, 244–49. This study will not attempt to engage Hauerwas's critique at this level, since it is well beyond the scope of developing Hauerwas's critique itself. Nevertheless, Hauerwas's study seems in need of some qualification to be consistent in its discussion of Kant's intentions. Of course, this leaves aside the question of how Kant's intentions relate to the way he has been interpreted in the last two hundred years. Hauerwas is not without friends in his view of Kant.

68. Hauerwas, *After Christendom?* 97.

69. Hauerwas and Willimon, *Resident Aliens*, 100.

70. Ibid., 99–100.

Kant's great achievement was that he had made ethics democratic. His project was "to free the moral agent from the arbitrary and contingent characters of our histories and communities."[71] People could think for themselves and did not need to be trained according to a moral tradition to be ethical. They could in fact base their morality on their own rationality, on the principles discovered in their own mind.

> All you have to do to be moral, believed Kant, is to think clearly and to think for yourself, to get your basic, universally fitting principles right, and you will do the right thing. Being ethical is a matter of being more fully human, that is, more rational.[72]

The universality of Kant's ethic was grounded in his "categorical imperative."[73] The "categorical imperative," in the abstract, released people from the historical contingencies of their situations and allowed them to act according to universal principles that were applicable to all rational creatures, kings and peasants alike. In Hauerwas's understanding, such a release from contingencies is not merely a release from the messiness of dealing with arbitrary or unnecessary elements in ethical considerations. It is also, for the church, the release from all connection to the tradition of Christian history.

But the release from history did not come easily. People had been taught a place in the social structure that was accepted as, more or less, God-given. To be freed from this, they must be retrained in another community to recognize that freedom is only realized in the autonomy

71. Ibid., 98. Here, and elsewhere below, we see the difference between Hauerwas's interpretation of Kant and what may be called a neo-Kantian defense of Kant's writings. Hauerwas interprets Kant according to the emphasis seemingly placed in Kant himself and, moreover, in later interpreters of Kant, on the purer elements of his ethics. Accordingly, Kant is seen as primarily concerned with the abstract principles for morality, at times even appearing to ignore the empirical experience of humans. Robert Louden (*Kant's Impure Ethics*, 3–30) argues that Kant constantly couches his development of pure ethics in an awareness and inclusion of impure ethics, that is, the empirical nature of human contingency. Louden believes that Kant realizes an interdependence was always at work in his ethics, even as Kant was devising the means for discovering the universals of pure ethics. Unfortunately for Kant, the connection between the pure and impure and the full development of his impure ethics remained obscured by the incomplete nature of his later works (6–7).

72. Hauerwas and Willimon, *Resident Aliens*, 98.

73. Kant, *Foundations of the Metaphysics of Morals*, 39. For Kant, the single categorical imperative is "Act only according to that maxim by which you can at the same time will that it should become a universal law."

of the self.[74] The view of autonomy deriving from Kant cannot allow humans to live under the guidance or instruction of another. Indeed, the theme of Enlightenment freedom is release from all such external authorities and taking "courage to use your own reason."[75]

Obviously, this meant that the church could no longer engage in training the faithful as to belief or practice. Such training amounted to tutelage that was against the Enlightenment rejection of the external authority. Convictions that are defensible and personally attainable must be discovered in reason alone. Kant still wished religious instruction to play a role, but it could not be a primary source for religious conviction. Religious conviction or belief could serve as data informative to the reason of the individual, but it could not be formative over that reason. This was especially true with regard to scriptural devotion. Scripture was not necessary for human moral development.

> [S]ince the sacred narrative, which is employed solely on behalf of ecclesiastical faith, can have and, taken by itself, ought to have absolutely no influence upon the adoption of moral maxims, and since it is given to ecclesiastical faith only for the vivid presentation of its true object (virtue striving toward holiness), it follows that this narrative must at all times be taught and expounded in the interest of morality; and yet (because the common man especially has an enduring propensity within him to sink into passive belief) it must be inculcated painstakingly and repeatedly that true religion is to consist not in the knowing or considering of what God does or has done for our salvation but in what we must do to become worthy of it. This last can never be anything but what possesses in itself undoubted and *unconditional* worth, what therefore can alone make us well-pleasing to God, and of whose necessity every man can become wholly certain without any Scriptural learning whatever.[76]

As Hauerwas points out, this move, for Kant, makes morality "the 'essence' of religion, but ironically it is understood in a manner that makes positive religious convictions secondary."[77] What also

---

74. As Hauerwas points out, even a historically contingent theology like liberation theology can still succumb to the subtle attractiveness of such a conception of freedom. See Hauerwas, *After Christendom?* 50–55.

75. Kant, "What Is Enlightenment?" 85.

76. Kant, *Religion within the Limits of Reason Alone*, 123. Emphasis Kant's.

77. Stanley Hauerwas, "On Keeping Theological Ethics Theological," 20.

should be noted is that moral knowledge can be discovered 'without any Scriptural learning whatever.' While this may not seem a surprising statement coming from Kant, it is somewhat telling that Hauerwas makes no mention of it.[78] This may be understandable since Scripture is not essential to the argument that Hauerwas is making. Nevertheless, its absence may also serve to indicate an aspect in Hauerwas's thinking in which he is still implicitly Kantian. Hauerwas, like Kant, has little, or at least not a primary, place in his thought for Scripture as a formative element in moral training.[79] Hauerwas is being consistent in this regard, since he believes that the community of the faithful (i.e., the church) is the primary place where religious formation takes place. Scripture is secondary in nature and only becomes a part of the process as Christians are taught to read Scripture correctly within the community that has substantiated traditional interpretation.[80] Scripture, then, becomes a formative element alongside other elements in the tradition. However, it is not an external element exerting authority over those in the community. It is a part of the tradition and has formative authority only insofar as it is read in and with that community. In this respect, Hauerwas does not appear to be reflecting a Kantian sense of freedom from external constraints. Hauerwas's objections to Scripture appear to

78. Hauerwas's use of Kant's quote in "On Keeping Theological Ethics Theological," 20, leaves off the last sentence concerning Scripture. This seems strange coming from Hauerwas, given that he knows and seems to concur with Barth's assessment of revelation in Scripture. See Hauerwas, *With the Grain of the Universe*, 150–51. Here Hauerwas quotes approvingly Barth's discussion of God's place as primary in the revelation found in the Bible. See Barth, "Strange New World within the Bible," 43.

79. More will be said on this in chapter 4 in our discussion of tradition and the church. One response that Hauerwas may give is that he expects people to read his work alongside active involvement in the church. In saying this, he could escape the criticism of not using Scripture in a formative manner in his own work, since people are expected to receive it at church. However, I am not sure such a response so easily escapes the point here.

80. It is not coincidental that Hauerwas is attracted to an authoritative papal role in this regard, since the Roman Catholic Church has traditionally epitomized the notion that one must be taught to read the Scriptures. He has little patience for the Protestant ideologies of "freedom of access" and perspicuity. While he is certainly not opposed to Christians reading the Scriptures, Hauerwas believes that reading, like any other craft, must be taught by those who read well to those who would wish to be able to rightly read the Scriptures. See Hauerwas, *Unleashing the Scripture*, 15–44. For an interesting comparison on the formation of contemporary saints in literature to Hauerwas, see Gerber, "Virtuous Terrorist," 230–34.

be more in line with a Wittgensteinian/Fishian rejection of the notion that Scripture can be understood as an autonomous text apart from a community of interpretation.[81] I believe Hauerwas is right that Scripture is not such a simple document that it can be read well without training. Indeed, even a conservative Protestant history of preaching would affirm the need for further explanation alongside exhortation to give the layperson a complete understanding of the Scriptures. This does not render laypeople incapable of understanding Scripture, nor does it remove the Scriptures from their hands, but it does make clear that training is necessary for a right handling of Scripture. Hauerwas seems to see that formation through the discipleship of lives influencing one another instead of, or at least more primarily than, the influence of text on a life is implicit within Scripture. He would be well served to find such a premise explicitly in Scripture. Obviously, this does not destroy the narrative effects of Scripture as text in the formation of believers. On the contrary, it indicates the manner in which Scripture comes to life in the performance of the text in the lives of believers. Ultimately, the life of Jesus comes to us in two forms: in the text and in people who have been formed by the life of the church. Hauerwas does not significantly address how the two correlate. This raises the question for Hauerwas as to what language the church uses in its formation. Perhaps Hauerwas does not address such a question in any detail because he believes the question to be premised on a false dichotomy. Certainly, in a Wittgensteinian sense, scriptural language should be the primary formative language of the church, and in that sense should create a dialectical relationship between text and practice. In this relationship, practice would rightly take on the burden of forming and shaping the performance of the text in the lives of believers, but it can never do so

81. Hauerwas, *Unleashing the Scripture*, 19–28. I am here referring to Hauerwas's affinity for Stanley Fish's rejection of meaning that can be found in a text qua text, separate from the reader. Though it is beyond the scope of this study, an interesting comparison and contrast could be made between the way in which Scripture is used by Hauerwas in the formation of believers and the way in which Aquinas regards it as a first principle. See Thomas Aquinas, *Summa Thelogica*, I.I.8. Hauerwas would wish to argue, with MacIntyre (*First Principles, Final Ends and Contemporary Issues*, esp. page 7) that, for Aquinas, first principles are not known to be true *a priori*. Instead, they are "judgments grasped intellectually through participation in the activity in which they are embedded" (Hauerwas, *With the Grain of the Universe*, 209 n. 7).

in a consistently Christian manner without the text of Scripture being its primary language. As Hauerwas explains,

> The main reason I write so much, however, is because I do not believe that any theory can be, or should be, developed that is more determinative for understanding the truth of what we believe as Christians than the language we actually use as Christians.[82]

On the other hand, Hauerwas does not appear to go as far as Fish does with regard to the authority of a text discovered solely in the resonance of the reader (which is, ironically, merely a furtherance of Enlightenment autonomy, whether individualized or communalized). Since the church has held to a strong sense of inspiration in the Scriptures, tradition would seem to compel us to regard the text as authoritative in spite of the reader's response to it. In this, the community of faith can still serve as a necessary corrective guide in the interpretation of the text. However, one hardly comes to the text alone. Every time a person reads Scripture, the act of reading and understanding is a product of his/her history, not merely a continual process of discovery. A dialectic, of sorts, arises between text and community in such a way that an interdependence exists between them. In other words, I believe meaning is to be found in an appropriate rendering of the text, which implies a reading done in the community of faith. This is something Hauerwas seems to practice as well, though he appears, on occasion, to lean more toward Fish in his "theory" of interpretation.[83]

We return to Hauerwas's discussion of Kant. One of the primary connections he makes between Kant and liberalism is the ahistorical nature of Kant's thought. Kant worked to excise all historicity from primary moral consideration.[84] He worked diligently so that

---

82. Hauerwas, "Where Would I Be Without Friends?" 316. Though Hauerwas would surely not wish for his understanding of Christian language to be limited to the language of Scripture, he cannot escape the historical evaluation of Scripture as the church's primary document and language. Theology may at times go beyond Scripture or even ignore Scripture, but the church cannot easily escape its connection to Scripture, nor would Hauerwas wish for it to do so.

83. See Hauerwas, *Unleashing the Scriptures*, 47–62.

84. As mentioned above, Kant did have a place for the empirical in his ethics. However, the way in which the majority of interpreters, specifically Hauerwas, have read Kant leads to the conclusion that the empirical plays a role subsequent to that of pure principle.

> [I]n the end religion will gradually be freed from all empirical
> determining grounds and from all statutes which rest on history
> and which through the agency of ecclesiastical faith provision-
> ally unite men for the requirements of the good; and thus at last
> the pure religion of reason will rule over all, "so that God may
> be all in all."[85]

History was an encumbrance for Kant that needed to be expunged from
religion in order to get at the reasonable ground for morality. This was
the only way he believed he could arrive at an account of morality that
would be universal. As Hauerwas points out,

> It was Kant's great enterprise to free morality from the arbi-
> trary and the contingent, in order to secure at least minimal
> agreement between people of differing beliefs and societies.
> Moreover, Kant tried valiantly to free the realm of morality
> from the determinism he thought characteristic of the natural
> world. He sought to guarantee the "autonomy" of morality by
> grounding morality neither in religious or metaphysical be-
> liefs, nor in any empirical account of humanity, but in ratio-
> nality *qua* rationality. . . . [The categorical imperative] renders
> the contingent history of the agent irrelevant in moral judg-
> ment and evaluation; it demands that the justification for our
> decisions be given from the perspective of anyone.[86]

Such an ahistorical approach to rationality means that, for Kant,
all moral judgments can, and must, be based on the universal. Only
insofar as any reasonable person can recognize the moral universal in
contingency can an act be considered right or wrong. This neutrality
with regard to contingency leads the moral agent to affirm a moral objectivity that is unencumbered by the historical. Even further, such objectivity, as with the observer in any of the physical sciences, is deemed
necessary for an ethical claim to be considered rational. The subject has
become both the locus and determining agent in moral claims. Thus, in
the objectivity of Enlightenment rationality, the democratic nature of
ethics is finally achieved. As Alasdair MacIntyre states,

> To be a moral agent is, on this view, precisely to be able to
> stand back from any and every situation in which one is in-
> volved, from any and every characteristic that one may pos-

85. Kant, *Religion within the Limits of Reason Alone*, 112.
86. Hauerwas, *Peaceable Kingdom*, 10–11.

sess, and to pass judgment on it from a purely universal and abstract point of view that is totally detached from all social particularity. Anyone and everyone can thus be a moral agent, since it is in the self and not in social roles or practices that moral agency has to be located.[87]

Thus, for a rational mind weaned on individual autonomy, any communal affiliation is unnecessary for moral reasoning. In other words, the church doesn't matter, as least not substantively, for ethics, which is the same thing as theology for Hauerwas.

Two ironies stand out as substantive critiques of Kant's universal ethics. The first has been mentioned already: Kant's ethic is also a tradition, and to assume otherwise is simply an illusion. Though Kant worked to excise all contingency from moral consideration, he did not recognize that such a goal was a historically contingent presumption. As Hauerwas rightly surmised, "There is simply no place to start thinking prior to being engaged in a tradition."[88] Kant's efforts reflected the modern desire for sure knowledge based on the objective and abstract, while at the same time presuming such a thing could be discovered. Both scope and intention were historical constructions, though they both sought to escape such an encumbrance. Such things were still the product of a society—a social context, that is, the society of Enlightenment rationality and autonomy. As James Gustafson notes, even "If a community of autonomous rational moral agents, that fictive denomination into which many contemporary moral philosophers seek to convert us all, were actualized, it too would share [historical/communal] characteristics."[89]

The second irony of Kant's presumed neutrality is found in its inability to avoid the very conflicts it is intended to alleviate. Moral

---

87. MacIntyre, *After Virtue*, 31–32. MacIntyre's statement helps illustrate the permeating nature of autonomy in that even universal theological assertions would finally be subject to the assent of the individual. In other words, as Hauerwas puts the matter, humanity suffers from the problem of "anthropodicy" (Hauerwas, *God, Medicine, and Suffering*, 62).

Wells (*Transforming Fate into Destiny*, 169) identifies Hauerwas's aversion to such an "observer" as the reason that Hauerwas cannot develop further the ironic and eschatological tendencies within his theology. Both tendencies, if explicitly acknowledged, tend toward an ability to see beyond the historical.

88. Hauerwas, *Better Hope*, 131.

89. Gustafson, *Ethics from a Theocentric Perspective*, 317–18.

disagreement can presumably be resolved on the basis of agreement concerning the universal principle and its subsequent application. However, one must ask, what happens when such agreement cannot be reached? What happens when the universal is not obvious to all rational creatures? It is at this point that Kant's ethic seems most incongruous to his desires for individual freedom, since anyone who disagrees cannot be seen as anything but an irrational creature. As Hauerwas makes clear,

> An ethic claiming to be "rational" and universally valid for all thinking people everywhere is incipiently demonic because it has no means of explaining why there are still people who disagree with its prescriptions of behavior, except that these people must be "irrational" and, therefore (since "rationality" is said to be our most important characteristic), subhuman.[90]

According to Hauerwas, Kant is careful not to become distracted by the particulars of people's lives. He would rather be able to stand at a distance and keep the contingencies of human history from disrupting his own pursuit of enlightened morality. In this sense, Kant's respect for the other, even in his "categorical imperative," is but a way to preserve his own well-ordered solitude. "Kant's respect for the other is but the respect of universal reason in his breast, not the contingently real historical person."[91]

Hauerwas believes much of modern theology, and in particular, theism, has gone the way of Kantianism. It has largely embraced Kant's thought, particularly the notion of a universal abstractness that dissociates the church from its own particular history in the person of Jesus Christ. Though Hauerwas does not qualify his critique of Kant by offering extensive critique of others who may have paralleled Kant's thought, it seems fair to read in Kant that Christian convictions have been subsumed into something called "religion," whose primary pur-

---

90. Hauerwas and Willimon, *Resident Aliens*, 101.

91. Hauerwas, *Vision and Virtue*, 32 n. 7. Cf. Murdoch, "Sublime and the Good," 42. Hauerwas was initially taken with Murdoch's critique of Kant and continues to rely upon it. However, he has also realized in recent years that simply because Murdoch's enemies are his enemies does not necessarily make them friends. Hauerwas believes that Christians must be historical in a way that Murdoch likely would not find attractive. See Hauerwas, *Wilderness Wanderings*, 155–70, esp., 156.

pose it is to make us a moral community of autonomous individuals.[92] Of course, as Hauerwas sees it, this means that Christian convictions and their consequent histories are made unintelligible. The church is simply a tool to make human social structures (i.e., the state) better. On this reading of Kant, it makes little difference whether the church is Christian or something else. Even some who have been critical of Kant are still bound to the project of maintaining social order. In the context of anti-Kantianism, the presumption of a common humanity necessary to sustain social function and congenial relations amongst those of differing beliefs still thrives.[93] Accordingly, the church "in the process of providing Christian support of democratic social orders, . . . became unable to sustain itself—in short, it became a 'knowledge' rather than a church."[94] Thus, the systematizing efforts in theology meant to bring about a knowledge construed as universal or final are but one more attempt to apply the Kantian project to knowledge of God in such a way as to transform such knowledge into anthropology/sociology. But Hauerwas cannot allow the church to give up its identity so quickly. For the church to remain church, it must hold fast to its convictions qua convictions. Even in the face of such comfortable options as democracy and political liberalism, Christians cannot lose their identity as a truly Christian community.

> Christians can therefore never lose hold of the affirmation that God will choose those whom God will choose in a manner that cannot help but be offensive to people with Kantian sensibilities, for whom the necessity of a people, Israel, or a person, Jesus, for salvation can only appear absurd.[95]

If left at this point, Hauerwas's understanding of historicity and his depiction of liberalism's abandonment of the historical person of Jesus Christ may sound rather inconsistent. Hauerwas has opposed

92. Kant, "What is Enlightenment?," 85. Cf. Kant, *Religion within the Limits of Reason Alone*, 98–99

93. Hauerwas, *Wilderness Wanderings*, 86. Hauerwas here critiques the lingering vestiges of Kantianism that seem to remain in Martha Nussbaum's critique of Kant and in her development of Aristotelian thought.

94. Hauerwas, *Dispatches from the Front*, 94. With this statement, Hauerwas is introducing his discussion of Walter Rauschenbusch's and Reinhold Niebuhr's support of democracy.

95. Hauerwas, *Wilderness Wanderings*, 86.

all presumptions of universality in "systematic" investigation but now seems to be advocating a universality of the historical. As mentioned above, Hauerwas believes that "All rationality, more than Kant realized, depends on tradition, is based upon a view of the world, a story and way of looking at things."[96] Pointing to the work of Oliver O'Donovan, Hauerwas further makes the point that "[O'Donovan's] is a historical theology that rightly begins with the fundamental theological *fact* that out of all the peoples of God's good creation Israel is God's promised people."[97] What these statements seem to indicate is that historicity (that is, the embedded nature of a community in its historical context) is a fact—even more, a universal fact. The historicity of the church, and of any other community for that matter, is a universal reality not unlike the universal reality of the abstract and ahistorical objectivity found in Enlightenment thought. Even though Hauerwas believes that the supposed neutrality of Enlightenment rationality was still tradition-bound, he appears to have simply exchanged Enlightenment universalism for the universality of the particular. Has Hauerwas escaped the bindings of liberalism only to be caught again in a universal maxim regarding historicity?[98] Hauerwas's attempt to ground his claim of historicity would undoubtedly entail a development of the narrative community of the church. But surely he doesn't wish to support the maxim of historicity based solely or primarily on the community of the church, as though the church were simply a microcosm of the way all reality is for all people. This would simply be to step back into using the church to underwrite a notion of historical neutrality, since in such a scenario the church maintains no historical particularities qua church. It is merely an illustration of the larger human context, which Enlightenment rationality has worked so hard to release from any historical contingencies.

96. Hauerwas and Willimon, *Resident Aliens*, 100.

97. Hauerwas, *Wilderness Wanderings*, 200. Emphasis mine.

98. Kroeker ("Peaceable Creation," 138–39) makes a similar point with regard to how far Hauerwas has actually distanced himself from the liberal project. By accepting "the liberal dualism between nature and history" (138), Hauerwas has remained entrenched in the modern tendency to describe humanity in extrabiblical terms. Therefore, Hauerwas's choice of narratives for his anthropology seems somewhat capricious. Kroeker argues for a unification of nature and history in a "dramatistic cosmology" (139). Hauerwas would likely respond that he, like Aquinas, no longer makes such a strong distinction between nature and history. See Hauerwas, *With the Grain of the Universe*, 25.

Hauerwas would thus, like Reinhold Niebuhr, be grounding his theology in an anthropology (i.e., in the human qua human).[99] Hauerwas seems hooked on the horns of a dilemma at this point. He cannot attempt to ground his claims for historicity only in the community of the church, since this would be to make the church a mere sociological reality similar to any non-Christian human community, implying a universal anthropology.[100] On the other hand, he cannot simply state such a historical maxim and leave it as though it is obvious to all rational creatures. Perhaps the only way out of such a dilemma is through an appeal to revelation. Though Hauerwas is typically apprehensive about such an appeal, it may be his only out. The history of the church is historical and unique because God (and the church) says it is (e.g., through the incarnation). In a sense, this is precisely what Hauerwas does by appealing to such doctrines as creation and the resurrection.[101]

99. See Hauerwas's critique of Niebuhr and Bultmann, "On Keeping Theological Ethics Theological," 24.

100. As mentioned above, Hauerwas believes the commitment to a universal anthropology was only one way in which Niebuhr remained entrenched in liberalism. One wonders at this point in the study if Hauerwas has actually escaped such an anthropological foundationalism himself. As will be seen below, Hauerwas addresses this problem by appealing to the sacraments as practices that elevate the human community of church beyond itself. However, this appeal seems inadequate in that the sacraments have limited scope and power for character formation.

If Hauerwas is guilty of maintaining a universal anthropology as a foundation for his theology, this could open him up as well to the criticism of immanentism. In other words, if Hauerwas presumes an anthropology as the universal on which all contingency rests, God is finally subject to being discovered only in and through human existence. In my estimation, such a construal could qualify as a form of immanentism.

101. What I mean here by revelation is not simply an appeal to the text of Scripture. Rather, it would seem consistent for Hauerwas to make an appeal to something like the incarnation as warrant for, at least, the historicity of the church. Of course, the stronger and broader doctrinal support is going to be found in a "doctrine" of creation. Hauerwas even goes so far as to say that a defense of God's activity as creator and upholder of creation is the primary purpose of much of his work. See Hauerwas, *Wilderness Wanderings*, 7. Such an appeal to creation may seem somewhat circular, but if God is real and "really" did create, then such circularity is moot. In other words, the charge of circularity presupposes an external rationality on which to support the reality of God's creation, as if the external reality were somehow "more real." The church can appeal to no such rationality since it believes God really did create all that is out of nothing. The church's final appeal can only be to God. Within the church's context as church, that is sufficient. With such a context in mind, the "givenness" of the particular is perhaps better thought of as "gift." This is Hauerwas's way of affirming a form of theological realism.

Conclusion

Hauerwas demonstrates and convincingly argues for liberal theology's inability to construct a Christian theology that is historically Christian. Further, though liberal theology does not have the substance to support the theology that Hauerwas believes the church must have to be church, it is nonetheless quite permeating in its sway over the church. Hauerwas believes that the church, especially the western church, has embraced liberalism and is still held fast in its embrace. He believes this is the case due to the permeation in the church of the modern project of systematic theology. Hauerwas is opposed to system, as it makes theology a mere knowledge about an object called God. Such a move makes the historicity of Jesus somewhat unnecessary. Further, systematic theology does not build a strong bridge from mind to character, as was seen specifically in Hauerwas's rendering of the relationship between religion and ethics in Kant.

On the other hand, Hauerwas does maintain a system within his own theology, but not in the modern sense of having a foundation prior to theological reflection. Instead, Hauerwas's system is one founded on specific doctrinal realities. For Hauerwas, these are presuppositions. The sectarian critique, built upon the fact that Hauerwas uses Christian doctrine as the foundation for his realism, becomes a moot point in that he believes that these presuppositions are, or perhaps will be in the eschaton, self-verifying. In other words, Hauerwas rightly sees that the reality of Christian doctrine is not a point of speculation, nor is it a point for evaluation; Christian doctrine is simply the way God has made things. They are a given, or better, a gift.

In this chapter, we have seen that Hauerwas came to believe the predominant understanding of theology as knowledge was a mistake deriving from Enlightenment rationality, especially from Kant. Following Wittgenstein, Barth, and some of his own professors, Hauerwas understood that theology must become embedded in history, particularly in

---

Hauerwas makes his appeal to the doctrine of the resurrection explicit in his response to James Gustafson's conception of time and history. "I remain stuck with the problem of history in a way different from Gustafson because I remain stuck with the claim that through Jesus' resurrection God decisively changed our history. Therefore, I believe we must continue to begin with the 'particular,' with the historical, not because there is no other place to begin, but because that is where God begins" (Hauerwas, *Wilderness Wanderings*, 79). Cf. Gustafson, "Response to Critics," 194–96.

the history of Jesus of Nazareth, in order to be regarded as authentically Christian. In other words, action, or contextualization in the practices, including language, must become, at the least, a part of Christianity's epistemology. As will be evident later in our discussion of narrative, such a move implies an equivalence between rational epistemology and moral epistemology. The historicization of theology in church practice had been compromised by liberalism, focusing as it did on creating a rational epistemology available to any rational creature, from which a moral epistemology could later be derived. Such a move domesticated the message of the gospel for the church, transforming it into the mere political ideology of western democracy. System represents the rational epistemological framework on which liberalism was able to build its de-historicized knowledge. By removing the historical context (i.e., action and the practices of being church) from the knowledge of theology, systematicians believed they were arriving at knowledge that was universal, or final. Discovering truth was then merely a matter of corresponding the principles extracted from a historical context with the overarching principles of universal knowledge organized in a system. Hauerwas rightly sees that such an understanding of knowledge is docetic in that it makes the life of Jesus unnecessary. Hauerwas's critique sets out to demonstrate such moves are recent conventions of modernity and are not representative of the history of Christian theology. Throughout his critique Hauerwas is careful to avoid falling into the trap of replacing one system of universal knowledge with another. However, he cannot avoid the implication that his own theology also would make claims that are equally overarching. Though he never describes or attends to such claims of universalism, they become apparent and do reflect a way in which Hauerwas remains attached to claims of knowledge that are universal.[102] As will be seen in a later chapter, these claims seem warranted to Hauerwas because they are statements affirmed by and embedded in the history of the life of the church, even in the life of Jesus. Therefore, though he is not opposed to making such claims, Hauerwas believes he is avoiding the systematic tendency of liberalism to found its knowledge on authorities external to itself. In the next chapter, atten-

---

102. Contrary to his own intentions, we will see in the next chapters how Hauerwas's narrative seems to presuppose a universal notion of anthropology deriving from sources other than a Triune conception of God, leaving him open to the critique that his own narrative is a "mere" anthropology.

tion will be given to the alternative Hauerwas proposes, and to voices more directly influential in helping him discover his own emphasis on narrative.

In his attempt to help Christianity maintain its convictions in the face of a permeating liberal tradition, Hauerwas employs the critical help of various theological and philosophical figures, particularly premodern figures, and those he believes have returned to a more premodern rendering of theology. Some have more prominence in his thought than others, but attending to a few figures that shape Hauerwas's positive reflections will help us to grasp both his critique of liberalism and the alternative that he offers. We have already seen the way in which Hauerwas employs the thought of some of his teachers and his contemporaries. It is to a few historical figures we must now turn our attention.

4

Whose Tradition? Which Narrative?

Hauerwas's Alternative to Modern Systematics

Introduction

ONE COULD PRESUME FROM THE CHAPTER ABOVE THAT HAUERWAS'S theology is primarily a critical theology built specifically on a critique of modern liberalism and on an implicit trust in the continuation of the church's tradition "somewhere." Hauerwas himself lends some credibility to such a presumption, in that he seems constantly to be about a sort of deconstruction of the modern project as it is discovered in theology. When this is coupled with his constant avoidance of system, he could even appear haphazard in his approach to theology. However, a closer reading of what Hauerwas offers as an alternative to the modern project demonstrates that he is hardly haphazard. Hauerwas's answer to modernism is at once cogent and consistently theological.

This chapter will attempt to outline Hauerwas's conception of narrative as he applies it to theology. Certainly he does not believe theology is or should be merely an academic discipline; however, it yet requires a certain quality of reflection that Hauerwas finds most adequately represented in the approach of narrative. Narrative is most conducive to providing a theology for the church, in that it is centered on action as epistemologically primary. This means the church's everyday life—as it is discovered in the practices of the church—has value in determining the veracity of theology. In a manner similar to other narrative theologians, Hauerwas does not find truth located primarily in statements. Instead, knowledge and truth are measured in the crucible of the life of the church. One marked difference between some other narrative theologians and Hauerwas is that Hauerwas sees little reason to "spell out" his method or to justify it for anyone who might wish to observe or evaluate it. In this sense, Hauerwas truly believes himself to be writing theology for the church.

A Brief Synopsis of Hauerwas's Narrative Approach to Theology

Hauerwas's response to the universalism and individualism of modern liberalism is grounded in an understanding of Christian narrative. It is in the living of our various stories, insofar as they are connected to the story of Jesus told through the church, that we find meaning and truth. Prone as Hauerwas is to avoiding definitions, he does not provide a theory of narrative. Nevertheless, as has been seen already in the chapters above, he does give many suggestive descriptions of how narrative relates to the historical reality of human lives and to knowledge. Early in his career, Hauerwas was willing to provide certain definitional language to give insight into his understanding of narrative.

> [My and David Burrell's] argument put in traditional terms is that the moral life must be grounded in the "nature" of man. However, that "nature" is not "rationality" itself, but the necessity of having a narrative to give our life coherence. The truthfulness of our moral life cannot be secured by claims of "rationality" in itself but rather by the narrative that forms our need to recognize the many claims on our lives without trying to subject them to a false unity of coherence.[1]

Here we see that narrative is foundational not simply for understanding or doing theology. Indeed, it is at the very heart of the "nature of man." Though certainly narrative includes the language of history in order to describe our past, it goes deeper in that it also includes the actions and habits that make our past and present coincide. Further, as will be seen below with regard to Aristotle, in narrative, actions and habits take epistemological primacy over thought, or theoretical knowledge. We can only come to understand the self through its history of formation in specific practices. In other words (and Hauerwas would still seem to affirm this today), narrative, that is, the formative community, is the best avenue to explore when attempting to describe the human

1. Hauerwas and Burrell, "From System to Story," 177.

person, particularly with regard to epistemology, or how humans come to know what they claim to know. Hauerwas believes that humans do not need narrative merely to claim our histories as our own but even to understand and assimilate knowledge. This would especially be the case when it comes to theological knowledge, since theology is ethics.

> The reason [stories are more than simply entertaining, offering a moral,] lies with the narrative structure, whose plot cannot be abstracted without banality, yet whose unity does depend on its having a point. Hence it is appropriate to speak of a plot, to call attention to the ordering peculiar to narrative. It is that ordering, that capacity to unfold or develop character, and thus offer insight into the human conditions, which recommends narrative as a form of rationality especially appropriate to ethics.[2]

As noted in the previous chapter, Hauerwas believes narrative formation is the universal condition of all knowledge, present and past. Kant's attempt to escape historical contingency was irretrievably flawed, due to its inability to account for its own historical contextualization and contingencies. Ironically, the knowledge derived from such systems, particularly in theology, is suspect precisely due to its lack of historicization. Hauerwas wishes to replace universal knowledge based on abstract principles of rationality with a knowledge based in the contingency of human history. The way in which he escapes relativism is by a continual appeal to the rootedness of human narrative in the narrative of God himself. This conversion from system to story that Hauerwas believes necessary bears repeating here.

> The standard account's project to supply a theory of basic moral principles from which all other principles and actions can be justified or derived represents an attempt to make the moral life take on the characteristics of a system. But it is profoundly misleading to think that a rational explanation needs to be given for holding rational beliefs, for to attempt to provide such an account assumes that rationality itself does not depend on narrative. What must be faced, however, is that our lives are not and cannot be subject to such an account, for the consistency necessary for governing our lives is more a matter of integrity than one of principle. The narratives that provide the pattern

---

2. Ibid., 179–80. This quotation and the previous one are surely too theoretical for Hauerwas to make today. Nevertheless, he still seems to implicitly subscribe to them in his understanding of narrative.

of integrity cannot be based on principle, nor are they engaging ways of talking about principles. Rather, such narratives are
the ones which allow us to determine how our behavior "fits"
within our ongoing pattern. To be sure, fittingness cannot have
the necessitating form desired by those who want the moral life
to have the "firmness" of some sciences, but it can exhibit the
rationality of a good story.[3]

It would be misleading to leave Hauerwas's concern for narrative
at this point. He certainly sees it as the only alternative to the abstract
systems that he believes so devastating to human epistemology and ethics. However, a narrative anthropology, or a narrative understanding of
what humanity is, is hardly his goal. Hauerwas wishes to employ narrative because he believes it the only way in which the contemporary
church can truly become what it is intended to be: the body of Christ.
In order to accomplish its fulfillment as body of Christ, the church must
become a part of the narrative of Jesus. In other words, it must become
a part of his history in a way no theory could accomplish. Hauerwas
believes, and he says he learned this from Aristotle and Aquinas,

> What is required for our moral behavior to contribute to a co-
> herent sense of the self is neither a single moral principle nor a
> harmony of the virtues but, as I have already said, the formation
> of character by a narrative that provides a sufficiently truthful
> account of our existence. If I can show this to be the case, then
> at least I will have found a way to make intelligible the Christian
> claim that understanding the story of God as found in Israel
> and Jesus is the necessary basis for any moral development that
> is Christianly significant.[4]

The tradition of the church is the narrative in which we find ourselves
already being molded and shaped into the likeness of the One whose
name we bear: Jesus Christ. In a Thomistic turn derived from Aristotle,
Hauerwas views believers as apprentices learning a life from masters,
who are ultimately being conformed more into the image of The
Master. Narrative is but another name in Hauerwas's language for the

---

3. Ibid.,170–71.

4. Hauerwas, *Community of Character*, 136. By "understanding the story of God"
here, Hauerwas means far more than simply a cognitive assent to historical facts. He
means a kind of assimilation of the story that makes it one's own.

community that forms and shapes the self to be virtuous. Further, this community is, of course, the church.[5]

Being formed according to the tradition of the community of the church (i.e., discipleship) has implications for the role of the church as it seeks to fulfill its mission. The church functions in the world to witness of the reality that Jesus's life and message are its own. The mission of the church is not simply to make the world a better place. Indeed, the church's task is to "be the church" and "help the world understand what it means to be the world."[6] The world will not like to hear of the distanciation, but the church's identity is found precisely in the gap. "After all, it is not just a conversation the church is having with the world—it is hopefully an argument."[7]

We have already observed the ways in which certain figures have influenced Hauerwas's critique of modernity. To assist him in the "discussion" of how and why narrative is the way to "do" theology (since he dare not give an explication), Hauerwas enlists the help of his own masters. Some were his professors or had a dominant influence on him in his school or in his teaching. Others were those who filled the role of "theologian as a servant of the church" in years, even centuries, past.

5. Note here that the community is prior to the self in the definition of formation of the self.

6. Hauerwas is quite fond of quoting this throughout many of his works. For a good example of this with some contextual development, see Hauerwas, *Peaceable Kingdom*, 99–102. Cf. Hauerwas, *Wilderness Wanderings*, 2–3; and Hauerwas, *Character and the Christian Life*, 223; and recently, Hauerwas, *Matthew*, 25.

One wonders if Hauerwas's church needs the world in order to exist. One might question whether he in fact holds a dualistic or antithetical view of the church/world relation. Hauerwas would likely respond that his reflections on the world as helpful for understanding what the church "is" or "is not" is simply what it's like to be "between the times." What the church is experiencing is the "already/not-yet" aspect of the kingdom of God. As such, the church cannot help but struggle to maintain and build its identity, particularly in the face of such a tempting assimilation as that offered by the world. Hauerwas would go even further to say that the world's appeal is why patience is a key virtue for the church in its contemporary context. The church is now in a context in which hope should be its "mode of being." The temptation for Christians is to "set up" or "build" the kingdom in the world. The church does not have the patience to wait for Christ to establish his kingdom. But, in fact, that is the reality in which the church finds (or should find) itself. The church is waiting for the eschatological kingdom, and until that day, we are called to continue as a distinct witness to the life, death, and resurrection of Jesus. See Hauerwas, *Peaceable Kingdom*, 101–6.

7. Hauerwas, "Storytelling," 169.

Since this is not meant to be a study of every influence on Hauerwas's thought, we will try to limit our discussion to a few dominant figures.[8]

Karl Barth: Ecclesiology as Narrative

One might expect, given the period in which Hauerwas studied theology, that Reinhold Niebuhr might have been a predominant influence on him.[9] In fact, Niebuhr did have tremendous influence on Hauerwas, but Niebuhr's lapse into liberal presuppositions left his thought unusable as Hauerwas continued his critique of liberalism. As is mentioned above in chapter 3, Niebuhr did not go far enough in his rejection of liberalism. The more influential figure in Hauerwas's thought, the one who provided him with an overarching way in which to think of theology and the church, was Karl Barth.[10] For Hauerwas, Barth provides a useful critique of the modernism creeping into the church. On the other hand, Barth also provides a substantive alternative to modernism. Because of Barth's ecclesiological and christological emphases, Hauerwas seems able to adopt much of Barth's thought without revision or explanation.

8. Though I make occasional reference to John Howard Yoder and Alisdair MacIntyre, I do not consider their influence on Hauerwas in a separate section here. I have chosen instead to focus on the historical figures to which both of these more contemporary influences also point: Barth, Aristotle, and Aquinas. This is not to say that the influence of Yoder or MacIntyre on Hauerwas has been slight. Indeed, it has been significant. However, they too have intentionally focused primarily on the historical figures mentioned, making the influence of the historical figures that much more prominent.

9. Reinhold Niebuhr died the year before Hauerwas matriculated in what was then known as a Bachelor of Divinity degree at Yale University. Though Niebuhr spent his career at Union Theological Seminary, his influence was widespread in theology as well as politics. Hauerwas could not avoid the influence of Niebuhr on American Protestantism.

10. It is significant to note that Hauerwas spent a good deal of time on Barth in his PhD dissertation at Yale. This dissertation was later revised and published as *Character and the Christian Life*. See *Character and the Christian Life*, 129–78, for Hauerwas's discussion of Barth's methodology for ethics. Though some obvious Barthian sensibilities remain in Hauerwas (in fact I think his appreciation of Barth has increased over the years), Hauerwas's own theoretical tendencies in his dissertation make it fairly unrepresentative of his recent thought. Perhaps a better way of stating this would be to say that Hauerwas has found a quite-different way of putting his profound emphasis on character. One interesting way in which Hauerwas seems to parallel Barth is that Hauerwas believes "Barth's work cannot be understood by trying to pin down the intellectual influences in his background. When all is said and done, he simply did theology as if it mattered" (Hauerwas, *With the Grain of the Universe*, 150).

Due to the extent of Hauerwas's positive appropriation of Barth, his influence on Hauerwas is treated here, rather than in the above chapter on Hauerwas's critical engagement with liberalism. Perhaps the best place to begin our discussion of Hauerwas's appropriation of Barth is with Barth's "unsystematic" tendencies.

Barth serves Hauerwas's purposes well, because Barth was comprehensive in his rejection of liberalism. Comparing Niebuhr and Barth, Hauerwas makes it clear why he finally found Barth more compelling than Niebuhr:

> Niebuhr, far more than was seen at the time, continued to be essentially a liberal theologian. His emphasis on the sinfulness of man in his magisterial *Nature and Destiny of Man* led many to associate him with the "neo-orthodox" movement of Bultmann, Brunner, and Barth. Yet Niebuhr never shared Barth's theological rejection of liberalism as a basic theological strategy; he, like Bultmann, continued liberal theology's presumption that theology must be grounded in anthropology. Thus his compelling portrayal of our sinfulness, which appeared *contra* liberal optimism, only continued the liberal attempt to demonstrate the intelligibility of theological language through its power to illuminate the human condition.[11]

It is both Barth's substantive objections to liberalism and his methodological (if it can be called that) response that attracted Hauerwas. Taking first the matter of Barth's "methodology," the similarities between Hauerwas and Barth are unmistakable. "Indeed, one of the things [Hauerwas] most like[s] about Barth is that his position defies summary because he was so determinedly unsystematic, making it almost impossible to know what it would mean to be a 'Barthian.'"[12] Barth was not attempting to provide a rationality on which to "hang" his theology. Instead, Barth's purpose was to explicate the message of Scripture through repetition of Scripture in traditional theological language. "Barth saw that theology is incapable of saying everything at one time. So any attempt to wrap everything up in one concept that is continually unfolded simply will not work."[13] As Gerhard Sauter quotes Barth,

---

11. Hauerwas, "On Keeping Theological Ethics Theological," 24. Emphasis Hauerwas's.

12. Hauerwas, *Dispatches from the Front*, 58.

13. Ibid., 59.

describing Barth's theology is like trying "to trace the bird's flight."[14] In many respects, reading *Church Dogmatics* is an effort not unlike engaging the characters in a novel.

> I think it is not so odd to compare Barth's work with that of a novelist. For just as any good novel cannot be captured by a summary of its plot, by a description of the characters, or by trying to say what it is about, so Barth's theology cannot be summarized. There is no substitute for reading *Church Dogmatics*, just as *Church Dogmatics* reminds us that nothing can substitute for reading the Bible.[15]

Aligning himself with Hans Frei, Hauerwas believes Barth's project was to train his readers in the reading of Scripture. As Frei states,

> [Barth] took the classical themes of communal Christian language moulded by the Bible, tradition and constant usage in worship, practice, instruction and controversy, and he restated or redescribed them rather than evolving arguments on their behalf. It was of the utmost importance to him that his communal language, especially its biblical *fons et origo*, which he saw as indirectly one with the Word of God, has an integrity of its own: it was irreducible. But in that case its lengthy, even leisurely unfolding was equally indispensable.[16]

In the telling of the doctrinal (biblical) story, Barth was teaching his readers how to place themselves into the narrative of Christian historicity. "Through repetition, Barth forces his readers to attend to the story

14. Sauter, "Shifts in Karl Barth's Thought."

15. Hauerwas, *Dispatches from the Front*, 59. Unfortunately, Hauerwas does not heed as well as he could have Barth's emphasis on the explication of Scripture. Though certainly Hauerwas does wish to be Scriptural in his theological investigations, he seldom engages in any significant Scriptural discussion. Even when he does discuss Scripture, it more typically is a discussion of someone else's interpretation. Perhaps Hauerwas wishes to maintain a sense of modesty, given that he is not a Scripture scholar. However, I do not see that he can escape the engagement with Scripture so easily. Perhaps Hauerwas could also make the case that he has been discussing Scripture on every page of his written works, but the connection would seem a bit strained. It is the intention of this study to make such an engagement more explicit by bringing the Scriptures to bear on Hauerwas' emphasis on ecclesiology by giving a fuller account of the Scriptural discussions of pneumatology as the substantive doctrine necessary for his ecclesiology to work.

16. Frei, "An Afterword," 110–11.

of God. . . . Barth knew repetition was a way to train Christian readers."[17] His was not simply an academic exercise. Instead, Hauerwas believes that Barth was always striving to be a theologian for the church. Theology was not simply another idea amongst the many options available at the university. Hauerwas learned from Barth that to be a theologian is to fulfill an office that attempts to faithfully serve an institution maintaining the name of Jesus across centuries.[18]

Barth's substantive response to liberalism was to ground the church once again in the historicity of the person Jesus. Combined with his "method" of restating Scripture, this concern gave his theology a uniquely traditioned (i.e., historical) sense. Of course, this also distinguished Barth from many of his contemporaries, who were somewhat ambiguously lumped together in "neo-orthodoxy." As Hauerwas explains,

> Tillich and Bultmann, two premier "modern" theologians, were not so modern. They both bought into the notion, conventional wisdom at least since Schleiermacher (no, since Constantine), that the challenge of Christianity was primarily an intellectual one involving the clash of two different systems of belief: how to make old Christianity credible to the new modern world. Which explains why Karl Barth was much more "new" than Tillich. Tillich still thought that the theological challenge involved the creation of a new and better-adapted systematic theology. Barth knew that the theological problem was the creation of a new and better church. Tillich hoped that, by the time one had finished his *Systematic Theology*, one would think about things differently. Barth hoped that, by the time one had plodded through his *Church Dogmatics*, one would *be* different. . . . So the theological task is not merely the interpretive matter of translating Jesus into modern categories but rather to translate the world to him. The theologian's job is not to make the gospel credible to the modern world, but *to make the world credible to the gospel*.[19]

It was perhaps primarily because of Barth's own historical context that he countenanced such a strong disjunction between the church and the world. Liberal theology was unable to withstand the test of Nazi

17. Hauerwas, *Wilderness Wanderings*, 183.

18. Hauerwas, *Dispatches from the Front*, 19.

19. Hauerwas and Willimon, *Resident Aliens*, 23–24. Emphasis Hauerwas and Willimon's.

Germany. Liberalism had compelled the church to forget the historicity of a Jew called Jesus.

> Liberal theology had spent decades reassuring us that we did not have to take the Jewishness of Jesus seriously. The particulars of this faith, the limiting, historically contingent, narrative specifics of the faith, such as the Jewishness of Jesus or his messianic eschatology, were impediments for the credibility of modern people and could therefore be removed so that we could get down to the real substance of Christianity. Jesus was not *really* a Jew, he was the pinnacle of the brightest and best in humanity, the teacher of noble ideals, civilization's very best. It was a short step from the liberal Christ-the-highest-in-humanity to the Nazi Superman.[20]

Barth countered such thought by attacking the liberal notion that humanity had moved beyond its need for a living God, or that theology was merely anthropology in Christian dress. "God is not 'man' said in a loud voice," was Barth's reply to such thought.[21]

Hauerwas finds it very significant that the Barmen Declaration is rather exclusive, even imperialistic, with regard to the lordship of Christ.[22] Such exclusivity is consistent with Barth's, and Hauerwas's, conviction that the liberal church had totally accommodated itself to the world. Indeed, as they would say, proclaiming the lordship of Jesus is the scriptural role of the church. "[The church] exists . . . to set up in the world a new sign which is radically dissimilar to [the world's] own manner and which contradicts it in a way which is full of promise."[23] However, this is not an exclusivistic (sectarian) goal.

20. Ibid., 25. Emphasis Hauerwas and Willimon's.

21. Ibid. Hauerwas and Willimon intimate that this quotation is from Barth's commentary on Romans; however, they give no specific bibliographic reference.

22. Ibid., 43–44.

23. Barth, *Church Dogmatics* IV/3.2, 779. This quotation of Barth is found in Hauerwas and Willimon, *Resident Aliens*, 83. It should be noted that Hauerwas is particularly attracted here to Barth's section in *Church Dogmatics* on "The Holy Spirit and the Sending of the Christian Community." Though by no means is Hauerwas's attraction to Barth exclusive to this section, this is where Barth devotes specific attention to the church/world distinction and to the Christian call to be church. I call attention to this merely to point out that Hauerwas fails to make clear the connection Barth has in mind between ecclesiology and pneumatology. Barth obviously sees the activity of the human community of the church as best embedded in the context of the Holy Spirit. Though Hauerwas does occasionally make note of this, he fails to give a full account

> [C]alling for the church to be the church is not a formula for a
> withdrawal ethic; nor is it a self-righteous attempt to flee from
> the world's problems; rather it is a call for the church to be a
> community which tries to develop the resources to stand within
> the world witnessing to the peaceable kingdom and thus rightly
> understanding the world. The gospel is a political gospel.[24]

Barth likewise believes the community of the church is intended
to live as a witness to the world around it, and this as a recognition that
Jesus is Lord of all. This is a community rooted in human history.[25] This
is eminent love of neighbor.[26] Hauerwas makes it clear that Barth's is
also his own position, as he uses Barth explicitly to support his notion
of the church as church in the world; not a ghetto Christianity but a
Christianity rooted in the natural human community of the church.[27]
This is not a triumphalist kingdom theology, since Hauerwas still holds
to an eschatological kingdom that awaits. The church, therefore, points
to the reality of that coming kingdom. But would not Hauerwas be better served by spelling out the relationship between history and eschatology? In other words, can church function as a sign for the world of
the eschatological kingdom without developing the way in which the
history of the church contributes to or detracts from the reality of a
coming historical kingdom? If the church is real history, does this in
any way detract from its capacity to be an eschatological sign? What is
the relationship of the historical nature of the church to the reality of
the coming kingdom in history? Hauerwas is not willing to explain the
relationship, and may not be able to give an explanation on purely rev-

---

of its import for ecclesiology. I do not believe this to be the fault of Hauerwas, since
I do not believe Barth sufficiently accounts for the relationship of ecclesiology and
pneumatology. Hauerwas is aware of Barth's belief that the church is first presented as
unnecessary in the grand scheme of witness to Jesus. However, Hauerwas also comes to
discover that Barth indeed believed the church to be the crucial element in witness. See
Hauerwas, *With the Grain of the Universe*, 192–204.

24. Hauerwas, *Peaceable Kingdom*, 102. Wells (*Transforming Fate into Destiny*, 139)
picks up on this as he summarizes Hauerwas's position: "There is no question of with-
drawal: the community of character is surrounded."

25. Barth, *Church Dogmatics IV/3.2*, 763–95.

26. Ibid., 831–901.

27. Hauerwas, *Peaceable Kingdom*, 166–67. He is here citing Barth *Church Dogmatics
IV/2*, 721, 723.

elational grounds. However, his commitment to the historical community of the church as anticipatory of the kingdom needs clarification.

Pannenberg's Eschatology and its Thin Connection to History

The theologian we have chosen as a conversation partner for Hauerwas picks up on the notion of church as sign, but incorporates it into his theology in a more intentionally systematic fashion. Eschatology likewise becomes the hinge on which Pannenberg locates the connection between the historically conditioned human community of the church and the timeless truth of a doctrine of the eschatological kingdom. However, whereas Hauerwas seems to leave us with a weak link to the church's affirmation of the doctrinal truth of eschatology, Pannenberg's connection to doctrine appears to be finally made at the expense of historicity.

Pannenberg believes the human community to be an overly contingent and obscure context in which to develop a doctrine of ecclesiology. Therefore, his ecclesiology remains theoretical or abstract, with application to any human community being somewhat arbitrary, or "merely provisional."[28] The church is a community in which the lordship of Jesus is expressed and celebrated, but the church does not yet exist as the kingdom of God. As such, it cannot rightly be considered a permanent expression of Jesus's lordship, in that it is now only representative of the collective of Christians who will one day rightly express his lordship.

> [The church's] relation to the kingdom of God, as an anticipation of the future fellowship of the humanity renewed in this kingdom, must form the context for an understanding of the church as the fellowship of believers that is grounded on the participation of each in the one Jesus Christ.[29]

The church then serves as an anticipation of the eventual reality of the kingdom. This parallels Hauerwas' understanding of a fundamental distinction of the church—practicing the lordship of Jesus before a watching world.[30] This "anticipation" of the kingdom's reality would

28. Pannenberg, *Systematic Theology*, 3:19 n. 51.

29. Ibid., 20. Cf. ibid., 3, especially Pannenberg's discussion of Barth.

30. E.g., see Hauerwas, *In Good Company*, 249–50 n. 12; and Hauerwas with Michael Baxter, "The Kingship of Christ: Why Freedom of 'Belief' Is Not Enough," in *In Good Company*, 216. Perhaps the parallel here between Hauerwas and Pannenberg's concern

seem to make the kingdom an event without connection to the historical reality of the church. In other words, does the church still matter if
the consummation of fellowship with God and his people is yet a future
event? Pannenberg's answer is to make eschatology a present reality
with a future consummation (i.e., a prolepsis).

> The church, then, is not identical with the kingdom of God. It is
> a sign of the kingdom's future of salvation. It is so in such a way
> that this future of God is already present in it and is accessible
> to people through the church, through its proclamation and its
> liturgical life.[31]

Thus, the future is brought back to the present without doing fundamental damage to the future kingdom as an eschatological event. The
means for accomplishing this is through the church, which is the community of the Spirit.[32] "In the eschatological consummation, the Spirit
is active as the enabling and transfiguring power that gives creatures a
share in the glory of God."[33] Pannenberg believes, and I think Hauerwas
would agree, that the Spirit has always been understood in this sense:
as an "eschatological gift and . . . his working in the community is an
eschatological event."[34] Consequently, as the Spirit works to bring glory

---

for the display of Jesus's lordship, which, incidentally, is also Yoder's concern, is best
traceable to Barth's mentoring, as he desired to heighten the lordship of Jesus in his
own theology.

31. Pannenberg, *Systematic Theology*, 3:37. Cf. ibid., 45, 47.

32. Pannenberg tends to equivocate a bit as to how the kingdom becomes a present
reality. As seen above, he believes it is through the church. At the same time, he affirms
that the means through which it is accomplished is the Spirit. While I am attracted to
such an equivocation precisely because of what it does for an understanding of the
Spirit, I am wary of embracing it, due to Pannenberg's own individuated understanding
of the Spirit in humanity. I am afraid ecclesiology is once again reduced to a collection
of individuals.

33. Pannenberg, *Systemaic Theology*, 3:4.

34. Ibid., 7. Cf. ibid., 16–17. This systematic move parallels the ecclesiological move
that Hauerwas makes with regard to the eschatological nature of the witness of the
church. The lordship to which the church attests is the lordship that will one day be
affirmed by the world as well. See Hauerwas, *In Good Company*, 249–50 notes 12–13.
What both Hauerwas and Pannenberg are reflecting here is the way in which the
historical nature of God's activity *must* permeate their doctrine of his lordship over
creation. Since history is awaiting its culmination, his lordship must, therefore, also
be awaiting a fuller revelation, at least as it regards creation. Pannenberg would argue
that the lordship of the Father expressed by the Son was certainly complete. But the
lordship of the Son, being worked out by the Spirit in creation, is yet to be fully realized.
Hauerwas seems, implicitly at least, to agree with such notions.

to Jesus and to establish his lordship in the human community of the church, the Spirit is ultimately confirming in the present history what will finally be consummated in eschatological reality.[35] The community of the church is an eschatological sign by means of its being indwelled by the Spirit. The Spirit's presence within the church makes the church an eschatological people.[36]

While I am attracted to Pannenberg's avoidance of anthropological reductionism by maintaining a distinction between the human and the Holy Spirit (contra Friedrich Schleiermacher and, as will be seen later, Hauerwas) and his protection of the kingdom as a future event, both intentions seem to erode or minimize ecclesiology. Of course, the more interesting point of making ecclesiology an eschatological reality is that it is not entirely a retreat into theory. By allowing the historical human community of the church to participate in God's fellowship and in the confirmation of Jesus's final lordship, Pannenberg has made room for ecclesiology as history in a way that a more purely theoretical or abstract account of ecclesiology as knowledge would not. Unfortunately, Pannenberg, like Barth, appears to have little confidence in the historical reality of the church. In his discussions of the real human community and its relation to doctrine, Pannenberg's church still amounts to a, more or less theoretical development.

> The church is not in and of itself the saving mystery of the rule of God either in its social constitution or in its historical form. It is so only in Christ, therefore only in the event of participation in Jesus Christ as this takes place in its liturgical life. Of itself the church is not at once seen to be the sacrament of unity in which the future unity of humanity in the kingdom of God finds anticipatory representation and is historically at work for human reconciliation. The divine mystery of salvation achieves only broken manifestation in the church's historical form. Perversion results from the failures of Christians, not least those in office

---

35. Though he uses more biblical terminology, Pannenberg has here made a move similar to Hauerwas's critique of Kant. Hauerwas believes modernity's project, particularly as it took shape in Kant's thought, allowed the individual to maintain autonomy in the face of God's sovereignty. It was in fact, as Hauerwas calls it, the problem of "anthropodicy" (see Hauerwas, *God, Medicine, and Suffering*, 62). Pannenberg seems to waver on this a bit at times, still giving preference to the individual in his ecclesiology. Nevertheless, he consistently affirms that lordship was the central thrust of Jesus's message. See Pannenberg, *Systematic Theology*, 1:310.

36. Pannenberg, *Systematic Theology*, 3:13.

in the church, and from the related divisions that have arisen in
its history.[37]

Pannenberg has no enduring tradition or historicity of formation on which he can base the ongoing affirmation of the church in
its commitment to the lordship of Jesus. All such representation of the
eschatological reality is based on the immediacy of individual participation in Jesus. Such a reduction to theory seems to directly contradict
Pannenberg's confidence in the church as the means by which salvation
has always been offered to humanity since the first century. "If we ignore the first band of disciples, the fellowship of individuals with Jesus
is always mediated by the church, by its proclamation and its adminis-
tration of the sacraments."[38]

In the end, Pannenberg seems unable to escape a precommitment
to the individual in his definition of the self in relation to Jesus, making
his ecclesiology inconsistent on this point. Hauerwas offers Pannenberg's
theology the option of a more thoroughgoing ecclesiology without doing fundamental damage to Pannenberg's eschatology, pneumatology,
(or perhaps more important), to his Christology. Whereas Hauerwas
is certainly more historical than Pannenberg (i.e., he has a real human
community in mind in his ecclesiology), he would likewise wish to affirm the final consummation of human history in the eschatological
confirmation of Jesus's lordship. However, instead of basing his affirmation on the security of a promise of the coming future kingdom,
Hauerwas bases it on the insecurity of the contingent community of
the church. What is needed then is not better theory or doctrine but
"thicker" narrative. For this we must return to Barth.

Barth's Ecclesiology as History Also Insufficient

Hauerwas believes that Barth was rightly concerned to reshape the
narrative in which the church was defined. The liberal church had accommodated itself to the world. Accordingly, it needed to recover the
narrative that constituted it historically in the person of Jesus. Barth attempted to do this by pointing to the need, not for a renewed statement
of the church in contemporary terms, but for a conversion of those
from the world into the church.

37. Ibid., 42–43.
38. Ibid., 24.

Barth was really more "new," more "radical," than Tillich in his determination to get the church accommodated to the gospel rather than the gospel adapted to the status quo in the world. In Barth we rediscovered the New Testament assertion that the purpose of theological endeavor is not to describe the world in terms that make sense, but rather to change lives, to be re-formed in light of the stunning assertions of the gospel. Each age must come, fresh and new, to the realization that God, not nations, rules the world. This we can know, not through accommodation, but through conversion. As Barth noted, sanctification and justification go hand in hand. We cannot understand the world until we are transformed into persons who can use the language of faith to describe the world right. Everyone does not already know what we mean when we speak of prayer. Everyone does not already believe that he or she is a sinner. We must be taught that we sin. That is, we must be transformed by the vision of a God who is righteous and just, who judges us on the basis of something more significant than merely what feels right for us.[39]

This means for Hauerwas that a more true narrative must be found than the one given the church by the world. The church must recover its own sense of what it means to be a people with a history of worship. This is not the typical theology of the modern church as it seeks for the essence of Christianity in rational belief (i.e., systematics). Instead, it is to be found in the telling of the Christian narrative, the story of Jesus who came *from Nazareth*. Here is a theology with a time and a place, with the historicity that can ground it in the real life of the church. Hauerwas, following Frei and Barth, came to realize that the narrative of Jesus found in Scripture was a better christological rendering of his life and significance than the more "orthodox" Christologies.[40]

But Hauerwas became increasingly aware that Barth could not ground this narrative as well as the Hauerwas would have liked. Barth seemed to lack a narrative in historical reality to ground his ecclesiology. Instead, Barth turned to a more universal rendering of ecclesiology, which finally leaves his theology rather theoretical when contrasted with narrative. Though certainly Barth "feared that any account of humanity in the abstract, even the humanity of Christ, could not help but

39. Hauerwas and Willimon, *Resident Aliens*, 28.

40. Hauerwas, *Peaceable Kingdom*, xxi. Hauerwas seems to have more systematic renderings of Christology in mind here.

be an invitation to return to Protestant liberalism,"[41] he was unable to sufficiently ground his understanding of ecclesiology in a real historical community. Comparing Barth to the novelist Anthony Trollope with regard to the virtue of honor, Hauerwas finds that Barth leaves his readers with a general account of honor that is relatively "thin." The readers must compensate for the "thinness" by inserting their own sense of what honor ought to be.[42] Hauerwas believes that Barth's conception of honor is correct. The problem is simply that Barth leaves readers without any sense of where this honor might be found.[43] Barth's discussion of honor remains too general. By refraining from placing his account in the concrete human community of the church, Barth is succumbing to the modern temptation to be universal. Barth is still entrenched in the tendency of liberalism to make the Christian ethic an ethic for all humanity. Hauerwas cannot allow such an endeavor to pass without notice. Though Barth's method is notable in its intention to form readers through repetition in the Christian narrative, nevertheless, he is unable to escape the liberal aspiration to be universal.

> Modern moral philosophy [including Barth at this point] tries to underwrite [living unashamedly] by its insistence that moral actions can be justified only when reasons can be given that are anyone's. But, ironically, that results in the creation of the kind of moral anonymity that destroys a society capable of sustaining Puddicombes [a character in Trollope's novel]. For impersonal principles, or even commands of God, are not sufficient to replace the flesh and blood of Puddicombes. . . . Barth simply fails to provide any conceptual or empirical account of how honor requires the existence of such a community. As a result, his account of honor is susceptible to an individualistic interpretation that his theological program is meant to counter.[44]

41. Hauerwas, *With the Grain of the Universe*, 160.

42. Hauerwas, *Dispatches from the Front*, 66–67.

43. Ibid., 77.

44. Ibid., 78–79. Hauerwas finds such a lack of empirical account in Barth perplexing given Barth's struggle against totalitarianism. Totalitarianism is fostered by precisely the kind of individualism and secrecy that Trollope's novel counters and that real communities make impossible.

For a more detailed account of the relationship of Barth's ecclesiology with his social ethics, see Hauerwas "On Learning Simplicity in an Ambiguous Age," 43–46. For a more thorough comparison of Barth's ecclesiology with Hauerwas's, see Hütter, *Evangelische Ethic als Kirchliches Zeugnis*.

The temptation toward a theoretical universal in Barth may also be due to his dissatisfaction with the human community of the church. In other words, Barth may be driven to the theoretical because of the historical reality of the church in Germany. What we find in Barth's ecclesiology is a "bifurcation" of the church, in that he makes a clear distinction between the church in its essence and the human church with all its encumbrances. Barth believes the Scriptures portray a church that is pure, or at least that is becoming purer, in contradiction to what he saw in the human church of the twentieth century. This made him reticent to emphasize the humanness of ecclesiology beyond what can be said in a somewhat christological sense. However, this finally left his ecclesiology in the rather awkward position of being merely theoretical. Thus, as Nicholas Healy notes, "Barth avoids the error of a one-sided sociological description of the church's identity by making the opposite error, presenting us with a one-sided doctrinal description."[45]

Without a narrative community to establish the veracity of theological commitments, Barth's program leaves Hauerwas without sufficient grounding for the historical reality of the church and a clear witness to the person of Jesus. Thus Hauerwas is left without the "thickness" he would like in a theology that purports to tell the story of the church and that has the capacity to sustain an ongoing rehearsal of a true narrative of the life, death, and resurrection of Jesus.

Interestingly, Hauerwas himself chooses to counter his dilemma with figures from a Trollope novel rather than to recount happenings from a concrete community.[46] The fictional nature of the novel makes it a questionable comparison, since the characters can be shaped in ways that may or may not be "true to life."[47] Of course, the response to such a

---

Hauerwas seems to have changed his mind a bit on this recently (see Hauerwas, *With the Grain of the Universe*, 194–95 n. 46). Though he seems ready to acknowledge that Barth did have the resources for presenting a "thicker" account of the church and its indispensable nature for witness to the reality that it is, i.e., body of Christ, I remain unconvinced that he should abandon his critique altogether. Barth did have a strong conception of the church as the essential material witness, as Hauerwas delineates for us (*With the Grain of the Univese*, 193–204); however, the question remains, for Barth, where is this church? In other words, Barth's historical context seems to prevent him from identifying this church in more than theoretical terms.

45. Healy, "Logic of Karl Barth's Ecclesiology," 263.

46. See Hauerwas, *Dispatches from the Front*, 58–79.

47. Cf. Holland, "Mennonites on Hauerwas," 145–46 n. 9.

criticism is likely to be that precisely because we can resonate with the humanness of the characters, they become "true to our lives." In a sense, we can join in their story because we feel that their lives are like our own in some ways; our aspirations and expectations become a part of the character development. Unfortunately, such a response seems to underwrite the implicit universalism of human experience that Hauerwas has fought so hard to remove from his theology. Perhaps one cannot read too much into Hauerwas's use of a fictional work for the sake of illustration. However, in Hauerwas's words,

> [I]f lives like Dag Hammarskjold, Martin Luther King, Jr., Clarence Jordan, Charles Ives, Sarah and Jonathan Edwards, Dietrich Bonhoeffer, Dorothy Day, Coffee Martin Hauerwas, and James William McClendon do not exist then what we Christians practice cannot be true. The attempt to do theology as if such lives did not need to exist is now at an end. God has forced us to see that there is no "foundation" more sure than the existence of such lives.[48]

Hauerwas seems to realize that it is the stories that are "true to life" that can make us "true to His life." Nevertheless, he struggles with telling the story of moral virtue (e.g., honor) so that it will "come out right." Perhaps that is because he knows that real lives are a bit too "messy" for the comparison to be clear; or perhaps it is because there are so few lives that emulate the kind of honor Hauerwas sees in Barth's narrative. What

---

48. Hauerwas, "Church's One Foundation is Jesus Christ Her Lord," 161–62. The first eight names are those that shaped the theological works of McClendon, to whom the book is dedicated as a *Festschrift*. The article that Hauerwas contributed to this work was a compilation of three sermons, each given in the context of real lives in real places. The last sermon was especially poignant, being the sermon that Hauerwas delivered at his father's funeral. Each of these "stories" was a celebration of real lives made even more real by the reminder of death and how a person's death serves as a culmination of his life, rather than as a disconnected ending.

As mentioned in the introduction, emergent-church theologians have attempted to co-opt narrative epistemology by theologizing in novels and other fictional stories. Their attempts seem to fall prey to the same critique given here. We can and should no longer pretend, with liberalism, that a universal anthropology is a satisfactory substitute for a *real* ecclesiology. This seems to be the trap into which fictional works fall: expecting a narrative resonance with all humanity (i.e., anthropology) to be sufficient grounding for ecclesiology. Though fictional works may be interesting and less messy than the lives of real people, their value seems limited to a bolstering of the theoretical. In other words, fiction is merely illustrative, which finally does little to overcome liberal theorizing.

may be needed in Hauerwas's "true-life stories" is a narrator to make them more to the point; but, of course, having a narrator implies a sense of objectivity or distance that may be more rationalistic than Hauerwas wishes. He is not so bold as to think narrative theology should attempt such a universalistic approach in response to the universalism of rationality—as his comments with regard to John Milbank and Alasdair MacIntyre indicate:

> There is a very serious problem about the character of Milbank's whole project as he attempts to supply a counternarrative to that of liberalism. Does he reproduce exactly the violence of liberalism by trying to write such a grand narrative of how we have gotten in our peculiar straits today? In that sense his project is not unlike MacIntyre's project in *Whose Justice? Which Rationality?* Obviously, in my own work I have tried to chip away at liberalism one piece at a time. Milbank, however, may be right that you can only counter a totalizing narrative with another narrative that is equally totalizing, but I fear that in the process the Gospel cannot help but appear as just another "system" or "theory."[49]

As will be seen below, Hauerwas's response to the compulsion for totalizing narratives is to situate his narrative in the life of the real human community of the church. Thus, theology and ethics are subsumed into the practice of living as church. This is no less totalizing than Milbank's or MacIntyre's projects, but it is distinct in its location as a real community, rather than a communal theory. The question remains, however, whether Hauerwas is consistent in the application of his intentions.

Hauerwas is faced with another problem: where to locate the Christian community. He, like Barth, could well be asked, where is the real community to be found? Is it only in novels? Is it only sporadically found here and there? Hauerwas's work represents an attempt to show what such a community looks like, but to the extent that he draws from several communities and authors, some of which are dubiously Christian, he seems to underwrite the very pluralism he abhors.[50] Hauerwas appears to have the ability, or prerogative, to pick and choose which stories he finds most illustrative of his point. While this may be

49. Hauerwas, *Wilderness Wanderings*, 197–98 n. 7.

50. Ibid., 3.

a useful (efficient?) literary and academic tool, it seems a bit abstracted from real life. Even if a story is true, that doesn't mean that it fits well with the rest of the stories that make up the narrative of the church. Although certainly I recognize the value of including both positives and negatives, the point is that not everyone's story seems to matter in Hauerwas's conception of the ongoing narrative. Hauerwas seems to be rewriting the narrative by picking and choosing which elements of the narrative best "carry" the story, always searching for the right characterization. But picking and choosing which stories best illustrate the point seems counternarrative. It seems instead that Hauerwas here has an overarching story that dictates the "fittedness" of each contribution from individual narratives (i.e., a preexistent metanarrative, or perhaps even systematic doctrine of the "universal church"). Hauerwas seems to struggle with precisely this issue, particularly as it regards historical Christian traditions. He is prone to associate himself with a broad theological spectrum in his search for the kind of community that best emulates his ecclesiology. In this sense, he may finally find himself a victim of the "consumer preference" mentality that plagues modern liberal theology in its many faces.[51]

Hauerwas has little answer to this dilemma, other than to say that recognition of past accomplishments and problems is not so much a "pick-and-choose" approach as it is a form of learning from past communities, from tradition. It is a learning that is accomplished not so much through the recognition of similarity in belief as through similarity in facing the enemy that is the world. We are sort of thrown together by our similar contexts. The church today needs to find a voice to respond to the powers that challenge its commitment in ways very similar to those in the days of Constantine, and others. What is particularly useful for Hauerwas is that this mixing of historical horizons helps blur denominational, as well as chronological lines.[52] He can then claim to be in service to the whole church. The further question that remains, of course, is, is that what Methodists do, or is this a somewhat speculative recommendation?[53]

51. Ibid., 184. Here, among other places, Hauerwas identifies himself as a "High Church Mennonite."

52. Ibid., 185.

53. Hauerwas may wish to respond that this is what he does with his students, and it is what he calls the Methodist church to do. But he cannot respond in such an individu-

In order to find this real narrative community and the inherent practices that sustain it, Hauerwas looks to two figures highly influential in providing theoretical development for the historically grounded communities that sustained the Greek state and the Christian church, and that eventually also helped to provide a narrative accounting of the virtuous Christian life—Aristotle and Aquinas.[54]

Narrative Epistemology in the Ethics of Aristotle and Aquinas

As an antithesis to Kant's ahistorical universalism, Hauerwas employs the contingency of Aristotle's communalism.[55] Hauerwas finds in Aristotle the recognition of context necessary to counter the historical forgetfulness of modernity.[56] Hauerwas is concerned to demonstrate

alistic or speculative manner, since to do so would be to admit that he is still a liberal, or perhaps even a sectarian.

As will be discussed later, it may be the permeating notion of grace in Wesleyan theology that allows Hauerwas some liberties in this regard, but I am not convinced that such an appeal works, particularly since grace in Wesleyan theology is often used for very different purposes, e.g., to maintain the freedom of the individual.

54. This is a narrative suggested by many critics of the modern problem, but perhaps the most influential for Hauerwas is Alasdair MacIntyre. Cf. MacIntyre, *After Virtue*; and MacIntyre, *Whose Justice? Which Rationality?* Hauerwas continually acknowledges MacIntyre's influence on his own work. Hauerwas's own thought shifts a bit when he turns more decidedly toward Aquinas. Nevertheless, even his reading of Aquinas is rather MacIntyrean.

55. It seems a bit ironic for Hauerwas to find historical contingency in Aristotle, in that Aristotle maintained a sense of universality that seems a bit antithetical to Hauerwas's narrative. Perhaps Hauerwas would be willing to admit such universality; even, as was seen above, he once did admit to the universal nature of narrative for humans and their knowledge of God. Unfortunately, Hauerwas no longer addresses such themes.

56. Quinn, "Is Athens Revived," attempts to attack Hauerwas's use of Aristotle by accusing Hauerwas of employing a pagan philosophy in developing Christian ethics. Quinn sets out to demonstrate that Aristotle and Augustine are far apart on important Christian themes. In the process, Quinn employs his own philosopher to support his scheme of Christian ethics. As a defender of Kant and of divine-command ethics, Quinn wishes to return to a duty ethic. His support for such an ethical scheme is that it seems to be at least acknowledged, if not even proposed, by all who are familiar with Christian ethics. While I remain skeptical that duty ethics is so universal in contemporary theology, I am quite convinced that it is not the ethics of the New Testament. Having left the law behind in its legalistic sense, Christians are called to move into a relationship with the law which is based on the new covenant. The Holy Spirit writes

that the Christian life is a life primarily dedicated to the development of character and virtue. As Hauerwas became "armed with [the belief that the Christian's life of morality is best characterized in the language of character and the virtues] [he] began a serious study of Aristotle and Aquinas."[57] Aristotle provided the means to ground the virtues in history through the polis and the formative nature of the community on the morality of those within it. "Why choose Aristotle? At least one answer is that Aquinas found Aristotle such a fruitful resource for his account of the virtues—and [Hauerwas] believe[s] Aquinas's account of the virtues remains unmatched in Christian theology."[58] While not uncritical of Aristotle's program, Hauerwas believes it to be only relatively "translatable" into Christian terms.[59]

Aristotle's primary goal was to make the community a better place by making those within it better people. They were to become virtuous people so that they might live the "happy" life. "Aristotle's means of describing and navigating the journey to the destination of happiness (a destination understood as of a journey and not as of a trip) is the

---

the law on believers' hearts and causes them to walk in God's statutes (Jer 31; Ezek 36). The question, of course, is how the Spirit does this. Since I am convinced that duty ethics cannot answer this question well without slipping back into some form of legalism, I will attempt to outline a more plausible approach in chapter 7 below.

57. Hauerwas, *Peaceable Kingdom*, xxii.

58. Hauerwas and Pinches, *Christians among the Virtues*, xiii. Cf. Hauerwas, *Wilderness Wanderings*, 156.

59. I have placed the word *translatable* in quotation marks because I know it is a concept that Hauerwas deplores. Translation implies that tradition is merely an idea that can be "explained" in other words. Hauerwas believes that a tradition is hardly able to convey itself to a "foreigner" by rendering itself into some universal symbols. The idea that Aristotle's thought was merely given a Christian rendering is completely foreign to Hauerwas's conception of tradition-determined reality. (On this, cf. Hauerwas, *Wilderness Wanderings*, 145ff.) Hauerwas makes it clear throughout his work that Aquinas did make several critical changes in Aristotle's thought, pagan as it was. See Hauerwas and Pinches, *Christians among the Virtues*.

Nevertheless, it is interesting to ponder whether Aquinas was doing something new in the *Summa Theologiae*. Obviously, he was shaped and changed by his contact with Aristotelians. But one wonders if this was his formative community. Was Aristotelianism enough of a tradition for Aquinas to be formed by it, or was it more of an idea he confronted in texts? Cf. Hauerwas, *Character and the Christian Life*, 35–82. Of course, the same question could likewise be asked of Hauerwas's appropriation of Aristotle and Aquinas.

virtues."[60] He does not wish to accomplish this by the reductionistic means of universal principles or theories. Instead, it is through the influence and expectations of the community itself that such things are accomplished. It is through training that virtue is accomplished. Hauerwas notes how this is contrary to the work of Kant.

> [Kant's] general project of finding a foundation for morality has gone hand in hand with an aversion to the particular and the contingent. Why has ethics the sudden need for a "foundation" and in particular a foundation that is characterized by universality and necessity, when it seems that such a demand distorts the very nature of moral judgment? As Aristotle reminds us, ethics by its nature deals with matters which can be other—that is, particular matters. Confronted by the fragmented character of our world, philosophers have undoubtedly tried to secure a high ground that can provide for security, certainty, and peace. It is a worthy effort, but one doomed to fail, for such ground lacks the ability to train our desires and direct our attention; to make us into moral people.[61]

In Hauerwas's reading, Aristotle believed that the community's purpose was to make the community better. Humans are formed by the community in which they live. "Aristotle rightly argued that descriptions of our activities are correlative to the kind of person we are. It is not enough that we do the right thing rightly, but we must do it for the right reason, with the right feeling, and at the right time."[62] In order to be a moral person, one must therefore be a part of a moral community. "Aristotle argued that the primary purpose of the *polis* is the creation of people who are better than they would be without the aid of the *polis*."[63] Further, the community must foster morality in its people by teaching them to be moral. One cannot teach oneself. It is through instruction, and that primarily in the practices of virtue, that one is made moral. It is by doing virtuous things that one becomes virtuous.

60. Hauerwas and Pinches, *Christians among the Virtues*,19.

61. Hauerwas, *Peaceable Kingdom*, 11. Hauerwas is here thinking specifically of Aristotle, *Nicomachean Ethics*, 1094b15–27.

62. Hauerwas and Willimon, *Resident Aliens*, 11–12.

63. Ibid., 32. It was through consideration of Aristotle's "understanding of *phronesis*, the kind of politics necessary to sustain an ethic of virtue, and the corresponding historicist perspective required by each that led me to appreciate [John Howard] Yoder's significance" (Hauerwas, *Dispatches from the Front*, 22).

The idea of character, therefore, involves the complex question of the relation between our "reasons" and the "corresponding action." Aristotle was fond of saying that "virtues develop from corresponding activities," which implies that it is possible to establish a rather direct relationship between the virtue and a certain set of actions that have a publicly agreed on description (*Nicomachean Ethics*, 1103a21).[64]

Of course, this does not mean that simple repetition can make a person virtuous. Simple obedience to the "laws" does not necessarily make a person moral, since these activities do not by necessity reflect a virtuous character. Aristotle does not wish to allow someone's activities, however right they may be, be called virtuous if they are not done from a virtuous character. As Aristotle makes clear, "People may perform just acts without being just men."[65] Hauerwas clearly understands that Aristotle believed virtuous acts must also come from a virtuous character.

Aristotle maintained that one could not become virtuous simply by copying the actions of a virtuous person, but rather one could only become virtuous by acting in the manner that a virtuous person acts. Crucial for Aristotle was that what we do must come from a firm and unchangeable character. That is, virtuous persons are those who would not choose to do other than what they have or have not done, since what they have or have not done is consistent with who they are. Their actions, so to speak, are not what they do, but confirm what they are. Thus, virtuous persons do not feel what they do to be onerous, though in fact it may involve hardship and may even be life threatening, because what they do is commensurate with what they are. They could not nor would they want to choose to be or do other.[66]

This means that the virtues are difficult to transfer from one generation to the next since they cannot be simply "written down" or told to

64. Hauerwas, *Vision and Virtue*, 59. Hauerwas is quoting from Aristotle's *Nicomachean Ethics*.

65. Aristotle *Nicomachean Ethics* 1144a13.

66. Hauerwas, *Christian Existence Today*, 192–93. Notice the implicit definition of self emerging in Hauerwas from Aristotle. Self is defined in the actions of a person, which expose the character. Character is not necessarily prior to those actions but is in a reciprocal relationship to them. Thus it seems plausible to define self as communal and, as such, as at least reciprocal with, or perhaps even more primary than, the individual self, since action requires communal participation.

the next generation, though certainly such things may help. Instead, Aristotle believed that the virtues must be impressed upon a person by another person who had mastered them. This was particularly the case in Aristotle's situation, since his concern was primarily with the politics of the *polis*. Political judgment could not be subject to a simple set of rules or principles, being typically rather historically contingent to a specific time, place, and situation. Therefore, politics must be entrusted to men (Aristotle was not inclined to think of women in political terms) who had developed the character to make virtuous decisions. Such development came with time and with extensive apprenticeship at the feet of a master in virtue. Simply providing a list of the virtues for someone to read or to attempt to enact was useless. This must be the case in politics, since "politics, like ethics, involves judgment about contingent matters and thus requires people of wisdom which comes only by being well formed through the virtues."[67] This means for Aristotle that ethics, and politics, is more a craft than a set of statutes to be obeyed, much in the same manner that medicine is a craft. As Hauerwas notes,

> Aristotle was fond of using the example of the experienced physician to elicit the sense of wisdom he thought necessary for knowing how to live well. Aristotle suggested that physicians often know the right thing to do even though they do not know—at least "know" in the sense of being able to give a general principle—why they do what they do. That is why the professions can never be learned abstractly but require apprenticeship, for only by being initiated by a master do we gain some idea of the kind of people we need to be to be capable of judgments.[68]

What is obvious to Hauerwas, given this reading of Aristotle, is how distinct Aristotle is from Plato and Kant. Both Plato and Kant attempt to provide a grounding for morality in something separate from action, making habits a mere outgrowth of a rightly ordered mind. Commenting upon the work of Lawrence Kohlberg, Hauerwas believes that Kohlberg rightly understands the difference between Aristotle on the one hand and Plato and Kant on the other.

67. Ibid., 193.

68. Ibid., 141. This is not to say that Aristotle devalued the place of schooling. He certainly believed that novices needed to be trained, and training needed to begin somewhere, particularly with the wisdom of those who had gone before.

Kohlberg rightly seems to see that there is a deep connection between Plato and Kant, as each in quite different ways tries to provide a "foundation" for "morality" that makes the acquisition of "habits" secondary. Aristotle's insistence that "morality" must begin with habits simply assumes that there is no "foundation" for "morality" abstracted from historic communities.[69]

But that leaves us, as moderns, with the question: where are we today? How are we being taught to be moral? Hauerwas illustrates that the peasants of premodern days, and perhaps today, likely had some of the best training for being Christian. "Peasants are often suspicious of intellectuals because they rightly worry about 'ideas' that come from people who do not work with their hands."[70] It is in the doing that we are and become Christian.

Since there is no such thing as traditionlessness (the fallacy of Kant's supposed neutrality), we are a part of a tradition. In our modern context, particularly in America, the language of "individual rights" is what shapes our morality. Each individual self is accorded the right to choose his or her own moral destiny by exercising the basic right of freedom. Even Christians are taught that the freedom of the individual is a basic moral presupposition that must be accounted in every moral strategy.

69. Hauerwas, *Community of Character*, 273 n. 20. Hauerwas is here citing Kohlberg, "Education for Justice," 59. Aristotle was gravely concerned, as was Kant and Kohlberg, that the right thing be done for the right reason. But as Hauerwas sees it, "Where [Aristotle] differs from Kant is in his characterization of the kind of reason that forms our agency so we are capable, not just of acting, but of becoming moral through our activity. A formal principle of rationality could not be sufficient, as the self must be formed to desire and act as a man of virtue desires and acts. Even though . . . Aristotle distinguishes between the intellectual and moral virtues, the latter are only formed rightly when they are the result of practical wisdom" (Hauerwas, *Community of Character*, 138).

Note also the use of "historic communities" as a sort of foundation or grounding for moral training. Hauerwas has not left foundationalism totally behind; he has abandoned only foundationalism's modern commitment to rational principles as primary, from which moral virtue can then be derived.

Hauerwas seems to believe that such a grounding of practice or historical rootedness existed, in varying forms perhaps, from Aristotle through Aquinas and still exists in places today. I would qualify this as a type of practical foundation for moral training, which is distinct in form yet similar in function to modern foundationalism's use of rational principles.

70. Hauerwas, "Sanctified Body," 21.

Most contemporary Christians cannot say enough good about rights. The way to ensure the "freedom of the individual" as well as to create a limited state is to protect the "rights of the individual." It has thus become our unquestioned assumption that every human person has the "right" to develop his or her own potential to the greatest possible extent, limited only to the parallel rights of others.[71]

Hauerwas learned from Barth, among others, that such individualism is not correlative to the salvation found in the church. Indeed, for Barth, it seems impossible for a Christian to conceive of a definition of the self that is prior to the community of church.

[The Christian] is not in [the church] merely in the sense that he might first be a more or less good Christian by his personal choice and calling and on his own responsibility as a lonely hearer of God's Word, and only later perhaps optionally and only at his own pleasure, he might take into account his membership in the church. If he were not in the church, he would not be in Christ. He is elected and called, not to the being and action of a private person with a Christian interest, but to be a living member of the living community of the living Lord Jesus.[72]

Hauerwas wishes to overcome Schleiermacher's synopsis of the difference between Protestant and Catholic views of the relationship between the individual and the church—a synopsis based in Protestantism's commitment to the liberal self as primary. Schleiermacher surmised that Protestantism "makes the individual's relation to the church dependent on his relation to Christ" whereas Catholicism "makes the individual's relation to Christ dependent on his relation to the church."[73] Hauerwas would certainly affirm Mangina's conclusion regarding the mediation of the gospel through the church, "If the church mediates [the gospel], then in some sense it forms a unity with Christ that stands prior to the individual's *credo*."[74]

Of course, what we believe to be freedom may not be freedom at all. The "removal of all constraints," as freedom has been defined at least since the Enlightenment, may in fact be simply another means to mas-

71. Hauerwas and Willimon, *Resident Aliens*, 33.
72. Barth, *Christian Life*, 188.
73. Schleiermacher, *Christian Faith*, 103.
74. Mangina, "Bearing the Marks of Jesus," 293.

querade the influence of certain powers. In the language of Scripture (i.e., the book of Judges), a society founded on individual rights easily becomes a society in which "everyone does what is right in their own eyes." Kant attempted to place boundaries on the human propensity toward selfishness by taking into consideration the rights of others, but this is hardly a boundary when others are not present to advocate their own welfare.[75] "Our society, in brief, is built on the presumption that the good society is that in which each person gets to be his or her own tyrant (Bernard Shaw's definition of hell: Hell is where you must do what you want to do)."[76] Freedom of the individual turns out to be but another form of slavery.

Aristotle's conception of the relationship of morality to the individual was something quite different. He did not have room for the no-

75. Hauerwas believes that humans, if left to their own recourse, will seek their own interests ahead of others. Though Hauerwas is by no means attracted to rights language, it is an assumption of this nature (i.e., that people will not "naturally" seek the good of another, thus requiring in democratic societies a check-and-balance system based in either character formation or rights language) that makes me suspect that Hauerwas, like Kant or Niebuhr, still has an anthropology of sin lurking in his politics. The presumption of human goodness for more than temporary necessity is not an option within Hauerwas's conception of modernity. Therefore, he rightly assumes a position of total (pervasive) depravity, aligning himself well within the tradition of Christian belief.

Hauerwas seems to be acting here on the presumption of a predisposition within humanity toward idolatry. He cannot engage such a tendency in universalistic (i.e., doctrinal) language. Nevertheless, Hauerwas seems to presuppose a human tendency toward this type of sin. I suspect that he would wish to argue that such an idolatry is a learned thing, making it a product of western democracy's ideology. But to make such a case may take Hauerwas into places he would rather avoid, since "learning" idolatry sounds somewhat akin to Locke's notion of a *tabula rasa*. Though it is obvious that Hauerwas could not advocate such a thing, the question of why Christlikeness is impossible without training in some Thomistic/Aristotelian sense still remains. Why doesn't righteousness just happen "naturally"? Hauerwas is certainly in good company within the church tradition to answer, because humans are sinful and predisposed to sinfulness from birth. But such an answer may sound too much like Niebuhr's anthropology of sin for Hauerwas to claim. Of course to say nothing at all leaves Hauerwas without much of a theological tradition on which to attach his own theological discussion. Hauerwas is willing to admit that he holds to a universal understanding of human sinfulness, but only as it can be christologically construed as embedded in the context of the story of Jesus's death and resurrection. He does not elaborate extensively on the distinction between his own view of sin as a doctrine applying to all humanity and Niebuhr's anthropology of sin. See Hauerwas, *Better Hope*, 192–99.

76. Hauerwas and Willimon, *Resident Aliens*, 33.

tion of an individual choosing where to begin and what moral options they might like to do or not do. Instead, his was a morality of training, even of discipleship.

> Aristotle taught that the moral life is life lived on the basis of example. A person becomes just by imitating just persons. One way of teaching good habits is by watching good people, learning the moves, imitating the way they relate to the world. For Aristotle, apprenticeship was essential to the task of morality— an ethically inexperienced person looking over the shoulder of someone who was good at it. Aristotelian ethics were thus "elitist" and not democratic, in the sense that such ethics presuppose people who are better at morality than other people.[77]

Hauerwas translates the Aristotelian model of moral training quite easily into the Christian language of discipleship.

> If Christian ethics were only a matter of doing what anyone knows to be right or wrong on the basis of reason qua reason, then such imitation and observation would not be so necessary. . . . Christian ethics arise out of the formation of the peculiar community engendered by listening to scripture like the Sermon on the Mount and attaching ourselves to a master like Jesus.[78]

Aristotle provides Hauerwas with the resources to address his own concern that our morality be rooted in the historicity and reality of a historical person (i.e., of Jesus). But this doesn't mean we can simply give Aristotle's virtues Christian names, translating them into the Christian tradition without reservation. What is needed is "a different understanding of the virtues (and different virtues as well) than that

---

77. Ibid., 98–99. Hauerwas's choice of words is interesting at this point. The word *elitist* typically rubs us wrong precisely because it does not accord with our sense of fairness. However, fairness is what Hauerwas is arguing so vehemently against. We do not all share equally in morality, as if we all exercised the same capacity to be moral on any occasion. Such equality in moral capacity (i.e., fairness) is but the product of an Enlightenment ethic of individual choice, premised as it is on simply the evaluation of options and information available to all rational creatures. Instead, we must be trained to be moral by someone who is capable of greater morality than we are. Hauerwas's rhetoric is meant to challenge our own liberal sentimentalities.

78. Ibid., 99. Again, Hauerwas appeals to Scripture, but only "methodologically." He does not engage us in the reading of Scripture, instead relying on the presumption that we will get that elsewhere, or that at least we will know what he is talking about.

offered by Aristotle."[79] Obvious for Hauerwas is that this need for something different from Aristotle does not mean that Aristotle is rendered
unusable. Indeed, Hauerwas, like Aquinas, finds the work of Aristotle
very attractive. But one must proceed with caution when approaching
a foreign or "pagan" context. Hauerwas cannot simply adopt Aristotle
without some critical interaction. Nonetheless, Hauerwas finds "Aristotle
more of a help than a hindrance."[80]

Of course, Hauerwas's appropriation is hardly something new.
In fact, it has already largely been accomplished by Thomas Aquinas,
which has allowed for its practice in certain communities for several
centuries. As mentioned above, Hauerwas believes Aquinas's development of the virtues has not been matched in theology since. Therefore,
the best Hauerwas can do is point us to the master, that is, master
Thomas. Hauerwas also makes it clear that Aquinas's work was not a
simple adoption of Aristotle, but rather a reworking that resulted in a
thoroughly Christian masterpiece. In a remark critical of MacIntyre's
work, Hauerwas states

> We [Hauerwas and Pinches] cannot, then, begin with Aristotle's
> virtues and fill in the gaps with Christianity, nor can we, as
> Christians, defend virtue first and Christianity later, the strategy
> we find prevalent in MacIntyre. . . . We are convinced that the in-
> sights about virtue offered by Aristotle and other ancient Greeks
> are indispensable in any true and subtle treatment of Socrates'
> fundamental question regarding how one should live. Yet as
> we believe the great Christian thinkers such as Saint Paul and
> Saint Thomas meant to teach us, Greek accounts of the virtues
> are there to be *used* by Christians, not *built upon*. These name
> two quite different things. To use requires that one apply a thing
> within a framework significantly other than the one in which
> it originally appeared, which is precisely what Christianity re-
> quires insofar as it refounds human life on the life, death, and
> resurrection of Jesus Christ, God made flesh.[81]

79. Hauerwas and Pinches, *Christians among the Virtues*, x.

80. Ibid., 27. Hauerwas and Pinches go on to actually attempt such an appropriation later in the book. The point here is simply that it cannot happen uncritically, since
Aristotle was hardly concerned about a man called Jesus.

81. Ibid., 68. For further critical interaction with MacIntyre's use of Aquinas, see
190–91, n. 11. Though MacIntyre's effort may seem here at odds with Hauerwas's own
intentions with regard to Aristotle and Aquinas, Hauerwas acknowledges a great indebtedness to MacIntyre for helping him see why Aristotle's conception of virtue even

Aquinas, for Hauerwas, is the pinnacle of moral teaching. He combined the thought of many significant moral teachers, while still maintaining a thoroughly Christian context. Aristotle was especially predominant for Thomas, which helps make Thomas's thought all the more attractive to Hauerwas.

> Aquinas in many ways is the high point for reflection on virtue, as his compilation combines the influence of Plato, Aristotle, the Stoics, and Augustine in an extraordinarily complex manner. Though his account of the nature of the virtues as habits and how we acquire them is primarily dependent on Aristotle, he attempted to correlate the individual cardinal virtues with functions of the soul.[82]

A primary aspect in which the thought of Aquinas and Aristotle is complementary to that of Hauerwas is in their presumption of the community as a prerequisite to moral (and spiritual, for Aquinas and Hauerwas) transformation. Hauerwas believes that Aquinas's and Aristotle's analysis of how the virtues are acquired and form the self presupposed as well as required a narrative.[83] The obvious difference between Aristotle and Aquinas is found in the manner in which Aquinas simply assumed the formative narrative would be the church. Aristotle's community was the polis. With regard to modernity, Hauerwas laments the fact that Christianity's primary narrative is no longer the church; it is now the world, and in America, it is an ideology of the democratic society committed to preserving the individual self. Such a context means that knowledge of God is no longer regarded as real knowledge without some type of rational justification. Aquinas is further useful

matters for a Christian understanding of what it means to be moral. E.g., see Hauerwas, *With the Grain of the Universe*, 18–26. As a more personal note, I recall being told by Hauerwas to reread MacIntyre's *After Virtue* as a prelude to his seminar in theological ethics. Though Hauerwas is doing some rather unique things ecclesiologically, the way was being paved for him by MacIntyre's appropriation of Aristotle and Aquinas's ethics in philosophy. The formative nature of a narrative community in Aristotle and Aquinas was by no means original with Hauerwas, nor does he claim that it is.

82. Hauerwas, *Community of Character*, 122–23.

83. Hauerwas argues that though Aquinas and Aristotle did not have an explicit affinity for narrative, it seemed to underlie their understanding of virtue and self. Hauerwas is, somewhat anachronistically, dissatisfied that neither make the step to give explicit reference to the necessity of a historical community in order to accomplish an understanding of the virtues. Nevertheless, he believes it remains implied in their thought. See Hauerwas, *Community of Character*, 135–52.

for Hauerwas in that Aquinas was never tempted to succumb to such a narrative. Aquinas presumed that knowledge of God—particularly revealed knowledge—was real knowledge, and all other knowledge was to be judged by it.

> Aquinas's characterization of the knowledge that is proper to theology—that is, knowledge that "comes through revelation"— seems to name for many today a knowledge that is incapable of rational defense. Yet Aquinas assumes the opposite. For Aquinas, knowledge attained by "natural reason" is not more certain than that attained by revelation; "natural" and "revelational" do not name epistemological alternatives. Thus, those who attempt in the name of Aquinas to develop a "natural theology"—that is, a philosophical defense of "theism" as a propaedeutic for any further "confessional" claims one might want to make—are engaged in an enterprise that Aquinas would not recognize.[84]

Hauerwas finds himself in good company by appealing to Aquinas as an authoritative point in the tradition where knowledge of God is not subject to suspicion *prima facie*. Instead, revealed knowledge "provides more certain and complete knowledge" than knowledge discovered through reason.[85] This does not mean that knowledge through reason, even knowledge about God, is impossible or untrue.[86] It simply means that "*sacra doctrina* could and must stand in judgment on the other sciences."[87] But what, then, becomes of moral knowledge, i.e., virtue? Is revealed knowledge a knowledge separable from, and perhaps prior to, the narrative of the church in forming the virtues in the self?

The apparent circularity in Aristotle and Aquinas with regard to how one acquires virtue (i.e., that one must already be morally virtuous to some degree before he or she can act in a manner that contributes to moral growth) may leave one with the impression that virtue cannot even be identified, leaving aside the possibility of acquiring it. Hauerwas's solution to this problem, and perhaps the solution implicit in both Aristotle and Aquinas, is to argue that all virtuous activity is

---

84. Hauerwas, *With the Grain of the Universe*, 25.

85. Smith, "Thomas Aquinas's *De Deo*," 135. Cited by Hauerwas, *With the Grain of the Universe*, 30, n. 36.

86. Thomas Aquinas, *Summa Theologiae*, I.I.

87. Hauerwas, *With the Grain of the Universe*, 24. Cf. Aquinas, *Summa Theologiae*, I.I.6.2.

grounded and displayed in a formative narrative. Christians become part of the church and find themselves immersed already in the process of formation (i.e., discipleship).

> Aristotle and Aquinas are right to think that moral growth is dependent on the development of character sufficient to claim one's behavior as one's own. But they were incorrect to assume that the development of such a self is but the reflection of the prior unity of the virtues. What is required for our moral behavior to contribute to a coherent sense of the self is neither a single moral principle nor a harmony of the virtues but, as I have already said, the formation of character by a narrative that provides a sufficiently truthful account of our existence. If I can show this to be the case, then at least I will have found a way to make intelligible the Christian claim that understanding the story of God as found in Israel and Jesus is the necessary basis for any moral development that is Christianly significant.[88]

The turn to narrative gives Hauerwas the warrant to develop a tradition-formed accounting of the virtues, as well as a narrative accounting of moral knowledge. Since "For the Greeks, as well as the Christians, virtue was the central concept for moral reflection,"[89] then such an accounting must be developed within the parameters of an appropriate context. In fact, the virtues must be understood as context, or tradition, laden. Just as theories of action falter when they "isolate and abstract 'action' from the narrative contexts that make an action intelligible,"[90] so also any account of virtue in a theoretical sense suffers from an inability to display its claims. This is particularly the case in Christianity, since

> The sign and substance of this infusion of Christian virtues is always participation in the body of Christ. This involves our reception of the sacraments of baptism and Eucharist, but also includes (and entails) immersion in the daily practices of the Christian church: prayer, worship, admonition, feeding the hungry, caring for the sick, etc. By these we are transformed over time to participate in God's life.[91]

88. Hauerwas, *Community of Character*, 136.

89. Ibid., 111.

90. Ibid., 262 n. 11.

91. Hauerwas and Pinches, *Christians among the Virtues*, 69. Cf. Hauerwas, *Prayers Plainly Spoken*, 126–27. Though developed in no significant sense by Hauerwas, the notion of participation in God is important for his theology. For the narrative to be

Being incorporated into a narrative (though incorporate may not be the best word since it presupposes a self-defined *a priori* to the community) is the manner in which Christians are made capable of identifying their "selves" as children of God. It is also through this narrative that Christians are capable of making the story of Christ their own story. For as Christians begin to see themselves as part of an ongoing narrative, of which they are a part, they can begin to take ownership of their identity as Christians. As Hauerwas explains,

> I am suggesting that descriptively the self is best understood as a narrative, and normatively we require a narrative that will provide the skills appropriate to the conflicting loyalties and roles we necessarily confront in our existence. The unity of the self is therefore more like the unity that is exhibited in a good novel— namely with many subplots and characters that we at times do not closely relate to the primary dramatic action of the novel. But ironically without such subplots we cannot achieve the kind of unity necessary to claim our actions as our own.
>
> Yet a narrative that provides the skill to let us claim our actions as our own is not the sort that I can simply "make mine" through a decision. Substantive narratives that promise me a way to make my self my own require me to grow into the narrative by constantly challenging my past achievements. That is what I mean by saying that the narrative must provide skills of discernment and distancing. For it is certainly a skill to be able to describe my behavior appropriately and to know how to "step back" from myself so that I might better understand what I am doing. The ability to step back cannot come by trying to discover a moral perspective abstracted from all my endeavors, but rather comes through having a narrative that gives me critical purchase on my own projects.[92]

---

rightly aimed, it must be directed toward a Christian existence that is somehow "caught up" into the divine. It cannot be left as merely a human community. Hauerwas provides little more than rhetoric in this regard. He leaves readers with no theological or biblical means with which to support a justification for participation in the divine by the human community called church. His attempt through the sacraments is a useful start but relies heavily on the mystical, in the negative sense of mysticism. As will be seen in the chapters below, an ecclesiology formed and filled by a thoroughgoing doctrine of the Holy Spirit can do in theological terms what Hauerwas is unable to do in more purely anthropological narrative terms.

92. Hauerwas, *Community of Character*, 144–45. It should be acknowledged that Hauerwas may wish to disown some of the "self" and "step-back" language he uses in this quotation, since it is from his early thought. Nevertheless, it is apparent his

But much of this language sounds terribly individualistic, so much so that one wonders whether the narrative is only about "me" and excludes others from participation in it. In other words, doesn't asking the question about formation of the self require an *a priori* conception of self as prior to the formation in a way that destroys narrative? If left at the level of self and community, such may be the case. Hauerwas answers this problem by understanding the narrative in the context of the name *Christian*, and all its incumbent implications. As will be displayed in the next chapter, only in the context of the church can Christians claim their actions as their own and as significantly a part of the ongoing narrative that is God's story.[93]

Conclusion

To demonstrate the veracity of his critical engagement with modernity, Hauerwas has employed the substantive resources of three historically contingent moral epistemologies. He bolstered his critique of liberalism discussed in the last chapters by displaying the church/world antithesis so crucial to Barth's theology. This made the commitment by the church to certain ideologies or tendencies of the world clearly destructive of the church's identity and mission as church. However, the real purchase of Hauerwas's turning to Barth was to display the necessity of an ecclesiology grounded in its existence qua ecclesiology. Barth could supply Hauerwas with the theoretical, and even some biblical, support for such a move. However, Barth was finally unable to affirm an ecclesiology that is historically grounded in a community in history. For this, Hauerwas must turn elsewhere.

Aquinas's adoption and transformation of Aristotle's ethics provided Hauerwas with a theory of historical grounding necessary to affirm a community in history. Aristotle's, and Aquinas's, moral epistemology

emphasis on narrative as the most appropriate manner in which to understand a Christian's participation in the church, and ultimately in the life of God, has never waned. Likewise, I believe Hauerwas would still affirm that narrative is prior to voluntarism in the definition of self. Unfortunately, Hauerwas does not develop sufficiently here the further priority of the narrative before the individual, i.e., a corporate definition of the self.

93. Hauerwas intimates our final goal as becoming part of God's story in his discussion of relating our "past" to our "present." This appears to be the same manner in which we finally make the history of the man Jesus our own. See Hauerwas, *Community of Character*, 147.

required the existence of such communities in that narrative was the necessary context for moral formation. Discipleship required that a master apprentice students through the process of learning morality. Learning, in such a context, was not mere observation and abstraction into principles. Instead, learning was the imitation of virtue by seeing and attempting to duplicate action, attitude, intention, and motivation. This creates an obvious contradiction with the modern mindset of the individual as primary and of individual rights as the context for moral formation. Hauerwas's response to this contradiction is to persuade the church to remain the church. His argument for the church as the only context in which a Christian can or should affirm any claims regarding reality has been asserted as a foundation, of sorts, for his theological/moral epistemology. What remains to be seen is how and if Hauerwas has the theological support for such an argument, specifically for the connection between an understanding of the Trinitarian God and the human community of the church. For this we must turn to the particulars of how Hauerwas understands the church to be church.

To this point, Hauerwas's critical interaction with liberalism and his narrative alternative seem both consistent and convincing. He has made a strong case for presupposing revelational knowledge as real knowledge in the face of rationalism's claims to the contrary. Unfortunately, Hauerwas does not give a clear indication of where this revelational knowledge is located. Perhaps he, like Barth, would see it as broadly encompassing Scripture and creation, culminating in the incarnation. However, since he does not (he would say he cannot) spell this out in any detail, he is finally left with a fairly abstract notion of revelational knowledge with regard to its content, source, and locus.

Hauerwas persuasively demonstrates that narrative is at once both more historical and more epistemologically useful for theology than is a foundational system. Narrative expands epistemology so that it includes ethics in its determination of knowledge. The determination of truth in epistemology then becomes more than simply a matter of evaluating the correspondence of statements with objects or with rational demonstration. Truth is now intertwined with the truthfulness of the person making truth claims. In other words, as Aristotle would have it, truth is bound up with character. This fits well with the church's claim that truth is bound to the person of Jesus. To know truth, one must know him and participate in his life. This happens as one is apprenticed in the Christian life, that is, as one is made part of the church. The narrative epistemology derived from Aristotle, Aquinas, and finally Barth seems most appropriate for a church committed to demonstrating the witness of the lordship of Jesus before a watching world. Hauerwas's aim (to give the church back its voice in proclaiming the gospel message by being church) demonstrates that he aspires to more than mere consistency or coherence with his critical project. Indeed, Hauerwas' work breathes new life into the church when liberalism appears to have domesticated it. The following chapter will attempt to demonstrate that Hauerwas, while having a remarkably dynamic ecclesiology, does not develop sufficiently how his narrative can escape the criticism of being a mere anthropology. This critique will then be answered in the following chapters by attempting to provide Hauerwas with a biblical pneumatology as robust as his narrative ecclesiology.

5

Practice Makes Perfect

The Church and Its Connection to the Divine

Introduction

THROUGHOUT OUR DESCRIPTION THUS FAR, WE HAVE SEEN HAUERWAS aiming at providing an ecclesiological epistemology—that is, a narrative epistemology specifically for the church—though he would obviously be reluctant to use such language. In other words, Hauerwas wants Christians to affirm their real existence as Christians and to find verification of their status as Christians without appeal to any external criteria. Further, Hauerwas wishes for the church to affirm Christian history as the only reality. This is the realism and epistemology he has hinted at in developing a metaphysic embedded in witness rather than premised on explanation.[1] Though such a metaphysic is not, for Hauerwas, prior to theology, it certainly must clearly be displayed in theology.

Hauerwas attempts such a display by providing a "thicker" definition of the church than is typical. This is seen in two respects in Hauerwas's work. The first is his substantive work in ethics.[2] Here he provides numerous accounts of lives that have been shaped into a witness of Jesus and that are also capable of shaping us into the life of Jesus. The many stories of real lives who have suffered, triumphed, or simply (but not merely) continued is likely the truest form of witness that Hauerwas could provide. The second form of this display is his occasional comment on how the witness of these lives can and should

1. Hauerwas, *Wilderness Wanderings*, 168 n. 8.

2. E.g., see Hauerwas, *Suffering Presence*; *Dispatches from the Front*; and *God, Medicine, and Suffering*.

affect the lives of others. Hauerwas does provide some doctrinal and even theoretical development of the ways the church is to be church. Without delving into theoretical construction destructive of his narrative "methodology," Hauerwas gives careful consideration to what it means for sinners to be transformed into worshipers, and what it takes to accomplish such a transformation. Here he must not only spell out a more complete ecclesiology in human community but also must affirm the reality of the foundation for such a community: the Triune God.

In this chapter, we will be dealing more directly with Hauerwas's argument rather than discussing the sources of his position. The first three sections will provide a more detailed examination of Hauerwas's ecclesiology. Here we will see that Hauerwas rightly believes the church is its own epistemology, and as its own epistemology such as it works to form its people according to the practices of the faith. This narrative formation connects the church with its past in a way that makes faithfulness to the tradition the mark of truthfulness for the church. Theology, instead of being the knowledge that could be evaluated according to its correspondence to an object or according to its coherence with other knowledges (i.e., with systematics) serves as a guide to reflection on the practices. Further, theology may be seen as one of the practices that the church enacts in its process of training. This move makes Hauerwas's ecclesiology foundational for the formative community of believers. At the same time, it makes the church sufficiently historical to provide for a real narrative connection to its head, Jesus. This is hardly sectarianism, since the church will live its message as witness to the world that the church's object (i.e., God) is the only reality. In other words, the church claims universality in its claim to worship the God of the universe.

While Hauerwas's ecclesiological developments seem rightly placed, one point of internal inconsistency seems glaring. The church's connection to the Triune God is accomplished by Hauerwas through the sacraments and grace. Though certainly these points of connection may bear considerable merit, in my judgment, they are finally seen as insufficient for creating the kind of community that Hauerwas envisions as formative. The robust ecclesiology that Hauerwas rightly believes necessary must be placed in the context of an equally robust pneumatology. Hauerwas seems to hint that this is the case. However, as will be illustrated by the relative paucity of references to the Holy Spirit in Hauerwas, he never takes up the discussion. Such a lack of discussion about the Holy Spirit leaves Hauerwas in the perilous position of maintaining an ecclesiology that is primarily a sociological reality. In other words, Hauerwas's ecclesiology is finally in danger of being reduced to a mere study of the human qua human (i.e., anthropology).

The Church on Earth: Fleshing Out the Church as a Formative Community

Hauerwas believes that the purpose of the church is to be the church and to help the world know that it is the world. The questions that this statement elicits include the following: what, then, is the church? How will we know it when we see it? Or as it is also sometimes asked, where is the church? Hauerwas's response to these questions is, as expected, elusive— from the standpoint that it does not provide "rational" definitions. He has no explicit "doctrine" of the universal church on which to hang various qualifications.[3] Instead, he begins (though for Hauerwas there is no such beginning point for defining church) by pointing to the reality of the church, both as it is and as it should be. In this, his understanding of everything as somehow entrenched in a tradition is crucial.

> There is simply no place to start thinking prior to being engaged in a tradition. As Yoder says: "What must replace the prolegomenal search for 'scratch' is the confession of rootedness in historical community. Then one directs one's critical acuity toward making clear the distance between that community's charter or covenant and its present faithfulness."[4]

3. On this point, see Weston, "Invisible Church," 95–105.

4. Hauerwas, *Dispatches from the Front*, 22. Hauerwas is here quoting Yoder, *Priestly Kingdom*, 7. It is interesting to note Yoder's reliance on a church's charter or covenant, presumably a statement of faith in which the goals or purposes of a church are reflected and delineated in some fashion to define what faithfulness looks like, e.g., a catechism. The link between a tradition and such a statement seems to contradict the primacy that Hauerwas, and Yoder, give to a living tradition. The correspondence between the tradition and the charter or covenant raises the question of which comes first. Yoder indicates that the charter and faithfulness to it come after confession and rootedness. Nevertheless, they serve as a corrective to rootedness in a way that seems at least as authoritative as the community itself.

Perhaps Yoder envisioned a dialectical relationship between theology and the community, or between the external and the internal. He would certainly not be alone in proposing such a relationshi E.g., cf. Lash, *Theology on the Way to Emmaus*, 114–17. Hauerwas (*Better Hope*, 167–68) makes explicit reference to this possibility in refer-

This historical community is, of course, the church. But this is not an ethereal church that might appear as an ideal in some doctrines of the church within a more systematic approach to theology. Instead, the church is the real community of people who are rooted in historical reality, and who exist in the formative nature of the church's practices.

> The church, therefore, is not some ideal of community but a particular people who, like Israel, must find the way to sustain its existence generation after generation. Indeed, there are clear "marks" through which we know that the church is church. These marks do not guarantee the existence of the church, but are the means that God has given us to help us along the way. Thus the church is known where the sacraments are celebrated, the word is preached, and upright lives are encouraged and lived.[5]

These "marks" of the church are not meant to be some standard against which we measure the church to see if it corresponds to the ideal.[6] Rather, these marks are meant to indicate the shape that the practices of the church should take in order to mold its people into faithful worshipers of God. If the church is to resemble, at least in some practical fashion, the *polis* of Aristotle, in which masters train apprentices toward moral perfection through the practices of morality, then it must train its people in and through worship.

It is on this point of the marks of the church that must be maintained to remain faithful to tradition that Hauerwas appears to lapse

---

encing Rowan Greer's dialectic between the growth of knowledge and the growth of virtue.

5. Hauerwas, *Peaceable Kingdom*, 107. It should be noted that these "marks" appear rather abstract if left in this definitional form. One could even venture to regard these marks as a doctrine or theory of the church. In fact, I believe Hauerwas would hesitate to state this in quite such an abstract manner today, since he is not in the habit of giving "definitions." However, I do not see how he can escape employing such marks, even if implicitly or secondarily, in order to determine the historical accuracy of the tradition maintained by the church.

6. This is Todd Whitmore's ("Beyond Liberalism and Communitarianism in Christian Ethics," 215–19) critique of Hauerwas as Whitmore questions how Hauerwas can legitimately include those on the fringes in the community called Christian (i.e., those who follow a just-war tradition). Whitmore does not believe Hauerwas has room in the Christian community for just-war proponents precisely because they do not fit with his own conception of what it means to be truly Christian, or truly church. Such uncooperativeness leads Whitmore to believe that Hauerwas is reflecting an absolutism reminiscent of the Enlightenment.

back into the type of systematic analysis he has worked hard to avoid. Though he gives little indication as to how one measures the veracity of such marks within an existing community, it appears crucial that such marks be present in order to distinguish between what is truly church and what is merely a human community. Hauerwas would likely appeal to tradition here to substantiate the reality of an ongoing presence of the marks in specific communities throughout history, but such an appeal would simply underline the question as to where the tradition is found, or which communities' tradition is to be revered. It does not appear as though he can escape an appeal to something universal.[7] Perhaps, as will be seen later in this chapter, this is why he finally appeals to the doctrine of the Trinitarian God as the theological marker for which communities are to be considered church.

Hauerwas believes that to be a Christian is to be made a part of the narrative that we describe as "God's story." Indeed, it is to be made a part of the community that is God's community, even his body.

> To be a Christian is to be joined, to be put in connection with others so that our stories cannot be told without somehow also telling their stories. Through such telling and retellings we believe that God makes us part of God's story.[8]

Thus we are not only a narrative community, but the narrative that is the church is also made part of God's own narrative through Jesus. By being a part of the community that we call church, we become a part of his body, i.e., we are made Christian. And it is through the church and its continued practices that church continues as church. This is the only means through which the church can survive in the world: as it exists as church.

7. See Gustafson, "Response to Critics," 195–96; and Muray ("Confessional Postmodernism and the Process-Relational Vision," 86–88. Gustafson believes that Hauerwas must resort to a type of universalism to finally identify the church he is attempting to describe. Muray accuses Hauerwas of having an "essentialist" understanding of Christianity because Hauerwas purportedly believes "there is an unchanging core to the tradition" (86). In order to maintain the veracity of the church community from generation to generation, Hauerwas seems unable to escape the necessity of an implicit, at least, doctrine of the universal church. Hauerwas would rather ground these marks in the practices, but the question remains, why these practices and not others?

8. Hauerwas, *In Good Company*, xiii.

> [To challenge the political liberalism of the world] you will need a community of people who have the ability to transmit across generations the skills necessary for survival. That community we call church; it names a reality that is constitutive of, and not simply incidental to, being Christian. In short, that is why there is no salvation without the church.[9]

In a world that would like to render the church impotent by characterizing it as merely another idea in the marketplace of ideas, it takes solidification of the reality of the church to make it a distinct witness to the reality that is encompassing of all realities. The church's witness to the reality that Jesus is Lord is not something the world wishes to hear, but it is a reality that the Christian believes is true not only for Christians but also for the whole world. In other words, Christians tell the world that Jesus is Lord, regardless of the world's acceptance of such a fact. Of course, for Hauerwas, "telling" is not a fair characterization of the Christian witness. Practices are the skills that train Christians to be Christian in the world. But they are not simply a way to prepare Christians for the Christian life. Indeed, they are also the actualization of the Christian life. That is why Hauerwas

> [E]mphasize[s] the importance of practices, which may of course involve "doctrine" as well as "called membership," since practices provide the material specifications that help us resist the endemic character of modernity, bent as it is on turning faith into just another idea.[10]

To be a Christian is to be a member of a community of people who are called out of the world to witness the reality of Christ's kingdom through their very lives. Christianity is not simply another theory or idea. Ultimately, it is a way of life, or better, it is life. "Indeed, it was exactly the attempt to make Christianity 'true', without the necessity of witness, that produced the systems which made Christianity appear as 'thought.'"[11] The practices of the church teach us who we are and who we are to be. It is not a matter of choosing to engage in certain practices in order to become who we want to be. The practices are the church's

9. Hauerwas, *Wilderness Wanderings*, 31.

10. Hauerwas, *In Good Company*, 73.

11. Hauerwas, "Storytelling," 173.

means of embodying the life, death, and resurrection of Jesus Christ.[12] It
is only as we participate in the practices that we can know what it means
to be Christian. As we have seen, Hauerwas learned this from Aristotle's
conception of actuating the virtues in order to learn the virtues.

> For the things which we have to learn before we can do them
> we learn by doing; men become builders by building houses,
> and harpists by playing the harp. Similarly, we become just by
> the practice of just actions, self-controlled by exercising self-
> control, and courageous by performing acts of courage. . . . In a
> word, characteristics develop from corresponding activities. For
> that reason, we must see to it that our activities are of a certain
> kind, since any variations in them will be reflected in our char-
> acteristics. Hence it is no small matter whether one habit or an-
> other is inculcated in us from early childhood; on the contrary
> it makes a considerable difference, or, rather, all the difference.[13]

We finally see here that Aristotle's epistemology (and Hauerwas's,
for that matter) is the reverse of Kant's. Whereas Kant appears to emphasize thought as preceding action in moral epistemology,[14] Aristotle
seems to indicate that action precedes thought. While certainly a dialectic may be present in both Kant and Aristotle regarding the relationship
of thought and action, the preference by each is clear. Action as primary
in Aristotle opens the door for Hauerwas to make extensive use of a
preference for action in his call for Christians to be formed by the practices of the church, in order to "know" theological truth.

But even further than being the way Christians and the church as
"body of Christ" are formed, it is only as we exhibit our Christian commitment in the practices that we witness to the reality of Christ's Spirit
in the midst of the community called church, since "our practices, more
than our arguments, reveal and shape what is truly important to us."[15] It
is through the practices that the church makes the faithful be faithful.
It trains them to be a part of the church when the world tells them
they should be otherwise. That is why Hauerwas wants "to be part of a

---

12. Cf. the Apostle Paul's desire to participate in (and indeed to complete what was
left incomplete in) Christ's suffering in Col 1:24.

13. Aristotle Nicomachean Ethics 1103a30–1103b25.

14. Kant, Foundations of the Metaphysics of Morals, 23–25, 28–29, 57.

15. Hauerwas, with Berkman, "Trinitarian Theology of the Chief End of All Flesh,"
186.

community with the habits and practices that will make me do what I would otherwise not choose to do and then to learn to like what I have been forced to do."[16]

The church is, or at least it should be, unashamed about its intentions to transform people into imitators of Jesus. After all, teaching is one of the practices that helps form the faithful. Teaching is not the presentation of options from which the "student" chooses.[17] Rather teaching is about shaping apprentices (i.e., sinners) into worshipers of the God who made them: "Teaching is practice that cannot help but seek to change lives. The teaching goal of the church is to 'indoctrinate.'"[18]

An example of how practice is formative for Christian life and commitment can be found in Hauerwas's understanding of sin. Far from being a universal condition of humanity (à la Niebuhr), recognition of sin is rather a practice in which the church trains us. We could not know sin without the church. As Hauerwas states plainly,

> Sin is not a universal condition. Rather, it is the refusal of some to believe when confronted with the Gospel of Jesus Christ. The very assumption that we can know what sin is prior to knowledge of Christ is but a form of our sin, of our attempt to claim that we can comprehend the meaning of our existence.[19]

It is in the worship done by the church that we learn what sin is and what our response to sin should be as Christians. Through recitation of the creeds and confession of our sins, we are trained to name sin as it is, an affront to a holy God. Sin is, consequently, only knowable through the practices of confession, reconciliation, and forgiveness. Practices such as these are recognizable only in the context of "an account of the virtues and corresponding moral psychology."[20] They cannot be divorced

16. Hauerwas, *In Good Company*, 75.

17. It should be pointed out here that Hauerwas would not be opposed to choice as a means of deciding. What he is opposed to is the notion of choice as the point at which an individual without bias weighs objectively the many options presented him or her. Hauerwas, following Aristotle, would still believe we make choices, but these choices have become, for those who have been rightly trained, instinctive action based on habitual formation. In other words, we choose things based on how we have been trained. Our choices are the consequence, not the progenitor, of our formation.

18. Hauerwas, *Wilderness Wanderings*, 173. This is one reason why Hauerwas organizes his Christian Ethics course according to the Methodist order of worship.

19. Ibid., 44.

20. Hauerwas, *In Good Company*, 158–59.

from the historical contingencies of the church and its claim to a "high" definition of sin. Sin cannot simply be redefined in such terms as immoral behavior or social immaturity, as though it were something that every rational creature who is honest could identify if given enough information and the time to reflect upon it. Sin is a theological accomplishment that must be learned.

> Put differently, "sin" is not a natural category, that is another way of talking about a failure of "moral development" or immoral behavior, but rather a theological claim about the depth of the self's estrangement from God. That is why we are not just "found" to be sinners, but that we must be "made" to be sinners.[21]

Through the practices, Christians are trained to be Christian, and consequently, given the language to name sin. In the midst of the onslaught of alternative traditions offered by the world, it is important that Christians be appropriately trained to name the things of the world and the things which are rightly God's.

> To be Christian means that we must be embedded in practices so materially constitutive of our communities that we are not tempted to describe our lives in the language offered by the world, that is the language of choice. Only then will Christians be able to challenge an all too tolerant world that celebrates many gods as alternatives to the One God who alone is worthy of worship.[22]

As should be clear from this statement, one of the fundamental practices for Christians to learn is a new language. Notice here the connection that Hauerwas finally makes between Aristotelian practice and Wittgensteinian formation through language. Hauerwas was "convinced (and [he] thought [he] learned this from Wittgenstein) that we can only see what we have been trained to see through learning to say."[23] As was mentioned above in chapter 2, Hauerwas began to learn this as a young student under Paul Holmer. It was then that he was introduced to Wittgenstein and became convinced that this was the way in which one became "religious." As Hauerwas states, "Holmer was slowly changing my idea of what it meant to be religious. He did so by forcing us to

21. Hauerwas, *Community of Character*, 270–71 n. 9.
22. Hauerwas, *Wilderness Wanderings*, 116–17.
23. Ibid., 156.

read Wittgenstein. I was learning that to become 'religious is, in part, a matter of learning a new language.'"[24] Hauerwas was quite taken with Holmer's rendering of Wittgenstein, displaying, as he did, the primary importance of "being" the truth before possessing the truth. As Holmer puts it, "There can be no substitute for being the truth, no matter what the quantity of the truth we may possess."[25] This means that what someone says is not as important as who is saying it. Hauerwas's comments on Holmer's statement and its context are instructive.

> Of course, Holmer's statement does not mean that questions of truth do not matter; instead, it is a reminder that people, not sentences, make truthful claims. Our claims, moreover, are shaped by the way we have learned to speak, and our speech is constituted by concepts that are capacities. What it means to be a self is therefore more like the naming of a set of skills than it is a "what," which should not be surprising once we remember that the self is not so much a name as a relation.
>
> Big words like "God," "sin," and "salvation" are likewise best thought of as capacities, that is achievements. That means, as Holmer says in *Making Christian Sense*, "Most of us have hardly any concept of God at all." All this began to make me understand why Holmer kept inquiring whether I was praying enough. Indeed, it made me wonder whether I actually ought to go to church for, as he reminds us, "the use of religious language requires participation in the religious life and this involves exposure to the community of believers."[26]

Hauerwas was learning the fundamental importance of primary religious language. To put it in Wittgensteinian terms, he was coming to recognize that the church is "the primary set of language games not only in which Christians learn to speak, but in which our speech already is

---

24. Ibid., 145. Hauerwas is here quoting Holmer, *Theology and the Scientific Study of Religion*, 163.

25. Holmer, "Christianity and the Truth," 40.

26. Hauerwas, *Wilderness Wanderings*, 145–46. Hauerwas is here quoting Holmer, *Making Christian Sense*, 118; and *Theology and the Scientific Study of Religion*, 109. I believe that Hauerwas and Holmer are right on this point, as I have stressed for years, and perhaps I learned it from Hauerwas, that ethics begins at the level of naming. Cf. my *This Is My Father's World*, 141–42.

a practice with a significant difference."[27] Within this context, worship becomes the primary language of the Christian's reality.[28]

Enfleshment Becomes the Rationality of Witness

A primary aspect of Hauerwas's emphasis on worship is the way in which such formation of the community relates the church to the world. Hauerwas's emphasis on worship as the primary language of the church may seem rather exclusive. As was mentioned above, Hauerwas is often accused of being a "tribalist," or "sectarian."[29] From his discussion of worship as the primary language for the church, this charicterization may seem warranted. However, Hauerwas is not interested in speaking the language of the world in order to secure the church a place in world politics. As will be seen, the church is a politic in its own right, and this through the witness of worship.

> Just as suddenly as Christians have been gathered they are sent forth with God's blessing. I again return to the Troeltsch's and Niebuhr's typologies to suggest that sending out of the church means that the church can never be a "sect." For Christians it is never a question of whether to serve the world but how they are to be of service in the world. We can never forget that worship is the way God has given us to serve the world.[30]

27. Hauerwas, *Wilderness Wanderings*, 3.

28. One might wonder if Hauerwas's granting primacy to the language of worship is correct, given the church's traditional affirmation of Scripture as inspired. In other words, should not Scripture be considered the primary language of the church? Hauerwas would likely respond that the reading and preaching of Scripture is included in the language of worship, but that worship language should not be limited to Scripture. While I would agree with such an inclusive understanding of worship language, I am not convinced Scripture could be so easily dismissed. It would seem that Scripture has played a role similar to that of other forms of theological/worship language; however, it has always also been regarded as more formative and more authoritative than other forms of language. Creeds, though highly useful and perhaps even more declarative of the church's faith than Scripture, are rarely cited by theologians throughout history as an inspired authority. Hauerwas would seem to affirm this implicitly by granting primacy to the formative narrative of Jesus in the gospels over "orthodox Christologies" (See Hauerwas, *Peaceable Kingdom*, xxi.) However, he is reticent explicitly to allow Scripture a place above other practices in the church.

29. See chapter 1, n. 29 above.

30. Hauerwas, *In Good Company*, 162–63.

Thus, the church is neither a tool of the state nor an authority over the state (as in Constantinianism). Rather it is a witness to the state: "God does not only make possible the church as a community of memory: the church is God's memory for the world."[31] In the times in which Christians find themselves, the "in-between" times, this is a tension that cannot be resolved. Christians are not called to resolve the tension between church and state. Instead, such tension is left profoundly unresolved until Christ returns to confirm the lordship Christians practice in the presence of the state.[32] This does not mean that worship is a retreat to a cloistered existence as a "tribe." Rather, it is a call to share what we have discovered in worship with those who would come to realize the kingship of Christ over all the world, for that is truly what Christianity has taught since its inception. This is "good news" for all the people.

> Obviously, Christians think what we have learned from our worship about living well is true for anyone. That is why we have the obligation and joy of witnessing to what God has done for us. But the very notion of witness means we cannot presume that those to whom we witness already have learned what we have learned by the necessity of our being gathered.[33]

This may lead one to conclude that Hauerwas's scheme of Christian witness is intolerant of other traditions, even destructive of them. To a certain extent, Hauerwas recognizes this to be the case, but he sees no alternative. If Christians really believe the language they have been taught to affirm in worship, then they cannot escape the implications in the world. The affirmations of Christians in worship go well beyond mere internal concerns of the church, though certainly the internal life of the church is of primary importance. Christians make claims that are unmistakably political in nature.

> If the church's first task is to make the world the world, that is its fundamental social and political task. Such a claim is often resisted because it sounds so intolerant, which of course it is, but it is an intolerance based on charity that would have the world saved by knowing that it is the world. If the church does

31. Hauerwas, *Better Hope*, 151.
32. Hauerwas, with Baxter, "Kingship of Christ," 216.
33. Hauerwas, *In Good Company*, 158.

not worship rightly, how can the world know that it is the world exactly to the extent it does not willingly glorify God. As Yoder puts the matter in *Body Politics*, "stated very formally, the pattern we shall discover is that the will of God for human socialness as a whole is prefigured by the shape to which the body of Christ is called. Church and world are not two compartments under separate legislation or two institutions with contradictory assignments, but two levels of the pertinence of the same Lordship. The people of God is called to be today what the world is called to be ultimately. . . . The phrase found in the title, *body politics*, is of course partly redundant. Yet each term does say more than the other would alone. 'Politics' affirms an unblinking recognition that we deal with matters of power, of rank and of money, of costly decisions and dirty hands, of memories and feelings. The difference between church and state or between a faithful and an unfaithful church is not that one is political and the other not, but that they are political in different ways."[34]

Worship is politics as it is witness. As Christians affirm the reality of God in their community and in the world, they are telling a story of the world that the world will not recognize based upon its own language. Christians are, in a very real sense, teaching the world a different language. Christians should not attempt to find a "lowest-common-denominator" type of worship language that could assuage the tension between the claims of God's control and the controls of the world. "Our task, as Christians, is not to offer . . . theoretical alternatives, but rather to be an alternative."[35] Indeed, if we were able to offer a theory of truth "more determinative than the Christian witness to Trinity . . . then we should worship that theory rather than praise the Trinity."[36] The temptation for Christians is, of course, to wish to rule the world, or in the very least, to establish Christ's rule for him. Hauerwas makes it clear that this is not, and should not be, our desire in the "in-between" times.

Learning to live by one's wits is a skill acquired by those who, as a people, have discovered how to survive without ruling. We

34. Ibid., 249–50 n. 12. Hauerwas is here quoting Yoder, *Body Politics*, ix.

35. Hauerwas, *Wilderness Wanderings*, 122.

36. Ibid., 193. Hauerwas seems to have learned this from Barth, as Barth declares "a proved God is world, and a God of the world is an idol" (Barth, *Theology and Church*, 243). Hauerwas quotes this claim from Barth in Hauerwas, *With the Grain of the Universe*, 149–50. Of course, Barth likely learned such a notion from Aquinas. Cf. Hauerwas, *With the Grain of the Universe*, 164 n. 50.

believe that however much Christendom may have at certain times and in certain places represented the church's faithful and unfaithful witness, that day is now behind us. Wilderness, not rule, is where we presently dwell as Christians. As we know from Jesus' own temptations, wilderness means learning how to live under conditions of great testing. It means living a life that continually calls for the deployment of the "survival skills" of witness and mission and prayer. For those who think they are in control, who are convinced that they are called to rule, these skills cannot help but atrophy.[37]

It is within this context that worship is rightly understood. The church is called to be the church, and as such it does not seek to *use* its worship to motivate itself to social action or political posturing. Rather, its worship is a politics. As the church displays itself in worship, it is a politic in the world. This is seen nowhere more clearly for Hauerwas than in baptism and the Eucharist, both of which are very physical displays of the church's commitment to the "body" of Christ.

> These rites, baptism and Eucharist, are not just "religious things" that Christian people do. They are the essential rituals of our politics. Through them we learn who we are. Instead of being motives or causes for effective social work on the part of Christian people, these liturgies *are* our effective social work. For if the church *is* rather than has a social ethic, these actions are our most important social witness. It is in baptism and Eucharist that we see most clearly the marks of God's kingdom in the world. They set our standard, as we try to bring every aspect of our lives under their sway.[38]

It is in statements like these that Hauerwas's metaphysical claims regarding ecclesiology (though he would still not wish to engage in the conversation such a term implies) become perhaps most apparent. He is obviously not committed to discovering in the church a reality that corresponds to what we see in nature or what can be rationally defended according to some set of *a priori* principles regarding what can be said to be intelligible belief as opposed to that which is simply irrational or fideistic. Hauerwas's ecclesiology is his own form of realism (though

37. Hauerwas, *Wilderness Wanderings*, 217.
38. Hauerwas, *Peaceable Kingdom*, 108; italics Hauerwas's.

certainly he does not claim to be doing something new).[39] He is dissatisfied with the dichotomy that has typically resulted from discussions of
the modern conception of rationality.

> I have put quotes around "antifoundational" to indicate my un-
> ease with the widespread assumption that epistemologically
> our only two options are foundationalism or antifoundational-
> ism. Though my sympathies lie with the antifoundationalist, if I
> have to choose, I am bothered by the assumption that the foun-
> dationalist—that is, those people vaguely associated with the
> Cartesian project—have the right to set the terms of the debate.
> Thus I have tried to argue for a kind of realism that assumes that
> that which is known requires a corresponding transformation
> by an ongoing community of people.[40]

Hauerwas's appeal for the church to be church may seem like a
somewhat quaint approach to social life in the world, particularly when
coupled with Hauerwas's use of worship as the primary language in
which social engagement occurs. Nevertheless, Hauerwas believes this
must be the manner in which Christian theology conducts itself. As
Hauerwas states with regard to Pope John Paul II's use of terms found
in ancient Greek philosophy and with regard to Pope Leo XIII's en-
cyclicals, "Such language may seem foolish or naive in the face of our

39. One could easily question whether Hauerwas is really doing anything epistemologically distinct here, given his remarks about the "qualification of the self" (Hauerwas,
Christian Existence Today, 230). Here Hauerwas states that "To know the truth requires
correspondence to the truth" (230). Though the notion of persons corresponding to the
person Jesus in their lives is not the typical function of the correspondence theory (i.e.,
correspondence between belief or statements of belief and external facts or objects), it
is a bit curious that Hauerwas still adheres to somewhat traditionally modernistic epistemological categories. Of course, such language dates to earlier in Hauerwas's career.
It is likely he would be reluctant to use such language today. For a brief discussion of
Hauerwas's use of this in regard to the virtues, see Jenson, "Hauerwas Project," 286–88.

40. Hauerwas, *Wilderness Wanderings*, 94 n. 2. Though he does not use the language,
one could plausibly assume from this statement that Hauerwas employs some form of a
performative theory of truth.

Hauerwas appears here to be attempting to redefine realism by focusing on the reality of the human community. Hauerwas still wishes to affirm the human community
of the church as the true body of Christ (i.e., infused by God to become the people of
God). However, I am not sure that the discussion needs to be centered on the terms
foundationalism and *realism*. Hauerwas would likely wish to restate this today as well.
Nevertheless, his meaning remains clear. Realism, for Christians, is the belief that the
church and its theology are the clearest representation of the reality that is "behind the
curtain of history and anthropology," that is, the reality of God.

so-called political realities, but I think there can be no greater realism."[41] Such is the rationality of witness, as Hauerwas makes clear with regard to Barth.

> In his life and in his work, Barth sought nothing other than to be a witness to God's reconciling and redeeming work in Jesus Christ. He therefore did not try to "explain" the truth of what Christians believe about God and God's creation. He understood that such an explanation could not help but give the impression that the explanation is more than the witness.[42]

Contrary to the common understanding of witness as something that attests to the veracity of something else (e.g., a statement of fact or a truth claim), witness is a form of rationality unto itself. As the church is the church, particularly as it is in worship, so it attests to the reality that it believes is itself, i.e., the body of Christ. This focus on the human community of the church does not negate the fact that the church is also a testimony to the work of a God who is outside creation, but rather attests that God can only be known as he is given substance in the community we call church. As Hauerwas states in response to the thought of Tristram Engelhardt, "Engelhardt assumes that witness is what you need when your position cannot be rationally defended. I, in contrast, assume that witness is one of the most determinative forms of rationality."[43] Such an understanding of witness may seem circular in nature, but of course the accusation of circularity presupposes that something must exist external to the "rationality" of the church on which to base its veracity—a presumption that Hauerwas obviously cannot grant. It is to the evaluation of the church's truthfulness in witness that we must now turn.

---

41. Hauerwas, *In Good Company*, 133.

42. Hauerwas, *With the Grain of the Universe*, 146. Cf. ibid., 193 n. 44. Mangina notes that though Barth does emphasize the church's role as witness, he does not make clear the connection between witness and specific practices: "[W]hile Barth emphasizes the church's task as a witness to Christ, it is not clear that the church *as a configuration of human practices* makes much difference to this task" (Mangina, "Bearing the Marks of Jesus," 278, emphasis Mangina's).

43. Hauerwas, *Wilderness Wanderings*, 117.

The Church as the True Enfleshment of Jesus

One of the more frequently asked questions of Hauerwas, and one obviously related to the issues discussed above, is, how do we know that
the church of today is the real church? In other words, what makes the
community we call church a *true* enfleshment of the body of Christ
and, more important, how will we know it? Hauerwas offers answers to
these questions that may not satisfy those who are searching for some
way to measure the veracity of the community according to principles
available to any rational person, since he does not believe a standard set
of rules or principles exist against which the church could be compared.
Such questions cannot be answered "in principle."[44] Instead, the church
can only be called faithful when it practices the traditional teachings
that have been handed down through church practice for generations.
Truth is not discursive (Hauerwas has no list of which traditions or
teachings are to be practiced), but is a person; faithfulness is measured
as lives that "are church" become true to the person of Jesus, not as individuals enact the right principle.[45]

As mentioned above with regard to Kant's rational project, traditionlessness is an impossibility. Everyone is part of a tradition, whether
they realize it or not. But it is not enough to simply find a tradition.
Christians must be certain that the tradition they affirm is one that may
be regarded as true.

> Our selves are shaped, our thoughts arise out of a tradition. In
> our world, where so many feel rootless, detached, and homeless,
> many people are out shopping for a "tradition." And this trend,
> wherein people search for their roots, recover their past, and
> affirm tradition, is often seen as good and healthful. But just as
> the Christian faith has no stake in people being a part of just any
> old community, so we have no stake in people affirming any old
> tradition. Traditions can be less and more true.[46]

44. See Hauerwas's discussion to this effect in *Wilderness Wanderings*, 148–49.

45. This somewhat awkward way of putting the matter is meant to indicate the
way in which Hauerwas is transforming the word *church* into a verb. He wishes to see
church become something that we do, rather than something that merely exists.

46. Hauerwas and Willimon, *Resident Aliens*, 100–101. It may be pertinent to point
out that though Hauerwas is occasionally accused of being a communitarian, he has
no wish to defend the notion of community in any abstract sense. See Whitmore,
"Beyond Liberalism and Communitarianism in Christian Ethics," 207–25. Michael
Quirk ("Beyond Sectarianism?" 78–86) demonstrates that while Hauerwas may have

But if traditions can be less or more true, how then do Christians know that they are part of the right one? Hauerwas answers this by pointing to the only thing that is true. Instead of asking where Christians can find truth, the questions needs to be, rather, who is the truth?

> We are called to base our lives and actions on something which, to Kant, seemed woefully contingent—a Jew from Nazareth. Our claim is not that this tradition will make sense to anyone or will enable the world to run more smoothly. Our claim is that it just happens to be *true*. This really is the way God is. This really is the way God's world is.[47]

The Christian tradition is not one that is to be measured by criteria established elsewhere. It is its own criteria. The Christian tradition is the embodiment of the life of Christ in the community called church. It is maintained and carried on throughout history as the church engages in the practices that make it church. "The various sets of exercises through which Christians learn to understand and live appropriate to the story of God's dealing with them in Israel and Jesus may be called tradition."[48] As Christians continue to practice the habits that make them distinctly Christian, they are providing a true witness to their Lord. Hauerwas knows he inherited such a concern from Barth. "The *Church Dogmatics*, with its unending and confident display of Christian speech, is Barth's attempt to train us to be a people capable of truthful witness to the God who alone is the truth."[49] All of this rests, finally, on the existence of a church that has a history sufficiently grounded in the life of Christ to withstand the pressures of change and challenge over time.[50] The

---

some characteristics of communitarians such as MacIntyre, Sandel, Walzer, Taylor, and Sullivan, his strong ecclesiology prevents him from being "aligned with this movement" (79). For a brief discussion of this issue, also cf. Rasmusson, *Church as Polis*, 271–74.

47. Hauerwas and Willimon, *Resident Aliens*, 101.

48. Hauerwas, *Community of Character*, 150. The life of Jesus is finally the only measure of truth we have for the community of the church.

49. Hauerwas, *With the Grain of the Universe*, 176.

50. Though Hauerwas is obviously reluctant to rely on something known as the "universal church," he appears to have something like this in mind here. Since he is hesitant to say tradition must be found in the Methodist Church, or in the Catholic Church, or the like, he remains a bit unclear as to exactly which church has provided the faithful witness throughout history. In this respect, church remains little more than an "idea" in Hauerwas's theology, at least insofar as it can be anybody's church. As will be discussed in the next chapter, Hauerwas finds himself in the awkward position ad-

church is, finally, the historical extension of the One who claimed to be "the way, the *truth*, and the life" (John 14:6). But of course, the church is not a thing to be examined as one might examine a theory or a historical "fact." The church is the people who worship and live in Christ every day.

> [T]he justification of our moral principles and assertions cannot be done from the point of view of anyone, but rather requires a tradition of moral wisdom. Such a tradition is not a "deposit" of unchanging moral "truth," but is made up of the lives of men and women who are constantly testing and changing that tradition through their own struggle to live it. The maintenance of such a tradition requires a community across time sufficient to sustain the journey from one generation to the next. The Christian word for that community is church.[51]

The true church is not one that attempts to keep itself in line with traditional beliefs by constantly asking itself "what" it believes. Rather, the true church is one that is constantly telling itself and the world, in word and action, "who" it believes. In this way, the church is found to be true as it continues to align itself with the life, death, and resurrection of Jesus, who is its life. Even further, the church is that community that is more than itself due to its participation in the reality of God's own Triune relationship.

The Trinity as the Locus of Worship and Ground of Narrative Formation

But someone may well ask, who is it that you worship? Hauerwas's response would likely be "Come, let me show you. Let's go to church." With that, he would introduce the questioner to the worship of the God we know as Father, Son, and Holy Spirit in the church. Doctrine plays a distinct role for Hauerwas in his theology. It is still instructive, but not as to content or as a body of knowledge. Hauerwas finds George Lindbeck's conception of doctrine helpful:

> Too often "doctrine" is relegated to the world of thought and ideas. Church doctrine is one of the crucial *practices* of the

---

vocated by Barth as well. Neither seem able to state clearly where they find the church to be located.

51. Hauerwas, "On Keeping Theological Ethics Theological," 33.

church necessary to sustain the church's identity. I think George Lindbeck's "rule-theory" of doctrine at least reminds us that doctrine is meant to do some work and is therefore not "about" something in and of itself.[52]

Though Hauerwas does not seem to believe doctrine is only regulative, it can serve the church in a regulative capacity as it directs the church toward right worship. But this regulation is not something that happens anew each time doctrine is given serious meditation in worship. In other words, even the regulative capacity of doctrine is tradition-dependent. David Keck's understanding of doctrine is instructive on this point:

> First, as a historian, I am astounded by [doctrine's] endurance through the centuries. Many impressive thoughts have not survived, and many that have, have lost all power today. Second, and more personally, I am thankful for doctrines because I believe that only through the faithful transmission of the church's traditional teaching is it possible to have hope for my mother; for my father, her primary caregiver; and for the rest of the world which suffers from sunrise to sunset. Hence, as I use the term, orthodoxy is not only about doctrine or guiding principles; it also denotes a kind of existence to be desired in itself. Orthodoxy is a longing to align one's own life and memories with the life and memories of the church.[53]

What Lindbeck lacked in his conception of doctrine as "rule-theory"—that is, the grounding of such a practice in a tradition-formed community—Hauerwas provides with a thoroughgoing ecclesiology. It is impossible to conceive of a doctrine outside of its traditional use in the history of Christian theology. In this, the doctrine of the Trinity is paramount, since Christians can only know God as Trinity. For instance, even the doctrine of creation is not doctrinally subsumed under the rubric God. Instead, it is to be understood through the lens of Trinitarian worship.[54]

---

52. Hauerwas, *In Good Company*, 220 n. 19. Hauerwas is cautious not to completely subscribe to Lindbeck's understanding of language usage in doctrine. Perhaps Hauerwas recognizes that language is not so tidily limited to one use or definition.

53. Keck, *Forgetting Whose We Are*, 82. For a good summary of the way Hauerwas relates suffering to ecclesiology, see Lammers, "On Stanley Hauerwas," 128–142.

54. Hauerwas, *Wilderness Wanderings*, 9.

Trinity is, for Hauerwas, not some ethereal doctrine contemplated by ancients in purely speculative terms. To characterize the doctrine of the Trinity in this way would be to make the Trinity into a type of image. Instead Hauerwas wishes to understand the Trinity as it is most profoundly revealed, i.e., in the community of the church. Trinity becomes the personalization of God in the "body" that he knows as his own. It is only as God has acted and become known in the community of the church that we can know him. He is not abstracted to the point of contemplation. Instead he is realized in the company of the faithful.

> I do not believe that the Trinitarian Father, Son, and Holy Spirit is an image. Rather, Trinity is a name. Christians do not believe that we first come to know something called God and only then further learn to identify God as Trinity. Rather, the only God Christians have come to know is Trinity: Father, Son, and Holy Spirit.[55]

Hauerwas has no doctrine of the Trinity "as such." He believes that Trinity, to be rightly "understood," must be first embodied in the life of the church before Christians can appropriately name God as Trinity. With this in mind, Hauerwas believes that Christians, in order to rightly understand and rightly display their knowledge of God, must live lives of witness. Knowledge of God rests finally on the work of the Spirit in the lives of believers to bring about the display of God's character in humans.

> The truth of Christian convictions can be known only through witnesses because the God Christians worship is triune. If the truth of Christian convictions could be known without witnesses, then that truth would no longer be the work of the Trinity, and those who espoused it would no longer be Christians. . . . [William] James did not understand that the lives he admired were the lives of witnesses, and that there can be no witnesses without the One to whom they witness.[56]

James McClendon's theological method is attractive to Hauerwas in precisely McClendon's aversion to defining God before turning to the life of Jesus.[57] McClendon wishes to introduce people to the reality of

---

55. Ibid., 29.

56. Hauerwas, *With the Grain of the Universe*, 211–12.

57. Hauerwas, *Wilderness Wanderings*, 180.

God in Trinity rather than provide some grounds by which to identify a thing called God, which can then be attributed to various expressions in history. McClendon even acknowledges his intent to lead readers slowly along the path, pointing to the marks of God, but never saying "there he is." McClendon's project is never to presume to "define" God. Indeed, such a presumption cannot help but lead to idolatry.

> The results [after almost 300 pages of reading McClendon's *Doctrine*] will disappoint some. Spheres of action for Jesus' God have been indicated, and names for God named, some familiar, some strange. Yet "God" has not been defined here, or God's essence described, apart from the Israel-Jesus-church story itself.[58]

What such an understanding opens up, particularly for Hauerwas, is the possibility of a thoroughgoing ecclesiastical Trinitarianism. What is most significant for our purposes is the way in which the Holy Spirit plays a part in drawing humanity into the Trinitarian "circle." Hauerwas finds the thought of Milbank useful here.

> Creation is not a finished product but rather God's continuously generated *ex nihilo* in time. Creatures thus do not assist God in creation but participate in God's continuing creation as Trinity. In this respect, one of the most interesting ways to think of *Theology and Social Theory* is to interpret it as an extended reflection on the work of the Holy Spirit. The materiality of the Spirit's work is the reason Milbank can make the astounding claim that theology must be its own social science. It must be so exactly because Christian convictions are necessary for us to locate the final causes shaping our history as God's ongoing work of creation.[59]

Hauerwas believes, with Milbank, that this must be the case since the Christian's only understanding of reality must be ecclesiologically formed. It is only as the Christian is made a part of the church's story that he or she can become a part of God's story.[60] The Holy Spirit's "in-

---

58. McClendon, *Doctrine*, 294.

59. Hauerwas, *Wilderness Wanderings*, 192.

60. The limiting nature of such a claim is obvious. There is no salvation outside the church. Correlatively, one wonders, for Hauerwas to remain consistent, if there is any grace outside the church. While it is certainly a Christian affirmation that God is Lord of all that is and Creator of all that is, can a Christian call "grace" the things that happen in the world outside the church, or must they remain nameless?

dwelling" makes possible the Christian's joining the community, though this term, *indwelling*, may not be the best description of the work of the Holy Spirit since *indwelling* makes such a Trinitarianism sound rather gnostic. (*Indwelling* may sound gnostic if the word points to the implication that the work of the Spirit is thus primarily internalized; such an implication ignores or demotes the material reality of the Spirit in the human community.) Instead, the work of the Holy Spirit seems to be *identical* with the practices of the church, at least insofar as they are rightly formed. Hauerwas's observation of Milbank makes this clear.

> Milbank is not suggesting that a Christian sociology can be deduced from the Christian doctrine of the Trinity in and of itself—because there is no doctrine of the Trinity in and of itself. A distinguishable Christian social theory is possible only because there are Christian practices. Put in terms of Christian dogmatics, Milbank's position assumes that Christian theological reflection "begins," insofar as Christian reflection has a beginning, with ecclesiology.[61]

Such an ecclesiological understanding of the Trinity suits Hauerwas's purposes quite well. Such an ecclesiological understanding of the Trinity allows him to avoid any speculative work on the "doctrine" of the Trinity, since Trinity can only be known as it is enacted in the church. Christians, as they enact the practices of the church, embody the Holy Spirit as he draws them into participation in the Trinitarian community. Such may be seen as an "enfleshment" of the Trinity, though that sounds a bit too docetic. Instead, it may be better to say that the community of the church is the consummation of the Christian community with the God they name as their own.

What this language is struggling to describe is the way in which Hauerwas can claim such a strong ecclesiological description of Trinity and human participation in the Trinity, and yet attempt to avoid the criticism of anthropological reductionism, that is, of reducing the

---

61. Hauerwas, *Wilderness Wanderings*, 192. Though it is beyond the scope of this study, an interesting comparison could be made between, on the one hand, Hauerwas's and Milbank's notion of theological reflection on the Trinity beginning with ecclesiology and, on the other hand, Pannenberg's conception of the Trinity's being built up "from below," that is, the notion that the Trinity is only conceivable based on the revelation of Jesus's life and message. All could be understood as reversing the classical theological method of beginning "from above," i.e., with the theistic presupposition of God's unity. Cf. Olson, "Wolfhart Pannenberg's Doctrine of the Trinity," 185.

Trinity to merely the human community. As indicated above, I am not sure this is a criticism that Hauerwas can avoid or that he addresses sufficiently; moreover, I am not sure it is a criticism that he even finds interesting. Nevertheless, since Hauerwas believes "one of [theologians'] primary tasks today is to help the Christian people be confident speakers of the language of the Church,"[62] it seems incumbent upon Hauerwas to provide some of the language the church has either lost or not yet articulated well. Hauerwas's vague references to the work of the Holy Spirit do not seem sufficient warrant for claiming the work of the Holy Spirit as the answer to his reductionistic problem.

Pannenberg's Social Trinity and Human Participation

Hauerwas's position may be clarified and enhanced at this point through dialogue with the thought of a more systematic thinker on the social nature of the Trinity. Though it may be understandable that Hauerwas wishes to avoid specific doctrinal assertions in the abstract, I believe it evident by this point in our study that he makes extensive "use" of doctrinal assertions when they further his purposes. Wolfhart Pannenberg is equally concerned with developing an ecclesiology that is more than superfluous. For Pannenberg, as the Spirit indwells believers in the church, they become a part of the body of Christ, but even further, they are a part of the intratrinitarian fellowship of God. Like Hauerwas, Pannenberg calls such a notion "participation."

> The gift of the Spirit to believers in which the Father and the Son work together follows only from its mediation by the fact that believers, linked by faith and baptism to the Son revealed in Jesus Christ, become members of his body, so that sonship in relation to the Father finds manifestation in them, too, as participation in the sonship of Jesus and therefore in the intratrinitarian life of God.[63]

This "participation" means not only that believers are a part of intratrinitarian fellowship; they are also caused to become a community of human fellowship on account of their fellowship with God. Humans can reach the full potential of such fellowship by participation in the community of the church.

62. Hauerwas, "Where Would I Be Without Friends?" 317.
63. Pannenberg, *Systematic Theology*, 3:11.

> The only criterion of authentic spirituality is the relation to con-
> fession of Christ (1 Cor. 12:3), and the relation to the one Lord
> means commitment to the unity of Christians in the church's
> fellowship, not in the denial of the plurality but by mutual par-
> ticipation and love in the unity of the body of Christ.[64]

This is not an attempt to raise all human fellowship to the level of fellowship in the Spirit. Indeed, Pannenberg is careful to distinguish the
humanity of the church from its communal existence in Jesus.

> The Spirit must not be viewed as the church's common spirit
> after the manner of the esprit de corps that characterizes other
> forms of human fellowship and binds the members together,
> even though due attention be given to the specific grounding
> of the church's sense of fellowship on the basis of its existence
> in the person and history of Jesus Christ. The church and its
> members do not control the gift of the Spirit as though it were
> their possession. The gift remains linked to the foundation that
> they have outside themselves in Jesus Christ.[65]

Pannenberg is here critiquing the common spirit of Schleiermacher.
He believes Schleiermacher has mistakenly blurred the lines between
a common human fellowship and that of the Spirit. By clinging to a
grounding outside the human community—an external or transcendent point of reference—Pannenberg is avoiding the anthropological
reductionism he believes characteristic of Schleiermacher (and I believe
characteristic of Hauerwas) in his understanding of the Holy Spirit.

> This "outside" is what distinguishes the church from other fel-
> lowships and their common spirit. It is essential to the significa-
> tory character of the church as a fellowship. But Schleiermacher
> takes too little note of it, for he regards the church's participa-
> tion in Christ only causally from the standpoint of the effect
> deriving from him. Hence he does not sufficiently weigh the
> difference between the eschatological nature of the salvation
> event in Christ and what is always the merely provisional form
> of the church.[66]

64. Ibid., 18.

65. Ibid., 19.

66. Ibid., 19 n. 51. One will recall that the gift of the Holy Spirit is an eschatological
gift. Therefore, the work of the Spirit is located in the externality of the eschaton.

Pannenberg attempts to avoid lapsing into a common spirit himself by maintaining that it is the Holy Spirit who draws people into fellowship and raises humans above their humanity to participate in the fellowship of the divine. However, Pannenberg still relies on an inherent individualism to accomplish it. Though certainly he believes the church is a necessary component of the Spirit's work as the entry point for humans in connection to the divine, he yet appears to begin with the ontological priority of the individual.

> By the Spirit creatures will be made capable of independence in their relation to God and at the same time integrated into the unity of God's kingdom. . . . The form of the gift does not mean that the Spirit comes under the control of creatures but that he comes into them and thus makes possible our *independent and spontaneous entry* into God's action of reconciling the world and our participation in the movement of his reconciling love toward the world.[67]

In this, Pannenberg appears to remain entrenched in the belief that the ecclesiological community is, in a primary sense, a collection of individuals. He attempts to qualify such a beginning point by claiming that the Spirit's indwelling in individuals lifts them above their own particular existence as individuals.

> The gift of the Spirit is not just for individual believers but aims at the building up of the fellowship of believers, at the founding and the constant giving of new life to the church. For by the link to the one Lord by which all believers receive a share in his sonship, and hence also in the Spirit of Christ, they are at the same time integrated into the fellowship of believers. Each by faith is related to the one Lord and hence to all other believers. By the Spirit each is lifted above individual particularity in order, "in Christ," to form with all other believers the fellowship of the church.[68]

Certainly, Pannenberg recognizes the value of a corporate fellowship and identity, but his ontology of what constitutes the self and its relation to the community of faith seems reflective of an individualistic beginning point. Pannenberg appears to share with Hauerwas a concern that the individualized self be somehow subjected to the community of

67. Ibid., 12; emphasis mine.
68. Ibid., 12–13.

faith, i.e., that it become the singular "body of Christ." As demonstrated above, Hauerwas has diligently illustrated one way, at least, in which corporate identity may take precedence over the individual. In other words, the definition of self becomes a subsequent question to the development of ecclesiology. Pannenberg is, I believe, at a disadvantage in retaining the preeminence of the individual, precisely because church can then be largely reduced to the individual. Thus, while he avoids anthropological reductionism, he still seems to struggle with a form of anthropological psychologism true of many more modernistic depictions of the Spirit's indwelling, as will be seen in the next chapter. Though certainly he qualifies his commitment to the individual, by beginning with the priority of the Spirit's indwelling in the individual, Pannenberg does not appear to escape the critique of defining the individual's nature as Christian qua human. Fellowship in the community of church, instead of being the constitutive element he wishes it to be, could easily become, as it has in certain voluntaristic ecclesiologies, an option or elective choice of the individual.[69] He rightly points to the Holy Spirit as an external connection to a God who, though certainly immanent within history, remains outside of creation. Nevertheless, Pannenberg seems to fall short of providing an adequate account of how the church, as Christ's body (note the singular unity here), can become part of the intratrinitarian fellowship *as one body*, rather than as parts of the body.[70]

A primary issue related to this discussion is whether the existing church's pneumatology can bear the sociological enfleshment given it in Hauerwas's ecclesiology. Does he have, as Pannenberg seems to have, a tradition of the Holy Spirit in doctrinal or scriptural language that is sufficiently developed to avoid the accusation that his ecclesiology is merely an anthropology? It is the contention in the following two sections that he still lacks the language necessary for such a doctrine to be affirmed as the church's own. This language we will attempt to provide

69. I am here mindful of the voluntaristic nature of many parachurch groups that exist, particularly amongst western Protestants, as well as of the somewhat voluntaristic nature of salvation in some conservative Protestant theologies (e.g., Wesleyan Arminianism).

70. This seems an appropriate way of phrasing the matter given Paul's emphasis on unity taking precedence over particularity in 1 Corinthians 12. More will be said on this in chapters 6 and 7 below.

in the chapter below. For now, we must finally turn to the manner in which Hauerwas attempts to avoid a reduction of the church to mere anthropology.

The Tenuous Nature of the Sacraments in Hauerwas's Church as the Point of Connection between the Human and the Divine

Worship is the central practice of Christians, since it is within the context of worship that Christians embody and name the God they know as the One true God. It is primarily in this context that truthful language is possible and that truth-telling creatures are formed. In his Christian ethics classes, Hauerwas's goal is to begin to give students a taste of this training by ordering and modeling his classes within the framework of worship.

> Gathered Christians greet one another in the name of the Father, Son, and Holy Spirit. Accordingly, I remind my students that any account of the Christian moral life begins and ends with the question of the God we Christians worship. The God Christians worship is known through initiation into the practices of a tradition which are necessary to know how rightly to name God—that is, Father, Son, and Holy Spirit.[71]

The formation of Christians and the Christian moral life in worship is not coincidental. As Hauerwas understands worship, it is the place where Christians learn holiness and what it means to live as virtuous people. This is the primary goal of Christian ethics. Instead of being about the various issues that ethicists typically present in discussions of morality, Christian ethics is first and foremost about teaching Christians to "live up" to their calling.

> [T]he formation of Christians through the liturgy makes clear that Christians are not simply called to do the "right thing," but rather we are expected to be holy. Such holiness is not an individual achievement but comes from being made part of a community in which we discover the truth about our lives. And

---

71. Hauerwas, *In Good Company*, 158.

"truth" cannot be separated from how the community worships,
since the truth is that we are creatures made for worship.[72]

Hauerwas does not believe that worship is something that "comes
after" getting theological conviction right. Instead, worship is, part and
parcel, the language and activity in which theology is rightly done.
This means that worship comes before any conception of God. It is as
Christians are trained to stand in awe of God that right speech and right
thinking are made possible. As Fergus Kerr puts it,

> [I]t is because people exult and lament, sing for joy, bewail their
> sins and so on, that they are able, eventually, to have thoughts
> about God. Worship is not the result but the precondition for
> believing in God. Theological concepts are rooted in certain
> habitual ways of acting, responding, relating, to our natural-
> historical setting.[73]

This means that worship cannot be relegated to a mere rehearsal
of what is discovered in theological reflection. Instead, it is in the midst
of worship that "theology" actually happens. This is obviously counter
to the typical approach to theology and worship in modernity. In the
modern context, theology is left lifeless, a rational explanation, without
the changing power of a community that is shaped by the practices.
Consequently, it has no "meaning." This is why Hauerwas is drawn
away from referential or representational language.[74] Representational
language has the limiting effect of creating a theology that is largely
powerless to change lives. Certainly it can change minds, but it is to the
church's detriment that we have said "That is sufficient for us." Indeed,
worship in the modern context, as it is primarily reflection on a body
of knowledge, is gnostic by its very nature in that it denies the material
necessity of physical human participation. This is not to say that this is

72. Ibid., 155. Notice the way in which Hauerwas relies on a doctrinal point of
anthropology in order to sustain his epistemological point. He seems not entirely opposed to foundationalism in his method; he seems opposed only to the way in which
foundationalism has been joined to a rationality that is independent from the church
and its life.

73. Kerr, *Theology after Wittgenstein*, 183.

74. Hauerwas's affinity for Wittgenstein conforms with his desire that language do
more than simply function in a representational sense. Nancey Murphy spells this out
more clearly than Hauerwas in theoretical terms; however, Hauerwas would appear to
concur. See Hauerwas, Murphy, and Nation, *Theology Without Foundations*, 14–15.

true of all modern worship. However, as knowledge is exalted to a primary level, worship becomes a product of the mind, even the individual rational mind. The church is then expendable in the modern church's worship. In contrast, for Hauerwas, worship is theology that comes to life, even changing the lives that are formed by it. It is in the change that meaning is discovered. Such change can only take place in the context of a community that forms and molds us into its likeness. That is finally where ethics is, or at least should be, done. As Samuel Wells summarizes Hauerwas's thought,

> It is [the church in worship as "it is made a part of God's praise and joy"] that principally distinguishes the church from the world. The task of ethics is "to assemble reminders from the training we receive in worship that enable us to rightly see the world and to perceive how we continue to be possessed by the world.[75]

Thus ethics, as worship, serves to remind us how far we have yet to go in ridding the church of its embrace of the world.

Central to Hauerwas's demand for worship as the locus of theology are the sacraments. It is in the context of worship that Christians can truly be said to embody the presence of Christ in the world, and this particularly as they celebrate the Eucharist. The Eucharist is so integral to worship that Hauerwas can hardly conceive of a true Christian community without the real presence of Christ celebrated in the midst of the community through the miracle of the bread and wine.[76]

Through the sacraments, a believer becomes engrafted into the life of the community, ultimately into the story which is God's. We do not choose how much or whether to become God's own. We are

---

75. Wells, *Transforming Fate into Destiny*, 122. Wells is here quoting Hauerwas, *In Good Company*, 156.

76. See Hauerwas, *In Good Company*, 76. Here Hauerwas chides his Anabaptist friends for denying the miracle of the Eucharist and thus for failing to articulate well their identity. I am not convinced that Hauerwas has rightly located the miracle of divine presence. Since to locate it in the Eucharist remains a rather mystical and sporadic appeal, I believe he would be better served to locate the miracle of the divine as it is coupled with the human precisely in the indwelling presence of the Holy Spirit in humanity. Indeed, since I do not hold the sacraments to be miraculous, I believe the memorial view could serve as an even better rendering of the pedagogical nature of the bread and wine, and baptism. Hauerwas is finally left with but a momentary experience of the miraculous on which to hang the remainder of the community's remembering.

made such through the participation that the sacraments provide: "To be baptized in Christ's death and resurrection is *to be made* part of a people, part of God's life, rendering the language of choice facile."[77] As Christians participate in the sacraments, they become part of the divine drama that is God's story. Through the sacraments they make God's story their own story. This is how the practices serve to make the narrative of Jesus "real" for Christians.

> The sacraments enact the story of Jesus and, thus, form a community in his image. We could not be the church without them. For the story of Jesus is not simply one that is told; it must be enacted. The sacraments are means crucial to shaping and preparing us to tell and hear that story.[78]

To speak of the church as the enactment of the story of Jesus, as Jesus's body, is Hauerwas's way of answering the question, where is the church? The church is located precisely in the practice of the Eucharist, since it is there that the church becomes more than itself; it becomes, in more than a figurative sense, the body of Christ. Quoting Milbank, Hauerwas reasons that

> It is only in the Eucharistic celebration that the church is body exactly because there a ritualistic distance obtains that distinguishes the church from itself. Thus, in Milbank's words, the "Church is first and foremost neither a programme, nor a 'real' society, but instead an enacted, serious fiction." So the answer to the question "where is the church?" is to found it "on the site of the Eucharist, which is not a site; since it suspends presence in favour of memory and expectation, 'positions' each and every one of us only as fed—gift from God of ourselves and therefore not to ourselves—and bizarrely assimilates us to the food we eat, so that we, in turn, must exhaust ourselves as nourishment for others."
>
> Milbank is, I think, rightly struggling to find a way to remind us that the church is the body of Christ only by the gift of the Holy Spirit—a Spirit clearly not under our control. The

77. Hauerwas, *Wilderness Wanderings*, 115; emphasis Hauerwas's. Unfortunately, Hauerwas fails to recognize the compromised nature of baptism in modernity, at least in western countries. Prone as modern Christians are to identify the community as simply a collection of individuals, baptism hardly represents a significant identification with a body any longer.

78. Hauerwas, *Peaceable Kingdom*, 107–8.

problem, then, is how to say that without becoming ecclesiologically docetic or politically domesticated.[79]

With his turn to the Eucharist, what Hauerwas, like Milbank,
seems to be struggling with is how to locate the reality of God in the
community known as church. This he must do without equivocating
between the human and divine, because the transcendence of God is
reduced to the human if all we finally have is the human (i.e., anthropological reductionism). Thus, the real presence of Christ in the Eucharist
makes it possible for Hauerwas to infuse the human community with
the transcendent reality of God.[80]

79. Hauerwas, *In Good Company*, 29. Hauerwas is here quoting Milbank, "Enclaves,
or Where Is the Church?" 342. Cf. Hauerwas, *Matthew*, 219.

80. It may be pertinent at this point to address how the charge of anthropological reductionism is related to the charge of sectarianism. This can be done best by discussing
reductionism in the context of sectarianism. Hauerwas has little interest in appealing to
human experience as the locus of God-talk. Instead, he wishes to ground the totality of
his narrative in the Jesus story. Thus, appealing to the Eucharist as primary for communal formation allows Hauerwas to remain internally consistent. Nevertheless, this does
not seem to provide an escape from anthropological reductionism, since Hauerwas's
God is merely "added on" to the already existing human community. A more thoroughgoing doctrine of the Holy Spirit would provide for fuller interaction between
the divine and human, providing Hauerwas with a means to escape the problem of a
preexistent human community that is only subsequently made divine.

Holland (Holland, "Problems and Prospects of a 'Sectarian Ethic,'" 165–67) criticizes Hauerwas for not engaging the obvious commonality of human experience in
language and action. However, Holland's own modernistic arrogance can be seen in
his belief that morality is discovered in the commonality of pluralism. "One need
not be a foundationalist to concede that there is moral wisdom beyond the text and
tradition of one's community" (166). The question for Holland is how such pluralistic
moral wisdom fits into his ecclesiology. Holland's ecclesiology appears to be too inclusive to be called distinctly Christian.

Holland's main concern appears to be that something called god, which phenom-
enologists have told us is common to all human experience (i.e., theism), is absent from
Hauerwas' public discourse (167). Hauerwas' response would likely be "Why talk about
god? Let's talk about Jesus."

A further problem for Holland (Holland, "Mennonites on Hauerwas," 147–51) is his
notion that the "public conversation must precede the writing of an ecclesiology—not
simply because communities of discourse precede the church, but because in Scripture
the grand story of creation precedes the story of the church" (147). Besides the problematic presupposition of public being a more primary category than ecclesiology in
Holland's statement (i.e., anthropology comes before ecclesiology), it is theologically
questionable and perhaps even a bit positivistic to presume the precedence of the doctrine of creation over ecclesiology based on chronology.

One wonders if Hauerwas, and Milbank, has accomplished a real joining of God's transcendence with the human by locating the presence of Christ in the community precisely at the point of eucharistic meal. Hauerwas seems to believe that this maintains the reality of a God distinct from the human community, but the claim that the church can then still be identified as the "body of Christ" remains a bit tenuous. Hauerwas appears to have merely added the divine onto the already existent human community, and in a rather sporadic sense at that, since the sacraments are only temporal points of training. He lacks a thoroughgoing sense of the divine within the human community.[81]

What Hauerwas needs, and looks to the sacraments to provide, is a way to avoid the criticism that his human community is preexistent to the divine community. This stems from the necessity that the human community of the church be more than merely a human community. It must have a strong connection to the Triune God in order for Hauerwas to avoid reducing the church to anthropology. The Eucharist is the point on which he hangs this connection. However, the Eucharist seems insufficient as the encompassing connection needed to warrant the kind of narrative formation that Hauerwas desires from the church. What is needed is a constant presence of the divine within the human community.

With his turn to the Eucharist, what Hauerwas, like Milbank, seems to be struggling with is to locate the reality of God in the community known as church. This he must do without equivocating between the human and divine, because the transcendence of God is reduced to the human if all we finally have is the human (i.e., anthropological reductionism). Thus, the real presence of Christ in the Eucharist makes it possible for Hauerwas to infuse the human community with the transcendent reality of God

---

81. Hauerwas may wish to argue that since the Eucharist is celebrated around the world in various places at differing times, a constant or continual celebration of the Eucharist is happening someplace in the world every moment of every day. While this may allow him to say that such an appeal to the Eucharist is not then sporadic, it leaves him once again affirming a type of universal church with which he is clearly uncomfortable.

The Missing Element of the Holy Spirit in Hauerwas's Church

Hauerwas has made clear that the Triune God must be the central point for Christian identity and formation. As detailed above, the Trinity is central for Hauerwas's conception of church, not as a conceptualization of God, but as a name that guides our formation in worship. The only manner in which humans can approach the divine is through the revelation of God provided in the economic Trinity. Hauerwas, like Barth, makes the incarnation central in this revelation. However, Hauerwas becomes almost binitarian in his forgetfulness of the Holy Spirit as the agent causing the church to become Christ's body. The Holy Spirit is finally only given lip service as a part of Hauerwas's formative narrative community.[82]

The discussion concerning anthropological reduction of the human community of the church qua human seems to turn on Hauerwas's understanding of the work of the Holy Spirit. Hauerwas does seem to collapse the distinction between the notion of an immanent and economic Trinity with statements like "the nature of God's love for us cannot be separated from the story of God's activity with humans."[83] Nevertheless, he, with Aquinas, also maintains an external or transcendent reality of the Holy Spirit. When describing some of the differences between Aristotle and Aquinas, Hauerwas intimates that the Spirit is an external reality exerting external influence.

> We need a way to describe at least some of these differences as non-incidental and resilient, but we do not find it in Aristotle. As we suggest, the New Testament language of gifts of the Spirit is much better equipped here. First, it does not presume all virtues are received in the same way and intimates, as Aquinas later codifies, that some gifts (for Christians all of the virtues are gifts) are not so much acquired by habituation and learned in a friendship in which one is presented a model after which to

---

82. One will notice the relative paucity of comments by Hauerwas in this section on the Holy Spirit. The references to the Holy Spirit are exhaustive of Hauerwas's work in approximately the last fifteen years. Study of works prior to that would not reflect a more detailed treatment of the Spirit, but neither might such works be reflective of Hauerwas's current thought. While Hauerwas has devoted extensive attention to ecclesiology, he has only occasionally mentioned pneumatology, which is one of the primary reasons for the work offered in the chapters below.

83. Hauerwas and Pinches, *Christians among the Virtues*, 44.

follow, but rather they are *directly bestowed by God*—"*infused*" as Aquinas would have it.[84]

Hauerwas clearly believes that the moral life for the Christian on earth is "the work of the Spirit who enables us to submit ourselves one to the other and to God. The Spirit trains us up into the obedience of Christ."[85] Though Hauerwas may be loathe to provide any systematic presentation of the Spirit, he readily invokes the reality of the Spirit in both existence and power in his prayers.[86] The transcendence of the Holy Spirit is important for Hauerwas in that it would enable him to avoid the accusation that the divine is totally humanized, that is, that theology is finally anthropology. To make the life of the divine community equivalent with the human community, without any theological qualification, comes dangerously close to identifying the divine with the human community (Scleiermacher). This is the problem we have called anthropological reductionism. Hauerwas fails to provide the theological qualifications necessary in his rather scant discussions of the Holy Spirit. This seems to be a problem similar to what Barth's theology faced in his determination to connect the reality of ecclesial community with the divine. As Reinhard Hütter notes,

> The relation between Holy Spirit and church turns out to be the core problem. Although Barth did renew theology as a serious practice within the church, namely as 'church theology', he was himself only able to develop this theology charismatically, that is, only in his own personal practice of it; yet he was unable to give it any pneumatological-ecclesiological foundation by demonstrating why this ecclesial discursive practice is necessary in

84. Ibid., 188, n. 12, emphasis mine. Hauerwas has purposely chosen Aquinas in this respect to counter the prominent understanding of Aquinas as a natural-law theorist. See Hauerwas, "On Keeping Theological Ethics Theological," 32–33. Here Hauerwas cites Aquinas, *Summa Theologiae*, I–II.106.2. It is interesting that Hauerwas does not further address the issue of "fruit of the Spirit" in Galatians, since the listing of character attributes there would seem to lend itself well to the notion of training and habituation.

85. Hauerwas and Pinches, *Christians among the Virtues*, 148.

86. For an example of such a dependence on the Holy Spirit in his prayers, see Hauerwas, *Prayers Plainly Spoken*, 24, 44, 56, 80, 109, 132. Hauerwas undoubtedly wishes his prayers to be a formative language for the practice of all those who participate in them. Prayer shapes much of our lives theologically, that is to say, ethically. See Hauerwas, *Better Hope*, 103.

the first place and in what way it is tied to church doctrine or makes such doctrine necessary.[87]

It is conceivable that Hauerwas may be relying on the notion of church as eschatological sign to avoid equivocating between theology and anthropology. He believes it is only in an eschatological sense that the kingdom of God will be fully realized. Christians live between the times, and so wait for the kingdom to be established by Christ.[88] When his belief in an eschatological kingdom is combined with the belief in the reality of a transcendent Spirit who gifts Christians with virtue, Hauerwas can avoid being accused of a thoroughgoing reduction to anthropology. The divine nature of the Holy Spirit is not, in this eschatological sense for Hauerwas, totally socialized. Further, the social reality of the Spirit as it directs the church toward its eschatological goal could yet be considered a primary emphasis of Hauerwas's work.[89]

Early in his career, Hauerwas was prone to think of the work of the Spirit as a part of Christology. Sanctification must be understood, in the context of the Spirit's working, as a necessary counterpart of the doctrine of justification.

87. Hütter, *Suffering Divine Things*, 13. Hütter is here offering a synopsis and critique of Barth's response to Peterson in a conversation between E. Peterson and A. Harnack. Though Barth agrees with Peterson, he cannot finally find a way to account for the materiality of Peterson's ecclesiology.

88. It is a significant point for Hauerwas to emphasize that God's story is not finished and will not be finished until the lordship of Christ is established over all peoples and over all the earth. Of course, what looks like an ending may be only another beginning. But the point to be made here is that Hauerwas explicitly acknowledges the reality of an eschatology that is at best only being partially realized in the church and cannot be fully realized without the presence of Christ. E.g., see Hauerwas, with Berkman, "Trinitarian Theology of the Chief End of All Flesh," 195–96. As seen previously, by affirming eschatology, Hauerwas's thinking bears marked similarities to the theology of Wolfhart Pannenberg; Pannenberg believes that the doctrinal claims about God, though universally true, will finally be ratified in the eschaton. E.g., see Pannenberg, *Systematic Theology*, 1:259–336.

89. Here I am obviously giving a fairly charitable reading of Hauerwas's understanding of the Spirit. I am not sure he would choose the word *transcendent* to describe the work of the Spirit; however, I do not see how he can escape it and still remain orthodox, at least orthodox in his understanding of Thomas. Hauerwas dares not develop a "doctrine" of the Spirit, but it may be to his benefit to at least discuss in more detail how Aquinas viewed the work of the Spirit in the world.

Hauerwas's own theology seems rather lacking in mention of the Holy Spirit. However, his prayers are quite full of the Spirit's presence. See Hauerwas, *Prayers Plainly Spoken*.

Thus justification and sanctification are but two modes of the one work of Christ for the believer. They cannot be separated, because that would result in abstracting the Christian life from its source. Yet, equally important, they cannot be mixed or confused; that would diminish the significance of one in favor of the other. They are rather two essential, interdependent aspects of the one work of Christ.[90]

To aid him in developing what this connection meant, Hauerwas employs the thought of Calvin and Wesley. Wesley is especially useful in that he makes it quite clear how justification and sanctification "hang together." They are both grounded in the grace expressed most clearly by Christ at the cross. "Despite Wesley's progressive view of sanctification, no stage acquired independent significance apart from Christ's work of atonement."[91] As Harold Lindstrom makes even clearer, "The grace of salvation is in Wesley the common foundation of all phases in the process of salvation. Of everything that man undertakes on the path of salvation it is true to say that without God he can do nothing."[92] Wesley's characterization of salvation as permeated by grace affords Hauerwas the opportunity to ground character in the very human reality of community. It is also likely, and perhaps even more likely, that Hauerwas's discussion of grace as the grounding or source for the human connection with the divine in the community of the church derives from Barth's discussion of Aquinas and the Roman Catholic position on the relationship of reason and grace. According to Barth's reading of Aquinas, grace permeates all human nature to such an extent that it is impossible to separate the human qua human from the working of God in humanity through grace.[93] Understanding grace in such broad terms has been something that Protestants were wary of attempting, since it could be interpreted as a reduction of the supernatural work of God in his elect through the Holy Spirit to something that could be finally seen as merely human. In other words, in some interpretations

90. Hauerwas, *Character and the Christian Life*, 186. I am taking for granted here that Hauerwas believes sanctification to be likewise a work of the Holy Spirit.

91. Ibid., 188.

92. Lindstrom, *Wesley and Sanctification*, 212. Hauerwas quotes Lindstrom in *Character and the Christian Life*, 188.

93. For Hauerwas's discussion of Barth's thoughts on grace, see Hauerwas, *With the Grain of the Universe*, 163–64 n. 49.

what may be due to the grace of God in humanity may be interpreted as human accomplishment in other interpretations. If one cannot distinguish between human work and the grace of God in a particular action, then one cannot be assured that God is the primary agent. Therefore, Protestants have pursued a more supernatural means of God's movement discovered in the Holy Spirit (i.e., means beyond human control). Justification then becomes a work specifically attributable to God, with human participation left only thinly described. However, Hauerwas is uneasy about leaving the relationship between the human and the divine a mystery here. He would rather see the extension of grace to humanity more clearly credited.

> The problem does not focus so much on the notion of "mythical union" [in justification] with Christ, but rather on the inability to characterize the human side of that union. Protestant theology has resisted spelling out this union for fear that any attempt to explain or make this union intelligible in terms of a concrete view of the self would make the mystery of grace disappear in some reductionist form of empirical psychology. It may well be that grace is a mystery, but mystery is hardly preserved by resisting any attempt to understand the nature of the self that is graced.[94]

My own hesitancy about relying on grace as the point of connection between the human and divine in ecclesiology is that the church is always more than simply a human community. The divine nature of the formative community of church cannot be reduced to grace as the point of connection, though certainly grace is always *a* point of connection. Grace is a gift shared by church and world alike, but the church must always be more than world in this regard. By appealing to grace as the means of divine connection to the human, Hauerwas seems to lose some of the qualification he has made for the church as distinct from the world. He is left with the question, how is the grace that makes the church more than a human community different from the grace that is common to all humanity? In my estimation, ecclesiology must, therefore, be bound up in pneumatology if it is to be understood according to the communal identity to which it lays claim—the body of Christ. Hauerwas seems to concur, as his discussions of Milbank's development of the Holy Spirit in relation to the Trinity and the Eucharist above in-

---

94. Hauerwas, *Character and the Christian Life*, 193.

dicate, but he hardly makes this distinction clear in such theological terms.[95] If left at the level of "mere" grace, though "mere" is hardly a term I wish to use of grace, ecclesiology seems reduced to anthropology. In other words, if we leave the connection between the divine and the human community of church at the level of grace that is common to all humanity, we have succeeded only in reducing the church, once again, to the world.[96]

Hauerwas's strong emphasis on the pervasiveness of grace in the whole process of salvation—in both justification and sanctification—allows him to pursue the notion that the work of the Spirit is, in fact, a sociological reality in the human community of the church; i.e., that the work of the Holy Spirit has primarily to do with human activity as found in the community of the church qua community. Unfortunately, he seems to fall into the trap of believing the work of the Spirit is nothing more than this sociological reality.

> In loving and sanctifying us, [God] does not act contrary to or above his creation, but through and in it—i.e., the sanctification of men does not happen apart from the way we as men form ourselves through our acts and deeds. To be sanctified is to have one's character formed in a definite kind of way. What distinguishes Christian sanctification from the way men's lives are generally shaped and formed is not the process of formation itself but the basis and consequent shape of that formation.[97]

Hauerwas seems to believe the grace that works in forming Christians is the same grace that sustains the whole of humanity in the process of learning and being formed by specific actions and habits. Of course, this seems to blur the notion of grace as an agent distinct from the Holy Spirit throughout historical theology. The work of the Spirit in sanctification has, throughout theological history, consistently been

95. See Hauerwas, *Wilderness Wanderings*, 192; and *In Good Company*, 29. Both passages, as quoted above, indicate that Hauerwas wishes to interpret Milbank's social theory as a form of pneumatology. Unfortunately, Hauerwas only mentions this possible interpretation in passing. He does not explore it in any detail, nor does he make the direct link to his own work as an attempt at pneumatology.

96. One could perhaps read Hauerwas's last chapter in his Gifford Lectures as an attempt to move beyond grace to pneumatology, particularly in his discussions of Marshall's *Trinity and Truth*. See Hauerwas, *With the Grain of the Universe*, 207–15, especially 213 n. 16. However, Hauerwas never makes such a move clear or explicit.

97. Hauerwas, *Character and the Christian Life*, 194–95.

bounded as work only within and amongst the believing community of the church. It seems as though Hauerwas wishes to say that sanctification is both the Holy Spirit and grace without spelling out the doctrinal issues involved. Above we observed that the Holy Spirit is transcendent and infuses certain gifts on believing humanity. Here we see that the work of God through the communal work of the Spirit is completely socialized to such an extent that the only difference between the human community qua human and the human community divinely indwelled is the final appearance; ultimately the process is the same, leaving the church indistinct from the world. Hauerwas seems to equivocate between the work of the Holy Spirit and the permeating effects of grace in humanity, leading me to associate, at least, his pneumatology and ecclesiology with a thoroughgoing anthropology. Hauerwas appears, at times, to have become more sensitive to a transcendent reality of the Holy Spirit in his recent work, perhaps sensing the need for a defense against the critique of being a sociologist of religion rather than a theologian. However, he also still seems to be firmly planted in his belief that the work of the Spirit is only to be understood in terms of the narratively formed human community. I believe that Hauerwas's emphasis is rightly placed, in that the transcendent reality (i.e., the Spirit) has taken up a very real internal dwelling place; and this indwelling is not to be overridden by a more gnostic understanding of the reality of the Spirit as an ethereal being who has no material existence. For the church truly to be the "body of Christ," it must be more than a shell that is somehow "spatially" filled by a different spirit. Instead, the Spirit is to be discovered precisely in the activity of humans as they practice the life of Christ. This is why worship becomes such an important practice of the Christian community and why ecclesiology is central in all theology. Unfortunately, Hauerwas does not (indeed, according to his own narrative epistemology he cannot) spell this out in pneumatological or biblical terms. His perception that a systematic or more theoretical development of the doctrine of the Spirit would somehow destroy the narrative character of moral development will be taken up and answered in the next chapters, as we try to do the theology necessary to provide the theological and biblical language that Hauerwas has attempted to give us, albeit briefly, in sociological terms.

Conclusion

What we have seen in this chapter, as well as in the previous chapters, is a continued conversation with Hauerwas regarding his own theological evolution and the results of his pilgrimage out of liberalism. This conversation has allowed us to see that his own narrative has been shaped and formed by people who have "apprenticed" him in his theological work. It has also, through interaction with his aversion to modern metaphysics, forced us to reconfigure the way we go about construction in the theological project. Indeed, I suspect Hauerwas would be quick to say that he has no conception of the theological project. What he has instead is the church, in which we worship and are trained to rightly name the God we worship and to rightly live as people called by that name. Hauerwas provides little theory to critique and offers little construction to evaluate. What he would rather offer is his own life and the lives of those whom he has trained as servants in the church.

Nevertheless, some helpful points have been examined regarding the way Hauerwas views the church and about the way he understands incorporation into it. We have seen that Hauerwas is committed to a thoroughgoing ecclesiology, and that this entails the church rendering itself distinct from the world. The church must be church so that the world can know it is the world and is in need of redemption. The church becomes church by practicing the habits it has inherited over generations from the faithful through training. Thus, Hauerwas is attracted to Aristotle's epistemological ordering, granting precedence to action. Though Hauerwas provides little opportunity for critical interaction with statements of doctrinal belief (indeed he believes he cannot provide this), he does still rely on some theological claims that demonstrate he has not entirely distanced himself from foundationalism. The reversal of modern epistemological primacy, from thought to action simply means that Hauerwas now uses specific practices as his foundation, rather than specific statements of fact. Hauerwas sees the primary function of doctrine relating to its usefulness in training and giving language for worship. However, he does not consider the value of doctrine to be limited only (merely?) to a regulative role. For example, he has a rather explicit dependence on the doctrinal assertions associated with the Eucharist. Likewise, the doctrine of the universal church seems to always lurk implicit within Hauerwas's narrative as it is continually transmitted through tradition.

In spite of certain minor inconsistencies pointed out above, Hauerwas's ecclesiology seems largely appropriate for depicting how the church should regard itself, its activity as church, and its acquisition and understanding of knowledge. On the other hand, one major problem still appears to exist for Hauerwas. He understands the community of the church to be epistemologically and doctrinally sustained as a divine community by an appeal to the miraculous nature of the sacraments. Since the sacraments seem sporadic (i.e., they only happen once a week) and geographically limited (i.e., they only happen at church) with regard to narrative formation of the human community, the extent of their effect is questionable. In the end, the practices of the sacraments appear to be mere additions onto an already completed accounting of the interaction of God and humanity through a more purely sociological or anthropological development of ecclesiology; that is, divine implications are simply added onto a preexistent human community qua human. This would seem to open Hauerwas to the criticism of his work as reductionistic. In other words, his theology is finally left with a church whose connection to the divine is rather thin, causing Hauerwas to rest his doctrinal and epistemological assertions primarily on a sociological understanding of the church. What is needed to answer this critique is for Hauerwas to place his ecclesiology in the context of pneumatology—thereby avoiding the mystical characterization of the effects of the sacraments and providing for a more doctrinally thoroughgoing account of the interaction between the human and the divine. The transcendent reality of the Holy Spirit, when combined with a strong emphasis on human activity as equivalent with the Spirit's activity, provides one with the language in which to develop Hauerwas' theological realism regarding the church in history. Unfortunately, Hauerwas fails to substantial develop his themes in either biblical or theological language, causing a gap between his intentions and the tradition with which he wishes to link himself. Bridging this gap is the goal of the following chapters.

6

Locating the Narrative Question
on a Doctrinal Plane

Introduction

SINCE HAUERWAS WISHES TO MEASURE THE VERACITY OF DOCTRINE
and community in terms of the history of the community of the church,
we must attempt to discover if the history of the church can bear such
consideration. In other words, is the church's understanding of itself
as a formative community sufficient to warrant any comparison to
Hauerwas's narrative community; or perhaps more to the point, has the
church conducted itself in such a way as to require or even warrant
emulation? Hauerwas's answer to this question would likely be that the
church has "in places." In other places, the church has not lived up to
its calling. It would be impossible to evaluate *the* history of the church,
since many histories make up the life of the church. Hauerwas delves
deeply into lives that he believes warrant consideration. However, this
chapter will not pursue the various biographies that Hauerwas has delineated as a personification of the truthfulness of Jesus. Instead, we
will attempt to introduce a doctrinal element that could begin to bridge
the gap that Hauerwas purports between narrative and systematics.
Doctrine still serves a purpose in narrative thought, at times even rival-
ing the foundationalism of systematics. This chapter intends to briefly
introduce thoughts hinted at by others in the question of how best to understand the divine/human connection. Barth's instincts were correct in
the way that he turned the theological community toward Christology.
However, as the same community begins to attempt to understand how
this Christology impacts the lives of the faithful in the community of

the church, we are in need of a language in which to help describe appropriately what is occurring. Doctrinal language is needed in order to "tell the story" of the human community's connection to the divine. This chapter and the next are intended as the beginning of a conversation in which this language can be developed and understood.

Locating the Doctrinal Question Historically

A Brief History of Pneumatology and Hauerwas's Appropriation of It

It is significant that much of what little historical development we have of the doctrine of the Holy Spirit and its relationship to ecclesiology arose during the centuries in which the Constantinian presumption of membership in the society was equivalent with membership in the church. The Holy Spirit's activity was understood to be bounded by the sanctioned practices of the church under the rule of the sovereign governing authority, whomever that might have been in a given location.[1] Such a context required little doctrinal development of the relationship between pneumatology and ecclesiology, since ecclesiology was, more or less at times, presupposed as the guiding context for all doctrinal reflection, and was based more purely on the foundation of grace rather than on a specific doctrine of the Holy Spirit. The relationship between ecclesiology and pneumatology was simply a given for theologians and kings alike, who were both a part of the church.[2] Protestantism changed this to the extent that the indwelling of the Spirit and the incumbent responsibilities of having the Spirit were no longer explicitly subject to

1. I recognize that at least three positions existed during the Middle Ages with regard to the relationship between church and state. These included the papalist, or Guelf, position, and the imperialist, or Ghibelline, position, with a third mediating position defended in the fourteenth century by John Quidort of Paris. For a brief discussion of these three positions and their proponents, see Weisheipl, *Friar Thomas D'Aquino*, 191–92. Cf. Dulles, "Spiritual Community of Man," 144–46.

2. To say that it was a given is not to imply that discussion did not take place on the subject. However, most of the discussion in the Middle Ages was instigated by and centered on the question of whether the existing church was the community of the Holy Spirit, or if people should be looking for another more perfect community in the coming future. Thomas argued against the Joachimites, believing as he did that the existing church was the community of the Holy Spirit. See Dulles, "Spiritual Community of Man," 129–33.

political or to ecclesiologically institutional concerns, although obviously this move away from institutional qualification of those who were indwelled by the Spirit certainly carried political ramifications. Prior to the Reformation, the location or identifying characteristics of the Spirit's indwelling were, more or less, a settled issue, since theologians expected all citizens in good standing to be members of the body of Christ in some sense.[3] Following the Reformation, the work of the Holy Spirit came to be understood in a more directly applicable manner for Protestant laity.[4] The interaction between the human will and the directives of the Spirit became a prominent concern as each person, in some respects, became responsible for his or her own spiritual awakening and growth. While persons may have still had membership in the community or institution of the church, such personal responsibility also brought with it a certain amount of self-determinism. It is debatable whether this new self-determinism can rightly be called the origin of

3. Along these lines, several theologians have made the bold claim that Thomas Aquinas had no developed ecclesiology. Though other factors play a role in such a claim, one of the primary reasons for such an assertion is the belief that Thomas didn't need to develop an ecclesiology, since all humans shared in God's grace, and since the community of Christendom was the umbrella for all the known "civilized" world. See Kleutgen, *Institutiones theologica*, v; and Dempf, *Sacrum imperium*, 230–31. Dulles challenges such a notion, delineating the permeating nature of Thomas's ecclesiology throughout all his theology. See Dulles, "Spiritual Community of Man," 125–53. Dulles also demonstrates that the primacy of the internals over the externals of the church for Thomas evolved, and was reversed within Catholicism by the sixteenth century. However, the nineteenth and twentieth centuries have seen a return to Thomas's concern that the inner working of the Spirit be given preeminence over the institution of the church (146–51).

4. By stating the matter as a Protestant issue, I do not mean to imply that Catholicism today or prior to the Reformation was without consideration of the work of the Spirit in the lives of individuals. Killian McDonnell, ("Communion Ecclesiology and Baptism in the Spirit," 671–93) provides an interesting discussion of the ministry of the Spirit within and outside the sacraments. Tertullian makes a good case study for McDonnell, since Tertullian appears to link the baptism of the Spirit directly to the sacraments at the heart of ecclesiological communion. Likewise, John H. Wright ("Church," 25–44) argues strongly for the communal aspect of the church displayed particularly in the fact that the church is sacrament, in that it encompasses all seven of the generally recognized sacraments. For a short history of pneumatology as it was related to ecclesiology in Catholic theology in the last two centuries, see Hinze, "Releasing the Power of the Spirit in a Trinitarian Ecclesiology," 347–81.

the Enlightenment; nevertheless, it is true that the spiritual autonomy of Protestantism was fertile ground for Enlightenment individualism.[5]

What seems further apparent in the Reformation is that much of Protestantism rejected the pervasive nature of grace so prominent in pre-Reformation theology. One would thus expect a turn toward the Holy Spirit as a primary source of divine power.[6] Such was not the case, as Protestantism moved toward the primacy of Word over Spirit.[7] Of course, one of the primary exceptions to this rejection of grace in Protestantism was Wesley. Although Wesley could perhaps prove fruitful for Hauerwas due to his permeating understanding of grace and the possibility of wedding this understanding of grace to the work of the Holy Spirit, Hauerwas makes little explicit use of Wesley. Perhaps Hauerwas expects his audience to make some of the connections, given that he speaks from within the Methodist tradition. However, Hauerwas is prone to search elsewhere for his sources.[8]

5. It is interesting to note that those, including Hauerwas, who criticize the Protestant Reformation as the historical circumstance that spawned the Enlightenment seem to be implying a return to Constantinianism (by *Constantinianism* I mean an understanding of ecclesiology in which the church is equivalent to the kingdom of God on earth) by advocating a form of Thomistic primitivism. Though Hauerwas would be quick to object that a Constantinian context is well beyond his vision of how the community of the church is to function in the world, he cannot seem to escape the fact that his church, or polis, seems quite like the church of pre-Reformation centuries in many respects. Perhaps the similarity is only due to Hauerwas's vehement dislike of Enlightenment rationality. Nevertheless, the traditioned church in our contemporary context cannot help but ask, which tradition? Hauerwas seems to have settled on the church envisioned in Thomas's theology, though not on Thomas's historical circumstances. One wonders if such an approach to Thomas's theology makes it merely an idea or system to be applied to a different context, rather than a tradition that remains in existence today.

6. Though common grace still played a role for Reformers like Luther and Calvin, and for later theology, they almost unanimously rejected the notion of such a grace having any salvific efficacy. The possible exception to this is the Arminian strand of theology, which still maintained a doctrine of prevenient grace. Likewise, following the Reformation, reason quickly replaced a reliance on grace, especially in Protestant circles. See Placher, *Domestication of Transcendence*, especially chapter 5.

7. For an excellent summary of the impact of such a divergence between Catholics and Protestants on the doctrine of the Holy Spirit, see Moltmann, *Spirit of Life*, 1–14. Moltmann's proposed "Trinitarian pneumatology," which serves as his response, embodies and parallels many elements developed below in this chapter.

8. One may nonetheless wonder if Wesley is the best choice for Hauerwas. Obviously, being a Methodist, Hauerwas seems to have little "choice" in the matter. Nevertheless, Hauerwas says little about Wesley's own espousal of Enlightenment ideals and the relative ease with which his followers became an institution unto themselves. Hauerwas

What we are left with in Hauerwas is a rather "thin" description of the Holy Spirit. His more implicit narrative epistemology does not provide a space in which to offer such a description "in itself." As previous chapters have shown, for Hauerwas to engage in such a theological activity would contradict his "method." Certainly Hauerwas could make use of a doctrine of the Spirit in a grammatical sense, but such a doctrine could not provide him with any sure knowledge of what the Spirit and his relations with humanity are finally like. On the other hand, on occasion, Hauerwas does seem to intimate at an implicit doctrine of the Spirit within the context of his ecclesiology.[9] Without such a development of the Spirit as the dynamic within the formative community of the church, Hauerwas's ecclesiology is finally seen as merely anthropology.[10]

What remains to be seen in our study is how or if the anthropological or sociological understanding of ecclesiology that Hauerwas gives can fit with a somewhat systematic and specifically biblical rendering of the Spirit, and how the human may be included in a "doctrine" of the

---

is ultimately forced to look elsewhere for some important elements of what his tradition requires, thus being driven into Catholicism, and into Protestant communities that demonstrate a dynamic and permeating ecclesiology, i.e., the Mennonites. What Hauerwas could gain from his Wesleyan tradition is a more permeating notion of grace. True to the Arminian tradition, Wesley allowed for a thoroughgoing acceptance of prevenient grace, making his theology elide more easily with Thomism in this regard. It should be noted that prevenient grace is not the same thing as the common grace of which Calvin occasionally spoke. Cf. Calvin, *Institutes of the Christian Religion*, II.3.3, II.2.14, II.2.15, III.14.2. Keen chides Hauerwas for not using the notion of prevenient grace more thoroughly in Hauerwas's own understanding of how the Holy Spirit effects holiness in Christians. See Keen, "Human Person as Intercessory Prayer," 43.

9. Certainly Hauerwas would wish to affirm the dynamic ministry of the Holy Spirit as key to his ecclesiology. Unfortunately, as seen above, he does not make it explicit. In the systematic and scriptural work below, this study intends to show both the necessity of a permeating doctrine of the Spirit and what such a doctrine would look like.

10. Though it is well beyond the scope of this study, an interesting comparison could be made at this point between Hauerwas and Reinhold Niebuhr on the doctrine of the Holy Spirit. Niebuhr seems to have remained committed to certain liberal presuppositions regarding the way in which God interacted with nature, making it impossible for him to affirm any supernatural or miraculous workings of the Spirit. As a consequence, the Holy Spirit was largely absent from Niebuhr's theology. Perhaps Hauerwas's own commitment to certain anthropological presuppositions likewise prevents him from exploring pneumatology in any significant sense. Cf. King, *Omission of the Holy Spirit from Reinhold Niebuhr's Theology*.

Holy Spirit in such a way that such a doctrine allows for, even demands, the sociological treatment that Hauerwas offers.[11]

The Necessary Human Agent in Pneumatology

In order to accomplish a correlation between the scriptural witness and an anthropological or sociological rendering of the Holy Spirit, that is, to offer a narrative formation grounded more specifically in human interaction, this study intends to call for a reexamination of a critical part of the doctrine of the Holy Spirit. Karl Barth called for a significant change in emphasis in Christology in 1956 with his address to the Swiss Reformed Ministers' Association, a speech titled "The Humanity of God."[12] In this address, Barth critiqued the prevailing mood in theology toward Christology as being overly concerned with the deity of Jesus at the expense of his humanity. While not challenging the affirmation of Jesus's deity, Barth concluded that his deity must in fact include his humanity as a significant element. Thus as a corrective to what Barth believed was perhaps an emphasis on Jesus's deity among neo-orthodox theologians (an emphasis that diminished the value of his humanity), Barth launched a new emphasis in the study of Christology. Jesus's humanity could no longer be regarded as secondary to his deity.

Something akin to Barth's shift in emphasis needs to take place in the doctrine of the Holy Spirit. An emphasis on the human as a significant aspect of pneumatology seems warranted. Further, it seems necessary as a complement to the ecclesiology of Hauerwas. Barth recognized that "The church is the historical form of the work of the Holy Spirit and therefore the historical form of the faith."[13] However, as

---

11. This study is by no means alone in an attempt to connect contextualized theology, like Hauerwas's, to a thoroughgoing Trinitarianism through the Spirit. For example, one could easily read the intentions of this study in parallel with the work of D. Lyle Dabney in his lectures at Canberra in 1999 in a colloquium on the Holy Spirit titled "Tracking the Spirit in Tradition and Contemporary Thought." His lectures are published in *Starting with the Spirit*, in the Task of Theology Today series, edited by Gordon Preece and Stephen Pickard, 3–110. For a brief summary of his intentions see 22–27.

12. This address, along with two other related addresses, has been reprinted in Barth, *Humanity of God*, 37–65.

13. Barth, *Church Dogmatics II/2*, 160.

Hauerwas notes, "Barth never quite brings himself to explain how our human agency is involved in the Spirit's work."[14]

One would have expected Barth to have launched a similar emphasis upon the relationship of the human to the Holy Spirit, given his own concern for ecclesiology.[15] However, what we find in Barth is a "bifurcation" of the church, in that Barth makes a clear distinction between the church in its essence and the human church with all its encumbrances. The Scriptures indicate a church that is pure, in contradiction to what Barth saw in the human church. Thus Barth was reluctant to emphasize the humanness of ecclesiology beyond what can be said in a somewhat christological sense. Thus, as Nicholas Healy notes, "Barth avoids the error of a one-sided sociological description of the church's identity by making the opposite error, presenting us with a one-sided doctrinal description."[16] Barth apparently believed that he must shield his ecclesiology from the kind of deep rootedness in history that Hauerwas so clearly embraces. While Barth does protect his ecclesiology, he is finally left with an ahistorical doctrine of the church. As Joseph Mangina makes clear, "Barth purchases this high ecclesiology at a high price, namely that of dehistoricizing the church."[17]

Ironically, Barth remains too abstract in his description of the church for his use of the Holy Spirit to become subject to the frailty of human history. Barth's pneumatology could not overcome this abstraction in order to make the connection between the supernatural of the Spirit and the supposed natural of ecclesiology. Barth is finally left with abstractions on both counts. However, as Stephen Sykes rightly makes clear, "The language of sociology and the language of theology may be separate, but the reality of divine and human power is not. It is not parallel, or merely co-ordinated; it is inevitably, and dangerously, mixed."[18]

14. Hauerwas, *With the Grain of the Universe*, 145.

15. This was Barth's desire, as indicated by his statement regarding his wish to pursue "the possibility of a theology of the third article" (Barth, *Theology of Schleiermacher*, 278). Unfortunately, Barth never takes up the development of such a theme as intentionally as he did other subjects. However, he laid some helpful groundwork by placing his understanding of the church in the confines of pneumatology. "In *Church Dogmatics* IV, 1–3, I at least had the good instinct to place the church, and then faith, love, and hope, under the sign of the Holy Spirit" (278).

16. Healy, "Logic of Karl Barth's Ecclesiology," 263.

17. Mangina, "Bearing the Marks of Jesus," 270. Cf., 280.

18. Sykes, *Identity of Christianity*, 207.

Barth's human church cannot serve as a model for the intertwining of the human and divine in the work of the Holy Spirit, since to make use of any specifically human community as a model for the Spirit's work would compromise the sovereignty of God. Thus the work of the Spirit must remain rather abstract for Barth, and the church must remain a theory.

Alongside this criticism of Barth lies the question of Barth's identifying the Spirit within the doctrine of the Trinity. Robert Jenson argues that Barth lapses into a form of binitarianism by identifying the Spirit as the bond between the Father and the Son, rather than as something distinct from, yet like, the Father and the Son.[19] George Hunsinger attempts to defend Barth against such an accusation, but only seems to confirm that Barth's doctrine of the Spirit is wanting with regard to its distinct personhood.[20] Barth was so focused on the cross of Christ as the culmination of God's salvific history that the eschatological nature of the church is underestimated. As Mangina points out,

> Since Barth treats the cross as bringing history to a close, the Spirit's work is 'short-circuited'. The Spirit can only appear as a predicate of Christ's reconciling work, a *manifestation* of the latter rather than an *agency* of its own.[21]

Thus far in recent theology's study of the Holy Spirit, particularly amongst conservative Protestants, emphasis has been placed on the supernatural elements of the Spirit's being and work.[22] While this study does not wish to diminish the reality of the supernatural in the Spirit's work, this study presumes that the working of the Spirit in the natural has been overlooked or ignored, and that the supernatural work of the Spirit has been overemphasized, especially as the Spirit relates to humanity and as the Spirit retains an identity both within the human and juxtaposed to the human.[23] In essence, the doctrine of the Holy Spirit

19. Jenson, "You Wonder Where the Spirit Went," 296–304.

20. Hunsinger, *Disruptive Grace*, 148–85. This chapter was previously presented by Hunsinger at AAR. Buckley critically interacts with the earlier presentation in Buckley, "Field of Living Fire," 81–102. Also cf. Hütter, "Church as Public," especially 340–45.

21. Mangina, "Bearing the Marks of Jesus," 270; emphasis Mangina's.

22. For a brief history of the various emphases in pneumatology, particularly amongst conservative Protestantism, see Bloesch, *Holy Spirit*, 98–209.

23 As will be seen below, some reaction against Schleiermacher's blurring of the lines between the human spirit and the Holy Spirit also undoubtedly contributed to this

in the twentieth and twenty-first centuries has become a doctrine of an invisible force or power distinct from the church—a power that can be accessed by individuals primarily and by the church secondarily, if at all, in a supernatural way that overpowers or removes the human as the primary active agent in sanctification.[24] As Berkhof has noted,

> For many Protestants it is difficult to understand that the Spirit has anything to do with the institutional and organizational character of the church. The reason is that they have such an individualistic and spiritualistic or, at best, personalistic conception of the Spirit that they do not understand that God created structures as well as persons and that in his saving work he is also interested in structures insofar as they can serve his purposes. The New Testament has not the slightest trouble in

aversion of the Spirit's being identified in the natural elements of human community.

This study will make no attempt to relate to ecclesiology other aspects of the doctrine of the Holy Spirit, which may be more directly attributable to supernaturalism in total. Such aspects as the work of the Spirit in creation, justification, intercession, and the like may be useful topics of related discussion, but are beyond the scope of this study. Here, we will focus primarily on the interaction of the Spirit and the human in human action, specifically in human sanctification.

Likewise, this study will make no attempt to distinguish between a Jewish and a Greek rendering of the Spirit. While I am confident that a discussion of an Old Testament theology of the Spirit would yield fruitful material for further examination, I will not pursue this avenue here. I suspect the conclusions of an Old Testament theology of the Spirit would be similar to the rather Greek rendering that this study places in a more Aristotelian context. I also know that in the amalgam of cultural influences of the first century, it may be impossible to entirely distinguish the Greek from the Jewish influences on Paul, for instance. Therefore, we will proceed with an examination of the Greek influences or parallels, knowing that such influences on first-century Christianity were by no means monolithic.

24. This can be seen explicitly in at least two popular models of sanctification in conservative Protestant circles. Both the Pentecostal and Keswick models of sanctification are intentional in the removal of the human element in the progression of holiness. Though their intentions are quite admirable, they unfortunately simply give further credence to the gnostic notion that sanctification is individualistic and rather mystical. See Horton, "Pentecostal Perspective," 127–35; and McQuilkin, "Keswick Perspective," 174–83. Cf. the Wesleyan, Pentecostal, and Contemplative views in Alexander, *Christian Spirituality*, 95–201. These views are primarily a passive response to the pursuit of holiness, leaving the human element out, or at best, suppressed. While I do not wish to engage in a debate regarding which view of sanctification is appropriate (my own view should be apparent from the remainder of this study), I simply wish to point out that the popularity of passive views is prominent amongst conservative Protestants.

seeing that the Spirit is connected with outward acts, ministries and organizations.[25]

This study wishes to propose that a more appropriate understanding of the Holy Spirit can be found precisely in a stronger ecclesiology.[26] The church is where the Spirit is predominantly active, and here in the natural processes of the human community rather (or perhaps more primarily) than in supernatural means that disregard the human. The Spirit is most active in the deliberate worship and training by the church of its members to be church. In this, Hauerwas has rightly emphasized ecclesiology. Unfortunately, he has developed his ecclesiological themes without extensive discussion of the Holy Spirit. A brief summary of his discussion may be warranted before this study proceeds into a substantive biblical discussion.

Hauerwas, though not inclined to demonstrate his project in epistemological terms, makes heavy use of an Aristotelian epistemology, in that the practices of the Christian community—particularly the sacraments—are what matter in order to discover (or, better, in order to become like) the Truth (i.e., Jesus). Hauerwas is not particularly interested in defending his program against Enlightenment criteria of truth. To make such a defense, he would need a rather developed theory of action. Though he once seemed intent to provide such a theory, he has since abandoned such projects as counterproductive.[27] His concern in recent work is primarily to help the church realize the impropriety of using theories of metaphysics (i.e., *a priori* categories) as foundational. The church's goal is not to emulate the world to such an extent that it is accepted or even admired as an integral part of the culture or society. This emulation of the world is what Hauerwas understands such theories as accomplishing.[28] Instead the church is to exist as church, so that the world might know the difference between itself and the church. By

25. Berkhof, *Doctrine of the Holy Spirit*, 51.

26. For a good, though brief, discussion of the relationship of the corporate nature of the Spirit's presence to the individual and the primacy of the Spirit's presence, see Winn, "Holy Spirit and the Christian Life," 47–57. This is, likewise, how I read Hauerwas's intentions, though he does not use such language to describe his work.

27. For Hauerwas's attempt to develop a theory of action, see his dissertation, Hauerwas, *Character and the Christian Life*, especially 83–128.

28. See most recently his discussions of how Christian ethics has had as its goal the success of Americanism. Hauerwas, *Better Hope*, 23–34.

being a community that exists as Christ's body, the church is practicing an epistemology of action. It should be noted that Hauerwas is not opposed to epistemology. He simply wishes to redefine where epistemology begins and ends; and for Hauerwas, the beginning and end must be within the church. To look elsewhere for verification of the church's life is idolatry.[29]

Some of the implications of Hauerwas's project thus far have been made apparent. A heightened ecclesiology allows for concentrated focus on the activities of the Christian community to such an extent that it is finally epistemologically foundational. One might say in Hauerwas's case that it is all his epistemology.[30] It could even be said that such an ecclesiology allows Hauerwas to complete his narrative system, since a fairly radical material ecclesiology is necessary for narrative to derive a consistent sense of the practice of doctrine. This is especially the case as he grounds his narrative epistemology (i.e., his ecclesiology) in the church's practice of worship. Hauerwas alludes to the notion that this might somehow constitute a doctrine of the Holy Spirit, but he cannot finally arrive at a doctrine in and of itself, since such a thing cannot exist for the church.[31] As was seen in the previous chapter, the closest he can come is to indicate that perhaps Milbank's sociological rendering of theology fulfills this needed development.[32] Unfortunately, Hauerwas only makes the suggestive comments concerning how pneumatology

29. This is why I find it somewhat ironic that Hauerwas has not spent more time developing the scriptural language that could provide the primary language for his ecclesiological concerns as they are connected to a Trinitarian doctrine of God. Though he does occasionally discuss scriptural passages specific to ecclesiology, Hauerwas spends little time discussing the import or further connection of the various passages, perhaps because he believes what can be said has been said, or because he wishes to avoid sounding like he is making some type of foundationalistic claim to a document rather than appealing to the tradition of the community. Unfortunately, either his readers are left to presume that the human community that he calls church has a legitimate divine connection, or they must make the connection themselves.

30. As has been noted several times already, Hauerwas has no explicit epistemology. Nevertheless, he gives an implicit nod toward an Aristotelian preference for the training that comes through the habituation of action and the primacy of action in a narrative epistemology. Doctrinal language finds its meaning in "use," in a Wittgensteinian sense, rather than in a simple representation of reality. Such a definition of his epistemology could serve as well for a definition of his ecclesiology.

31. See Hauerwas's comments with regard to Milbank's Christian sociology, Hauerwas, *Wilderness Wanderings*, 192.

32. Ibid.

and the narrative community might be connected; he does not develop the connection in any detail, nor does he indicate that his own narrative ecclesiology should be likewise understood.

As has been noted in the previous chapters, one of the primary problems facing Hauerwas is the critique that God's transcendent presence in the person of the Holy Spirit lapses completely into the material sociology of the church: in other words, the problem of anthropological reductionism. By stressing ecclesiology in such a strong manner, Hauerwas is left with little sense of an external, or transcendent, reality of the Holy Spirit. While he may not find this terribly problematic, since externality could be construed as implying theological or systematic independence, nevertheless it seems that historical and biblical considerations warrant at least an examination of how his "doctrine" of narrative ecclesiology informs and depends on a biblical rendering of the Holy Spirit.

Hauerwas could resolve this problem by articulating his understanding of the relationship between the Holy Spirit and ecclesiology, but as was seen above in chapter 5, he remains largely silent on the issue.[33] Whether this silence stems either from a presumption that anyone can see that the church is the divinely indwelled community precisely because it is the church (which begs the question), or from an unwillingness to "spell out" the doctrinal warrant for his position in order to avoid anything resembling foundationalism, we are finally left with a virtual absence of discussion on the subject. This leaves his doctrinal discussions wanting when it comes to the connection of the church to its object of worship. However a further problem arises when one turns to the biblical discussions of ecclesiology in that they seem interwoven with a discussion of pneumatology. So not only do Hauerwas's own doctrinal discussions come up short; he also seems to be reading the Scriptures rather selectively.

Conclusion

This brief chapter has pointed a way out of the corner into which Hauerwas seems to have backed. He wishes to have a robust ecclesiology epistemologically based in the life of the community itself. On the

33. See section 6 of chapter 5, titled, "The Missing Element of the Holy Spirit in Hauerwas's Church."

other hand, he wishes to maintain that this community is grounded in the life (and death and resurrection) of a man who lived two millennia ago. Further, this community is an enfleshment of God as it purely depicts, or performs, the life of Jesus. The connection in Hauerwas between the community of faith and the Lord whom it worships remains thin, in that Hauerwas is finally reliant on doctrinal considerations that seem somewhat sporadic (i.e., sacramental formation). Hauerwas has not explored the life of the church from a more traditional Trinitarian aspect in terms of the third person—the Holy Spirit. The humanity of the Holy Spirit may seem an odd or contrived inroad into pneumatology. However, as will be seen in the biblical witness in the next chapter, the human community is precisely the location in which one should explore pneumatology. In other words, pneumatology, as it relates to humans, is best understood as a subset of ecclesiology.

7

The Humanity of the Holy Spirit

Ecclesiology as Pneumatology in Scripture

Introduction: A Brief Word on Warrant for a Biblical Engagement

IT MAY SEEM SURPRISING TO ENGAGE HAUERWAS AT THE LEVEL OF biblical interpretation; however, I believe he would find such a discussion in line with his ecclesiological epistemology, not to mention the fact he would expect such a treatment from some of his Anabaptist friends. Hauerwas himself seems open to listening to the discussion, even if he does not wish to engage it in any detail. Hauerwas claims "To the extent that we [theologians] abandoned Scripture as integral to the theological enterprise, we allowed the Scripture to be separated from church-centered practice."[1] A scriptural development and discussion of themes raised by him seems a good beginning point for continuing the conversation he has begun.

Hauerwas has devised a compelling narrative ecclesiology but has yet to provide the scriptural language that may either attach it to theological tradition or distance it from what is accepted modernist theological teaching. It is not that he avoids Scripture or does not occasionally engage it. He actually does some very good work in scriptural

---

1. Hauerwas, *Unleashing the Scriptures*, 9. Hauerwas demonstrates throughout this work that he is fully in favor of Scripture's use as a primary document and language for the church. The problem, as he sees it, is that rather than human lives' being subjected to the Bible and to those who can read it rightly, the Bible has been subjected to the interpretive habits of people schooled in American democratic ideology. This chapter is an attempt to read Scripture rightly with regard to understanding the church and the Holy Spirit.

interpretation.[2] His problem is that he has not substantively engaged Scripture on the doctrine of the Holy Spirit, leaving his connection to the tradition rather tenuous.

On historical grounds, it is difficult to imagine a premodern theologian doing theology without a serious engagement with the text of Scripture. This is true for both Protestant and Catholic theologians, though at times more or less true for specific individuals in each tradition. Likewise, the church has relied on the Scriptures to establish the boundaries, even the very language in many instances, of theological reflection. One might expect that the fourfold method of premodern theology and biblical interpretation would create a context in which interpretation is as arbitrary as the modern context in which the interpreter is largely autonomous over the text and traditional teaching. On the contrary, what we find in some of the more widely known theologians of the premodern era is that they have a high regard for the text of Scripture over the imagination of the interpreter. Aquinas declares, "[N]othing essential to the faith is contained in the Spiritual sense of one passage which is not clearly expressed in the literal sense of another."[3] Thus, Aquinas establishes boundaries on scriptural interpretation and theological reflection based in a presupposed connection between the text of Scripture and theological teaching for the church.

Though a beginning point for the development and the discussion of doctrine in the dialectic between church and Scripture may be difficult to tease out of the conversation, scriptural reflection must be done. [4] In other words, though *an important question is* whether the queries posed to Scripture come first or whether the scriptural teaching comes first, a point in the conversation must come when discussion of the scriptural text becomes paramount. This is especially the case for Protestants but is by no means a secondary consideration for Roman Catholics. Therefore, the following discussion of Scripture is offered as

2. As noted above, Hauerwas's commentary on Matthew is masterful in its identification of many of the pressing cultural and theological themes running throughout Matthew's account of the gospel story. Plus, Hauerwas demonstrates an acute awareness of hermeneutical sensitivity.

3. Thomas Aquinas, *Summa Theologiae*, reprinted in *On Nature and Grace*, I, Q. I, 10, response to objection 1.

4. This is one of the primary thrusts of Hauerwas's work *Unleashing the Scripture*. See especially 15–18, 47–62.

a forum in which to place some of the debate about the indwelling ministry of the Holy Spirit as it relates to a thoroughgoing ecclesiology.

Along more substantive lines, Hauerwas raises several issues in his preference for narrative, particularly on an epistemological level. Specifically, his preference for narrative as primary in epistemology, and the way in which this preference places a distinct emphasis on ecclesiology, challenges several modern assumptions about the way in which theology should proceed. Such a reordering of theological epistemology raises several questions: Is a preference for the narrative community (Aristotle) over a preference for the individual (Kant) warranted, and how would one discover such warrant? Where is the locus of moral or spiritual formation? Is moral formation located in an individual's conscience, or in an individual's habits as observed by others? What is the relationship between the human and the divine in moral and spiritual formation, and how can this relationship best be expressed in theological language? What finally remains to be asked of our analysis thus far is how his theological enterprise fits with the tradition of the church, specifically with the tradition of the church as it is grounded in Scripture. While it may be beyond the scope of this study to engage in a historical discussion of theology (comparing several theologians to our central figure), the biblical avenue of study does remain open to us. Though this chapter makes no pretense of being a comprehensive treatment, several suggestions will be made as to how Scripture might best be understood, particularly in respect to the questions raised above by Hauerwas's reordering of the theological enterprise.

Scriptural language, though not the primary subject of this chapter, may be regarded as multifaceted. As was clearly seen above, Hauerwas was opposed to the immodest use of language in theology that purports to depict or describe the reality of a God who cannot be captured in human language. This is what Hauerwas believes systematics did to doctrinal language, (i.e., systematics limited it to the singular function of representation or reference). Hauerwas found descriptive language to be overly benign in that it does not "do" anything for or in the church. In this sense, systematic language appeared rather passive. Hauerwas affirmed a more active role for language, but in so doing seemed to waffle a bit on the connection language might have to literal reference. He did not wish to subscribe in a rigid fashion to language's having representational qualities, but he still used some doctrinal language as though it were representational (e.g., his understanding of the Eucharist).

The language of Scripture seems to encompass both the active and the passive senses of language, which seem to be a requisite part of any theology for the church. Scripture does at times seem to make referential or descriptive claims (albeit in a modest sense). However, scriptural language does not remain *merely* referential or descriptive. The pneumatological discussions in Scripture, seen below, confirm that action is a central locus for the "doing" of any good (i.e., biblically coherent, or biblically performative) theology. On this doctrinal point, Scripture displays an active language that affirms and yet significantly surpasses the passivity of mere literal claims of doctrine. This is, finally perhaps, a point at which narrative theology and systematics in a more modest sense may intersect.[5]

The Holy Spirit as he is described in Scripture is a rather daunting subject for concluding chapters in this study. Rather than attempting to develop every and all themes of pneumatology from Scripture, this study will focus more specifically on the question of the nature of the Spirit's indwelling ministry as it relates to ecclesiology. Some of the subjects discussed will derive specifically from issues that Hauerwas raises, in an attempt to demonstrate how his ecclesiology may more appropriately be located in a scriptural pneumatology. I intend to make

5. Since I do not wish to fall into the same trap as the systematicians that Hauerwas criticizes above, I will not attempt a theoretical defense of systematics per se. Instead, I will engage the language of Scripture on certain doctrinal issues with a view to expanding and revising pneumatology and ecclesiology to such an extent that that the interplay between Scripture and doctrinal reflection on the practices of the church encompasses Hauerwas's concerns. While this may seem like a retreat from epistemology, it is instead an attempt to conform to the epistemology that narrative theologians advocate, while at the same time incorporating a "cautious" doctrinal realism more akin to systematics. On "cautious realism," see Stiver, *Philosophy of Religious Language*, 23–29, 131.

Such an understanding of the systematic endeavor may coincide more closely with a conscious attempt to vacillate between the theology of scholastics such as Thomas and the theology of the Reformers. In more contemporary terms, I will be engaging in biblical studies more akin to biblical theology than to modern systematics. However, historically speaking, I believe such a method to be the most defensible and appropriate method for theological engagement within the church. While I do not wish to begin here a discussion of the relationship between the biblical texts and the community of the church, I recognize that it is in such a dialectic of interpretation that the primary source for theology is found, particularly for those from a conservative Protestant persuasion.

explicit in biblical and theological language what seems implicit in the thought of Hauerwas. Within this, we shall see how a critical (i.e., scriptural) adaptation of Hauerwas's understanding of ecclesiology is made stronger by doctrinal development in pneumatology. In the process, we will also see how such a combination of Hauerwasian ecclesiology and biblical pneumatology provides a corrective to some peculiarly modern emphases within the doctrine of the Holy Spirit. Given the way in which Hauerwas has established his position in contrast to specific modernistic tendencies that he finds problematic in the contemporary church, these subjects are perhaps best introduced through a series of questions about specific pneumatological issues: Does the Spirit primarily indwell the individual for work through and in the individual, or is his indwelling ministry directed primarily toward the community of the church, to work through and in the church? How does the community formed by the Spirit as church function—is it first a human community that is transformed into a supernatural community, or is it first supernatural, due to the indwelling of the Spirit, with its natural presence being merely circumstantial? What is the primary goal and function of the indwelling ministry of the Spirit in Scripture? With these questions as a point of entrance into the doctrine of the Holy Spirit, let us begin with an examination of the language of indwelling in Scripture.

Scriptural Development of Specific Themes in Pneumatology

The Indwelling of the Holy Spirit: Location or Authority?

One of the primary questions that seems to pinpoint the issue for Hauerwas is to ask, where is God presently? One might think the obvious answer to be "up there," wherever "there" might be. The transcendent nature of God so permeates our understanding that we cannot fathom his existence anywhere but in separation from us. Hauerwas attempts to resolve this by turning to an Aristotelian epistemology. This is also one of the fundamental problems we saw Pannenberg attempting to resolve in his discussion of the Trinity. He was attempting to derive the Trinitarian nature of God primarily from God's activity in creation, especially from revelation of himself through the Scriptures and preeminently in the incarnation. Ultimately, God's activity in creation is, for

Pannenberg, the only place that humans could hope to actually catch a glimpse of God. Locating God's identity in his activity was in contrast to what Pannenberg believed to be the traditional approach of beginning with a theory of the divine and deriving the nature of each member of the Trinity from that theory. What the following section is intended to accomplish is to take such an historical God seriously with regard to his activity as Holy Spirit. While it may be true that God's existence is something well beyond us, the incarnation and the coming of the Holy Spirit make God's presence a very human reality. What then do we mean when we say that the Holy Spirit indwells humans?

The concept of indwelling is not a particularly new subject, considering it is addressed in Scripture, many early church fathers, and is certainly present in the creeds as well, though the creeds were not significantly comprehensive. While the creeds do mention the Holy Spirit, it is with brief reference and little more than an acknowledgment of the Spirit's existence. One notable point to stress regarding the early church's conception of the work of the Spirit in human community is the order in which the Nicene Creed addresses the subject of the Holy Spirit. Interestingly enough, the Nicene Creed gives priority to the work of the Spirit in the community of faith over the discussion of the Spirit's essence. As Winn points out,

> Yet the Nicene creed, for all its brevity, does give first place to the life-giving role of the Holy Spirit, mentioning the Spirit's noetic work in a subordinate position. It has not been a good thing that our Western tradition has for centuries neglected this simple insight.[6]

As will be discussed below, the traditional approach to indwelling typically entails some type of spatial reference. It is possible that early Fathers like Basil laid the groundwork for such an approach, but indeed he was simply attempting to carefully restate the language of Scripture. "The Spirit is indeed the dwelling place of the saints, and the saint is a suitable abode for the Spirit, since he has supplied God with a house, and is called a temple of God."[7] What the spatial indwelling of the Holy Spirit refers to is the idea that he actually takes up residence within human flesh. In other words, he comes into humans in much the same

6. Winn, "Holy Spirit and the Christian Life," 51.
7. Basil the Great, *On the Holy Spirit*, 95.

way that someone would go into a house. Location then becomes the operative context for understanding the indwelling of the Holy Spirit.

The precedence for a spatial reference perhaps comes to us not only through scriptural references to humans as the "temple of the Holy Spirit" (1 Cor 3:16, 6:19) but also somewhat by default, or by analogy from, among other passages, an interpretation of the scriptural passage about the unclean spirit who leaves a person only to desire to return to that person (Matt 12:43–45).

> Then [the unclean spirit] says "I will return to my *house* from which I came"; and when it comes, it finds it unoccupied, swept, and put in order. Then it goes, and takes along with it seven other spirits more wicked than itself, and they *go in and live there*; and the last state of that man becomes worse than the first. That is the way it will also be with this evil generation. (emphasis mine)

This analogy of the person to a house has traditionally been interpreted spatially, as though the unclean spirits actually live inside the body of the person, animating limbs and controlling the connection between brain and body.[8] Such a concept of spirits dwelling spatially within people has likewise become the traditional interpretation of how the Holy Spirit indwells people. While the intent of this study is not to resolve the issues surrounding demonology, it may be useful to reconsider how the indwelling of unclean spirits takes place in order to provide insight as well into a better understanding of how the indwelling of the Holy Spirit takes place.

The inhabitation of demons has recently been explained more precisely as primarily an issue of authority rather than of spatial habitation. In other words, the way demon possession takes place in Scripture is that demons have the authority over humans first, and it is because of this authority that they can do things to and through humans. The issue of possession is more an issue of who has authority than of where the demons geographically or physiologically are located.[9] Certainly

8. The association with other passages regarding the physical impacts of being possessed by a demon or demons makes the physical presence of the demon a primary, if not *the* primary, concern.

9. Though still convinced that physiological location is important, Dickason does acknowledge that the primary issue in the scriptural examples of demonization is the control of the demon over the person (Dickason, *Demon Possession*, 37–40, 217–41).

demons still did spectacular deeds through and to humans (e.g., the child who fell into the fire and the water [Matt 17:14–18]; the demoniac who broke the chains with which the people had bound him [Luke 8:26–39]; the violent men who had their demons cast into the swine [Matt 8:28–34]). When Jesus addresses the issue of demon possession, each reference in Scripture says that he "cast them out" of people. This would seem to indicate that spatial reference is at least important. Nevertheless, the more pressing issue still appears to be authority. If one does not give one's allegiance to the demons, they will not be able to work their powers over humans. On the other hand, if one gives one's allegiance to demons (or at least remains uncommitted to the lordship of Christ), then that person is more susceptible to being duped into following after things that are not of Christ. This seems to be the point of the unclean spirit and the house mentioned above. Physical activities are more likely the result of a volitional control primarily, and of physical animation secondarily.

It may be profitable to reconsider the indwelling ministry of the Holy Spirit as a counterpoint to the issue of possession by demons. In other words, perhaps the indwelling of the Holy Spirit is not a spatial issue either but is likewise an issue of authority. By making indwelling an issue of authority over the believer, I do not mean to say the Holy Spirit inhabits people to work them like a puppet with strings and wires. Instead, the Holy Spirit works to establish the lordship of Jesus in his body—the church. To be "possessed" by the Holy Spirit, if we may use that term, is to give authority to the One who rightly deserves the allegiance of the church, that is the head of the body—Christ. This would seem to fit well with the primary goal of the Holy Spirit proposed by Pannenberg—"to glorify the Son".[10] This would also seem to fit well with Hauerwas's driving concern for the primacy of ecclesiology. The work of the Spirit is to make the church to be the church as it is witness to the world about the lordship of Jesus. Finally, conceiving the Spirit's

---

Dickason places strong weight on the issue of internal versus external influence for understanding and then dealing with the demonic. Nevertheless, Dickason does still focus on the issue of who has control over the person as the primary point of reference for the resolution of demonization.

10. See Pannenberg, *Systematic Theology*, 3:16–17. Pannenberg is by no means the only one to discuss this work of the Spirit as his primary office. Luther identifies it as such in his lectures on the Gospel of John. See Luther, "Sermons on the Gospel of St. John," 127.

indwelling as primarily an issue of authority could help us better understand the corporate nature of the Holy Spirit's indwelling, which is the subject of the next section.

Of course, a great distinction exists between demons and the Holy Spirit. Demons are spatial creatures, whereas the Spirit is not spatially confined. Due to their existence as finite creatures, demons are understandably limited to spatial reference. The Holy Spirit seems unbounded in this regard. Thus, any analogy between demon possession and the indwelling of the Spirit is rather limited in its ability to depict the indwelling of the Spirit. Certainly authority may be a primary issue in indwelling, but the comparison should not be pushed too far.

In order to engage more clearly the subject of the Spirit's corporate indwelling in the primary language of the church, we must now return our attention to the text of Scripture. This will be done by examining the way in which the indwelling of humanity by the Holy Spirit in specific passages in Scripture creates a context in which the human community of the church may be regarded as the contact point between the human and the divine, (i.e., the Holy Spirit constitutes participation of the human in the divine). As will be developed further, this is in contrast to the more typical, individuated contact point found through the Spirit (e.g., Pannenberg). In other words, as Hauerwas has painstakingly attempted to demonstrate, ecclesiology is the only context in which to "do" theology, both from a systematic approach (e.g., reflection on doctrine in language) and from a narrative approach. Though this assertion about the importance of ecclesiology for doing theology may not answer every question raised thus far, it should provide sufficient discussion for granting many of Hauerwas's ecclesiological concerns.

Indwelling as Body

One of the more thorough teachings on the work of the Holy Spirit in Scripture comes from the lips of the Lord Jesus Himself.[11] The Gospel of

---

11. A clarification should be made at the outset of this section. This study will simply presume the traditional authorship of the biblical books and attributions of certain statements to Jesus in the Gospels. While I am certainly aware of the debates about authorship and the reliability of narrative dialogue in the gospel accounts, I will attempt to keep any discussion of this to a minimum. This presumption will be glaring at times, such as in assuming the Pauline authorship of several epistles attributed to him. However, it would take this study well beyond the subject matter of the texts in

John records in chapters 14–16 several aspects of the Spirit's being and work. Jesus makes it clear here that the Helper (παρακλητον) who is to come to them will be one who is of the same kind as Jesus (αλλον— "another of the same kind"). This Helper will not merely be one who will assist or accelerate human capacities. On the contrary, he will actually be "with you" and "in you" (14:17). These phrases are typically used to support the notion of the Spirit's real presence in the physical bodies of believers.[12] While I do not wish to dismiss such an understanding of this passage out of hand, I nevertheless do find a significant problem with understanding John 14:17 as referring to individual physical bodies. Since the pronoun ("you") used with both prepositional phrases is plural (υμιν), it would appear as though this teaching is not directed primarily toward individual believers. One could respond that Jesus was merely using such a plural pronoun because he was speaking to more than one person. In other words, since Jesus was speaking to a group, he had to use the plural; but he was actually directing the teaching of the indwelling Spirit toward each individual person.[13] What such an interpretation represents is, at best, an unwarranted presumption of post-Enlightenment individualism and perhaps at worst an anachronistic foisting of the individual into a context that would not have conceived of things in primarily individualistic terms. It seems reasonable, given both an Aristotelian and Jewish context, to understand Jesus's use of the plural in this passage as intentional, in that he wished to speak to the disciples as a collective rather than as individuals.

On another note with regard to this passage, if the reference is spatial, then where is the Spirit, really? In other words, if the Spirit is spatially present in individuals, then where, physiologically or psychologically speaking, is he in the body of the believer? Since this question seems impossible to answer, and since we do not wish to dismiss the

---

question to attempt to establish the reliability of authorship in each case. Likewise, the issue of authorship does not enter significantly into the discussion of the interpretation of specific texts in this study.

12. Commentators are typically careful of making such an assertion boldly. Many have left their options open by claiming that these phrases could be referring to either individual believers or to the church (e.g., Morris, *Gospel according to John*, 577; and Beasley-Murray, *John*, 257–58). Nevertheless, many assert individuated physical indwelling as the most likely (e.g., see Barrett, *Gospel according to St. John*, 387; and Tenney, *John*, 220).

13. Barrett, *Gospel according to St. John*, 387.

concept of indwelling as merely metaphorical language, we must search elsewhere for an answer to the location of the Holy Spirit.

If we say that the Spirit is present in the plurality of Jesus's audience, does this necessitate some type of corporate spatial understanding of indwelling? Since Protestants have been reluctant to believe that the Holy Spirit indwells the church as a collective, instead favoring the notion of indwelling as individualistic, it is difficult to imagine a Protestant rendering of the corporate nature of indwelling. Nevertheless, it is not outside the realm of support from Scripture. In light of other passages in Scripture, discussed below, it may in fact be more plausible to understand Jesus's reference here neither to spatial indwelling in individual believers nor to spatial indwelling in a collective plurality but to the way in which the Spirit works authoritatively in the community of the church. This would mean that rather than on the way in which the Holy Spirit might indwell individual believers or a collection of individuals, attention should be given more directly to how the Holy Spirit indwells a community of believers qua community. In Hauerwas's terms, attention should be given to the narratively formed community, which is a reversal of the Enlightenment focus on the individual as primary. Ecclesiology must, therefore, be the context for pneumatology; community is epistemologically, and perhaps even ontologically, prior to the individual.

The metaphors of church as "body" (1 Cor 12:12–31) and "building" (Eph 2:19–22) are especially interesting in this regard. Paul's discussion of the metaphors in both cases focuses on the necessity for the church either to work together as one unit or to hold together as one structure, with Christ as the head and the cornerstone. Granted, the Apostle Paul recognizes that a community is made up of its individual members (1 Cor 12:27) but he never dwells on them as individuals qua individuals. Instead he views them continually as members of the collective, of the whole (1 Cor 12:7). Their role is not to exert their own identity but to submit their identity and self to the function of the community of the church as it further submits to the authority or lordship of Jesus.[14]

---

14. An analogy of a puzzle may help clarify this point. The individualistic mindset focuses on each piece of the puzzle, as if we have been given a piece and we analyze to the detail every aspect of the beauty of "my own" individual piece. Recognition of the purpose of each piece's fitting together into an entire mosaic is lost. Instead, individualism is content to be distracted by the characteristics and colors of each piece. The Holy

This seems well illustrated by the community of the early church in Acts 15:28. In the context of the first ecclesial conflict and first solution as a church body, it is more than coincidence that the "apostles and the elders, with the whole church" (15:22) should send a letter claiming the Holy Spirit's presence in their decision—"It seemed good to the Holy Spirit and to us" (15:28). While it is certainly possible that the Holy Spirit spoke to them directly, given the transitionary nature of the book of Acts, it is also as likely that the best decision of the apostles, the elders, and the rest of the church constituted the work of the Spirit. The apostles and elders seem to equivocate between their authority and the authority of the Holy Spirit. Further, what is instructive about this authoritative statement is that the restrictions placed on the Gentile believers are intended to identify them as a distinct Christian community similar to the way the Jewish community had been identified for centuries. The concern is not primarily the legal ramifications with regard to Torah, but how they would stand as a community of faith apart from the rest of the world, and in some ways even, apart from the non-Christian Jews.[15]

Another pair of passages at times understood as a reference to an individual's body comes to us from Paul's instructions to the Corinthians. 1 Corinthians 3:16–17 and 1 Corinthians 6:19–20 are both passages that mention the fact of the Spirit's dwelling "in" believers. However, once again, the pronoun used in both passages is a plural "you." In the first passage, the significance of the plurality is brought out by the context of constructing a building. In this passage, Paul uses the metaphor of a building and of the way one builds upon the foundation to point out that Christians must be careful in what they devote their lives to. In his discussion of the building, Paul uses the singular τις, τινος ("any person") and εκαστου ("each person"). However, when he moves back to his discussion of the indwelling of the Holy Spirit, he returns to the plural:

Spirit's goal is to draw the pieces together into a whole unit called body. The modern primacy of the individual makes this task difficult at best. Further, when individuals do gather together as church, it is only as a pile of pieces, not generally as pieces fit together in a specific fashion. In other words, the church is generally regarded as a collection of individuals rather than as a single unit. Cf. Mühlen, *Una Mystica Persona*, 199.

15. Hütter, "Church as Public," 357–60.

> According to the grace of God which was given to me, as a wise master builder I laid a foundation, and another is building upon it. But let each man be careful how he builds upon it. For no man can lay a foundation other than the one which is laid, which is Jesus Christ. Now if any man builds upon the foundation with gold, silver, precious stones, wood, hay, straw, each man's work will become evident; for the day will show it, because it is to be revealed with fire; and the fire itself will test the quality of each man's work. If any man's work which he has built upon it remains, he shall receive a reward. If any man's work is burned up, he shall suffer loss; but he himself shall be saved, yet so as through fire.
>
> Do you [*pl.*] not know that you [*pl.*] are a temple of God, and the Spirit of God dwells in you [*pl.*]? If any man destroys the temple of God, God will destroy him, for the temple of God is holy, and that is what you [*pl.*] are. (1 Cor. 3:10–17)

It would be easy to presume that the temple is the individual physical bodies of believers, since the Holy Spirit is said to dwell "in" them. However, it seems more likely, given the context of the building process with Christ as the foundation, to understand the plural "you" and the singular "temple" as references to the church as a whole.[16] This is especially the case given the fact that the letter continues in chapter 5 to outline the way in which one person (a man who has his father's wife [1 Cor 5:1]) is causing the whole church to be compromised. Thus, the last sentence in 3:10–17 above is best understood as setting the stage for chapters 5 and 6, and the discussion of how the community of the church—the "temple" and "body"—are to relate to the individual who is participating in immorality. This does not diminish the individual's participation in the whole in 3:10–15, but it does highlight the fact that the overarching context in which the indwelling work of the Spirit is to be understood is in the corporate nature of the church.

The second passage in question in this letter of Paul is 1 Corinthians 6:19–20:

> Or do you not know that your body is a temple of the Holy Spirit who is in you, whom you have from God, and that you are

---

16. Fee, *First Epistle to the Corinthians*, 146–47; Grosheide, *Commentary on the First Epistle to the Corinthians*, 88–89; and Robertson and Plummer, *First Epistle of St. Paul to the Corinthians*, 66.

> not your own? For you have been bought with a price: therefore
> glorify God in your body.

Again, the pronouns used for "you" are plural throughout this passage. The context of the passage in the immediately preceding verses is the use of a person's physical body for either moral chastity or licentiousness, the image of joining one's body with a harlot providing the vivid illustration of how one's use of one's physical body demonstrates how one practices immorality by joining with sin. This has led some to conclude that Paul is referring to physical bodies in verses 19–20, quoted above, making the place of residence for the Spirit to be the physical bodies of individuals.[17] However, such an interpretation misses the larger context in which Paul is attempting to address how the church should react to sin in its midst.

Chapters 5 and 6 of 1 Corinthians seem best understood as a single unit or thought, with chapter 6 functioning primarily as an illustration of Paul's teaching in chapter 5, and with 6:19–20 serving as a summary statement for the whole of both chapters. Back in 1 Corinthians 5:1, Paul bemoans the fact that a grievous sin exists in the Corinthian church: a man is living with his father's wife. The Corinthians are in fact proud that they have been able to overlook such a sin (1 Cor 5:2–6). Paul chastises them for not ridding themselves of the sin that is in their midst and implores them to eradicate it, so they might rightly come together as a community of fellowship in Christ. Paul closes this didactic section by quoting a repeated phrase from Deut 13:5; 17:7, 12; 21:21; and 22:21: "Remove the wicked man from among yourselves." (1 Cor 5:13). This wicked man is like the particle of leaven that, when mixed with the whole "lump" of bread dough, leavens the whole lump (1 Cor 5:6). Paul continues this thought of the community as *a priori* to the individual by illustrating how members of the believing community should work things out amongst themselves instead of going to unbelieving judges

---

17. Interestingly, the same authors who above rightly attributed Paul's reference of the temple to the church have here become distracted by the immediate references to sexual activity, not seeing such activity as illustrative of the larger point. See Fee, *First Epistle to the Corinthians*, 263–66; Grosheide, *Commentary on the First Epistle to the Corinthians*, 151–52; Robertson and Plummer, *First Epistle of St. Paul to the Corinthians*, 128. Grosheide comes the closest to recognizing Paul's return to the image of temple as church but doesn't finally recognize this passage as summarizing the whole of chapters 5–6.

(1 Cor 6:1–11), and by showing that allowing one vile person to remain in their midst is like joining themselves to impurity (1 Cor 6:12–18). These two illustrations are meant to demonstrate ways in which the community of the church is now a "new lump" of dough (5:7). They are the "unleavened bread" precisely because they exist as a different kind of *community*, though certainly individual participation in this community is still important.

The last illustration (1 Cor 6:12–18) is used by Paul to depict in graphic terms how such a sin affects the body of the church, (i.e., defilement). In chapter 6, verse 18, Paul finishes the illustration by stating, "Flee immorality. Every other sin that a man commits is outside the body, but the immoral man sins against his own body." (The use of "man" here instead of "you" implies a difference between verses 18 and 19: Verse 18 is still a part of the illustration, or may even be seen as a summary of the illustration in vv. 12–17; and verse 19 is the beginning of the summary for chapters 5 and 6.) Paul continues with language about the body in verse 19; however, he appears to have shifted his thought from a physical body to the body that is the church through his use of the plural "you" coupled with his change from the plural "bodies" in verse 15 to the singular "body" in verse 19. Paul appears to be using a play on words here, expecting the Corinthians to remember his reference to the church as temple back in 3:16. The connection does not diminish the admonition against joining oneself to a harlot but brings the illustration back to the context of sin in the midst of the church— the body of Christ, which is also a temple (a point to which Paul returns in chapter 12) is to be pure. As intense as the subject of promiscuity may have been for Paul and may be today, the reader should not be distracted from Paul's main point or isolate verses 19–20 from the overarching context, losing sight of his overarching point in the midst of his discussion of physical sexual sin. He is focusing primarily on the church in these chapters, not on sexual activity. He is still thinking ecclesiologically rather than focusing solely on personal holiness, though obviously his points on personal holiness are still quite valid. Paul summarizes chapters 5–6 by explaining that the body of the church is a holy place and is to be kept holy by casting sin from within its midst. This is how verses 19–20 should be understood.[18]

18. I do not mean to diminish the importance of physical human bodies by interpreting "body" here as "church" instead of as human bodies (see Fee, *First Epistle to the*

One final point needs mentioning before leaving these passages in 1 Corinthians behind. It may be somewhat confusing or disconcerting that in both passages Paul uses a plural pronoun but a singular noun: you (*pl.*) are a temple (*sg.*) (3:16); your (*pl.*) body (*sg.*) is a temple (*sg.*) (6:19). This may suggest that Paul is speaking about individuated bodies and temples (i.e., individual persons) rather than speaking communally. Perhaps again, he could even be understood to be speaking of the community as merely a collection of individuals. However, it would seem more plausible to understand these metaphors in the context of the plurality of the church. As mentioned above, Paul uses the metaphors of a building (temple?) and a body to refer to the church, not to individuals. Thus the use of the plural pronoun with singular nouns seems to be Paul's way of communicating his own view of the Corinthians as a collective unit, rather than as simply an amassed group of individuals, each with his or her own body or temple. Further, Paul's point later in 1 Corinthians 12 seems to be that the unity of the body is critical in pneumatology. Paul is conscious of the fact that there are not many Holy Spirits, but only one Holy Spirit. Those indwelled by the Spirit do not each have their own piece of the Spirit, nor are they indwelled by their own individuated Spirit. Instead, the church is said to have the one Spirit working in its midst to accomplish the goal of drawing the church into a right relationship with its head, Jesus Christ. Individual believers are still indwelled individually by the Spirit as they participate in his community (the church), but they are never able to sever themselves from the unity of the Spirit found in the fact that he is one Spirit for the church, not many Spirits for individuals. Paul's primary concern in all these passages is still the holiness of the church, and secondarily the holiness of individuals as they are part of the church.[19] Such a rendering of these chapters in 1 Corinthians seems to accord with the emphasis on community as prior to the individual seen above in Hauerwas.

Corinthians, 263–66). Paul seems to correct the inappropriate demeaning (gnostic dualism) of human bodies later in 1 Corinthians 15. However, here in the earlier chapters, he is still concerned primarily with the church as a whole.

19. For a useful discussion of the relationship between the individual body and the corporate body in 1 Corinthians, see Martin, *Corinthian Body*. Martin's discussion of 1 Corinthians 12 as nonmetaphorical is especially insightful in understanding the way in which the community gave identity to individual bodies.

Picking up again the theme of the ways that the Holy Spirit could possibly indwell the church as a unit primarily (and perhaps individuals secondarily), the notion of authority mentioned earlier may allow some room for understanding this more clearly. Just as demon possession in Scripture appears more clearly to be an issue of authority rather than an issue of spatial inhabitation, so too an understanding of the church as under the authority of the Holy Spirit may be a more plausible way of interpreting the plural nature of the Spirit's indwelling. This would help to alleviate some of the anthropocentrism associated with the individualization of the Spirit's indwelling ministry in our modern context. A new emphasis on the authority of the Spirit for the church would also make the indwelling ministry of the Spirit more consistent with the Triune relationship between Jesus and the Spirit that Pannenberg suggested above. Since it is the primary task of the Spirit to glorify Christ (John 16:14), and since Paul names Christ as the "head of the church" (Eph 5:23), the indwelling ministry of the Holy Spirit should be directed primarily toward causing the church to come under Jesus's headship.[20] Obviously this emphasis on the Spirit's bringing the church under Jesus's headship does not exclude the glory that Christ receives from the holiness of individuals, but the primary metaphor used to describe the relationship that Christ has with believers is as bride and Lamb (Eph 4:25–33; Rev 19:7–9). The holiness of individuals becomes a part of the marriage only as individuals are part of the church. In other words, what we seem to be discovering in Scripture, as Hauerwas has rightly seen, is that community is epistemologically, and perhaps even ontologically, prior to the individual.

How the Church Becomes Body

This seems an appropriate place to deal more carefully with the issue of the reality of the Holy Spirit in individuals' lives, since what I have

20. It would be compelling to construct (indeed this seems to be what Hauerwas is attempting to do) a theological anthropology based not on a theology of creation per se but on the lordship of Jesus over all creation. Holland seems to miss this point when he pushes for an anthropology based on shared human experience in a pluralistic community. See Holland, "Mennonites on Hauerwas," 142–51. Hauerwas's anthropology, following Barth, is christocentric, whereas Holland would prefer an anthropology that remains anthropocentric. The question for Holland, in my mind, remains, why privilege the doctrine of creation over the lordship of Jesus? This seems theologically arbitrary, and perhaps even idolatrous.

highlighted thus far has been the corporate nature of the Spirit's work. A corporate context is not meant to exclude individual participation in the work of the Spirit. On the contrary, I mean to demonstrate that it is only as individuals become part of the living community called church that they can actually become a part of the work of the Holy Spirit. Hauerwas's critique of the self as defined in particularly modernistic terms seems right in this regard. In other words, the definition of the self is, scripturally speaking, best subsumed into the definition of ecclesiology. This is not an exclusion of individual participation; however, the individual is recast as secondary rather than primary. Again, the focus for this issue is perhaps best centered, in theological terms, on the indwelling of the Holy Spirit.

As mentioned above, the transcendent nature of God's existence has tended to dominate theology, including pneumatology. This could easily lead to a distancing of the Spirit in such a way as to cause his ministry to be too easily differentiated from the activity of humans in community. While it seems incumbent upon theologians to preserve the transcendent nature of God's existence in the person of the Holy Spirit, such transcendence must not be preserved at the expense of a participation of Christians in the divine through the Spirit—a participation] that is constitutive of their very existence. If Christians really believe in the indwelling ministry of the Holy Spirit, we have to say that he exists in the materiality of the church, not in the air like some invisible force or ghost.[21] The Holy Spirit is found enfleshed in the lives of those who are part of the church, drawing them further into the church by providing them the context in which they can learn what it means to be church. In the words of John Zizioulas,

> The Spirit is not something that "animates" a Church which already somehow exists. The Spirit makes the Church *be*. Pneumatology does not refer to the well-being but to the very

21. Nicholas Lash believes that this is, unfortunately, the way many people within the church view the Holy Spirit, precisely because of the word association in our liturgies and theological traditions. See Lash, *Believing Three Ways in One God*, 84. Here he asks, somewhat sarcastically but with some seriousness as well, "Do you believe in ghosts? Only in the Holy Ghost. Supposedly sophisticated and well educated Christians ignore, at their peril, the influence on our imagination of connotations such as these. Words take their meaning from the company they keep and, in our culture, 'ghost' and 'spirit' keep close company with what we now misleadingly call 'supernatural' entities hovering at the twilit margins of our world" (84).

being of the Church. It is not about a dynamism which is added to the essence of the Church. It is the very essence of the Church. The Church is *constituted* in and through eschatology and communion. Pneumatology is an ontological category in ecclesiology.[22]

In other words, the Holy Spirit can be found in the natural workings of the church, or in Hauerwas's words, in the formative nature of the narrative community—discipleship, instead of the supernatural or the miraculous movements often associated with the work of the Spirit in the first century. The human community of church is the dwelling place of the Spirit. To put this in biblical terms, the church is the place where individuals are "being built together into a dwelling of God in the Spirit" (Eph 2:22). By making community ontologically prior to the individual, I am understanding the supernatural nature of the Spirit's work in humans to be composed primarily of the natural workings of the human community.[23] Of course, this sacrifices nothing of the Spirit's

22. Zizioulas, *Being as Communion*, 132, emphasis Zizioulas's. One would expect Zizioulas to hold to a strong materiality of the Holy Spirit, and in a sense he does when he makes the ordained bishop to ontologically become the communion of Christ with Christ's body, the church (225ff.). However, he wishes to maintain a distinction between the Son, who *becomes* history, and the Father and Spirit, who are *involved in* history. The distinction is maintained so that the Spirit can still function according to its role in the economy of the Trinity (130).

Perhaps due to a need to defend the supernatural economy of the Spirit, or perhaps due to an affinity for mystical qualities of the Spirit, Zizioulas seems to stake too much on the historicity of only the Son. Obviously, I do not wish to deny such historical concreteness with regard to the Son. However, I do wish to open up the notion of the historicity of the Spirit. Certainly Zizioulas, and Pannenberg for that matter, are right that the final historical nature of the church will be discovered in the eschaton. Nevertheless, as Pannenberg's emphasis makes clear, it must likewise be a historical reality throughout history as well. I am not here arguing for some form of animism or duality of participation between the church and the Spirit. Instead, the church is the real presence of the Holy Spirit. Zizioulas seems to want to say this but is still encumbered with a prior commitment to an ahistorical ontology of the Trinity.

23. This would perhaps be a good place to explain why I believe the social role of the Spirit is prior to the individual's reception of the Spirit. Certainly I am not denying individual participation and responsibility. However, taking my cue from what I perceive to be the epistemological priority of the community in the Greek city-state for both Plato and Aristotle, particularly in regard to moral formation, or discipleship, I believe Christians are primarily body of Christ before any individual element is given extensive consideration. It is not that remote to perceive an Aristotelian influence in both Jesus and Paul, and also to perceive Jewish identity as community prior to the individual in the Old Testament. Indeed, as Hauerwas would see it, a communal identity

person, since I am not attempting to equivocate between the person of the Spirit and the human community. I am instead equivocating between his activity and the activity of humans in community. Thus his transcendence is maintained. As shall be discussed below, this distinction between the transcendence of the Spirit's person and the limitation of his activity to the human community is best understood in terms analogous to the kenotic activity of the Son in Philippians 2:1–11.

By reexamining the supernaturalism of the Spirit, I must emphasize that I am not arguing for some type of naturalism like that of Benedict Spinoza or David Hume.[24] This appears, at times, to be where Hauerwas has left his notion of the working of the Holy Spirit, in that he at times appears to have simply adopted the human community as the church. Thus as was seen, Hauerwas opens himself to the criticism of reducing ecclesiology to mere anthropology.[25] Instead, I am arguing for a supernatural indwelling of the church that makes the natural

---

is evangelism—introduce and invite people to join the community. It is only in retrospect that one sees one's own self as self. One of Hauerwas' intentions, and I believe it is appropriate, seems to be to redefine the self as communal first and individual second. This obviously reverses the Enlightenment definition of the self, which seems to be anachronistic in attributing a preference for the individual in biblical interpretation.

24. One can easily illustrate the denial of the supernatural by both Spinoza and Hume through their rejection of the miraculous as impossible in light of the governing of all activity by natural laws. Miracles could not have occurred, since natural laws cannot be broken. See Spinoza, *Theologico-Political Treatise*, 1:83, 87, 92; and Hume, *Enquiry Concerning Human Understanding*, 10.1.122–23.

25. I am hesitant to assert of Hauerwas that this is where he has "left" his understanding of the Spirit, since he is quite reluctant to "spell out" a doctrine of the Holy Spirit per se. Nevertheless, it does seem apparent, at least from his neglect of doctrinal development, that he remains subject to such a critique of his thought. By not making his doctrine of the Spirit more explicit, he leaves himself open to the charge of lacking theological or biblical support for the primacy of narrative. I am not asking for foundations here. I am simply observing that nonfoundationalism, or even antifoundationalism, not only removes Enlightenment traditions from theology but also potentially disengages theology from its more solid traditional moorings. Of course, a response to such a charge would likely be to assert the formative and critical nature of the narrative community aligned with tradition as the place in which the treasure of theology lies. Herein, once again, is revealed the problem: To appeal to the human community, without any appeal to the power of such a community existent outside of the community (i.e., a transcendent Spirit) leaves one open to the charge of reductionism, in that God's activity through the Spirit is limited strictly to the human qua human. I am attempting to alleviate such a charge by making explicit a doctrine of the Spirit that seems, at times, to be implicit in Hauerwas.

supernatural.[26] One could plausibly argue this on the grounds of grace permeating the natural to such an extent that a further supernatural indwelling is rendered moot.[27] Yet without a supporting or complementary doctrine of the real indwelling of the Holy Spirit, this notion of permeating grace sounds dangerously like the common human spirit of Protestant liberalism (e.g., Schleiermacher). Liberalism depended on the innate goodness of humanity as foundational for human moral activity. When moved to the realm of action, this innate goodness in humanity resembled the righteousness depicted as the working of the Holy Spirit in Scripture; the resemblance was near enough for liberal Protestant theologians equivocate between the two.[28] However, without

26. One may question whether this is an appropriate dichotomy to articulate. However, I am not devising it from speculative sources. Instead I am attempting to respond to those who would argue vehemently for one side or the other. As can be observed from the many references throughout this study in this regard, I am not alone in attempting such a thesis. However, a fully developed discussion of the relevant material is yet wanting. Howe makes an admirable effort at developing just such a theme (Howe, "Holy Spirit and Holy Church," 43–57). However, his presupposed affinity for the natural comes at the expense of the supernatural and is left with little more than speculative support. In contrast, I wish to lay out a development of the natural from the source of Scripture, while at the same time presuming that the natural is not merely an effect of the supernatural but *is* the supernatural. As will be seen below, the fruit of the Spirit provides a good testing ground, since the fruit are not natural to those who remain under the curse of original sin.

It should also be noted that though this study may qualify as a form of incarnational ecclesiology with regard to sanctification, it is by no means incarnational in regards to soteriology. The church is still a witness to Christ and his power to save. I am merely developing the theme of how the church might more clearly be understood as Christ's body and might live as such subsequent to the realization of election. Cf. Saucy, "Evangelicals, Catholics, and Orthodox Together," 193–212.

27. Certainly grace permeates the activity of God in all of creation, but this seems an awkward locus for human participation, at least from a scriptural perspective. Scripture seems to portray the Spirit as the agent of change in humanity, not grace, though certainly the Spirit's work can rightly be understood as a movement of God's grace in his creation. Such a permeating notion of grace is likely why Hauerwas can rest so much weight in his formative theology on the sacraments.

28. Karl Barth wondered aloud whether this is perhaps the best way to understand Schleiermacher's universal spirit (see Barth, *Theology of Schleiermacher*, 276). Instead of finding the Holy Spirit in the common human spirit of Schleiermacher, Barth seems drawn more toward a strong differentiation between the two, with the common human spirit being insufficient to effect righteousness (cf. Barth, *Church Dogmatics II/2*, 538, 541).

It is significant to note that though Schleiermacher's Holy Spirit seemed to have lapsed into the human spirit, Schleiermacher was still quite conscious (for obvious

188 SYSTEM AND STORY

the transformation of the human community beyond itself qua human, it cannot legitimately be called church. This does not deny the natural occurrences of human community in the everyday living of the community of the church. By investing these actions with theological significance (in Hauerwasian terms, by naming them; or in the terms of this study, by naming them biblically) and by doing them at the right time, in the right way, and for the right reasons, they become the work of the Spirit and are lifted beyond simple naturalism.[29]

On the other hand, the reality of the Holy Spirit's activity within the community must also be affirmed. The Spirit himself is actively working to glorify the Son in the church. Thus the accusation of the church's being *merely* a human community (i.e., anthropological reductionism) is explicitly avoided. The question then becomes, how does the Spirit work in the church? It is the contention of this study that he does so, though certainly as still an external agent, primarily through

---

reasons) of the presence of the Spirit being identified primarily in the community of the church. See Schleiermacher, *Christian Faith*, 560–69. Of course, Schleiermacher's church was yet primarily a collection of individuals who had discovered their own self-consciousness. (see Barth, *Theology of Schleiermacher*, 67–68). Thus, a list of some of the contrasts, as characterized by Barth, between the conception of the Holy Spirit in this study and Schleiermacher's doctrine of the Spirit would include 1) Schleiermacher's still operating with a definition of the self as individual before moving to any placing of the self in the community; 2) Schleiermacher's disavowal of the supernatural nature of the Spirit is a descent into naturalism, his scientifically encompassing efforts loosing his theological footing (see Barth, *Theology of Schleiermacher*, 171–72); 3) the gathering of the distinctive community of the church by the Spirit as, for Schleiermacher, merely a gathering of self-aware humans (i.e., the identity of the church as distinctly Christian as immaterial for Schleiermacher [see Barth, *Theology of Schleiermacher*, 30]). Further, Schleiermacher's spirit is the spirit of autonomy in volitional ethics —the Spirit in Scripture is the Spirit of submission to the lordship of Jesus; Schleiermacher's spirit is subject to the reasoning powers of the independent rationality of the individual—the Spirit in Scripture is subject to the patterned will of God revealed in the Scriptures and in the ongoing narrative of the church.

It may be interesting to note that a similar criticism of reducing the Holy Spirit to the human spirit is leveled at Reinhold Niebuhr by Song, *Christianity and Liberal Society*, 78. According to Song, Niebuhr uses the Trinitarian language of Father, Son, and Holy Spirit but leaves his understanding of the Holy Spirit at the level of the human spirit.

29. Whereas Hauerwas would depict the sacraments as such activities, I am not sacramentalistic. The practices that I would affirm would include, among many others, such things as prayer, praise, preaching, forgiveness, church discipline and accountability, and self-sacrificing love—in other words, worship. While Hauerwas would also likely include these, they are not, for him, as primary as the sacraments.

natural means (i.e., through the human community of the church). The power of naming the practices should not be underestimated as merely semantics. Indeed, I believe a plausible argument could be made that ontology begins at the level of naming.

The problem remaining for this study is how yet specifically to overcome Hauerwas's reductionism and Schleiermacher's equivocation between the human and divine spirit without creating a doctrine of the Holy Spirit whose transcendence makes history meaningless. In other words, how can we possibly retain the transcendent or external nature of the Holy Spirit and yet attempt to draw an equivalence, of sorts, between the natural workings of the human community and the supernatural working of the Holy Spirit? Whereas Hauerwas has largely approached the issue "from below," a more systematic presentation—like Pannenberg's discussion of the Spirit as emanating from the Father and sent by the Son—opens the door for further discussion "from above." A solution to the problem of anthropology's overcoming the transcendence of the Holy Spirit could then be pursued from a comparison of the Son and the Spirit by way of analogy.

The biblical and theological precedent for the Son's kenosis is without question. The second chapter of Philippians makes clear the activity of the Son in taking humanity onto himself and in adding a human nature to himself. Within this kenosis, certain self-limitations took place. However, it has been orthodoxy in the church's theology since Athanasius, or better, since the first century, that the kenosis did not in any way inhibit or diminish Jesus's deity. In whatever manner Jesus's divine nature and human nature may have been related over the centuries, orthodoxy has not compromised either as they coexisted in the one man, Jesus.

To maintain the transcendent nature of the Holy Spirit, while at the same time affirming an equivalence between his activity and that of the human community of the church, I wish to propose an analogy between the kenosis of Jesus and a kenosis of the Holy Spirit. Just as Jesus took on humanity in the form of a human body and mind, so too the Spirit takes on human bodies and minds, in a sense (to use Paul's language) becoming the human body of Christ on earth. Such a self-sacrificing effort by the Spirit in taking on certain human limitation and imposing on himself certain restrictions over his divine activity seems to fit well both the intentions of his mission—to glorify the Son and not Himself—and the parallel between the Father's sending of the Son and the Son's sending of the Spirit.[30] The eschaton will confirm the work of the Spirit in humanity, even as it will confirm Jesus's deity over all creation. However, until then, both the Son and the Spirit are limited to the extent that humanity is the crucible for such confirmation. The end or goal of God's eschaton is never in question, but the means of confirming the history of humanity as a history directed by God (one could even say "the history of humanity as the history of God" as long as panentheistic overtones were left aside[31]) remain an ongoing work *within* human history. The Holy Spirit's self-limitation to the human seems an appropriate way of understanding the context of participation, that is, the meeting of the human and the divine.[32]

Having laid out a possible proposal for how the Holy Spirit can maintain his own transcendence and likewise be wholly identified with the human community of the church, I recognize that I have not yet resolved the question of the locus of the Spirit's work: whether it is individualized or corporate. Certain modern conceptions of the indwelling ministry of the Holy Spirit have adopted, in both theological and political renderings, a notion of the doctrine of the Spirit that relies on the innate goodness of humanity for personal righteousness or transformation.[33] The work of the Holy Spirit becomes individuated in holiness—a

30. For a concise treatment of the Trinitarian relationship at work here, see Pannenberg, *Systematic Theology*, 3:4–6.

31. The difference between this proposal of the Spirit's kenosis and process theology or open theism is that I am here not subjecting the divine to limitation based on the divine nature. Any limitation is self-imposed and is not necessitated by human freedom. On the contrary, limitation is not due to God's inability to know the future or control it. Instead, limitation is due to God's desire to draw humanity into his unfolding of the future. Though subject to the limitation of acting primarily within human form and function, the Spirit is still the Spirit that is directed by the Father and the Son and is drawing people toward the lordship of the Son. The transcendent nature of the Spirit's mission and identity is not diminished because of his enfleshment. As alluded to above, in contrast to Schleiermacher's understanding, this view the preserves a primary distinction between the Holy Spirit and the human spirit.

32. I was pleased to find that I am hardly the first to suggest such an understanding of the relationship between the human and the divine through a kenosis of the Spirit. Since it is not the intention of this study to engage in a systematic presentation of such a notion, we will leave aside extended development of the theme. However, for a fuller treatment of the subject, see Dabney, *Die Kenosis des Geistes*.

33. E.g., see Hauerwas's comments on Niebuhr in Hauerwas, *Wilderness Wanderings*, 51–54.

point that Hauerwas has identified as deriving from liberalism.[34] Even the most conservative of theologians still parallel this move by leaving the work of the Holy Spirit primarily to the individual so that morality is relegated to either personal choice or individual conscience.[35] It is believed that as the Spirit works in the individual's life, that person will be brought to a higher level of holiness. This supernatural work of the Spirit is more purely a work between the Spirit and the individual first. The church can be of assistance by providing further education for the individual, but the work of the Spirit is a supernatural power that comes from the Spirit to the individual directly, unmediated.

In conservative Protestant theology, this direct "meeting" of the Spirit with the human in an unmediated manner may take the form of a direct "revelation," or even of an audible voice, as in some more Pentecostal understandings of the Holy Spirit. In non-Pentecostal theology, the "meeting" usually takes the form of a mental impression, or a sensation of "peace" about a decision or change in an individual's life (i.e., a choice).[36] Such a mystical approach to the doctrine of the Spirit may reflect the more miraculous nature of the work of the Spirit in the first century, but questionable is whether this was to be the normative way that the Spirit would direct the church. Since the prophets and apostles were foundational in the church (Eph 2:19–22), it would seem that some transition would take place from the foundational nature of the

34. Ibid.

35. E.g., see Erickson, *Christian Theology*, 873–77. Being somewhat inclined toward progressive sanctification, Erickson still sees room for growth and development, i.e., through teaching. Nevertheless, he seems to leave much of this growth to an inner compulsion produced by the Spirit.

For an insightful probing of the public/private dichotomy facing the church and the church's affinity toward privatization in modernity, see Hütter, "Church as Public," 334–35. Privatization in sanctification (i.e., that my morality is my business alone) lends itself in almost a direct correlation to an emphasis on the Holy Spirit as relating primarily to the individual's conscience.

36. At least Pentecostals are consistent when claiming to hear the voice of the Spirit in an audible sense. Others within conservative Protestantism who may equate the Spirit's leading with "impressions" or "feelings of certainty" have little recourse to any external witness. In both cases, the legitimation of the Spirit's leading is unassailable. It is, at best, the well-intentioned purposes of fallible individuals and, at worst, the justification of sin in a realm of spiritual isolationism that is above critique. In the case of an individual or group's justification of sin, the legitimation of the Spirit's leading reflects the spiritual arrogance that may be seen when one says "If God has spoken, who are we (you) to question it!"

workings of the Spirit to the more typical functions in a mature church. Beyond this, the issue arises as to the damage such mysticism does to the everyday workings of the Spirit. If the Spirit's primary "meeting" with the human is only understood in periodic and not constant terms, this leaves the rest of human activity to the more purely natural realm. In other words, supernatural moments may exist, in which the Spirit is active, but he is relegated only to the miraculous or to times of crisis or decision (e.g., impressions or feelings of "peace"). Such a dichotomy of natural versus supernatural is at best an unhealthy rendering of God's sovereignty over human activity and at worst a relegating of God to merely certain provisional human activities; both are an affront to his lordship.

One could perhaps understand such mysticism in terms of the influence of Descartes on modern psychology. The dualism of mind and body lends itself to characterize spiritual progress (i.e., sanctification) in terms of spirit *versus* body. In gnostic fashion (i.e., spirit as higher than matter), this usually means that the body is subjected to the spiritual and even, at times, looked upon as an encumbrance to sanctification. Work has already begun in an attempt to "embrace and hold together everything that Descartes holds apart."[37] There is also the further problem of the individuated existence owing to Descartes, though by no means to him alone.[38] The individuated self in Cartesian gnosticism subjugates the communal self in ontological, epistemological, and ecclesiological terms. These two emphases together translate into a holiness focused on the spiritual development of the individual as primary, which can then perhaps be offered to the community as it comes together as individuals in a collective unit. What is lost in such a notion is the possibility of the community's being the primary locus of spiritual development. In other words, bodily existence in the midst of the community of faith is dismissed as the crucible in which holiness is formed. As Hauerwas is prone to complain, "The problem with modern readings of Paul, readings often meant to underwrite a concern with holiness, is that they are far too spiritual."[39] Certainly, in an individuated

37. Keen, "Human Person as Intercessory Prayer," 40. This is Keen's description of Hauerwas's project in his essay in the same volume.

38. Keen traces a brief history of the "self" from Descartes to Leibniz to Locke to Kant. See Keen, "Human Person as Intercessory Prayer," 45–48.

39. Hauerwas, "Sanctified Body," 27.

model of sanctification, communal living can reveal further work to be done in spiritual formation, but as long as the Holy Spirit works primarily in the individual, then communal living is only a place for testing what has been accomplished and should be corrected in the individual self. Dale Martin has begun a substantive attempt to correct such an emphasis on the individual by developing what he declares to be the Pauline model of body life.[40]

The unmediated and individuated understanding of the Holy Spirit (i.e., that the Holy Spirit comes directly to the individual and is not mediated through the community of the church) may be better understood as a means of defending the liberal notion of the goodness of humanity by appealing to the supernatural. In practical terms, the unmediated and individuated understanding of the Holy Spirit looks no different from the naturalism of liberal theology. The individual is still the primary referent. Education, primarily in the form of information, is again the way in which moral transformation takes place, since the individual simply needs information to make a choice that coincides with his or her Spirit-induced compulsion (in conservative theology) or innate compulsion (in liberal theology) to choose the good. And of course, the community of the church has no authority over the individual since individuals are largely autonomous over their own spiritual development. In such a context, ethics becomes largely a matter of the individual's conscience, and increased morality is subject to the choice of the individual. Though the individual may acknowledge the lordship of Christ over his or her life, that individual is still responsible for figuring out the ways in which Christ is directing his or her life through the Spirit. A defense may be offered for such a spirituality by claiming that those who have the Spirit are now able to make good decisions precisely because they have been made inherently good once again, but this claim does not accord with the scriptural teaching. Though Paul makes it clear that those who are in Christ are a "new creation" (2 Cor 5:17), he also acknowledges that the flesh still wishes to captivate believers and entice them into following after what is wrong, even though they may know what is wrong (Rom 7:7–25).

40. Martin, *Corinthian Body*. Cf. Powell and Lodahl, *Embodied Holiness*. The essays contained in *Embodied Holiness* are also directed at developing an understanding of holiness that is "founded" on bodily existence in a physical community, particularly in a Wesleyan community, though the emphasis is by no means exclusive to Wesleyanism.

What has been seen thus far in our discussion of Scripture is that the indwelling work of the Holy Spirit is perhaps better located in ecclesiological terms. This assertion fulfills the intentions of Hauerwas to discover epistemological primacy in the actions of the human community of the church without resorting (as he appears to do) to mere anthropology. The warrants given for describing the indwelling work of the spirit in ecclesiological terms have been 1) Paul's emphasis on the plural in his discussions of the indwelling ministry of the Spirit, and 2) the intended purpose of the Holy Spirit to draw humanity into the confirmation of Jesus's lordship over all creation.

Placing this discussion again in biblical language, one may ask, are you (as an individual) filled with or filled by the Holy Spirit (Eph. 5:18)? In order to answer this question, one would first need to evaluate his or her relationship to the community of the faithful. In other words, guidance and peace from the Holy Spirit is first a question of fellowship, not primarily an issue of personal peace or power. Further, such a communal rendering of the Holy Spirit counters the insidious individualism that has permeated many modern discussions of the Spirit. Though this communal redefinition of the indwelling Spirit by no means excludes individuals as participants in the Spirit's work, individualism is not the primary context in which indwelling is to be understood. Hauerwas has argued convincingly that definition of the self must be subsumed into ecclesiology. Now we must answer more clearly why a corporate preference in our rendering of the Holy Spirit is biblically coherent.

Church as School

In a modern consumeristic context, it is often difficult to imagine the church as anything other than a service organization intended for the betterment of humanity. Hauerwas has rightly surmised that the contemporary church has shifted in its mission. It now functions as primarily a service to meet people's needs rather than a place of training people to worship.[41] Such was not always the case. Historically speaking, even amongst Protestants, the church has enjoyed a more authoritative and constitutive role in the moral and spiritual formation of its people. The church historically, in order to learn what it meant to be in service to Jesus, has found itself, as Barth rightly claimed, "in the school of the

41. See Hauerwas, *Wilderness Wanderings*, 184.

apostles."[42] As John Calvin would have it, the community of the church is the school in which holiness of life is taught.

> But because it is now our intention to discuss the visible church, let us learn even from the simple title "mother" how useful, indeed how necessary, it is that we should know her. For there is no other way to enter into life unless this mother conceive us in her womb, give us birth, nourish us at her breast, and lastly, unless she keep us under her care and guidance until, putting off mortal flesh, we become like the angels [Matt. 22:30]. Our weakness does not allow us to be dismissed from her school until we have been pupils all our lives. Furthermore, away from her bosom one cannot hope for any forgiveness of sins or any salvation, as Isaiah [Isa. 37:32] and Joel [Joel 2:32] testify.... By these words, God's fatherly favor and the especial witness of spiritual life are limited to his flock, so that it is always disastrous to leave the church.[43]

If the church is for training, such training implies, at least, change from what is to what should be. In Scripture, the battle lines between the flesh and the Spirit are laid out by the Apostle Paul in several places, but perhaps nowhere more clearly than in Galatians 5:16–26.[44]

> But I say, walk by the Spirit, and you will not carry out the desire of the flesh. For the flesh sets its desire against the Spirit, and the Spirit against the flesh; for these are in opposition to one another, so that you may not do the things that you please. But if you are led by the Spirit, you are not under the Law. Now the deeds of the flesh are evident, which are: immorality, impurity, sensuality, idolatry, sorcery, enmities, strife, jealousy, outbursts of anger, disputes, dissensions, factions, envying, drunkenness, carousing, and things like these, of which I forewarn you just as I have forewarned you that those who practice such things

42. Barth, *Church Dogmatics IV/1*, 720.

43. Calvin, *Institutes of the Christian Religion*, IV.I.4. Calvin appears here to be making an allusion to Cyprian's famous phrase "He cannot have God for his father who does not have the church for his mother."

44. As is evident above, I am interpreting "Spirit" in this passage as a reference to the Holy Spirit. Those who understand this as a reference to the human spirit, thereby making this passage unconnected to the surrounding verses or reworking other phrases in the passage to suit such a "psychological" rendering, are at best engaging in special pleading for modern presumptions about authorship, about transmission of the text, and about environmental influences—to say nothing about surrounding context. E.g., see O'Neill, "Holy Spirit and the Human Spirit in Galatians," 107–20.

shall not inherit the kingdom of God. But the fruit of the Spirit is love, joy, peace, patience, kindness, goodness, faithfulness, gentleness, self-control; against such things there is no law. Now those who belong to Christ Jesus have crucified the flesh with its passions and desires. If we live by the Spirit, let us also walk by the Spirit. Let us not become boastful, challenging one another, envying one another.

Having established in the previous verses that salvation is an opportunity for service to one another through love (5:13–15), Paul opens this passage by first commanding the Galatians to "walk by the Spirit." It is no small thing that we should understand the imperative to "walk by the Spirit" in the context of service to one another. The whole issue of walking by the Spirit is sandwiched between the imperatives, "serve one another" (5:13) and "bear one another's burdens" (6:2). This would seem to set the tone for how we are to interpret what comes between. Paul is *not* intending to lay out some isolationistic teaching on self-improvement. On the contrary, he intends for his teaching on the Holy Spirit to be understood in the context of the body life of the church. Paul is teaching pneumatology, but only as a subset of ecclesiology. In fact, it may be plausible to understand Paul's teaching on the works of the flesh and the fruit of the Spirit to be his own commentary on 5:13 ("For you were called to freedom, brethren; only do not turn your freedom into an opportunity for the flesh, but through love serve one another"). Having stated this as his premise for how to live as church, Paul may be spelling out for his readers what this living as the church looks like in the everyday terms of living life together. Taking his cue from this passage, he provides his readers with a list of what it would mean to "turn freedom into an opportunity for the flesh" in verses 19–21. Then he turns to what it is like to "through love serve one another" by listing the fruits of the Spirit in verses 22–23. With this as the context surrounding this passage, let us turn our attention to the verses at hand: Galatians 5:15–26.

Consistent with the context of life in the ecclesiological community, Paul opens this passage by using the second person plural imperative to emphasize the fact that, as was seen above with regard to the corporate nature of plural imperatives, walking by the Spirit is not to be done as an individual or as merely a collection of individuals: "But I say, [you (*pl.*)] walk by the Spirit" (v. 16). In other words, Paul is telling us that sanctification is primarily a work of the Holy Spirit in the context of the community of the church. This is, of course, directly in line with Hauerwas's concern that ethics be derivative of a narrative community in action. Likewise, as will be seen below, this imperative fits well with the more "Aristotelian" elements in Paul's ethics. Such a fit is made specifically clear later in 6:1–2, but for now let us direct our attention to the relationship between the flesh and the Spirit.

The flesh is explained as that quality in humanity that "sets its desire against the Spirit" (v. 17). Likewise, the Spirit is against the flesh, "for these are in opposition to one another, so that you may not do the things that you please" (v. 17). Paul uses the contrast between flesh and service to one another in verse 13, implying that part of the definition of walking by the Spirit is, through love, to "serve one another." This use of the object "one another" makes it likely that Paul is not discussing a psychology of the self here. Paul already presupposes the primacy of the community over the self. What he is doing here is laying out the way(s) in which the old human nature may still be plaguing the community of the church as they live together as church. The "flesh" is a technical term for Paul, used to describe the sinfully inclined old nature that directs the life of the unbeliever and even still plagues the lives of believers, causing them to struggle with doing what they know to be right, or with what they "please" (cf. Rom 7:14–25). The flesh is not simply removed from the lives of believers once they receive the Spirit. On the contrary, believers still have to overcome constantly the temptation to sin and the enslavement to sin that once marked their lives (Rom 6:15–23). According to Paul, one overcomes the influences of sin by "walking by the Spirit." But again, this is not individuated holiness; it is corporate. The deeds of the flesh may be exhibited both corporately and individually; however, Paul's intent here is to address the impact these deeds have on the church. Likewise, as will be seen in reference to Galatians 6:1–2, Paul's remedy for holiness is to *be* the church, not some psychologized personal improvement plan for the self. The only question remaining then is, how does one walk by the Spirit? Or better, how does the church as a community walk by the Spirit?

Ignoring the ecclesiological context, some of the more traditional understandings of this passage follow the supernatural route, understanding "walk by the Spirit" as some type of inner compulsion or feeling generated by the Holy Spirit in the individual's life.[45] In order to attain this feeling or to discover the "leading" of the Spirit, one must diligently seek some type of inner voice or must wait for a distinct sign from God.[46] While I am not opposed to the self-discipline required for a person to remove worldly distractions from life, I do not find such a concept of spiritual leading in this text. What I do find is that just as the habits of the flesh are learned and "practiced" (Gal 5:21), so too the fruit of Spirit, which seem to be the performance of walking by the Spirit, must likewise be learned and performed.[47]

The habits (εργα) of the flesh are delineated in a lengthy list by Paul. These may best be depicted as habits precisely because Paul states that those who "practice" (πρασσοντες [present, active participle, likely indicating continual or habitual activity]) "such things shall not inherit the kingdom of God" (v. 21). If Paul's expectation here was that someone who had merely one infraction would not "inherit the kingdom of God," then we would be forced to expect perfection immediately upon receipt of the Holy Spirit. Instead, what Paul is identifying is those people whose moral natures are characterized by a repetitive engagement (thus the present tense) in activities that would indicate a lack of spiritual change in their

45. Though I am not denying that such an internal working is present, as promised in the prophecies of the new covenant (e.g., Jer 31 and Ezek 36), it appears as though emphasizing the primary working of the Holy Spirit as a supernatural "impulse" leaves the teaching of such passages vague and useless. E.g., see Bruce, *Commentary on Galatians*, 243; Fung, *Epistle to the Galatians*, 248–49; and Schmoller, *Epistle of Paul to the Galatians*, 136–37.

46. Fung, *Epistle to the Galatians*, 248–49. Fung is here relying on the statements of Ladd, *Theology of the New Testament*, 475. Though Fung would likely bristle at such a depiction of his Pauline ethic, he nevertheless leaves the reader, as do most commentators, with little development of how one is to walk by the Spirit. To say that [it walking in the Spirit] is internal and that the Spirit will give "constant, moment-by-moment direction, control, and guidance" (Fung, *Epistle to the Galatians*, 249) leaves it to the reader to discover how this takes place. Since we live in a moral culture of individual choice and an ethic primarily linked to personal conscience, walking by the Spirit has easily become merely a way to restate living by personal choice, albeit supposedly good choices. Thus, education, or providing people with good information, becomes the key to moral living. Such is the ethics of liberalism. Cf. Kant's equivocation between the human conscience and the Holy Spirit, Kant, *Religion within the Limits of Reason Alone*, 131 n., 136 n.

47. While not engaging in a detailed analysis of this point, Stephen Winward recognizes that walking by the Spirit entails practice and an active engagement toward performing the virtues listed as fruit in the community of faith. See his *Fruit of the Spirit*, especially 23–24.

lives. They do not resist the temptation to follow the flesh, nor do they wish to resist. What we are left with, then, is a group of people who constantly engage in activities that have become almost second nature for them. To complete the analogy, one might say they are "walking by the flesh."

Stepping back from the passage for a moment, we note that the imperative Paul gives to contrast the continual engagement in the deeds of the flesh is to "*walk* by the Spirit" (v. 16). It is interesting to note that the word is an imperative, meaning that the hearers are being called to action and not to passivity. Paul expects them to do something. This command (περιπατειτε [present, active imperative, again likely indicating ongoing activity]) implies a continual reliance on the provision of the Spirit. How the Spirit effects this moral transformation or how he gives the power to perform the fruits that accompany such walking is a bit uncertain, in that Paul uses no specific preposition. In other words, πνευματι could just as easily be understood in a locative sense ("walk in the Spirit") as in an instrumental sense ("walk by the Spirit"). The difference is perhaps minor, but does suggest another possibility for understanding how one walks in relation to the Spirit. Let us now address the question of how believers are to "walk by (or in) the Spirit."

It seems reasonable from both the preceding and the following context to suggest that Paul is here instructing believers to walk in the community of the Spirit (i.e., in the church). He is not telling them to isolate themselves from others so that the Spirit might somehow supernaturally direct them in a more moral path. On the contrary, he is telling them to immerse themselves in the church, so that they might learn the habits of the Spirit instead of succumbing to the temptations of the flesh (i.e., the temptations that are the community of the world). The corporate nature of this passage follows directly on the heels of the command to "serve one another" (v. 13). Likewise, a corporate interpretation seems to best fit the context of Galatians 6:1–2 (the chapter break here is unfortunate). Instead of understanding Paul as beginning a new teaching in chapter 6, Paul's teaching is perhaps better understood as a continuation of how to "walk by (or in) the Spirit." Galatians 6:1–2 states:

> Brethren, even if a man is caught in any trespass, you who are spiritual, restore such a one in a spirit of gentleness; looking to yourself, lest you too be tempted. Bear one another's burdens and thus fulfill the law of Christ.

Paul expects the community of the church to function as a body that would use its various parts to heal and restore an ailing limb. One does not simply cut the ailing limb off and wait for a new one to grow. Indeed, such a practice would again expect perfectionism from believers. Instead, one seeks to restore the person caught in the sin, so that the person might not continue in it. But it is not enough to simply direct a person out of a sin and to leave them in a state of neutrality. In other words, instead of simply teaching a person not to continue pursuing sin, the church must also teach that person what should be pursued. Absence of sin is not equivalent to holiness. It still does not come entirely natural to humans to pursue righteousness, even though they are no longer enslaved to sin (Rom 6:17–22). It is the influence of modernity that has taught us to believe, "Fruit [of the Spirit] is a natural outcome, by a process of steady growth, of a principle of life *within*."[48] On the contrary, believers must still be taught the habits or virtues that would lead to living a life reflecting the lordship of Christ over his church. In the formation of habits or virtues, the fruit of the Spirit enters in.[49]

The fruit of the Spirit is not passively obtained by just waiting around for it to be born in a person's life. Ethical passivity is the pre-

---

48. Gee, "Gifts and Fruit of the Spirit," 21, emphasis his. The passivity implied here is destructive of the very point of the passage, i.e., an imperative to practice the fruit of the Spirit in the community of the church.

49. I should point out that by using the terms "habits" or "virtues," I am not intending to make a direct parallel between the list of the virtues of Aristotle or Plato and Paul's writings, e.g., the fruit of the Spirit. Some modern Protestants have argued for such a comparison (Bultmann, *Theology of the New Testament*, 2:225–27). Though not enumerating the Aristotelian or Platonic virtues, Bultmann implies this when he argues that good Christian ethics are equivocal with good pagan ethics, since both represent the good toward which all humans seek. Others have argued against it (e.g., see Ridderbos, *Paul: An Outline of His Theology*, 297). I am not here concerned with what the "fruit" is specifically. Instead, I am focusing on how it is obtained. In this regard, I find Aristotle helpful. Interestingly, Ridderbos makes the further point that Christian virtue is focused more specifically on "brotherly communion and the upbuilding of the church, and not, as in the Greek ethic, . . . [on] character formation" (297). Ridderbos appears to imply that Greek ethics was primarily concerned with the individual, rather than the community. While I find such a reading of the "Greeks" incongruous with Aristotle's vision of the good polis, I do wish to resonate with Ridderbos's emphasis that Christian virtue, (i.e., the fruit of the Spirit) is focused specifically on the community of faith, rather than the individual. Though Ridderbos may not have read Aristotle well, he seems to have gotten Paul right.

dominant context in which this passage has been interpreted.[50] For instance, Ronald Fung states,

> [Fruit of the Spirit] directly ascribes the power of fructification not to the believer himself but to the Spirit, and effectively hints that the qualities enumerated are not the result of strenuous observance of an external legal code, but the *natural* product ("harvest") of a life controlled and guided by the Spirit.[51]

Fung is undoubtedly right that Paul is opposed to the external legal code. But Paul's opposition to the legal code does not warrant an assumption that the only other option is something strictly internal or passively attained. As will be argued below, Paul appears instead to have in mind life in the community of the church, which is certainly indwelled by the Spirit. That is why the "fruit of the Spirit" is sandwiched between teachings on life in the community (5:13–15 and 6:1–2). The church enacts walking by the Spirit as it trains its people in righteousness. Though not attributing Paul's aversion to the law specifically to a quote of Aristotle, F. F. Bruce still proposes that Paul may be here relying on an Aristotelian conception of virtue.

> In Aristotle (*Pol.* 3.13, 1284a) the statement κατα δε των τοιουτων ουκ εστι νομος is used of persons who surpass their fellows in virtue (αρετη) like gods among men. They do not need to have their actions regulated by laws; on the contrary, they themselves constitute a law (a standard) for others

50. A good example of this in brief can be found in Scofield's discussion of how the fruit of the Spirit is brought about in a person's life. See Scofield, "Personal Relationships and the Work of the Indwelling Spirit," 41. I happily admit that Scofield and others along this line of interpretation believed that Paul was commanding believers to "walk by the Spirit," understanding this to mean a closer connection to the power of the Spirit. They believed too that Paul was calling people to action. But in focusing on a closer connection to the Spirit, they have implicitly turned inward into the individuated self, since this is likewise where they have emphasized the Spirit's dwelling. I am not denying the personal indwelling ministry of the Spirit. What I am saying is that to focus on it to the exclusion of the dwelling of the Spirit in the community of the church is to parallel the Enlightenment turn to the subject and, subsequently, to transform the Spirit into the human conscience or a psychologized "feeling" of heightened spiritual awareness, both of which are human products—even worse, individualistically unassailable human products. Thus have many fundamentalists and evangelicals unwittingly pandered to the hermeneutic of experience. They have begun to sound all too much like the classical liberals who likewise attributed the work of the Holy Spirit to the mere working of the human spirit in the individual.

51. Fung, *Epistle to the Galatians*, 262; emphasis mine.

(αυτοι γαρ εισι νομος). Paul probably does not quote directly or consciously from Aristotle: the saying may have passed into proverbial currency, like many phrases from Shakespeare or the AV which are frequently quoted without awareness of their source. Aristotle's statement shows some (rather remote) affinity with what Paul says here; it has more in common with the observation in 1 Tim. 1:9 that "the law is not laid down for the just but for the lawless and disobedient.[52]

Fruit of the Spirit, like virtue, is not passively obtained. Accordingly, a person does not grow the fruit of the Spirit by simply expecting the Spirit to somehow supernaturally produce it in his or her life. Instead, the fruit of the Spirit ("love, joy, peace, patience, kindness, goodness, faithfulness, gentleness, self-control" [5:22–23]) is a composition of habits learned in the community of fellowship known as church. They must be taught to people by others who do them well (cf. Phil 4:9).[53] In this way, "walking by the Spirit" is seen best as an apprenticeship in which novices learn from masters. The biblical term for this is, of course, *discipleship*, a point already made for us above by Hauerwas.[54] An Aristotelian epistemology is helpful in this regard in confirming that the church cannot expect believers to learn the fruit of the Spirit by simply giving them the information and waiting for them to grasp it on their own, eventually becoming moral by making better and better choices as they maintain control over their own lives. Scripture does

52. Bruce, *Commentary on Galatians*, 255–56. Bruce's distancing of Paul from Aristotle is perhaps overstated if one views Galatians 6:2 ("Bear one another's burdens, and thus fulfill the law of Christ") as the climax of this passage. In other words, perhaps Paul is reflecting precisely on the notion that those who are in the church and are being taught how to be part of the church are in fact a law unto themselves, in that they are now pursuing and achieving virtue rather than merely conforming to external standards.

53. The presumption that not everyone is equal in this regard will undoubtedly be offensive to the modernistic sensibilities of those committed to the democratic nature of ethics based on inherent capabilities qua human. See Kant, *Foundations of the Metaphysics of Morals*, 397. Hauerwas is, rightly, opposed to the supposed equality implied and explicit in Enlightenment ethics, particularly in Kant. Cf. Hauerwas and Willimon, *Resident Aliens*, 98–103.

54. Interestingly, as a systematic contrast, Pannenberg's ecclesiology does not draw significant attention to the direct connection between ecclesiology and discipleship. It is, remarkably, absent in Pannenberg. For him, discipleship has more to do with proclamation and theoretical relations than it does with the ongoing human community of church in history. See Pannenberg, *Systematic Theology*, 3:91–92, 232, 241–42.

not pander to the preeminence of the self. The church must counter modern individualism and autonomy (i.e., liberalism) by training its followers to follow the lives of masters, to submit themselves together to the lordship of Christ. As seen in the last chapters, to suggest this notion of apprenticeship is what Hauerwas has intended through granting primacy to ecclesiology, that is, to the narrative community. Further, apprenticeship seems to be what Paul has in mind when he commands the Corinthians to "Imitate me as I imitate Christ." (1 Cor 11:1), and to "imitate" him since "in Christ Jesus I became your father through the gospel" (1 Cor 4:15–16).[55] The liberalism of modernity has taught people to object to such authoritarianism as an infringement on the rights of individuals to choose their own destiny. Likewise, such tutelage by imitation is precisely what the Enlightenment rebelled against when it rejected the church over two hundred years ago.[56] However, as Hauerwas has forcefully argued, the Enlightenment tradition is not the church's tradition. The language, even the realism, of the church is to be found in its alliance with the tradition as depicted in Scripture. Aristotelian apprenticeship into the fruit of the Spirit appears to be very much in line with the teachings of Scripture.

While this may seem like a leap in logic to connect the Pauline notion of imitation to Aristotle's model of apprenticeship in ethics, the two may actually have more in common than a simple conceptual parallel. The words Paul uses for "imitation" (μιμεομαι, μιμητης, and συμμιμητης) have their origin in Platonic thought. Plato's notion that the ideas or forms are enacted in reality required that some type of imitation occur as humans attempted to enflesh the idea or the "really real" ideal of the form. Aristotle moved beyond this in his ethics by positing that the ultimate in virtue was not a form or idea somewhere in the realm of the ethereal (i.e., a principle) but a human reality in the flesh of everyday activities done by virtuous people. Nevertheless, imitation re-

---

55. The notion of Paul's considering himself a father to the Corinthians, and thus worthy of imitation, is a useful comparison with Luther's notion of himself as a father of those who would follow his own teaching. It seems likely that the notion of church as school and of masters teaching apprentices is as strong in Luther as it is in Paul and in Aristotle. See Luther, "Lectures on Titus," 14–15. Luther does not, perhaps in contrast to post-Enlightenment Protestant expectations, support the primacy of the self. He recognizes the role the self must play, but he still grants primacy for moral transformation to the community of the church and to church leadership.

56. Cf. Kant, "What Is Enlightenment?" 85–92.

mained the key to becoming virtuous as people attempted to model the behavior seen in others who were virtuous. Such imitation was hardly a matter of simply copying behavior. Instead, it involved the enactment of the whole person in performing virtuous acts. Likewise, Paul has inherited this from both his Jewish roots (Deut 6:4–5) and his philosophical training. Though he may not be quoting Plato or Aristotle directly, Paul is using the same language in a very similar way for his Christian audience. Undoubtedly, Paul's education made him very aware of Greek thought. His use of language hardly seems arbitrary.[57]

A challenge to such a communal interpretation of Galatians 5:16–6:2 is found directly in the succeeding verses. Galatians 6:3–5 discusses the life of individuals who should examine themselves with regard to sin; the discussion climaxes with the statement that "each one shall bear his own load" (v. 5). This would appear to make the individual responsible for his or her own spiritual growth, "fruit of the Spirit," or removal of sin. However, if one recalls that Paul has used this same metaphor ("to bear") in an individualistic sense the preceding verses (5:10), then one discovers that there he uses the language of "bearing" with regard to judgment for sin, and not with regard to transformation by the Holy Spirit. Judgment of the individual for sin seems a better way to understand Galatians 6:5. While it may be true that judgment of sin is still accounted according to the works of the individual, and that each individual will face judgment alone, it also appears true that moral transformation by the Holy Spirit is to be the result of living within the community, or school, of the church.

Conclusion

This chapter has sought to provide the ecclesiological reflections of Hauerwas with the outline of a pneumatology necessary to make his church a divine community. The passages under discussion have dem-

---

57. For a development of the linguistic history and Paul's inheritance of it, see Michaelis, " mimeomai, mimhthj, summimhthj," *TDNT* 4: 659–74. Certainly, Paul does not see himself as the only model to follow, nor is he the perfect model. Jesus is Paul's perfect model to imitate. In other words, Jesus is the virtuous man. However, Jesus is not himself physically present in the sight of people any longer, having left the role of providing models to imitate to the apostles. Succeeding generations must likewise provide models of godliness to follow. Unfortunately, as mentioned above, liberalism has done its best to convince us we do not need such models.

onstrated that ecclesiology is epistemologically and ontologically prior to the individuated self. The Apostle Paul's thought on pneumatology (particularly his construction of metaphors), on ecclesial authority, and on formation through the practices found in the character habits of the fruit of the Spirit all accord well with Hauerwas's emphasis on the church as a formative narrative. Furthermore, Paul's emphases provide Hauerwas with a connection to the divine that lies outside a mere sociological depiction of the church. Thus, Hauerwas's ecclesiology can be consistent both in emphasizing the role of the divine in morally forming the human and in proclaiming that ecclesiology is its own epistemology.

The primary role of the Spirit—understood as bringing glory to Jesus—is given further credence and expansion by opening the role of the Spirit to a more corporate understanding. Whereas the individual has dominated most understandings of the notion of the Spirit's indwelling for the last few centuries, this study has demonstrated that Scripture may be better understood as locating the Spirit's indwelling primarily in the community of the church. Though by no means attempting a novel interpretation of Scripture, this study understands "church" as a living organism (i.e., as a body) that is the primary dynamic in forming those who are part of it. The church is not merely a collection of individuals. Instead, through the Spirit, it is made into more than it could be by itself. It is fashioned into the formative community that Hauerwas envisioned in his ecclesiology.

Finally, this study has intentionally attempted to spell out the necessity for seeing as identical the natural and the supernatural in the Spirit's activity in human sanctification. The humanity of the Spirit has been neglected as a theological conception of the way in which the activity of the Spirit in humanity should be understood. However, it seems that such a notion as the humanity of the Spirit is precisely in line with the scriptural teachings about an ontology of the church. The church is caught up, through participation, into the divine community of the Trinity. As it participates in this divine relationship, it does so not in some mystical or gnostic (i.e., nonmaterial) sense. Instead, the very relations of humans to other humans within the church ground the display of such a divine and human union. Thus, the human activity attributable to the Spirit becomes indistinguishable from the activity of the Spirit as supposedly supernatural. While this argument does not reduce the Spirit to anthropology (the Spirit maintains his own distinct personhood), it does allow the practices of humans within the church to take on theological significance.

Let us now place the emphasis of this chapter back into the context of the overall study. In chapters 1, 2, and 3 of this study, we reviewed Hauerwas's critique of system as a tool for those engaging in what he would term a more "liberal" strategy of theological investigation. Hauerwas rightly identified systematics as primarily concerned with discovering and justifying universal truth claims. Such justification is based on the rationality of theological knowledge. In other words, such knowledge is available to any rational creature and could only be counted as knowledge when divorced from any particularistic view-point. Consequently, knowledge that claims an attachment to history, including to the history of Jesus, was deemed too contingent to be considered true. Hauerwas demonstrates, by discussing Kant and others, that such a view of universal knowledge needs to be understood as a product of certain historical circumstances; understanding the notion of universal knowledge as itself contingent on history makes such a notion as universal knowledge self-contradictory. Hauerwas argues that what is needed is an epistemology that takes history into account—an epistemology open to the kind of claims theologians make about the relationship of knowledge to action, and to the claim of Jesus to be the Truth.

Chapters 4 and 5 set out to display Hauerwas's alternative to systematic knowledge. Here he provides the reader with a fairly "thick" depiction of what a narrative epistemology would look like and of how it would function in theology. By discussing Barth and placing Barth against the backdrop of Aquinas and Aristotle, we were able to see that Hauerwas's narrative epistemology reverses the Enlightenment primacy given to thought over action. In Hauerwas's reading of the Enlightenment, thought (or theoretical knowledge) was given the high ground with regard to what constituted knowledge, with action deriving from the principles of knowledge provided by thought. In contrast to this, Hauerwas sees action as primary in a narrative epistemology. Aristotle, as assimilated into Christian theology through Aquinas, was particularly helpful here. Aristotle rightly understood that moral training (which, by and large, is theology for Hauerwas) requires the kind of practice only apprenticeship affords. Therefore, the knowledge gained in apprenticeship derives not from thought but from the actions themselves. The impact of such an epistemological shift for Hauerwas is that now theology must be understood through the lens of the narrative, or formative, community, which is the church. Ecclesiology, then, takes on an epistemological role in any claims that the church might make about knowledge and truth. Rather than Rather than deriving from a historical vacuum, truth is now centered, as is theologically appropriate, on the person of Jesus. For the church to know truth, it must be truthful to his story. In other words, one of the more important elements that the church bears in demonstrating its veracity is its faithfulness to live the story of Jesus.

Chapter 5 in particular fleshed out the way in which the church demonstrates this faithfulness through its witness to the world of the lordship of Jesus. Here the full impact of Hauerwas's ecclesiology is seen. As the historical community of faith, the church submits itself to the headship of Jesus. This is not knowledge exclusive to the church, since the whole world is subject to his rule. The church's goal is to live his lordship in such a way as to call the world to acknowledge its place before him, as subject to him as well. The message of the church is not a message of bowing before a malevolent dictator. On the contrary, it is a call for all to participate in the loving relationship that marks the very heart of the Godhead itself. This notion of being drawn into participation in God is the way in which the church is raised to be more than itself. It is not a mere human community. It is a community that strives to be the very body of Christ.

It is on this point of the church's being a divine community that we discovered Hauerwas's most serious problem. While he makes an effort to provide the human community of the church with a divine connection through the sacraments, this remains a rather sporadic and mystical connection. It was argued that Hauerwas is far better served to ground the connection of the church to the divine in a robust doctrine of the Holy Spirit. This would give him the means to overcome the anthropological reductionism into which he seems to lapse. At the same time, pneumatology would provide him with greater warrant for making the claim to the church's divine participation. The church is finally made the body of Christ only through the Spirit.

In the face of many decades, at least, of emphasis on the supernatural working of the Spirit in the lives of individuals, this chapter provides a concerted theological effort toward a more precisely scriptural portrayal of the ministry of the Holy Spirit in the natural or human community of the church. The Spirit works primarily in the community of faith, and only secondarily in the individual. This does not dismiss individual participation in the activity of the Spirit. Instead, recognition of the corporate working of the Spirit brings needed humility to claims of the Spirit's presence in the lives of individuals. Training (or in Aristotelian language, apprenticeship) becomes the way in which people are invited into the community of worship. Ecclesiology is the proper context in which to place any discussion of the work of the Spirit (i.e., the connection between the human and the divine), since it is to the *head of the church—Jesus—*that the Spirit directs all people within the church. Just as the deity of the Son has often eclipsed his humanity, the supernatural work of the Spirit seems to have entirely covered his place in the natural working of the community of the church. While not denying the supernatural elements of the Spirit's ministry, this study has sought to show that the more primary locus of the Spirit's work is found in the activity of the church being church. This is perhaps the most obvious connection between the work of Hauerwas and the original discussions of the Holy Spirit offered in this chapter. Hauerwas has endeavored to demonstrate the primacy of churchly activities in his epistemological efforts. This chapter offers a depiction of the Spirit's working in the midst of the people of the church. As they themselves work to be church, their faithfulness to living the gospel lifts what might otherwise be considered common activities to the level of primary or foundational acts. Being church is the primary work of Christians. By theology's developing more thoroughly scriptural meditations on the Spirit, being church may also become the primary work of theology. Further, it is in development of ecclesiology (in the context of pneumatological participation of the church in God) that theology as life, instead of a purely academic discipline, can be regarded once again as primarily for the church.

8

Ancient Answers to Novel Problems

Introduction

SURELY OBJECTIONS WILL ARISE TO ANY PURPORTED THEOLOGICAL OR biblical novelties. This study does not pretend to be beyond criticism or correction. Undoubtedly certain things have been stated unclearly or perhaps without qualification. I may simply be wrong about some things. However, it seems incumbent upon the author to attempt an answer to some expected criticism before it too easily overshadows the primary thrusts of the study.

This chapter is intended to anticipate certain objections and to give a more detailed response than sporadic footnotes might provide. Here, the objections will include both direct problems associated with the scriptural interpretations presented above, and problems associated with certain presuppositions foundational to those interpretations. The first objection is a perceived difference between Paul and Jesus on the subject of the Spirit. The study will attempt to demonstrate that their teachings on the subject are consistent. Further, later in the study we will also see that the model of human formation through divine participation outlined above had effect for even Jesus himself. On the side of presuppositions, the study will attempt to define some of the cultural influences that may have been shaping the scriptural rendering of the Holy Spirit. We will see that Aristotelian apprenticeship in ethics seems consistent with Paul and Jesus's conception of formation by the Holy Spirit in the church. Finally we will demonstrate that Hauerwas's conception of church as church in contradistinction to the world is rightly placed as a proclamation of the lordship of Jesus over all creation.

Do Paul and Jesus Contrast In Their Understanding Of and Relationship to the Spirit?

Thus far our study has engaged, in a more technical manner, the teachings of Paul on how the church is to function according to the workings of the Holy Spirit. Not everyone would assume that Scripture is consistent in this teaching. Some may even wish to use other voices in Scripture to counter the Pauline argument constructed above.[1] Given his consistent emphasis that the primary formative story for the church is the life of Jesus, Hauerwas may even wish to counter that this study in pneumatology has focused on secondary teachings in Scripture, missing the central points of his narratively constructed epistemology and ecclesiology as they are depicted as ecclesiology by the authors of Scripture.[2] Further, one could anticipate the objection that what has been described in Paul is not the way the Holy Spirit actually worked in the life of Jesus. In other words, the depiction of the indwelling ministry of the Spirit given above is not how it actually occurred for Jesus (i.e., Jesus had no formative community to mediate the work of the Spirit), so why should we expect the work of the Spirit to occur in this way for other humans? To answer all these concerns, save the last (which will be discussed in a later section), our study must shift its focus to the Holy Spirit in the life of Jesus. This section of the study will demonstrate the consistency between Paul's teaching and the texts recording Jesus's words on the Holy Spirit. The next section will highlight a primary contextual influence regarding community and moral epistemology in the New Testament. This second section is a contrast to what this study perceives as the more typical anachronistic approach to Scripture through the primacy of the Enlightenment self. Finally, attention will be given to Jesus's own life and teachings about the Spirit.

---

1. Pannenberg finds several "differences" amongst the various New Testament books in their teachings on pneumatology. See Pannenberg, *Systematic Theology*, 3:6–7.

2. I do not mean to imply here that Hauerwas has a canon within the canon. His emphasis on Jesus and on Jesus's church as a living body is consistent with the emphasis seen in the scriptural texts related to ecclesiology. However, we are attempting to provide a way for his ecclesiology to be more than anthropology—thus the central focus on the Spirit.

JESUS AS SOURCE FOR PAUL IN GALATIANS

It seems reasonable to presume that Paul was not being original in using the metaphor of the "fruit of the Spirit." Indeed, the origins of such a metaphor may be attributed to Jesus himself. Jesus's primary teachings on the Holy Spirit are found in John 14 and 16. From the text of John, it is apparent that John 14–17 are all one discourse spoken by Jesus while he is at the table with his disciples. Two points stand out clearly as Jesus intertwines his teaching on the coming Holy Spirit with other teachings. First, sandwiched between his teachings on the Holy Spirit, Jesus uses the metaphor of the vine and the branches in John 15, including the notion of bearing fruit. This suggests, at least, that the life that the disciples would live in the Spirit after Jesus's departure would be one marked by fruit (or by the lack thereof), making the parallel metaphor of "the fruit of the Spirit" in Paul a relatively small step for Paul to make. Of course, one cannot be anachronistic here. Such a parallel relies on the presumption that Paul would have known Jesus's teachings on the subject of the vine and branches when he penned Galatians.

Since Galatians was likely written many years prior to the Gospel of John, the only means open to Paul for acquiring Jesus's teaching on fruit is oral tradition. Certainly oral tradition existed, as can be illustrated by observing certain statements that Paul attributes to Jesus—statements found nowhere in the gospel accounts. Paul quotes Jesus in Acts 20:35 as stating, "'It is more blessed to give than receive.'" While it may be plausible to believe that Paul is merely paraphrasing something found in the Gospels, it is perhaps more likely to find Paul here quoting a teaching of Jesus found in oral tradition. All this is to say that it is likely that Paul's primary source for Jesus's teachings in his early years of ministry was what he had been taught by the apostles and others. The fact that both Jesus and Paul discuss fruit does not establish Paul's reliance on Jesus' teaching for the metaphor of the fruit of the Spirit, but it does certainly make it a possibility. Such a conjecture of Paul's knowledge of Jesus' upper room discourse in John is perhaps further strengthened by a second characteristic of this passage to be noticed.

Jesus makes an issue of the disciples' relationship to the world in no uncertain terms. He explains that the world will "hate" them (15:18) and that they were chosen "out of the world" (15:19). Jesus even goes so far as to tell the disciples that the world will kill them (16:2). The disciples who are left behind to become the church have no part in the world, nor does the world have any part in them. The means for their survival and thriving as the church is precisely in becoming a part of the community called church that is rooted in participation in the community of the Trinity (17:21). In this regard, Hauerwas's emphasis on the church's commitment to ecclesiology is entirely biblical. Jesus begins to explain such a notion in John 13:34–35 by giving the disciples a new commandment to "love one another." He repeats this command in 15:12. His teaching on the role of community as a core teaching of the church climaxes in 17:20–26 (esp. v. 21) with Jesus's prayer for the unity of the disciples in their love for each other and for a communion with the Triune Godhead through participation in the love shared between the Father and the Son. Thus, Hauerwas's and Pannenberg's emphasis on participation as central to the communal identity of the church and to its moral formation is also a necessary component of a biblical ecclesiology.

If John 14–17 is an appropriate context in which to interpret Galatians 5:16—6:2, this context helps to explain the contrast Paul makes between the community of the flesh (world) and the community of the Spirit (church). Likewise, it deepens our understanding of what Paul has in mind when he discusses the community that "through love serve[s] one another" (Gal 5:13) and "bears one another's burdens" (Gal 6:2). This is the community that "loves one another" just as Jesus had loved them (John 13:34–35; 15:12), so that they might "thus fulfill the law" (or commandment, or even new commandment) "of Christ" (Gal 6:2).

JESUS AND THE SPIRIT IN EPHESIANS

By way of comparison to the imperative to "walk by the Spirit" in Galatians, another interesting imperative with regard to life in the Holy Spirit is found in Ephesians 5:18. Again using a second person plural imperative, Paul directs the believers at Ephesus to "be filled with the Spirit." Setting this passage in the context of the surrounding verses, we find that it appears to be speaking directly to the issue of living rightly in relationship to both Christ and fellow believers. Having just proscribed association with the "sons of disobedience" (5:3–14), taking special note of their immoral activities and of what such association would do to those who claim to be part of the church, Paul commends a better path to the Ephesians:

> Therefore, be careful how you walk, not as unwise men, but as wise, making the most of your time, because the days are evil. So then do not be foolish, but understand what the will of the Lord is. And do not get drunk with wine, for that is dissipation, but be filled with the Spirit, speaking to one another in psalms and hymns and spiritual songs, singing and making melody with your heart to the Lord; always giving thanks for all things in the name of our Lord Jesus Christ to God, even the Father; and be subject to one another in the fear of Christ. (Eph 5:15–21)

Two points about Paul's command to "be filled with the Spirit" deserve attention in light of the context of the whole passage. First, the Holy Spirit is apparently the agency of the filling rather than the substance with which believers are filled. The focus in this passage is not upon the wine and the Spirit as the substances of the filling. Instead the focus is on the way in which each one directs the will of the believer. Wine takes over a person's mind in such a way that one becomes enslaved to the whims of compulsion. That is why Paul calls the controlling effects of wine "dissipation." Those who are under its control do not have the capacity to direct their lives in a moral and prudent manner. Likewise, the substance of the Spirit is not what is at issue, but the way in which one is to be controlled by the Spirit and directed toward the Lord Jesus. One might even translate the concept of "filling" here as "be directed by the Holy Spirit." As Hauerwas and Pannenberg have made abundantly clear above, the Spirit's goal is to glorify Christ by directing the followers of Christ to live in community with one another: to join together in their worship and affirmation of the lordship of the Son. This is why Paul follows up his imperative to "be filled by the Spirit" with "be subject to one another" (5:21). Paul wishes the church to perform its filling of the Spirit by performing rightly the relationships that people in the church have with one another. This especially includes the relationships in which believers find themselves, whether as husbands and wives (5:22–33), as children and parents (6:1–4), or as slaves and masters (6:5–9). Each of these relationships is important, but they all serve only to illustrate the ultimate relationship that Christ is to have with his church (5:32). Though Paul is instructing believers here to compel each other to live in appropriate relationships with one another, the final relationship about

which he is concerned is that of Christ to the church. Other relationships are both illustrative and substantive. It is with this in mind that
our second point about Paul's directive to "be filled with the Spirit" must
be understood. The church is to be directed toward coming to Christ as
a "holy and blameless" bride (5:27). While it is evident that it is Christ
who makes the church spotless, nevertheless Paul compels believers to
live holy and blameless lives in their relations with one another. This is
the way that the church will be known as church: by their relationships
to one another, and not as the "sons of disobedience" found in the world.
Further, in the quality of relationships among believers, the "filling" of
the Spirit is made evident.

Jesus and the Spirit in Colossians

Though the strength of comparison may be called into question (since
it is unlikely that the readers of Ephesians and Colossians would have
compared their letters), nevertheless, presuming Paul's authorship of
each letter implies a strong sense of parallelism between the notion of
being "filled with the Spirit" in Ephesians and the "peace of Christ" and
the "word of Christ" in Colossians 3:12–17. The parallels between these
passages seem apparent, as one can observe in the following quotation
from Colossians 3:12–17:

> And so, as those who have been chosen of God, holy and be-
> loved, put on a heart of compassion, kindness, humility, gentle-
> ness and patience; bearing with one another, and forgiving each
> other, whoever has a complaint against anyone; just as the Lord
> forgave you, so also should you. And beyond all these things put
> on love, which is the perfect bond of unity. And let the peace of
> Christ rule in your hearts, to which indeed you were called in
> one body; and be thankful. Let the word of Christ richly dwell
> within you, with all wisdom teaching and admonishing one an-
> other with psalms and hymns and spiritual songs, singing with
> thankfulness in your hearts to God. And whatever you do in
> word or deed, do all in the name of the Lord Jesus, giving thanks
> to Him through God the Father.

It seems plausible to assume some parallelism here with what it
means to "be filled with the Spirit" in Ephesians, given the similarity of

the lists of "virtues" in both Ephesians and Colossians.[3] If one assumes parallelism between Ephesians and Colossians, then the communal nature of the "filling of the Spirit" becomes fairly obvious. "Bearing with one another," "forgiving each other," "teaching and admonishing one another," are all marks of what it means to be a part of a community in which the "peace of Christ" rules in hearts, and in which the "word of Christ richly dwells within" them. (Paul's listing in Colossians the character qualities of "compassion, kindness, humility, gentleness, and patience" makes this passage in Colossians an interesting "enfleshment" of the fruit of Spirit listed in Galatians 5:22–23. The parallel seems unmistakable.) This is a community of love, "which is the perfect bond of unity." This is the body of Christ. This is the church.

A final point to be noted about the conception of being "filled" with the Holy Spirit is that Paul uses a different word for being "filled" with the Spirit from the word Luke employs in the book of Acts. Luke typically uses the word πιμπλημι. This particular word emphasizes control and empowerment for action, even control of the mind, in this case the control of the Spirit over people and the use of their bodies for certain physical activities (e.g., Acts 2:4). Paul uses the word πληροω. This is a more general word for "filling" and does not seem to require such a strong possession of the person by the substance or object with which one is being filled. Being "led by" may be an adequate understanding of this word in Paul's use. While such a distinction could be attributed mere to two authors' differing views of the same activity, such a distinction may just as plausibly be seen as a development in the understanding of how the Holy Spirit worked in the early church. In other words, it may be plausible to understand the work of the Spirit in the early years of the church to be more direct and immediate, while in later years his work becomes primarily the work of the community of the church. In the later church, rather than direct and immediate, or unmediated, the work of the Spirit is mediated through the human community in which he is said to dwell.

---

3. Dunn, *Epistle to the Colossians and to Philemon*, 136–37. Dunn makes the comparison explicit but still maintains distinctiveness since the two lists are not exact, and the purposes for the lists are unique to each letter.

Can an Aristotelian Paradigm for Ethics Coincide with Scriptural Sanctification?

What has been observed thus far in our discussion is the fact that the Holy Spirit works primarily in the community of the church and that it is through human activity in that community (specifically through training in fruit of the Spirit) that one is brought to maturity in the faith. While these points do not deny the fact of the Spirit's powerful presence in the midst of Christ's people, they do emphasize the fact that a real indwelling ministry of the Spirit requires that he work through human agents to impact other humans. It is not mere coincidence that immediately following the initial indwelling of the Spirit in believers at Pentecost, they "had all things in common, and began selling their property and possessions, and were sharing them with all, as anyone might have need" (Acts 2:44–45). A strong sense of community and fellowship seemed to accompany the coming of the Spirit.[4] Perhaps this is why Paul calls believers to join in the "fellowship of the Spirit" (2 Cor 13:14; Phil 2:1). As people are continually apprenticed in the life of Christ, learning to live as his people to and for one another, they are brought beyond the elemental teachings of the faith to the more hearty, mature teachings meant for those who are ready to become mentors in the process of discipleship. Practicing the faith in communion with one another appears to be the cause of spiritual and moral maturity. Spiritual and moral maturity appears to be what the author of Hebrews has in mind in Hebrews 5:11–14:

> Concerning [Jesus] we have much to say, and it is hard to explain, since you have become dull of hearing. For though by this time you ought to be teachers, you have need again for someone to teach you the elemental principles of the oracles of God, and you have come to need milk and not solid food. For everyone who partakes only of milk is not accustomed to the word of righteousness, for he is a babe. But solid food is for the mature, who because of practice have their senses trained to discern good and evil.

The author makes it clear that it is not because of superior knowledge or position that one is able to live morally, (i.e., to live a life that is honoring to Jesus). Neither is morality due to one's ability to reason

4. Cf. McDonnell, "Communion Ecclesiology and Baptism in the Spirit," 674.

from principles what the best course of action may be, subsequently choosing the good, as though humans were either naturally endowed (liberalism) or supernaturally equipped (mysticism) to favor the good over the evil in the myriad of moral choices.

What such a passage seems to make clear is that an ethic focused on choice does not align with the scriptural method for sanctification. It is not that choices are inherently an inappropriate context for the doing of ethics. Choices need to be made in any ethic. It is the presumption of objectivity and the individuated isolationism often associated with choice that makes choice inappropriate as the primary context in which to discuss ethics. For Christians, no neutral position exists from which to make moral choices. Humans are either "slaves of sin" (Rom 6:17) or, "having been freed from sin," human beings are "enslaved to God" (Rom. 6:22). Scripture presumes, in contrast to the modern presumption of moral neutrality or innate goodness, that moral capacity is instead due to the habituation of the moral agent in the formative community to discern good and evil. The notion of "practice" (εξιν) has the connotation of a "skill acquired through exercise."[5] This means that moral discernment, which in the context of the passage seems to be equivalent with theological acumen, comes primarily from the continued practice of morality in the church.

As was seen in the earlier chapters, Hauerwas accomplishes the move to such a moral epistemology explicitly by appealing to Aristotle, at times directly and at times via Aquinas. The question before us now is whether Aristotle is the best context in which to situate Scripture and the teachings of Jesus and the early church.

Though no scriptural writers directly quote Aristotle, it seems apparent from the epistemological status given to action that Aristotle's influence managed to reach the authors of Scripture. Perhaps, as Bruce noted above, Aristotle had become "proverbial currency."[6] Whatever the case, with regard to the Hebrews passage discussed above, the parallel with Aristotle seems unavoidable. Aristotle makes it clear that

> Intellectual virtue or excellence owes its origin and development chiefly to teaching, and for that reason requires experience and time. Moral virtue, on the other hand, is formed by habit, *ethos,*

5. Bauer et. al., *Greek-English Lexicon,* 276.
6. Bruce, *Epistle to the Galatians,* 255–56.

and its name, *ethike*, is therefore derived, by a slight variation
from *ethos*.... [N]one of the moral virtues is implanted in us by
nature, for nothing which exists from nature can be changed by
habit.... Thus, the virtues are implanted in us neither by nature
nor contrary to nature: we are by nature equipped with the ability to receive them, and habit brings this ability to completion
and fulfillment.[7]

While it may be somewhat problematic to argue from Scripture
that all humans are given by nature the ability to receive the virtues
(although an attempt *to argue this* from the created image of God in
humanity may certainly be a plausible argument,[8]), it is nevertheless
true that those who are part of the church are "created in Christ Jesus
unto good works, which God prepared beforehand, that we should walk
in them" (Eph 2:10).[9] This means that those who are in the church are
created anew for the purpose of performing "good works," however the
notion of good works may be understood. While it would be superficial and textually questionable simply to equivocate between, on the
one hand, being created for good works and, on the other hand, having
natural capacity to receive the virtues (since Christians are specifically
created "*in Christ Jesus* unto good works" and since such a creation is
unique [i.e., not "natural"]), nevertheless the process for attaining virtue appears similar in Aristotle and the authors of Scripture. Aristotle
taught that people need to be instructed to be moral. In one of his more
known sentiments, Aristotle explains

It is by playing the harp that men become both good and bad
harpists, and correspondingly with builders and all other crafts-
men: a man who builds well will be a good builder, one who
builds badly a bad one. For if this were not so, there would be
no need for an instructor, but everybody would be born as a
good or bad craftsman. The same holds true of the virtues: in
our transactions with other men it is by action that some be-

7. Aristotle *Nicomachean Ethics* 1103a.15.

8. Although he uses a conception of common grace as derivative of the image of
God in humanity and does not use image language specifically, Hoekema supports the
notion that humanity's goodness, while limited by sin, is still generally seen in all humans. See Hoekema, *Created in God's Image*, 187–202.

9. I have little interest in defending the notion of morality per se, or, in other words,
morality that is characteristic of all humankind. Instead, for obvious reasons, what I am
interested in is the morality that is to be a distinctive mark of the church.

come just and others unjust. . . . In a word, characteristics develop from corresponding activities. For that reason, we must see to it that our activities are of a certain kind, since any variations in them will be reflected in our characteristics. Hence it is no small matter whether one habit or another is inculcated in us from early childhood; on the contrary, it makes a considerable difference, or, rather, all the difference.[10]

As the author of Hebrews notes, it is "through practice" that "the senses are trained to discern good and evil." The correlation to Aristotle comes at the point of training for discernment. In Aristotle, becoming virtuous comes by being taught by a master, and by doing virtuous acts. In Hebrews, becoming mature in Christ comes by training the senses through practice. The author of Hebrews seems to equivocate between the morality that comes through such practice and maturity in Christ—the point being, primarily through the living of a life purposed on moral practice, one knows who is mature and who is not. But what of the training in community paramount in Aristotle? Does the author of Hebrews deem such an apprenticeship necessary for moral formation, or can "practice" be accomplished merely at the level of the individual? While theological training (i.e., information) may be helpful in forming one's moral acuity, knowing information does not constitute maturity. Indeed, the definition of faith that the author of Hebrews later offers seems to indicate that it is not enough to simply have an intellectual trust in God. (In Hauerwas's terms, systematic knowledge cannot accomplish Christian maturity.) One must first have a life that displays trust in God in order to be considered mature. After giving a brief definition of faith in 11:1 and discussing at length the great lives of some of Judaism's heroes, the author of Hebrews draws a summary for readers: "Remember those who led you, who spoke the word of God to you; and considering the result of their conduct, imitate their faith. Jesus Christ is the same yesterday and today, yes and forever." (13:7–8) It would seem then that the community is necessary.

As Hauerwas makes clear through his critique of system and of Kant, Enlightenment sensibilities caused theology to presume that it must first have right thinking in order to produce right living. Morality, then, is merely the consequence of appropriate reflection, since morality is judged primarily on individual actions and not on

10. Aristotle *Nicomachean Ethics* 1103b.8–25.

the summation of actions displayed in a virtuous character. However, if one looks to the whole of life—to the character of a person—and begins to make moral judgment only on the basis of extended activity, then a clearer picture of the faith delineated in Hebrews 13:7 begins to come into focus. The epistle of James articulates a similar point with regard to faith's culminating in a life of morality:

> But prove yourselves doers of the word, and not merely hearers who delude themselves. For if anyone is a hearer of the word and not a doer, he is like a man who looks at his natural face in a mirror; for once he has looked at himself and gone away, he has immediately forgotten what kind of person he was. But one who looks intently at the perfect law, the law of liberty, and abides by it, not having become a forgetful hearer, but an effectual doer, this man shall be blessed in what he does. (James 1:22–25)

One implication of the imperative by the author of Hebrews to "imitate" the faith of those whose lives measure up is that faith may then be considered a learned practice. If it is to be imitated, then faith must be something that can be learned better through the emulation of those who have done it well (note the symbiotic, or even synonymous, relationship between conduct and faith). Scripturally speaking, this fits well with the notion of apprenticeship, developed above with regard to "walking by the Spirit." Paul did not simply command believers to live moral lives in isolation. He continually compelled them to follow the example of Jesus *as it was visible* in the lives of those who rightly followed after him (e.g., 1 Cor 11:1, Phil 4:9) Faith is not a static quality of trust felt by the individual in certain situations of life, such as in particularly difficult circumstances. Neither is faith only a supernatural gift that comes directly from God without any human intervention, though this may occasionally occur (Matt 16:15–17). In fact, faith can apparently be mediated through the instruction of those who do it well. Of course, faith is not merely the imitation of any person; rather, it is the imitation of Jesus. In other words, faith is defined, or better, described, in a person, rather than in a discursive account of doctrine. The life that is to be the primary life in moral formation is the life of Jesus, who is the *same* in the material existence of his body, the church, *today as* he was in his own physical body "*yesterday*" (Heb 13:8). This is the life we are to ultimately imitate.

Of course, the resources for such imitation may seem somewhat limited; after all, Jesus has ascended and no longer displays himself for personal observation. The response to this, often given by Protestants especially, is that he has left his revelation of himself in the Scriptures. While this is surely an excellent resource, the Scriptures themselves seem to be telling us that another at least as prominent resource is discovered in the lives of faithful people. Jesus's life is continually lived in the lives of his followers for others to follow in kind. That is why the author of Hebrews follows up the entreaty to "imitate their faith" with the claim that "Jesus Christ is the same . . ." Along similar lines, Paul compels the Corinthians to "imitate" him as he "imitates Christ" (1 Cor 11:1). Jesus is the one to whom all believers look for their ultimate model of conduct; He is Aristotle's "virtuous man." When one emulates the faith of someone who has done it well, he/she is ultimately emulating the life of Jesus. This can be seen further in Paul's command to the Philippians: "The things you have learned and received and heard and seen *in me, practice* these things" (Phil. 4:9, italics mine [πρασσετε: present, active, imperative]).[11] The issue of imitation is derived from the fact that Christ is mediated to those who are in the church precisely through others who are in the church. That is the climax of the indwelling ministry of the Holy Spirit. He has come to humanity, even come into humans, to glorify Christ. Imitation, then, is the means by which the life of Christ is mediated from one generation of believers to the next. Faith is learned. Transforming sinners into worshipers, which is the ultimate goal of the church, takes training. Again, the biblical word for this is *discipleship.*

Jesus's own testimony on the subject of training seems to likewise indicate an affinity for Aristotle's conception of a student's being apprenticed to become like the master.

> A disciple is not above his teacher; but everyone, after he has
> been fully trained, will be like his teacher. (Luke 6:40)

Here we see that Jesus acknowledges training to be the primary ingredient in maturing a disciple. Further, he sees such training as causing the disciple to become like the master who trains. Jesus makes the odd

---

11. It is instructive that Paul uses the same word here (with regard to the performance of what has been seen in him) as he does in Galatians 5:21 (with regard to the habits of the flesh). Such things are "practiced," or worked time and time again repetitively, for the sake of both demonstration and habituation.

statement in a parallel passage in Matthew 10:24 that "it is enough for the disciple that he become as his teacher." This seems odd because of the false humility of liberalism. Since liberalism compels moral agents to make choices based on good or bad information and consequences, each moral agent starts over again in every moral circumstance. Granted, some learning is intended from every occurrence of a choice, but this learning may or may not affect the choice in question. Thus, moral agents have the expectation that humans have unlimited moral potential, since each occasion is new. Likewise, the evolution of morality toward further moral goodness would seem to dictate that students are to be more than their masters. Thus, masters, though they may try hard, must finally admit they can never have as much potential as the next generation.

The answer to this dilemma seems to be found in Jesus's expectation that the church will live a morality that is marked by living between the times. In other words, because moral perfection and the evolution of social morality toward goodness are not expected by Jesus until the eschaton, he believes that we will become like those who taught us. Succeeding generations will not necessarily be better, nor will they necessarily be worse. The key is that here in Luke's gospel, Jesus seems to be subscribing to Aristotle's conception of apprentices who will be *like* their masters. If they have a good master, they will be well trained. If they have an incompetent master, they will likewise be incompetent. Jesus, Paul, and Aristotle seem to be in agreement on what training accomplishes and how it should be done.

One final point needs to be noted about Aristotle's conception of learned morality. While he allows room for the intellectual capacities to contribute to the moral development of a person, he does not wish for intellect to substitute for the activity of learning. True learning comes by doing, or as the author of Hebrews would have it, by practice. As Aristotle makes clear,

> Thus our assertion that a man becomes just by performing just acts and self-controlled by performing acts of self-control is correct; without performing them, nobody could even be on the way to becoming good. Yet most men do not perform such acts, but by taking refuge in argument they think that they are engaged in philosophy and that they will become good in this way. In so doing, they act like sick men who listen attentively

to what the doctor says, but fail to do any of the things he prescribes. That kind of philosophical activity will not bring health
to the soul any more than this sort of treatment will produce a
healthy body.[12]

Theoretical engagement is no substitute for the real learning that
comes through action. As Hauerwas has demonstrated, this is a reverse
of most Enlightenment versions of moral epistemology, which espouse
right thinking leading to right action. Instead, Aristotle seems to indicate that right action leads to right belief. What is most interesting about
this epistemological turn is what it can mean in the way we understand
Jesus's own claims about what is truth. When Jesus claims to be "the
way, the truth, and the life" (John 14:6), he is making an epistemological claim, as well as an ontological claim, about what can be known
and about what is valuable to know. Jesus is claiming to be the full revelation of the Father (14:7–10). He is also claiming that the only thing
worth knowing is himself. From a modern perspective, we may find his
statement suspect because he does not make available any standard to
which we might compare him, in order to see if he corresponds to the
truth. There is no external measure by which to test his claim. He does
provide some demonstration of his claim by means of the works he
has performed. These testify to his claim to be the Christ, but they are
not meant as evidence that could sufficiently grant his claims to be the
Messiah-King. Certainly Jesus did things expected of the Messiah—but
not everything that was expected. Indeed the final deeds of the Messiah,
such as the establishment of his kingdom, are still historically wanting
in Jesus. Instead of attesting specifically to his kingship, Jesus's deeds
reflect what type of person the Christ would be. Jesus's miracles point
to the fact that he lived up to what he claimed his character to be. What
Jesus wished for his followers to know was his own person rather than
simply some theory about truth or morality. As a consequence, the real
question seems to be, who is the truth?; not, how do we measure the
truth? What this means epistemologically for believers is that truth is
not some theory to be proven or derived from the principles of Jesus's
actions. Instead, we know him as a real, historical person who lived
and breathed and performed many deeds; this is the truth that is Jesus.
Likewise, we know each other to be truthful according to our living

12. Aristotle *Nicomachean Ethics* 1105b.9–18.

lives of activity in this world. We know each other in the church pre-, cisely as we live together as church. If we are to live as Christians, we are in fact living as the real presence of Christ to one another—another implication of the indwelling of the Holy Spirit in a very material way.[13] Indeed, living in such a way, we are living the Truth.[14]

Aristotle goes on to admit that reflection may have some value as a teaching tool for masters to share their wisdom with novices in morality. Perhaps he believes that learning must start somewhere. However, one cannot look here to retain a primacy of thought over action. For even when Aristotle affirms the power of undemonstrated reason, it is in the context of a life of demonstration.

> The intuitive reason then is at once beginning and end. It is from the truths of intuitive reason that demonstration starts, and with them that it is concerned. It is right therefore to pay no less attention to the undemonstrated assertions and opinions of such persons as are experienced and advanced in years or prudent than to their demonstrations; for their experienced eye gives them the power of correct vision.[15]

Hauerwas affirmed an epistemological primacy for action, which he derived explicitly from Aristotle. Hauerwas would certainly not deny the value of reflection placed in the context of an appropriate use of intuitive reason. Intuitive reason does not function apart from demonstration; however, it may become theoretical if used rightly by a virtuous man who has experienced or demonstrated a life of virtue. Only in such a context can intuitive reason be used theoretically. This is still far from the Enlightenment ethic available to any rational person. Nevertheless, it does raise an interesting point with regard to a seeming reciprocity in Aristotle between prudence and intuitive reason for one

13. Zizioulas, *Being as Communion*, 225–36. Zizioulas is here more concerned about the way in which the ordained ontologically become, in a real sense, the divine witness to the laity. Since I do not have such a strong sacramentalism or hierarchical ecclesiology driving my theology, I would rather apply this to all those who are a part of the community of the Spirit. Certainly I recognize this is a conservative Protestant shaping of the notion, which is to say I can do little other.

14. This is Hauerwas's understanding of how the church is to be the truth rather than to search for some criteria of truth external to the community in action. See Hauerwas and Willimon, *Resident Aliens*, 101; and Hauerwas, *Wilderness Wanderings*, 193.

15. Aristotle, *Nicomachean Ethics*, trans. by Welldon, 207. Reference in Ostwald is 1143b, 1–13.

who has attained the status of a virtuous man. Neither intuitive reason nor prudence exists in any substantive manner in a novice. When one has lived a life of virtue, both may be said to exist in fullness rather than in potential. Therefore, perhaps Aristotle would qualify his moral epistemology for the mature or "virtuous" man. In a virtuous person, thought and action may function in an epistemological reciprocity rather than in a linear relationship in which action is prior to thought.

The theological and scriptural parallel to Aristotle's notion of an "experienced eye" opening the way to some theorizing can be found in passages already cited above. In Hebrews 5:11–14, specifically, the author of Hebrews bemoans the fact that the readers are not able to teach because they have not practiced living holiness in such a way as to be able to discern good and evil. The lack of demonstrated practice makes their teaching impossible. While it may be debatable what constitutes teaching, teaching seems to include at least some theorizing about the relationship of the priestly natures of Christ and Melchizedek (5:1–10). This question does not directly parallel the moral theorizing discussed by Aristotle, but the method for evaluating the results of the Hebrews theorizing is the same as the evaluative method in Aristotle: Hebrews evaluates Christ's and Melchizedek's practice over time. Thus, while action may best be understood as prior to thought in an epistemology for the church (at least for the immature), an eventual reciprocity between action and thought may develop for masters (i.e., teachers) in the church. This eventual reciprocity does not warrant a reversal of the epistemological priority of action, but it does open the door for some extended use of theory for the sake of teaching novices.

On the basis of such a reciprocity between action and thought, with action remaining primary, theological reflection maintains a certain value within the church. Hauerwas, relying on Lindbeck and Wittgenstein, has argued for a regulatory, or grammatical, role for doctrinal language. Based on the reciprocal relationship discussed above and the use of theory by masters, this role seems to be warranted. However, it also seems somewhat deficient in regard to the appropriate use of regulatory language, if it is left at the level of mere Wittgensteinian limiting within a closed system of a language game. In other words, language without any reference to reality, albeit in a qualified or modest sense, is weakened in its power to perform any regulative function. This is particularly the case with regard to pneumatological language. If it does not affirm the realistic nature of theological language, then pneumatology remains at the level of anthropology. Pannenberg pertinently recognizes that we must say something, even if we must continue to revise what we have said. Modesty and moral maturity appear to be the hallmarks of a theologian who is able to engage in theoretical reflection. Thus, though theological language is certainly not democratic in such a scheme (and such democracy seems the aim of the theological rationalism of the Enlightenment), it is more than simply a "game."

Does the Holy Spirit's Work in Community Fit with the Life of Jesus?

Christian theology has had a slightly difficult time accounting for the work of the Holy Spirit in the life of Jesus. The primary affirmation needed in the early centuries of the church was that Jesus was both human and divine. The hypostatic union was explained in ontological terms but was left functionally nebulous. Thus discussions of Jesus's use of the Holy Spirit, particularly Jesus's human use of the Holy Spirit's power, have taken some time to develop. However, in recent years, it has become clearer that Jesus made extensive use of the Spirit in his life. While it may have been anathema to emphasize the humanness of Jesus in previous centuries, particularly when such an emphasis on humanness was understood as a challenge to his divinity, theology in recent years has emphasized the fact that Jesus relied heavily on the power of the Spirit so that he could show other humans the way to live in the Spirit.[16]

This can most clearly be illustrated in scriptural terms with regard to temptation. Since the author of Hebrews affirms that we have a high priest who "has been tempted in all things as we are" and yet remains "without sin" (4:15), it seems unreasonable to presume so great a distance between Jesus and other humans in their temptations. In fact, it is in his own temptation that Jesus demonstrates for humans how to survive temptation. Far from recommending the way out provided for him by affirmations of his deity (*non posse peccare*, "not able to sin"), Jesus's

---

16. See Erickson's (*Christian Theology*, 848–56, 870–77) treatment of the history of the doctrine of the Holy Spirit and of the Holy Spirit in the life of Jesus, which is immediately followed by his discussion of the Spirit's work in the rest of Christian humanity.

biographers illustrate the manner in which he (as a human being) relied on things available to humans in order to stand up under temptation (*posse non peccare*, "able not to sin").

After Jesus's baptism in the Jordan by John, the Spirit descends on him like a dove (Matt 3:13–17). Immediately after his baptism, Jesus is led out into the wilderness by the Spirit to be tempted (Matt 4:1). Jesus survives his temptation in each case by relying on means available to other humans, that is, on the power of the Holy Spirit, on Scripture, and on a resolute will to obey. It is significant to note that Jesus nowhere fell back on his divine nature, although this was a real possibility for him. Instead, Jesus uses three things to survive temptation that all Christians who wish to endure temptation without giving in have available to them. To acknowledge that Jesus subdued temptations with means available to humans is by no means to deny Jesus's divinity. It is simply an affirmation of his humanity.

Thus far in our discussion in previous sections of the work of the Holy Spirit in the church, we have focused on how the Spirit works through the natural in the narrative community of the church. While not excluding supernatural means, this focus opens the possibility that the natural workings of the community, when infused by the Holy Spirit, become the supernatural. In other words, we have discovered how the Spirit works through the training of people by other masters into living a life of worship to God. We have seen that such a task is by no means an individuation of the Spirit but is instead the way the Spirit draws the church closer into unity, causing it to function holistically rather than as a collection of individuals (cf. 1 Cor 12). A primary objection anticipated to such a conception of the nature of the work of the Holy Spirit is found precisely in the life of Jesus. Stated plainly, the objection expected is that Jesus used the Spirit in a supernatural way, receiving supernatural power and knowledge directly from the Spirit apart from any community. Therefore, it is impossible to imagine Jesus's being trained to live the way he did. Jesus walked in the Spirit immediately (i.e., without a formative community mediating any of the workings of the Spirit to him), and we should expect to receive the power of the Spirit without mediation as well.

To answer this objection, let us begin by first attempting to make the case for the notion of Jesus's unmediated formation and his individuated reception of the Holy Spirit. It seems evident that Jesus lived in two primary communities, both of which are also available to his followers. The first community in which he resided was the Triune relationship he had and still has with the other persons of the Trinity. Though Jesus had given up certain prerogatives of deity by becoming a human (Phil 2:5–11), he nevertheless had an intimate relationship with the Father through the Spirit. This was a supernatural relationship not accomplished through human means. Jesus consistently affirms that he has an intimate relationship with the Father. Even the fact that he calls God "Father" indicates an intimacy unbearable for the Jews of the first century (e.g., see John 5:17–18). Jesus also equates his own work with the work of the Father, or at least he sees both his Father and himself as colaborers (John 5:17–24; 10:22–39). This supernatural communion with the Father was Jesus's primary community in which he was formed and trained to be obedient. Even in the face of a dreadful death that he knew was coming, Jesus learned obedience without reserve (Matt 26:36–46). His prayer for deliverance from the cross was not simply for show. Jesus, as a human, could not have looked forward to the pain and humiliation of such a death. He really did not wish to go through such a dreadful experience. However, he was willing to learn obedience to do whatever the Father wished. Jesus learned in the community of the Trinity how to glorify the Father by being the Son. It is for this reason that the Father will highly exalt him (Phil 2:9), because Jesus "humbled Himself by becoming obedient to the point of death, even death on a cross" (Phil 2:8).

The relationship Jesus has with the Father through the Spirit in the Triune Godhead is quite obviously a supernatural relationship. However, it is important to note that he still learned through that relationship. He learned to survive temptation through means available to humans like himself. He also learned obedience to face a death that he did not want. Though a case could perhaps be made that Jesus's learning from the Father was yet mediated, it has traditionally been understood that his learning was immediate in that he was not shown by other humans how to do these things before he did them. In other words, Jesus does not appear to have been apprenticed by either people or circumstances in the humility required to face death on a cross, in spite of his sinlessness.[17] However, such is not the case with his followers. He is the "first fruits" (1

17. Though I do not wish to make a strong case for it here, Hebrews 5:8 seems to indicate that Jesus was apprenticed in his humility by the circumstances he faced. My point above is merely to demonstrate that the traditional approach is not without some merit.

Cor 15:23) and the "firstborn" (Rom 8:29) precisely because he provides a path for others to follow. He is also the great example set up for all his followers to imitate (1 Cor 11:1). Jesus's followers are apprenticed in that they are called to be like their master. They are not called to be masters by themselves, as if they could somehow create their own destiny and salvation, or devise their own moral life without conforming to Christ's image. Jesus's followers are called to do exactly that—to follow him.

Getting more to the crux of the matter, is it possible that becoming "conformed to the image" (Rom 8:29) of Jesus happens immediately, without any sort of training or apprenticeship? Since [his conforming to the image of his Father was presumably unmediated for Jesus, should confirmation to the image of Jesus] not be unmediated for his followers as well? Support for such a notion comes directly from Jesus's own conception of how his followers would be related to Himself and his Father. Pannenberg's development of the notion of participation is useful in this regard as well. Humans are able to participate in the Triune Godhead by means of their relationship to Jesus and the work of the Holy Spirit. Jesus prayed for all his followers, regardless of time, that "they may all be one; even as Thou, Father, are in Me, and I in Thee, that they also may be in Us" (John 17:21). Though the emphasis here and in the immediately following context appears to be on the unity that Jesus's followers will have with one another, nevertheless, a supernatural coupling of the human to the divine seems also in view. As Zizioulas states:

> [T]he Holy Spirit is not one who *aids* us in bridging the distance between Christ and ourselves, but he is the person of the Trinity who actually realizes in history that which we call Christ, this absolutely relational entity, our Savior. . . . Between the Christ-truth and ourselves there is *no gap to fill* by the means of grace. The Holy Spirit, in making real the Christ-event in history, makes real *at the same time* Christ's personal existence as a body or community. Christ does not exist *first* as truth and *then* as communion; He is both at once. All separation between Christology and ecclesiology vanishes in the Spirit. . . .
>
> Thus the mystery of the Church has its birth in the entire economy of the Trinity and in a pneumatologically constituted Christology. The Spirit as "power" or "giver of life" opens up our existence to become relational, so that he may at the same time be "communion" (κοινωνία, cf. II Cor. 13:13). For this reason the mystery of the Church is essentially none other than that of

the "One" who is simultaneously "many"—not "One" who exists first of all as "One" and *then* as "many," but "One" and "many" at the same time.[18]

But to argue for a coupling that overcomes the human to the point that it is no longer the activity of the human in action but the working of the Spirit—i.e., an exchanged life—seems to imply too much. Perfection should be the result if such were the case. Likewise to argue that the power of the Spirit is available but is simply not being drawn upon at all times by the believer is to presume too little. Since even Paul struggled with not being able to do what he wished at times (Rom 7:14–25), it would seem that if the way in which a human becomes moral is through the supernatural infusion of the Spirit's power, then the infusion is too weak or the Spirit too small to overcome our "old nature." While it is certainly true that the Holy Spirit is an enabler to help humans perform in a manner like Christ's, the Spirit is not, nor should he be expected to be, a cure-all for what ails humans. Even in his temptation, Jesus did not directly rely on the immediate working of the Holy Spirit. His greatest defense was an appropriate understanding of the teachings of the Word of God, which he used to counter the inappropriate renderings of Satan. Certainly it is possible that the Spirit brought these passages to Jesus's mind supernaturally. However, it seems more likely that Jesus already knew these passages from previous study and learning.[19] The case for Jesus's unmediated formation in Trinitarian relationship appears to leave too many issues open. Likewise, it creates a distance between Jesus and his followers that seems impossible to bridge. Finally, it does not answer the question of how the Spirit's work is identifiable and received by the human community. In other words, we are still left in the position of determining the work of the Spirit by means of feeling or personal desire.

18. Zizioulas, *Being as Communion*, 110–12, emphasis Zizioulas's.

19. Thomas Aquinas (*Summa Theologiae*, III.9.4) has an interesting discussion of just this subject, i.e., of whether Jesus had acquired knowledge and how that knowledge came about. Aquinas concludes that Jesus did have acquired knowledge (as opposed to infused knowledge) but that this happened primarily by means of his discovering this knowledge rather than by his being taught. Aquinas leans this way because learning by discovery is a higher form of learning than is learning by teaching. Though from the ecclesiological context I am defending teaching is the better way, I recognize Aquinas's position has similar intentions and, indeed, similar conclusions.

What seems to be left out of this equation is the context in which all these teachings were given. I wish to affirm with Hauerwas and Pannenberg that the Spirit does draw Jesus's followers into participation in the Trinity. He does this so that they might know the love between the Father and the Son, thus reproducing it in their lives (John 17:22–26). However, neither Jesus nor Paul nor any other biblical author expected believers to attempt this without participation in the community of the church. In fact, this is the point of Jesus's prayer in John 17—unity. Every biblical author expected that Jesus's followers would be apprenticed in the human community called church, since this was the way in which people learned. Those who wished to become masters at some skill or simply to be masters in life (e.g., a rabbi) were expected to go through the process of being trained by a higher master. We have already seen that Paul and the author of Hebrews expected this kind of training to happen for Christ's followers. Jesus likewise expected it, since he was continually calling those who wished to have what he offered to come and follow him. But the question remains whether Jesus himself was trained in such a way.

We know of Paul's training as a Pharisee (Phil 3:5–6). He did not count his training as something to gain him favor with God, but it is quite obvious that it prepared him well to write the things he did in the way he did. We also know of the training of the other apostles, at least at the feet of Jesus, if not elsewhere as well. But what of Jesus himself? Did he learn as a member of the human community?

It is easily established from Scripture that Jesus participated in and learned from the intimate relationship he had with the other members of the Trinity. At his baptism, the relationship was visibly and audibly demonstrated for human observation (Matt 3:13–17). Again at Jesus's transfiguration, the communion between the Son and the Father seems evident (Matt 17:1–8). But perhaps the clearest passages demonstrating Jesus's intimacy with the Father and his desire to learn from this intimacy are found in John 17 and Matthew 26:36–46. Jesus's high priestly prayer in John 17 is full of statements about his closeness to the Father (17:5, 10, 21, 22, 23, 26). It is important to note again that the intimacy Jesus shared with the Father is to be shared by those who follow him: "And this is eternal life, that they may know Thee, the only true God, and Jesus Christ whom Thou hast sent." (17:3); "I manifested Thy name to the men whom Thou gavest Me out of the world; Thine they were, and

Thou gavest them to Me, and they have kept Thy Word." (17:6); "[I ask] that they may all be one; even as Thou, Father, art in Me, and I in Thee, that they also may be in Us;" (17:21); "I have made Thy name known to them, and will make it known; that the love wherewith Thou didst love Me may be in them and I in them." (17:26). Jesus expects to return to the full relationship he had with the Father prior to his incarnation (17:5). However, during his ministry on earth, he still enjoyed intimacy that gave him the strength to do His ministry.

It is in the midst of this intimacy that Jesus learns from his Father the humility and obedience necessary to fulfill the will of the Father. In Matthew 26:36–46, Jesus agonizes over the fact that he must die. Though he knew beforehand what events must take place, he longed for another way. What we see in Jesus's prayer in the garden is his desire for a different means of accomplishing the purposes of his ministry; but alongside this is a willingness to submit to the will of the Father. This is the ultimate test of obedience, and in the three repetitions of his prayer, Jesus progresses in his thought from a desire to accomplish his mission another way to finally submitting fully to the will of the Father. That Jesus had wished for another way to fulfill his mission does not mean that he was unsubmissive earlier, but simply that he desired another alternative, "if it is possible" (Matt 26:39). Jesus knew the humiliating death he would be forced to endure. Likewise, he would be subjected to a very real break in intimacy between Himself and the Father (Matt 27:46). These were not things to be desired, but through enduring them, and through his submission to the Father's will, Jesus learned and displayed obedience (Phil 2:8). That is why the author of Hebrews concludes that Jesus, "Although He was a Son, He learned obedience from the things which He suffered" (5:8).[20] Such obedience does not diminish Jesus's deity but does accentuate his humanity. Obedience is something that Jesus apparently learned from the Father, yet he learned it, at least according to the author of Hebrews, through the agency of suffering. While it is possible that this suffering was from the blows of human hands, it seems more apparent in the context of Hebrews 5:1–10 that Jesus suffered due to his human limitations and from his being subjected to his role as the sacrifice for creation. He learned obedience in that he willingly subjected himself to the limitations of being human. For one who

20. See Ellingworth, *Epistle to the Hebrews*, 292.

had the prerogatives of deity at his disposal for eternity past, to become limited by a human existence would surely have brought suffering—not to mention the physical suffering that he endured in his death.

Jesus's humanness may seem theologically awkward because it makes God seem subjective or relative to human existence. We would prefer a God who could not be subject to such human limitation. However, in a christocentric theology, gone is the objectivity of a distant God who works through principles and rules (the theistic God of the Enlightenment). As Hauerwas has made clear, gone is the God who exists first as a theory of divine existence and only subsequently as a Jew in history. Modernity is uncomfortable with this God *in* history. But such is the way of the theology of the incarnation.[21] Barth argues against the God of modernity as he attempts to persuade his audience of the necessity that God's humanity be incorporated into his deity.

> We viewed this "wholly other" in isolation, abstracted and absolutized, and set it over against man, this miserable wretch—not to say boxed his ears with it—in such a fashion that it continually showed greater similarity to the deity of the God of the philosophers than to the deity of the God of Abraham, Isaac, and Jacob.[22]

The theological discomfort that makes the learning of obedience in Jesus' life a particularly hard thing to accept is likely due to theology's failure to grasp the significance of Jesus's humanness. By attempting to constantly defend Jesus from accusations of adoptionism, modalism, and the like, theology has become rather gnostic in its understanding of Jesus's humanity. It is all too easily regarded as merely an addition to his divinity. In making Jesus's humanity merely ancillary to his divinity, theologians have underestimated the humanity of Jesus and distanced Him from our own humanity in a way that sacrifices a material sanctification. This is nowhere clearer than with regard to the knowledge available to Jesus.

Theological problems arise when one affirms the deity of Jesus and likewise attempts to impose doctrines on Jesus that are more generally used to refer to the Godhead (i.e., the prerequisite nature of theism

---

21. I am beginning to open up the inference made earlier about the gains that Hauerwas could make by emphasizing more strongly a theology of the incarnation.

22. Barth, *Humanity of God*, 45.

involved in such characteristics as omniscience, omnipotence, and om-nipresence). A rather obvious discrepancy occurs when one attempts to apply the omnipresence of God to Jesus. Given that Jesus existed as a finite being, it is necessarily impossible to affirm that Jesus was omni-present during his earthly ministry. His status after the ascension may be another question to be answered in a manner different from his pre-ascended state; however, even his glorified body does not appear to be omnipresent. The point is simply this: the doctrine of God's omnipres-ence does not apply to Jesus during his earthly ministry as a finite being. A bit more difficult problem arises with regard to Jesus's omnipotence: Did he really have the power to accomplish anything he wanted while yet a human in his earthly ministry? His miraculous powers demon-strate that he was evincing more than just the normal human potential. The natural question, then, is why he did not exercise his powers when hanging on the cross, or even after the resurrection when asked, "Lord, is it at this time you are restoring the kingdom to Israel?" (Acts 1:6). Jesus apparently had the power available to him but chose not to use it. *Why* he did not use it has to do with God's dealings with the Gentiles (Luke 21:24). *That* He did not use it has to do with his humility in the face of choosing His own will or that of the Father. His humility is di-rectly reflective of His decision not to "grasp" at "equality with God" (Phil 2:6). Although Jesus had open to him the very real power of God at any time, he chose not to exercise that power to save himself or to establish his kingdom too soon. But what of his knowledge? Where was Jesus's primary community of learning?

We have already seen that Jesus learned from his relationship with his Father obedience and humility, albeit an obedience and humil-ity learned in a human context from human suffering. However, the intimacy between Jesus and his Father does not seem to be the only arena in which he learned. In fact, Jesus may have been trained in a very real way in the human community in which he grew up. This would seem to accord with Paul's notion of Jesus's kenotic setting-aside of the prerogatives of Godhood (Phil 2:5–8), including the setting-aside of omniscience.

Scripture affirms Jesus's supernatural birth, but it also affirms his human growth and development. Though the Scriptures spend very little time on Jesus's upbringing, we are told that he "continued to grow and become strong, increasing in wisdom; and the grace of God was upon Him" (Luke 2:40), and that "Jesus kept increasing in wisdom and stature, and in favor with God and men" (Luke 2:52). Since it is obvious that Jesus did not have the fullness of wisdom immediately, the natural question is, where did he get his growth in wisdom?

The succeeding phrase in Luke 2:40 ("and the grace of God was upon Him") may be taken to indicate that Jesus's wisdom came immediately from God.[23] While this may be plausible, it does not appear to be the best answer. Even if God did give Jesus wisdom immediately, God gave it over the course of time, and likely through various events in Jesus's life. In such a context, it would appear that even the immediate giving of wisdom would still have been mediated through circumstances. Likewise one cannot presume that "the grace of God" is a static state or a one-time gift. Peter implores his readers to "grow in the grace and knowledge of our Lord and Savior Jesus Christ" (2 Peter 3:18), implying that grace is not static. A more plausible explanation for Jesus's increase in wisdom is found in the story following Luke's statement.

Jesus was born miraculously without the joining of Joseph and Mary. Therefore, Jesus had no biological father. Nevertheless, Jesus did have an earthly father who raised him as his own son. It is likely that Joseph the carpenter was also a learned man, or even a rabbi.[24] Joseph is referred to as a "righteous man" (Matt 1:19). While Joseph's being "righteous" has often been taken simply to mean that he was a good man or a nice person, since he was going to separate from Mary "quietly" rather than to have her stoned, such an interpretation of "righteous" does not accord well with how first-century Jews would have understood such a

23. Nolland, *Luke 1—9:20*, 125. Nolland implies that such is the case since wisdom would naturally accompany the presence of the Holy Spirit in Jesus's life.

24. I am relying here on the thought of R. Steven Notley, professor and chair of New Testament backgrounds at Jerusalem University College. At the time of this writing, he has not yet published his studies in this area. Thus, I am citing our correspondence of October 27, 1998.

Notley states "There is evidence in the [rabbinic] literature that carpenters were known to be extremely knowledgeable. This does not answer the question of whether Joseph was a sage or not. However, I do feel confident he was." Sages of the first century typically had a physical trade by which they disciplined their bodies and provided opportunity for their minds to meditate. Far from being simply jobs in skilled labor, these trades served as part of the discipline of being a sage. Further, the relation between working a trade and practicing a discipline may be the best context in which to understand either Paul as a tentmaker or the fact that Jesus grew up as a carpenter and presumably practiced carpentry himself.

term. A first-century Jew would never be called a "righteous" man "unless they were also learned."[25] Given Matthew's intentions to write for a primarily Jewish audience, it seems likely that the meaning of "righteous" in this context is to demonstrate that Joseph was more than just a skilled laborer. This insight brings us to the important point that Jesus learned from the sages in the temple area and amazed them with his understanding and his own ability to teach and to ask questions (Luke 2:46–47). Perhaps Joseph was also a sage who would have participated in the type of conversations taking place in the temple area. While it is certainly possible that Jesus could have relied on a supernatural ability to individually grasp the teachings of the Scripture about himself and the future of God's plans for his people, it is as likely (if not more likely) that he was taught well by the best of the sages in all of Israel, both in Jerusalem and perhaps even in his own home.

An obvious problem arises when such an interpretation is confronted with the words of the Jews regarding Jesus in John 7:14–15. Here John records for us: "But when it was now the midst of the feast Jesus went up into the temple, and began to teach. The Jews therefore were marveling, saying, 'How has this man become learned, having never been educated?'" The presumption may be to think that Jesus was simply from an uneducated background, making statements in the temple that were discordant with his upbringing.[26] While this understanding is generally accepted, it may also be that Jesus's upbringing was only obscure to those in Jerusalem, where the major theological schools of the day existed.[27] It is very possible that Jesus had been trained well by his father, Joseph, without ever making an appearance in Jerusalem, other than the annual trek to the temple for the Day of Atonement and perhaps for other feasts. This would make Jesus's education and outstanding intellect rather obscure until he saw fit to reveal himself to those at Jerusalem. Another explanation may be found in the probability that Jesus's earthly father, Joseph, was dead by the time of Jesus's ministry (John 19:26–27). If this is the case, then people at the temple may not remember Jesus as Joseph's son, but as just another one of the hill people from the north. This would likewise make his educa-

25. Ibid.

26. This is obviously what the Jews thought; and it is what some commentators have accepted as well. E.g., see Tasker, *John*, 103–04.

27. Robertson, *Word Pictures in the New Testament*, 5:122–23.

tion obscure or even forgotten by those who were amongst the leaders of Jewish theological and biblical education in Jerusalem. Either case would allow for Jesus to have had a good education outside of the eyes of those in power in the hub of Jewish religion.

Of course, it is more difficult to say that Jesus's upbringing was obscure to those who knew him as merely "the carpenter" (Mark 6:3) or as the "carpenter's son" (Matt 13:55). Jesus's teaching in Nazareth seemed to draw a similar response from those who claimed to know all his family and him, apparently even from his youth. Again this response may not be amazement at the fact that they had thought him common before and that he has suddenly become wise. Rather it would seem that the people of Nazareth were astonished because he had not taught them before. In other words, they are not amazed because he has suddenly come upon this great wisdom. Instead they are amazed because they had never suspected him to have such wisdom. This does not necessitate that it was impossible for him to have gotten an education, particularly from his father Joseph. (Joseph isn't mentioned in any gospel account of Jesus in his hometown, implying his absence and perhaps even his death. Joseph may well have given Jesus a tremendous beginning in his education and then left him to continue on his own.)[28] The obscurity of Jesus's wisdom parallels the obscurity of his identity. In fact, he even wished to remain obscure with regard to his identity until his time had come. The same may be the case for his great understanding and wisdom. He did not wish to reveal himself before the appointed time.

Acknowledging that Jesus received a strong earthly education and training would allow affirmations of his humanity to be unqualified without diminishing his divinity. He was obviously divine in his being, but he chose not to exercise the prerogatives of deity, taking upon himself the fullness of humanity. Such an understanding of Jesus would rid the church of the latent gnosticism plaguing Christology for centuries. Jesus was fully God but chose to be fully human. Neither affirmation should be underestimated.

---

28. While it does seem the case that Joseph is dead by the time of Jesus's ministry (John 19:26–27) the mention of Jesus as "Mary's son" in both Matthew 13:55 and Mark 6:3 is more likely a slur against his birth. The Jews considered Jesus an illegitimate child. See Lane, *Gospel of Mark*, 200–203. This does not negate the probability that Jesus was trained by Joseph but may make the exclusion of his name from Jesus's identity less conspicuous.

This brings us back to our main point in this section. While it is certainly possible that Jesus learned immediately from the Spirit in a supernatural way, implying that we should also learn this way, it seems more likely from the text of Scripture that Jesus grew in his wisdom and knowledge in a very natural way. Points of the miraculous may exist in his knowledge or insight, but his primary learning was found in the community in which he lived. In like manner, humans in the church should expect to learn from active participation in the community of the church, rather than waiting passively for the Spirit to move in some supernatural way. I am not by any means excluding the possibility of the supernatural, but I am affirming that the supernatural is outside the norm in Scripture, even for Jesus's learning and wisdom.

Does Commitment to the Community of the Church Constitute Upholding the Common Good?

A further anticipated objection to linking the work of the Holy Spirit to the natural interaction of the community of the church is that such a linkage between the church and the Spirit's work makes the church the primary community in which Christians discover their full humanity. In other words, as Hauerwas has depicted it, the implication of such an affirmation is that the community of the church not only *is* but *should be* considered a distinct community from the rest of the world. In a modernistic context, this affirmation is troublesome for some. According to modernism, ecclesiology, and likewise pneumatology, must be subservient to the individual or to the society as a whole.[29] Why this criticism might arise deserves brief consideration.

Several presuppositions abound in such a criticism. First, it is presumed that society as a whole is the primary community. Attempting to discover some value for the New Testament writings with regard to society, Raymond George declares in his comments on the work of the Holy Spirit: "As we have already seen, a most important concept is that of the 'kingdom'; this concept does much to rescue the New Testament from the charge of being more concerned with the individual and the Church than with society as a whole."[30] Such a presumption reflects

29. This is what gives rise to Hauerwas's criticism of Christian ethics as merely an attempt to make the church more American. E.g., see Hauerwas, *Better Hope*, 18–34.

30. George, "Holy Spirit Transforms," 216–17.

a sort of universalism characteristic of much classical liberalism. Underlying such an affirmation of the larger society as the primary community of reference is the belief that theology has more to do with anthropological issues than with theological concerns. In other words, theology is really just another tribal language in which to explain the issues facing humanity as a whole. Therefore, theology's primary concern is, in actuality, to attempt to deal with the problems facing all of human society. We are all attempting to build a better society; we are just using differing languages and differing means. Thus, Nazi Germany could enlist the support of German Christians in their program. They were all simply trying to create a better social order. Some called it the kingdom of God, while others called it the Third Reich.[31] Why this is problematic, beyond the obvious reasons, will be discussed briefly below.

The second presumption deserving separate consideration is the notion that it is the church's responsibility to make society a better place. In other words, there exists some type of "common good" toward which the church, in communion with all other social groups, is responsible to direct its faithful. While this is similar to the first presupposition examined above, one distinction needs to be made clear. Not only is it the case for strategies upholding the common good that all human communities are just that, i.e., *human* communities; it is also the case that the church's moral goal should be to contribute to the welfare of the totality of human communities—i.e., to society. The notion of the common good in its present form derives, at least though not exclusively, from the era of Walter Rauschenbusch and the Social Gospel, who taught that it was precisely the church's goal to build a better society.[32] However, recent advocates of the same or similar notions regarding the common good have come from some unlikely sources.[33] Again, the belief in the value of the common good reflects a further belief that the totality of humanity is the primary social community in which such notions as justice, peace, goodness, and

31. For a good discussion of liberal theology's response, or lack thereof, to Hitler, see Hauerwas and Willimon, *Resident Aliens*, 24–26, 44. The authors here draw the distinction between the inclusive, anthropological nature of liberal theology and exclusive nature of Barth's christocentric theology.

32. For a good discussion of Rauschenbusch's goals and influence, see Hauerwas, *Better Hope*, 71–107.

33. E.g., see Mott, *Biblical Ethics and Social Change*. Mott would seem to fit within the conservative Protestant collective known as evangelicalism.

evil are to be considered and defined. Such scriptural teachings as Paul's words in Galatians 6:10 ("Do good to all men and especially those who are of the household of faith") are taken as a command about the responsibility of Christians to first see to their societal responsibilities and then, subsequent to that, to give attention to those in their own specific social group.[34]

The application of common-good doctrine is just as permeating a teleology for individuals as it is for social groups like the church: If one is transformed in one's own individual person, eventually such transformation will "trickle down" to a change in the rest of society as well. As George claims in his interpretation of the Spirit's transformation in the New Testament (especially Gal 5:22), "[T]he 'spiritual' change wrought in the human heart was bound to transform social relationships and thus eventually affect the whole structure of society."[35] Interestingly, even Luther would likely have had significant problems with such a rendering of Galatians 6:10. Early in Luther's career, he seems to have taken the position that doing good does have primary benefit for the recipients of the good.[36] Later in his writing, Luther demonstrates that the benefit is primarily for those who are doing the good work. The good work is not the issue in Luther, nor is the benefit to society what is at stake in Paul's command. Instead the focus is on how good works reflect on the community of the church—not only the works Christians do for others outside the church but also the works Christians do for those in their midst. What is at stake is their testimony as a community of the love of Christ.[37]

A third presumption has to do with the expectations about society. Those who believe that the church has primary social responsibility to society believe implicitly, and sometimes explicitly, that the social work of the church will effect social change—ultimately social betterment. An inevitability of progress is displayed in the belief that the church can actually accomplish some social change that will make the world a better place. Aside from the issue of whether bettering the world is the responsibility of the church, the larger issue at stake here is the reli-

34. Ibid., 36. Mott is here taking his lead from Ramsey, *Basic Christian Ethics*, 247.
35. George, "Holy Spirit Transforms," 214–15.
36. Luther, "Lectures on Galatians, Chapters 1–6 (1519)," 401.
37. Luther, "Lectures on Galatians, Chapters 5–6 (1535)," 128–29.

ability of such an expectation. As is well known among those familiar with the neo-orthodox movement, such expectations of the betterment of society fared poorly during World War I and World War II. How such a belief has been resurrected from the ashes of liberalism is another study. Our study will suffice to show that demonstrating scriptural precedence for such a presupposition is incumbent upon those who reflect on society as the first community for Christians. It is my contention that no scriptural warrant can be found for viewing society as the first community for Christians.[38]

The primary criticism to be leveled at each of these presuppositions is that they all reflect a belief that the church is actually the whole of humanity, or at least is merely a subset of the primary community of the totality of humanity. The implication of such a notion is that the church then should direct its efforts toward contributing to societal welfare. The work of the church as a community of love, joy, peace, and the like is, for those who subscribe to such presuppositions, equivalent to working to effect social change in society. For the church's primary social role to be the betterment of society, it must be understood as belonging first to that society, and only secondarily to an identity distinct unto itself.

Of course, such a broad notion of the purpose of ecclesiology is outside the parameters of how Jesus depicted the social role of his followers. While not denying the obligations of the church to do "good to all men," the New Testament makes it clear that the church is distinct from the rest of society in its primary social role. Its existence is "in the world" (John 17:11), but "they are not of the world" (17:14, 16). As a consequence, the world hates them, "because they are not of the world" (17:14). Jesus draws a direct line between the world or society and the church or his followers. The Apostle Peter makes a similar distinction when he affirms the status of the church in the world as "aliens" and "sojourners" (1 Peter 1:1, 2:11). The kingdom of God is yet to be revealed fully on the earth. Those who follow Jesus may still ask the question, "Is

---

38. Interestingly, George, though he is attempting to argue strongly for the social responsibility of Christians, seems to agree that Scripture is an unhelpful resource for supporting such a notion. The closest thing he can find to such a reference is the concept of kingdom. However, the explanation of kingdom in Scripture remains so nebulous as to leave him in no better a position than at his start. See George, "Holy Spirit Transforms," 214–24.

it at this time that You are restoring the kingdom?" (Acts 1:6). However, as Hauerwas (and Pannenberg as well) would affirm, the church still waits to see the final coming of the kingdom of God. The church's status while she waits is as a foreigner in a foreign land. Those who are part of the church live in communion with one another in a way that demonstrates (performs) the communion that exists among the members of the Trinity and between God and his people through the mediation of Jesus by the Holy Spirit. This is what it means to be church. This is what it means to be part of a community where the Holy Spirit dwells—or better, to be part of the Holy Spirit's community. Hauerwas is, finally, correct in his assessment that the church's main concern is not whether or not to be in the world, but how to be in the world: "The church need not worry about whether to be in the world. The church's only concern is *how* to be in the world, in what form, for what purpose."[39] That purpose is, finally, to affirm or perform the lordship of Jesus before a watching world, until the day of his appearing (Phil 2:12–16).

Conclusion

The objections raised in this chapter are directed primarily at the scriptural interpretations offered in the previous chapter. While it is certainly admitted that scriptural interpretation is subject to great debate, this study intends to provide readers with an interpretation of passages according better with the doctrinal renderings offered by Hauerwas above. The purpose of answering these objections is not to give the pretense that all problems have been resolved. Instead the purpose is to give readers an opportunity to examine the presuppositions behind each belief presented by the author of this study and by those who might object. Novelty is seldom orthodox, so this study has no intent to provide a new way to look at old problems. This study is attempting to look at the text of Scripture as it is best set into its cultural context. Thus, though it may seem at odds with Augustine, Luther and a host of other theologians to pursue an Aristotelian paradigm for interpretation, this seems to best accord with the culture of Jesus and Paul's day. To draw upon Aristotle is not to say that Aristotle had it right all along, or that Jesus and Paul simply borrowed from Aristotle. Instead it means that in God's providence, the culture of their day was a largely, though by

39. Hauerwas and Willimon, *Resident Aliens*, 43.

no means exclusively, Aristotelian, Jewish culture. The question before readers is, does this theological rendering of Scripture best account for what may have been the audience's understanding of the text? If it does, then we need to pursue both how best to understand the implications and to discover where we went wrong. However, instead of embarking on another long thesis, let us examine a final objection that may be raised. Would an apparent champion of individualistic theology agree with the rendering of Scripture set forth thus far? In other words, how might Luther respond?

9

The Protestant Problem

Martin Luther on Ecclesial Formation and the Holy Spirit

Introduction

BEFORE COMING DIRECTLY TO THE ISSUE OF THE INDWELLING OF THE
Holy Spirit in Luther, a brief note seems warranted as to why Luther is
important to this study. Since Luther is often turned to as the father of
Protestant doctrine and since he is given credit for championing the
priesthood of the believer, his understanding of the working of the Holy
Spirit is seminal for all subsequent Protestant thought. The man whom
Tillich called "Spirit-determined and Spirit-directed" is of tremendous importance and influence over every branch of Protestantism.[1]
Therefore, in anticipation of objections that this study is somehow antithetical to the thrust of the Reformers' meditations concerning the
Holy Spirit, it is important that a foundational understanding of Luther
be laid out about several aspects of the doctrine of pneumatology.[2] For
instance, Luther's understanding of the relationship between pneuma-

---

1. Tillich, *Systematic Theology*, 3:250.

2. One could easily argue that Calvin's work was much more comprehensive and
complete on the subject of the Holy Spirit than Luther's. While I am willing to accept
this as the case, I am here maintaining attention on Luther because of his parentage of
subsequent Protestant Reformation thought. Calvin studied and described the Spirit
in much more detail, but to focus on Calvin leaves the option open that Reformation
thought before Calvin (i.e., in its purest state) was distinctly unique. Calvin's thought is
well known and easily accessible. Luther's is a bit more obscure and more open to speculation. This study wishes to settle some of the speculation by delineating the fact that
Luther is not as individualistic as he is sometimes read to be by modern theologians.

tology and ecclesiology must be outlined. Would Luther be comfortable with a corporate or communal understanding of the indwelling work of the Holy Spirit, while yet affirming individual participation? His understanding of the level of mediation of the Holy Spirit in the "learning" of righteousness in good works must also be observed. Though Luther railed against the influence of Aristotle, was he really as anti-Aristotelian as post-Enlightenment readers might suspect? Finally, some time must be spent with the issue of Luther and individualism to discover Luther's relationship to later developments in Enlightenment modernism. It is the contention of this chapter that the Enlightenment, not Luther, represents a major shift in how the church now understands pneumatology. Luther maintained a high view of ecclesiology and the church's relationship to the workings of the Spirit, in spite of his objections to the abuses he perceived in the hierarchy of his time.

Indwelling in Luther

Luther's own understanding of the indwelling of the Holy Spirit has perhaps been overshadowed and skewed by other elements of his teaching regarding justification, sanctification, the issues surrounding indulgences, and the like. His comments on the Holy Spirit primarily comprise his lectures on the pertinent Scriptures relating to the Holy Spirit. In this sense, it may be questioned whether Luther had a developed doctrine of the Holy Spirit.[3] As Femiano remarks, "Luther never actually discusses *how* the Spirit dwells in the Christian. . . . [N]ever does he elaborate on what one might call the speculative implications of this indwelling."[4] Nevertheless, he does make several statements indicating his own view of the work and place of the Holy Spirit in the lives of believers.[5]

It was not a foregone conclusion in the days of Luther that one had the Holy Spirit dwelling within oneself. In fact, Luther had been taught

3. Carlson ("Luther and the Doctrine of the Holy Spirit," 135) makes it clear that "Nowhere has he systematically summarized his teachings on [the Holy Spirit]."

4. Femiano, "Holy Spirit in Luther's Commentary on Galatians," 43.

5. While some question exists whether the mature Luther held a different doctrine than the young Luther on virtually every doctrine (the Holy Spirit included), I am inclined to agree with Prenter that Luther never appears to have made any shifts in his thinking with regard to his understanding of the Holy Spirit. See Prenter, *Spiritus Creator*, xvi.

that it would be quite presumptuous to believe that the Holy Spirit was constantly present in a person. The corporate view of the Spirit's indwelling in the Catholic Church of Luther's day allowed people to believe that if the Spirit was present in other members of the Church, then he was also, in some way, present in them as well. Thus, the question of whether or not one had the Holy Spirit was relatively unanswerable by any individual. As Luther critically surmises,

> Thus I, too, lived and believed when I was a pious monk. And if any monk should be regarded as holy, then I, too, was holy! Nevertheless, if—after I had prayed most diligently every day, had confessed completely, had gone to Mass, and had done my best—someone had asked me: "Are you convinced that you have the Holy Spirit?" I would have had to join others in replying: "God forbid! How could I be so presumptuous? I am a poor sinner. To be sure, I have done this and that; but I surely do not know whether it satisfies God." Thus I and everyone else went along in unbelief. Yet they want to say boastingly of the Holy Spirit: "If He is not in me, He is not in others either." Still no one is able to say where He really is. Then where is He anyway? If neither you nor anyone else can say that He dwells in you or in this or in that person, then in the final analysis, He will evidently be nowhere at all.[6]

In contrast to such a position, Luther believes that true believers must have confidence that the Holy Spirit dwells in them. They are not subject to a whimsical God who may or may not be satisfied with the deeds done by them. Instead, the deeds are produced precisely by the working of the Spirit in their lives. Without the Spirit, they could do no good.

> If you want to be a Christian, therefore, you must conclude with conviction: "I have the Holy Spirit dwelling in me. I shall and must have Him; for I know, of course, that my Christ, with His blood, Baptism, and Sacrament, is holy, and consequently that the Gospel, which I preach with my mouth, hear with my ears, and believe with my heart, is also holy. And if I have this, I must also say that the Holy Spirit is in me. For you will surely have no faith, no good thought, no joy, and no comfort from Him—yes, you will neither hear nor preach a sermon, and thus also perform no work of love or of any real Christian vocation—unless

6. Luther, "Sermons on the Gospel of John," 129–30.

the Holy Spirit dwells in you and works and accomplishes all this in you. Of this you can cheerfully boast against the devil, who assails you with doubts and wants to rob you of this comfort, and against the world, which boasts against you of its possessions and condemns your faith, words, and works."[7]

It is the Spirit that accomplishes the good works that one does, though these good works are by no means able to secure the salvation of a person. Rather, they are the outgrowth of a life dedicated to Christ. One who truly believes will produce works in keeping with their belief, but these are not works accomplished by human effort. They are the fruits of the Spirit. Luther's comments on Galatians 5:22–23, ("But the fruit of the Spirit is love, joy, peace, patience, kindness, goodness, faith") are instructive here:

> Paul does not say "works of the Spirit," as he had said "works of the flesh"; but he adorns these Christian virtues with a worthier title and calls them "fruit of the Spirit." For they bring very great benefits and fruit, because those who are equipped with them give glory to God and by these virtues invite others to the teaching and faith of Christ.[8]

Luther seems to indicate that by not calling these "works of the Spirit," Paul does not mean that Christians passively obtain the fruits of the Spirit. On the contrary, the fruits of the Spirit are still actions done by humans, but they are neither the product of human ingenuity, nor are they simply inward attitudes. Just as the bad fruit is visible in those who practice the works of the flesh, so too the good fruit is evident of those who follow after the Spirit.[9] The point of saying that the fruit of the Spirit are not works is to make them unworthy of merit. Luther's contrast is not between works that are produced with effort and works that passively spring forth. Instead, his contrast is between works that are wrongly considered a contribution to salvation and works that are the product of salvation. In both cases, a person's works indicate what is already true in the heart of the person. If one seeks after the works of the flesh, one is giving in to what is already inside. If one seeks to bear the fruit of the Spirit, one is displaying the continued conquest of the

---

7. Ibid., 130.

8. Luther, "Lectures on Galatians, Chapters 5–6 (1535)," 93.

9. Luther, "Lectures on Galatians, Chapters 5–6 (1535)," 79.

Spirit over the temptations of the flesh, to continue following after what is still a temptation.[10]

However, it also still seems to be the case for Luther that the fruit of the Spirit is not humanly produced. In other words, it comes from a working of the Holy Spirit in a person's heart and mind, and springs forth with or without the moral training previously deemed necessary by the Scholastics. Speaking about the relationship of the believer to the law, Luther makes clear that the Spirit now replaces the law by making the things of the law a natural production of the Spirit.

> Thus [the law] is completely abrogated for them, first in the Spirit, but then also in works. It does not have the right to accuse them; for *spontaneously* they do what the Law requires, if not by means of perfectly holy works, then at least by means of the forgiveness of sins through faith. So a Christian fulfills the Law inwardly by faith—for Christ is the consummation of the Law for righteousness to everyone who has faith (Rom. 10:4)—and outwardly by works and by the forgiveness of sins. But those who perform the works of the flesh and gratify its desires are accused and condemned by the Law, both politically and theologically.[11]

The works accomplished through the Spirit are produced solely because of the Spirit's guidance and prodding, not because of human effort. As will be discussed below with regard to Luther's rejection of Aristotle, Luther may not have needed to go so far in his objections to training in righteousness. Of course, given his historical context, he may have had little choice. But if he were to rephrase it in a more neutral context, he may be more willing to allow for human action (i.e. training) to have a foundational role in living morally.

Thus far our study has focused on the issue of how Luther believes the Holy Spirit works in humans. Perhaps a better inroad to answering this question is first discovering where Luther believes the Spirit to be working. Is it in the hearts of individuals, in the community of the church, or in the movements of history by means of inaugurating the kingdom here on earth? Let us begin with the third question.

The reform-minded chiliasts (those who believed that the one-thousand-year reign of Christ described in Revelation 20:1–6 was

10. Ibid., 79–87.

11. Ibid., 96; emphasis mine.

beginning) believed they had found in Luther a defender of their conception of history. But Luther's reformation was of a different sort. His intent was not so much to change society as it was to change theology.

> Initially, Martin Luther was well received among chiliasts. They welcomed him as a prophet of transition to a new era and defender of the "new age," the age of the Spirit and of peace. But he disappointed them, for his reformation did not seek to transform society in order to prepare the way for the millennium. Bitterly, the militant "champions of God" turned away from him. Preeminent among them was Thomas Münzer, who had a large following of chiliastic prophets, all of them driven by the will to extirpate the "godless" in order to ensure that the reformation would be in place in time for the Day of Judgment.[12]

Because of Luther's belief that only God could establish his kingdom and bring about the righteous society marked by his rulership, he never allowed the tendencies of other Reformers to sway his efforts away from what he deemed the teaching of Scripture.

> [T]he Scriptures do not lead to a disclosure of the majesty of God's dominion, and they do not reveal His plan for the history of the world, in which the new man can simply take his place as the vanguard of freedom and progress.[13]

Luther was not at all in favor of the attempt to "build the kingdom." Others had such notions, but Luther had only just left a church that believed it had established the kingdom.

> The "modern" Zionists of Luther's time were the bishops and popes who placed their trust in temporal power in order to establish a papal state. Even more serious, the Roman curia claimed to be Zion, the unshakable foundation of God's kingdom on earth. From Luther's perspective, "Zionist reformation" meant the subjugation of all nations and empires under the dominion of Rome, a claim the papacy indeed adhered to until well into the sixteenth century.[14]

---

12. Oberman, *Luther*, 60–61.

13. Ibid., 225.

14. Ibid., 64. The Zionism spoken of here by Oberman is perhaps better understood as vestiges of Constantinianism. The Roman Catholic Church continued to express itself as the authority over both ecclesial and political matters, if not directly at least symbolically, in its crowning or criticism of various monarchs and their policies.

Luther's conception of the two kingdoms seems to imply that God is working not only to build his heavenly kingdom of the saints, but also to build an earthly kingdom in which his rule will reign supreme. However, Hagen rightly surmises that

> Since, however, the whole world is evil and that among thousands there is scarcely one true Christian ... it is out of the question that there should be a common Christian government over the whole world, or indeed over one land or company of people, since the wicked always outnumber the good.[15]

Likewise Luther was hardly the bastion of individual liberty and freedom. Though some Reformers were attempting to establish the rights and freedoms of the lower classes, Luther did not feel it incumbent upon himself to attempt to devise such a social program. Had he designed such a program, the Enlightenment may have come in a much greater rush. Indeed, as Oberman states, "Were it not for Martin Luther, the history of the Reformation could have become the glorious story of Germany's advance into the modern era."[16] It was figures such as Münzer and Zwingli who fueled the fires of individualism and the rejection of authority.

> Very much counter to the temperament of his age—and of later, "modern" times—Luther took a vigorous stand against all efforts to wrest from God His timetable, and to force—with sword in hand—the coming kingdom of peace. Contrary to the hopes of the party of national liberation, he opposed the rebellious imperial knights who wanted to terminate the regime of the self-serving prelates and princes.
>
> Even more problematic is his stand against the peasants who had for so long been demanding their rights and were now gathering to fight for the rights of God as well; Thomas Münzer was making one flaming appeal after another to put an end to the rule of the godless, and Huldrych Zwingli, that proud, pious citizen of Zurich, was uniting Europe to combat the Hapsburgs and thus do battle for the Kingdom of God.
>
> From differing perspectives, later generations considered these various groups and movements to be heralds of the future and of "progress": after all, the courageous knights dared to

15. Hagen, "Luther's Doctrine of the Two Kingdoms," 117. Hagen is here referring to comments made by Luther in his work *Temporal Authority* (see *Luther's Works*, 45:89).

16. Oberman, *Luther*, 66.

confront the princely clan; the oppressed peasants kindled the
early proletarian revolution; Thomas Münzer, the protagonist of
peasants' rights, was martyred for decrying the rule of the aris-
tocracy; and finally Zwingli, the reformer of Zurich, advocated
the establishment of democracy in Church and state.[17]

Such a kingdom on earth was impossible for an Augustinian monk
who had thoroughly digested Augustine's *City of God*. Luther's reading
of Augustine was as a parallel to his own situation. Just as Augustine
saw the church confronted with the allure of the Roman Empire, so too
Luther sees the church of his day tempted by the desire to take the reins
of control into its own hands. Like Augustine, Luther concludes that the
church must await the coming kingdom to be established by God in his
own time.[18] Of course, the parallel with Augustine may not be as easy as
this, even though Luther would have been inclined to follow Augustine's
lead. Indeed, Luther may have even been making a very different point
than Augustine, while still using a similar dichotomistic approach.
Without contradicting the point of Luther's disdain for establishing the
kingdom of God, Hagen points out that

> The two cities of Augustine's *City of God Against the Pagans* do
> not equal Luther's two kingdoms. The two cities for Augustine
> are two loves—one of the flesh and one of the spirit; the two
> cities represent the cosmic conflict between the divine and
> the demonic. The two loves and the cosmic conflict are also in
> Luther but do not equate with the two kingdoms of God and
> this world. Both kingdoms of God and the world in Luther are
> in conflict with the Devil.[19]

Luther never considers the kingdom of God to be a reality, or even
a possibility, without God's first intervening in history to establish it
himself.

Another issue related to where the Holy Spirit is, is the problem
of the individual. Some have bemoaned Luther's opening the door to
individualism.[20] Others have decidedly approved of it by making the

17. Ibid., 64–66.

18. Ibid., 66–67.

19. Hagen, "Luther's Doctrine of the Two Kingdoms," 103.

20. Though Hauerwas has said very little on this subject in print, since he does not
consider himself a qualified historian, he has much to say with regard to Luther in
his teaching and private conversations. (See the brief quotation on the Reformation

application of doctrine to the individual one of the fundamental tenets of Reformation advances in Christian doctrine.[21] However, whether detesting or admiring the rise of the individual, both sides seem to agree that it was the Reformers, and especially Luther, who inaugurated the preference for it. But what are we to make of this claim that Luther instigated attention to the individual, particularly with regard to his understanding of the Holy Spirit? Does the individual loom preeminent in Luther's conception of the Spirit?

One would expect to find Luther's most galvanized defense of individualism precisely in discussions of the indwelling of the Holy Spirit. Since the Holy Spirit's indwelling was the mark of a true believer's having been justified by faith alone through grace alone, then one would expect Luther to expound upon what the personal indwelling of the Spirit looks like. However, what we find in Luther is a somewhat different approach to the indwelling of the Spirit. His dichotomy of Spiritual indwelling is not drawn between the Roman Catholic Church and the individual. Instead, he attempts to outline the distinctiveness of the Reformers' church as the "true church,"[22] as opposed to the Church of Rome.

> In these words: "He dwells with you and will be in you" [John 14:17] and (v. 18): "I will not leave you desolate; I will come to you," the Christian Church or Christendom has a guarantee, a formal promise and a strong consolation from Christ that nev-

attributed to Hauerwas's *In Good Company* in *Christianity Today* [January 6, 1997], 51.) This subject specifically became a point of conversation while I was Hauerwas's student at Duke University. At that point, I believed Hauerwas to be a bit anachronistic in his reading of Luther. Nevertheless, Luther's emphases certainly provided a more open context for Enlightenment individualism. Of course, Luther was not the only one writing on such things. In fact, as discussed below, others from Luther's day seem to have been far more intent than he on pursuing individualism and personal autonomy.

Hauerwas has since seemingly changed his mind on Luther. Instead he attributes such individualism to the Westernization of Luther in the modern context, rather than to Luther himself. See, Hauerwas, "Sanctified Body," 23.

21. Henry, *God, Revelation and Authority*, 370. Henry does not cite Luther specifically but does approvingly attribute to the Protestant Reformers an emphasis on "the Spirit's relation to individuals." Interestingly, what may have been driving Henry's concern for individualism is the precommitment that he had to seeing the ideologies of the Western world succeed. While he may have wished to qualify such commitments, Henry saw such notions as democracy's holding out the best hope for the culture of the West. See Henry, "Has the West a Future?" 12–16.

22. Luther, "Sermons on the Gospel of St. John," 131.

er, till the end of days, will it be without the Holy Spirit. We can and should know that the Holy Spirit abides eternally and forever, and that He always has and preserves His Christendom on earth. Thus we also confess in the Creed: "I believe in God the Father and in Jesus Christ, our Lord, and in the Holy Spirit." For just as Christ remains our Lord and is believed in until the end of the world, so the Holy Spirit likewise. And so long as Christendom endures and the Day of Judgment tarries, this text must stand; and there will always be people who believe and confess it with all their hearts, through the Holy Spirit. . . . This text must be noted well, for it is exceedingly offensive and hard to believe. We must observe what we say and preach about it, because there are so few who are really Christians and have the Holy Spirit remaining and dwelling in them.[23]

In Luther's context, it would have been easy for him to base his notions of the indwelling of the Spirit on individual belief and individual justification. After all, he understood the Roman Catholic Church to be teaching that it had the Holy Spirit simply because it was the Roman Catholic Church.

The pope wields [John 14:17] with power and might. The papists shout and boast against us that the Holy Spirit is with them eternally. They say: "We are the Christian Church; when we assemble and decide or determine something, it is the Holy Spirit's decree; for it is unthinkable that the church should err and be mistaken." And with this text they have grown so strong, large, and sure of their cause that they bank on it like a wall of iron. Thus they have nullified this doctrine, which is our greatest comfort and strength, and have shamefully perverted and corrupted this text. For we ourselves must believe and declare that the Holy Spirit is with the church, and that the church certainly is and remains on earth; for the creed states: "I believe in the holy Christian Church, the holy communion."

Those who make this boast do have the numbers and the strength, and they give every appearance of being the apostles' successors. They have governed the church so long. Besides, they cultivate great holiness and the worship of God. We, on the other hand, are so few, so destitute of all reputation and all outward appearance, and, in addition, so timid that we ourselves cannot believe firmly enough. Our glory seems to us too great, and we seem too unworthy. Hence, we cannot have the courage

23. Ibid., 125.

which they display; nor can we boast, as they do, that the Holy
Spirit dwells in us and that what we say and do reflects the Holy
Spirit's speech and work.[24]

Nevertheless, having stated that his small group cannot auda-
ciously claim to have the Holy Spirit, Luther cannot leave the issue aside
as irresolvable. He does not wish to simply let the papists' claim remain
unchallenged. Luther believes that a way exists by which to observe
whether one has the Holy Spirit, and even to make such a claim with
boldness. Whether his remarks about being too few and too unworthy be taken as rhetoric or as an expression of humility, Luther does
eventually arrive at a means to determine who is the real church. His
opponents have made it impossible to know if a person truly has the
Holy Spirit. For whatever reason, Luther believes the Roman Catholic
Church would rather remain ignorant of their status with regard to the
indwelling of the Spirit.

> Furthermore, we are still involuntarily affected by the doctrine
> of the papacy. For even if they do defiantly boast, as said before,
> that their whole life and conduct proceed from the Holy Spirit,
> they cannot maintain this when it comes to the test, when ev-
> eryone is to say for his own person that he has the Holy Spirit
> and that his life and conduct are holy and pleasing to God. Then
> they become uncertain of their position; then their boasting is
> turned to water and is gone. For there is no one who could or
> dared say of himself with certainty that he is holy; but they do
> say that if they themselves are not holy, then others are holy and
> do what is right. "It is enough," they say, "that I am a member of
> that multitude of which a few are holy and have the Holy Spirit."
> Thus all their personal life and conduct are founded on doubt
> and uncertainty. Yes, they even teach the propriety of doubt;
> they say that it is impossible for man to be certain of being in a
> state of grace and of having the Holy Spirit.[25]

In light of this humility, or inability by the Roman Catholic Church
to identify the presence of the Holy Spirit in a person, the quotation
above becomes even more instructive.

> If you want to be a Christian, therefore, you must conclude with
> conviction: "I have the Holy Spirit dwelling in me. I shall and

24. Ibid., 126.
25. Ibid., 129.

must have Him; for I know, of course, that my Christ, with His blood, Baptism, and Sacrament, is holy, and consequently that the Gospel, which I preach with my mouth, hear with my ears, and believe with my heart, is also holy. And if I have this, I must also say that the Holy Spirit is in me. For you will surely have no faith, no good thought, no joy, and no comfort from Him—yes, you will neither hear nor preach a sermon, and thus also perform no work of love or of any real Christian vocation—unless the Holy Spirit dwells in you and works and accomplishes all this in you. Of this you can cheerfully boast against the devil, who assails you with doubts and wants to rob you of this comfort, and against the world, which boasts against you of its possessions and condemns your faith, words, and works."[26]

So finally, Luther does not wish to remain in doubt or ignorant humility about the presence of the Holy Spirit in those who are of the true church. Instead he has discovered, as he would have it, the means devised by Scripture and true tradition to determine if the Spirit is really present in a person. Though he began his remarks by contrasting the true community of the church with the false, he has arrived at a discussion of individual and personal application of the test for the presence of the Holy Spirit. It is finally "I" who must declare the presence of the Holy Spirit in my life, and "I" who must preach, hear, and believe the gospel. But does this focus on personal belief and justification translate so easily into the individualism we associate with later modernity?

Luther's Opposition to the Humanist (i.e., Autonomous) Individual

Luther clearly understands human believers to be yet subject to the authority and leading outside of themselves, whether to the authority of Scripture or to knowledge granted by divine gift, (i.e., by the Spirit). In believing that individuals are subject to outside authority, Luther separates himself from the autonomous reason of the humanists. He was quite clear that the human activities we associate with the Holy Spirit were by no means to be considered a human product. They were the result of the moving of the Holy Spirit and could be tested precisely as they accorded with what was considered glorifying to Christ. For instance, the teaching of doctrine by those in the church was not to be

26. Ibid., 130.

considered the product of human ingenuity or human work. Instead, it was the product of the teaching of the Holy Spirit, who pointed people directly toward the teachings of Christ. Indeed, the whole of the doctrine of the Spirit "is not discoverable by human reason but is revealed supernaturally from heaven itself."[27] Likewise, the individual who taught was not teaching as an individual with his or her own ideas and doctrines. Instead, they were the doctrines of Christ as found in the teachings of Christ in Scripture, to which the Holy Spirit directed the teacher's attention. In this sense, the autonomous individual is hardly emphasized by Luther. Speaking of Christ's statements regarding the Holy Spirit in John 16:13, Luther states:

> Thus He will speak exclusively of Me and will glorify Me, so that the people will believe in Me.
>
> In this way Christ sets bounds for the message of the Holy Spirit Himself. He is not to preach anything new or anything else than Christ and His Word. Thus we have a sure guide and touchstone for judging the false spirits. We can declare that it surely does not indicate the presence of the Holy Spirit when a person proclaims his own thoughts and notions and begins to teach in Christendom something apart from or in addition to what Christ taught.[28]

Even Luther's own claims of individuality (e.g., "Here I stand") cannot be understood as claims of his own prestige or understanding. He by no means considers himself autonomous. But does this amount to a subjection of the individual in Luther to the ecclesial community?

As will be developed further below, Luther still believes himself to be a working part of the church and to be a representative of the true doctrine of the Scriptures and the Fathers. He is not devising something new but is simply conveying what he believes has existed for centuries, at least since the first century. Certainly he was bold in his claims, but as he viewed his doctrine to be the true representation of what Scripture taught, he could be nothing less than bold. Though the church hierarchy of Luther's day may have drifted from the biblical and theological moorings of the early church, Luther was still optimistic that he was being true to the church's foundation that had existed for centuries and

27. Wood, "Spirit and Spirituality in Luther," 314.
28. Luther, "Sermons on the Gospel of St. John," 363.

still existed—he Scriptures. Luther wanted to reform ecclesiology according to the Scriptures, not to leave all ecclesiology behind.

> What an unknown monk in an inconspicuous cell in Erfurt was committing to paper here [Luther was recording his trust in Scripture above all else] would one day lead him to the historic pronouncement on the political stage of the Diet of Worms: "Here I stand, God help me, amen"—a statement that was not an affirmation of himself but an expression of his loyalty to the Scriptures, a loyalty conducive from the very start to generating clashes, even with the authorities.[29]

However, this is not all that can be said about Luther and the individual. Some implications of his teachings on justification's being based on a personal commitment to Jesus are fairly obvious. Without our delving into a lengthy discussion of justification by faith alone through grace alone, Luther's argument is that it is only on the merits of Christ's righteousness that a person can be saved. The application of this salvation is based strictly to the application of Christ's righteousness to the believer, not based on any works the believer has done, but solely on the grace of God.[30] So then, is a person granted salvation based upon their membership in the church? Not by any means. Instead a person receives salvation due to Christ's individual application of his righteousness to the individual personally. The individualistic implications are obvious. However, Luther was quick to counter such implications with his continued belief that "Apart from the church, salvation is impossible."[31] By this, Luther did not mean to imply that the church was the arbiter of salvation. Rather, salvation could only be truly experienced in its fullness as the believer became an active part of the body of Christ, partaking in the sacraments that Luther believed still effective for grace within the church.

Likewise, Luther's understanding of the relationship between the Holy Spirit and the human spirit could certainly lead to the conclusion that the Holy Spirit is a privatized force in the individual's life.[32] But the question remains whether Luther was intentionally attempting to indi-

29. Oberman, *Luther*, 160.

30. E.g., see Luther, "Bondage of the Will," 197–201.

31. Luther, *Luther's Works*, 21:127.

32. For a good discussion of the relationship between the Holy Spirit and the human spirit for Luther, see Wood, "Spirit and Spirituality in Luther," 317–19.

vidualize salvation or merely pointing out the extent of salvation to the level of every person who claims to be a Christian. In other words, was Luther advocating the exertion of individual claims to salvation? Was he teaching people to be self-determined about their life in Christ—to exercise their liberty from the authority of the church and to personalize their claims to righteousness?

As we further read Luther on the subject of liberty and individualism, it seems illegitimate to accuse him of inaugurating Enlightenment tendencies toward individual autonomy and personal freedom. Indeed, Luther hardly seems a modern at all in this regard. As Luther's objections to his teachers' and contemporaries' theology indicates, he was against many of the tendencies that mark the turn toward modernism in the latter half of the sixteenth century and early in the seventeenth. Luther's rejection of his Occamist teachers is perhaps the primary point at which his break with scholasticism, which Luther considers "modern," is most apparent. Luther attacks all of Scholasticism, including Thomas, without making terribly clear distinctions between the thought of each figure. Certainly exceptions existed for Luther, but he lumped Thomas in amongst the rest of the Scholastics that he attacked, even perhaps without having read Thomas firsthand.[33] However, in spite of Luther's lacking direct knowledge of Thomas, he numbers him among those who taught a Pelagianism of the worst sort. "Luther did not regard Thomist theological anthropology as differing substantially from that of his nominalist teachers."[34] Luther's understanding of Thomas was largely the result of his reading of Gabriel Biel. Luther's fundamental objection centered on the moral capabilities of humans.

> Luther attacks the proposition that it is possible to do what is morally good or avoid sin without the help of grace. He denies that human beings can love God supremely by the exercise of their natural moral powers or prepare themselves for the reception of grace. While Luther is directly attacking the theology of Biel and d'Ailly, he has also indirectly attacked at several points the theology of Thomas Aquinas as presented by Biel. While Biel's Thomas denies the possibility of loving God supremely

33. Steinmetz, *Luther in Context*, 47. Lortz bemoans Luther's lack of Thomistic training as the tragedy of the Reformation, believing that if Luther had known Thomas, the Reformation could perhaps have been avoided. See Lortz, *Die Reformation in Deutschland*.

34. Janz, *Luther and the Late Medieval Thomism*, 25.

without infused grace, he does teach the other propositions condemned by Luther.[35]

Luther's objections to the human capacity to do meritorious works extend to several of his contemporaries, with little exception. As he makes clear in his diatribe against the Occamists,

> For it is certain that the *moderni* (as they are called) agree with the Scotists and Thomists in this matter (namely on grace and free will) except for one man, Gregory of Rimini, whom they all condemn, who rightly and convincingly condemns them of being worse than Pelagians. For he alone among all the scholastics agrees with Carlstadt, i.e., with Augustine and the Apostle Paul, against all the more recent scholastics. For the Pelagians, although they assert that a good work can be performed without grace, at least do not claim that heaven can be obtained without grace. The scholastics certainly say the same thing when they teach that without grace a good work can be performed, though not a meritorious one. But then they go beyond the Pelagians, saying that man has the natural dictates of right reason to which the will can naturally conform, whereas the Pelagians taught that man is helped by the law of God.[36]

Luther cannot allow for human beings to have innately some capacity to accomplish works that are meritorious with God. In spite of the Scholastics' claims otherwise, Luther believes their theology to be inconsistent on this point. If humans can prepare themselves for the grace of God, then they are, however explicitly or implicitly, gaining favor with God. As Steinmetz observes,

> Luther admits that the scholastics teach that grace is needed for merit, but argues that they eviscerate this point when they teach that human beings can conform their wills to the natural dictates of right reason and so prepare themselves for grace. ... Luther appears to accept Biel's reconstruction of Thomas as a theologian who believes that free will and the *concursis dei generalis* (the natural causality of God) are all the sinner needs to prepare himself for grace and merit justification with a merit of congruity.[37]

35. Steinmetz, *Luther in Context*, 57.

36. Luther, *D. Martin Luther's Werke*, 2.394.31–395.6; translated by Denis Janz in his *Luther and Late Medieval Thomism*, 32. Cf. Luther, "Bondage of the Will," 210–11.

37. Steinmetz, *Luther in Context*, 57.

When Luther turns his attentions more specifically to the subject of the free will of humans, he is loath to allow humans the capacity to determine their own destinies. In the same way that Calvin did, Luther viewed even his position of Reformer in the church as a servant of the church, not as an individual. Comparing Luther and Calvin in this regard, Steinmetz concludes

> Like Luther, who appeals again and again to the office which he holds in the Church as legitimation for his reform activity, Calvin rejects the notion that he is merely exercising his own right of private judgment or pursuing a vocation which has no public authorization. He is an office bearer in the Church, standing in that valid succession which derives its legitimacy from faithful transmission of the ancient apostolic message.[38]

Indeed, it may even be plausible to interpret Luther as a man against the burgeoning tendencies of Enlightenment thought. Luther himself states that he was not up to the task of directing a free will.

> For my own part, I frankly confess that even if it were possible, I should not wish to have free choice given to me, or to have anything left in my own hands by which I might strive toward salvation. For, on the one hand, I should be unable to stand firm and keep hold of it amid so many adversities and perils and so many assaults of demons, seeing that even one demon is mightier than all men, and no man at all could be saved; and on the other hand, even if there were no perils or adversities or demons, I should nevertheless have to labor under perpetual uncertainty and to fight as one beating the air, since even if I lived and worked to eternity, my conscience would never be assured and certain how much it ought to do to satisfy God. . . . But now, since God has taken my salvation out of my hands into his, making it depend on his choice and not mine, and has promised to save me, not by my own work or exertion but by his grace and mercy, I am assured and certain both that he is faithful and will not lie to me, and also that he is too great and powerful for any demons or any adversities to be able to break him or to snatch me from him.[39]

Given Luther's opposition to self-determinism, free will, the human capacity to accomplish any good without grace, and given his desire to

---

38. Ibid., 91. Cf. Luther, "Sermons on the Gospel of St. John," 131.
39. Luther, "Bondage of the Will," 219–20.

view his own position as one who was still an officer of the church, it is hard to imagine Luther's making room for the autonomy and individualism associated with later Enlightenment thinking. Indeed some have posited that Luther foresaw the age of freedom and railed against its dawning.

> What Luther saw on the horizon were the dark clouds of divine judgment gathering over a world nearing its end, a world fettered and enslaved in a thousand ways, that insisted on self-determination before God, that dared to speculate about the "meaning of history" and to speak of the freedom of the will without being able to free itself from the paralyzing primeval fear of being trapped helplessly in the cage of an impenetrable world history.[40]

In contrast to the humanism swelling around him, which takes for granted the freedom of the will, Luther finds the freedom of the will to be one of the central issues in his theological debates, or at least indicative of what he considers the issue at hand.[41] Was Christ really the Lord of the church, or did humans and their own freedom to determine their fate rule the day? Luther's answer to this dilemma was a resounding no to the freedom of the human will, for "inasmuch as you maintain free choice, you cancel out Christ and ruin the entire Scripture."[42] The human was either, to use the words of the Apostle Paul, "enslaved to sin" or "enslaved to God" (Rom 6:15–23). In this regard Given Luther's opposition to the freedom of the will,]Oberman even sees Luther as a somewhat unique figure for his time.

> When God had long paled into an uncertain hypothesis and the Devil was no more than a medieval vestige and a childish memory of times past, Luther's slap in the face of humanist progress was still remembered: for Luther, man is *not* the mule that, stupefied by ignorance, cannot decide between two haystacks—education could help that mule. No, the condition of man does not depend on the breadth of his education but on his existential condition as a "mule," ridden either by God or the

---

40. Oberman, *Luther*, 218.

41. Luther, "Bondage of the Will," 225. Luther is here pleased with Erasmus—that he has focused the issue that Luther believes is the crux of the matter.

42. Ibid., 213.

Devil, but with no choice in the matter, no freedom of decision, no opportunity for self-determination.

This proclamation of man's total impotence on the eve of man's greatest scientific discoveries and enduring cultural achievements could only eliminate Luther as a point of spiritual orientation in the tumult of modern times.[43]

This point of Luther's objection to the free will of humans should be made further with reference to his debate with Erasmus. Without delving deeply into the full scope of the debate, a fairly substantive summary from Luther himself should confirm what we have seen thus far. As always, Scripture figures prominently in Luther's argument.

> This is how Paul, writing to the Romans, enters into an argument against free choice and for the grace of God: "The wrath of God is revealed from heaven against all ungodliness and wickedness of men who in wickedness hold back the truth of God" [Rom. 1:18]. Do you hear in this the general verdict on all men, that they are under the wrath of God? What else does this mean but that they are deserving of wrath and punishment? He gives as the reason for the wrath, the fact that they do nothing but what deserves wrath and punishment, because they are all ungodly and wicked, and in wickedness hold back the truth. Where now is the power of free choice to attempt anything good? Paul represents it as deserving the wrath of God, and pronounces it ungodly and wicked. And that which deserves wrath and is ungodly, strives and prevails against grace, not for grace.[44]

When he comes to the end of his response to Erasmus's defense of free will, Luther outlines in shorthand many of the arguments made in the bulk of the text. Since it serves as a good summary of his argument in total, quotation of the whole summary seems warranted.

> I will here bring this little book to an end, though I am prepared if need be to carry the debate farther. However, I think quite enough has been done here to satisfy the godly and anyone who is willing to admit the truth without being obstinate. For if we believe it to be true that God foreknows and predestines all things, that he can neither be mistaken in his foreknowledge nor hindered in his predestination, and that nothing takes place but as he wills it (as reason itself is forced to admit), then on

43. Oberman, *Luther*, 219.
44. Luther, "Bondage of the Will," 178.

the testimony of reason itself there cannot be any free choice in man or angel or any creature.

Similarly, if we believe that Satan is the ruler of this world, who is forever plotting and fighting against the Kingdom of Christ with all his powers, and that he will not let men go who are his captives unless he is forced to do so by the divine power of the Spirit, then again it is evident that there can be no such thing as free choice.

Similarly, if we believe that original sin has so ruined us that even in those who are led by the Spirit it causes a great deal of trouble by struggling against the good, it is clear that in a man devoid of the Spirit there is nothing left that can turn toward the good, but only toward evil.

Again, if the Jews, who pursued righteousness to the utmost of their powers, rather ran headlong into unrighteousness, while the Gentiles, who pursued ungodliness, attained righteousness freely and unexpectedly, then it is also manifest from this very fact and experience that man without grace can will nothing but evil.

To sum up: If we believe that Christ has redeemed men by his blood, we are bound to confess that the whole man was lost; otherwise, we should make Christ either superfluous or the redeemer of only the lowest part of man, which would be blasphemy and sacrilege.[45]

What can be seen in Luther then is a Protestant who remains relatively unimpressed by the modernistic offering of self-determinism and freedom of choice. In fact, he finds the entire notion of a free will contrary to all that Scripture has to teach about God and the lordship of Christ over his church. Luther considers himself subject to the authority of the Scriptures as they have rightly been interpreted by him, but also as they have been rightly interpreted historically. Luther appeals to the Fathers for his authority in interpreting the Scriptures. In other words, even in what appear to be his most individualistic efforts—his appeals to Scripture—he is still subjecting himself to the authority of the church, seeing himself as a part of the "true" tradition. Indeed, he must contextualize his argument in such a way to avoid being accused of using his own human reason after the fashion of the humanists. Nevertheless, while Luther is not a post-Enlightenment individual, he is also not a postmodern communitarian after the fashion of someone

45. Ibid., 224.

like Hauerwas.[46] This is perhaps most evident in Luther's disdain for Aristotle.

Works and Righteousness, or Works as Righteousness

Luther makes it clear that he has no regard for Aristotle early in his thought with his "Disputation Against Scholastic Theology" (1517). Because Christian theology had been wed to Aristotle in Scholastic theology, beginning with Thomas and developing through Luther's day, Luther believed he must attack it at its roots.[47] Luther begins his outline of the problems he has with Aristotle by stating. "40. We do not become righteous by doing righteous deeds but, having been made righteous, we do righteous deeds. This in opposition to the philosophers."[48] That this accusation is directed toward Aristotle becomes clear as Luther continues his diatribe by driving the point home further.

> 41. Virtually the entire *Ethics* of Aristotle is the worst enemy of grace. This in opposition to the scholastics.
> . . . 44. Indeed, no one can become a theologian unless he becomes one without Aristotle.
> . . . 50. Briefly, the whole Aristotle is to theology as darkness is to light. This in opposition to the scholastics.[49]

It appears from the context of these statements for debate that Luther's focus was particularly directed toward two issues: 1) the ability for righteous deeds to make one righteous; 2) the ability to devise a logic for faith.[50] Since the second issue (human reason's being sufficient

46. It is unfair to call Hauerwas a communitarian since he does not advocate the notion of community for its own sake. On this, see his *In Good Company*, 25–26; and *Dispatches from the Front*, 156–63. Nevertheless, community is obviously a central theme of his theology and the foundation for his ecclesiology. The question for Hauerwas is not whether or not community, but what kind of community. He has no theory of community per se. Instead, he has a fellowship of believers whom he wishes to describe. "Community" is, at times, a useful term in this regard, but it is not purely a definition.

47. Oberman, *Luther*, 158–61. Oberman traces Luther's dislike of Aristotle to his early days as a student at Erfurt studying Augustine.

48. Luther, "Disputation against Scholastic Theology," 16.

49. Ibid., 16. By the "whole Aristotle," Lull believes Luther is referring to Aristotle's logical and metaphysical writings (16, n. 7). Whatever other works may be included or excluded, it is obvious that Luther singularly disliked Aristotle's *Ethics*.

50. Ibid. The surrounding statements for dispute indicate that Luther was particu-

to accomplish faith) has been dealt with in summary fashion with regard to free will above, we will not address this issue further here. The first of these issues seems to stem from Aristotle's belief that a person's moral nature was formed specifically by the training received in the community in which the person lived. As Aristotle put it, "Hence it is no small matter whether one habit or another is inculcated in us from early childhood; on the contrary, it makes a considerable difference, or, rather, all the difference."[51] Aristotle taught that moral virtue was the result of habits gained by a person over years of appropriate training. Since conversion was hardly an issue for Aristotle or the Scholastics of Luther's day, given their Constantinian perspective on Christendom, it is easy to understand how Aristotle's program for moral virtue easily elided with Scholastic theology. Luther's concern centered on the issue of whether the development of such habits constituted righteousness before God. He was not opposed to the doing of good works, just the reliance upon them for the establishment of righteousness before God. Indeed, he encouraged works in keeping with the Spirit who dwelled in the believer. The Reformers were largely in agreement on this issue. As Steinmetz remarks about Calvin's response to Sadoleto when the Sadoleto made an attack upon the doctrine of the Reformers,

> Calvin also answers what he regards as Sadoleto's caricature of the evangelical understanding of justification by faith alone. Faith is not mere credulity, not a mere assent of the mind to true doctrine, but a committal of the whole self to God. To be justified by faith means to be united to Christ in a bond of mystical union (Luther had spoken of being baked into one cake with Christ). Naturally, anyone so possessing Christ and so possessed by him will perform good works. What is at stake is not the existence of good works but their status. Protestants deny only that these works contribute to justification or form even the partial basis for God's acceptance of the sinner. Good works are not merits in the Catholic sense, but only the fruits of faith.[52]

Like Calvin, Luther by no means disregards the value of good works, as long as they are rightly understood. Though works cannot

larly piqued by these two issues. Others may have lingered, but these are the focus of Luther's attention.

51. Aristotle, *Nicomachean Ethics*, 1103b. 23–25.
52. Steinmetz, *Luther in Context*, 93–94.

justify a person, they are still something that a person needs to accomplish. In a discussion devoted to demonstrating the agreement between Calvin and Luther, showing that they both knew each other's work and made explicit reference to their affinity for it, Steinmetz again writes

> The church has instrumental authority since we "cannot fly without wings." It leads believers to the sources of truth and life. But the church is not merely mother; it is also *school*. Even simple believers have a theological responsibility which they must assume. Like Clement of Alexandria, Calvin believes that every stage of the Christian life is justified only in so far as one is pressing on, however hesitatingly and ineptly, to the next stage. The faith that justifies is never static.[53]

Luther is hardly silent on this issue. He makes it clear that though works cannot justify a person, they are by no means unimportant.

> Our faith in Christ does not free us from works but from false opinions concerning works, that is, from the foolish presumption that justification is acquired by works. Faith redeems, corrects, and preserves our consciences so that we know that righteousness does not consist in works, although works neither can nor ought to be wanting; just as we cannot be without food and drink and all the works of this mortal body, yet our righteousness is not in them, but in faith; and yet those works of the body are not to be despised or neglected on that account.[54]

Luther is again reiterating his point with regard to the issue of justification, and in fact it does not appear that he can remove the issue of good works from this context. However, it should be noted that good works are not due to the effort of the individual. Rather they are the product of a person who has been changed by God. Thus Luther states, "Good works do not make a good man, but a good man does good works."[55] What Luther means by this statement is that the works a person do reveal what is already true in their inner being.[56] The person does not accomplish any of the work alone, but God accomplishes it through the person. As Luther states with regard to Romans 9:16,

53. Ibid., 93, emphasis mine.

54. Luther, "Freedom of a Christian," 624–25.

55. Ibid., 613.

56. Ibid., 596. Luther's "Freedom of a Christian" is divided between the discussion of the freedom of the inner, spiritual nature and the bodily nature.

"So it depends not upon man's will or exertion." This is not to be understood in the sense that this is a matter only of God's showing mercy, as if it were not necessary for a person to will or to exert himself, but rather that the fact that a man does will or exert himself is not of his own power but of the mercy of God, who has given this power of willing and doing, without which man of himself can neither will nor make exertion.[57]

The question that naturally arises is, how then does one become a good man? Luther answers this question by means of an analogy (contra Aristotle).

A good or a bad house does not make a good or a bad builder; but a good or a bad builder makes a good or a bad house. And in general, the work never makes the workman like itself, but the workman makes the work like himself. So it is with the works of man. As the man is, whether believer or unbeliever, so also is his work—good if it was done in faith, wicked if it was done in unbelief. But the converse is not true, that the work makes the man either a believer or an unbeliever. As works do not make a man a believer, so also they do not make him righteous. But as faith makes a man a believer and righteous, so faith does good works. Since, then, works justify no one, and a man must be righteous before he does a good work, it is very evident that it is faith alone which, because of the pure mercy of God through Christ and in his Word, worthily and sufficiently justifies and saves the person.[58]

Though Luther is attempting to speak to the issue of how both believers and unbelievers engage in good works, it seems clear that his concerns about unbelievers' meriting salvation is the paradigm of understanding works for both. Luther does not differentiate here between those who have the Spirit and those who don't.

But a further question remains as to whether becoming a "good man" after conversion is immediate (i.e., a gift) or a process (i.e., a work), or perhaps even both. Another way of asking the question might be, is sanctification effected internally or externally with regard to the believer? It seems as though the Spirit's activity is immediate in the be-

57. Luther, "Lectures on Romans," 388. Luther does not have all humanity in view here but only those who are believers, as he makes clear in the next sentence with a quote of Philippians 2:13.

58. Ibid., 613.

liever, but it also appears as though the Spirit's activity is yet mediated through the Scriptures, appropriately understood as the good news of God's salvation. As Steinmetz observes with regard to Luther's ethics,

> Good works are the spontaneous response of Christians to the need of the neighbor, as perceived by those who, following the mind of Christ, have put on their neighbor's situation. Good works spring from true and genuine love. Love is true and genuine where there is faith and confidence in the promises of God. Confidence in God is created by the proclamation of the Word of God, the good news of what God has done for the salvation of men and women in Jesus Christ. It is the Word of God which is the essential foundation and precondition for an authentic moral life.[59]

So then, though the inner working of the Spirit is certainly present in Luther, the believer is also sanctified by the external working of the Word and the sacraments. This was a major point of conflict between Luther and the "enthusiasts," who denied the external and relied solely on the internal influence of the Spirit and his gifts.[60] Against the subjectivism of the enthusiasts, Luther provides a much more balanced approach to the influence of both the internal and the external.[61] As Luther himself makes clear, "It is indeed true that the Holy Spirit alone enlightens hearts and kindles faith, *but* He does not do this without the outward ministry and without the use of the sacraments."[62]

The problem that arises in our understanding of Luther at this point is how to reconcile his acceptance, or even promotion, of the external with his ethics. If Arnold Carlson is right, Luther had left behind conforming to Christ through imitation in favor of an internal, dynamic assimilation of Christ's lordship over a person by means of the influence of the Spirit.

> Luther no longer thinks of the Holy Spirit in terms of the scholastic tradition as a transcendent cause of a new (supernatu-

---

59. Steinmetz, *Luther in Context*, 120.

60. Prenter, *Spiritus Creator*, 248. Cf. Wood, "Spirit and Spirituality in Luther," 319–20.

61. Wood, "Spirit and Spirituality in Luther," 321–22.

62. Luther, "Lectures on Genesis," 72. For a good discussion of the relationship between Word and Spirit, with preeminence given to the Word, see Runia, "Holy Spirit and the Church," 311–13.

ral) nature in man, infusing grace as a divine energy. Instead,
the Holy Spirit is proclaimed as the real presence of God. God
Himself, as the Spirit, is really present in the groaning of the
anxious and tempted soul held in the grip of death and hell.
... In imitation piety the believer is related to Christ as an ideal.
Christ is an example. He represents a way to be followed. He is
outside of us. The believer is himself the active one who exercises his own volition in choosing to follow Christ. In conformity,
by contrast, the living, present Christ unseats man's self-domin-
ion, so that the believer not only can but *must* say with St. Paul,
"I have been crucified with Christ; it is no longer I who live, but
Christ who lives in me." This activity of Christ within the believer as the new subject is, according to Luther, the direct result
of the Holy Spirit's activity.[63]

Carlson's understanding of Luther's dichotomy between external
imitation and internal dynamism does not seem to completely do justice to Luther's own commitments to the externals of Word and sacrament. While Luther does make explicit that the Holy Spirit is the one
who works in the heart, the Holy Spirit works in the heart only through
the externals of the Word and sacrament. Carlson seems (anachronistically) to draw a contrast between imitation and conformity that Luther
may not have recognized. In Carlson's scheme, the only two options
are either a dynamic, internal working of the Spirit or the Spirit as an
external "divine energy" that empowers humans to conform to the yet-
external example of Christ.[64] Carlson believes that Luther teaches only
the former of these options, objecting to the latter as the product of
human endeavors. Two questions must be put to Carlson's interpretation of Luther. Both will be answered simultaneously. First, does Luther
really believe that humans can function so ahistorically (i.e., without
any interaction with people and events of the world as instructive for
righteousness)? Second, does it have to be one or the other for Luther
with regard to the process of sanctification? In Luther's understanding
of the mediation of the Word, he recognizes the need for instruction
and correction from external sources, (e.g., teachers, pastors, mentors).
Luther does not simply free the individual to his or her own recourse,
saying, "Go with the Spirit." Instead he recognizes that while humans are
incapable of accomplishing Christ's righteousness in their justification

63. Carlson, "Luther and the Doctrine of the Holy Spirit," 140.
64. Ibid., 137.

without the dynamic working of the Holy Spirit, they are likewise incapable of accomplishing Christ's righteousness in their sanctification without appropriate instruction.[65] Such an understanding of sanctification does no damage to Luther's doctrine of justification. Neither does it diminish the work of the Spirit in humans. It is still the Spirit of Christ who accomplishes righteousness, and still Christ who receives the glory for it. What we find in Luther then is an understanding of the Spirit that would be akin to the notion that the Spirit cooperates with the human precisely through his activity in other humans. In other words, since the Spirit really indwells people, the way he accomplishes his work in a person is through other people, (i.e., through the community of faith).

One might wonder if Luther himself has the teachings of Aristotle in mind when he compares good works to a craft such as building a good or a bad house. If Luther does have Aristotle in mind in the above quotation, then Luther has, or those who taught him Aristotle have, perhaps misunderstood Aristotle. Aristotle did not teach that the craft itself would instruct the person in an art, as though the sculpture could tell the sculptor where to chisel. Rather, he taught that a master craftsman could apprentice a novice to teach the novice the art or craft. So too in morality, one could be apprenticed to a master and learn morality as one followed after the master. In this respect, like Aristotle, Luther does not seem to abandon his followers to a contextless arena in which they are left to make choices by themselves. Indeed, they are taught in faith by Christ through his Spirit. Luther makes it sound on many occasions as though this is a direct teaching by the Spirit. However, he does make room for this to happen through master Christians, in so far as they are appropriately aligned with Christ and rightly teaching the Scripture, and through specific constitutive practices of the church. Thus Luther can consider himself a teacher of those who follow him, as well as a student of another master.

> If there is to be only one father, then Christ is our father in Paul, in John, or in Peter. Thus all of us are sons in Christ, because John teaches nothing different from Peter. Therefore they can be called fathers in Christ, but not in themselves, because I listen to Christ speaking to me, not as the apostle himself speaks but as my Lord speaks through his mouth. And so I call Paul "father," not for his own sake but for Christ's. Thus he says to the

65. Luther, "Lectures on Titus," 14–15. Cf. 1 Cor 4:14–16.

Corinthians (1 Cor. 11:1): "Be imitators of me as I am of Christ,"
not merely "of me" but "of me as, etc." Here he unites himself
with Christ, so that there is one example and pattern which both
Christ and Paul set forth. In this sense we are fathers, provided
that our fatherhood redounds to Christ our head. For through
the apostles He speaks to us and rules us.[66]

Luther doesn't spend a lot of time addressing moral instruction, at
least not in the Aristotelian sense. It appears to be the context in which
he advocated training in how to learn to be righteous. However, his concern was primarily with his diatribe directed against the way in which
this teaching had become a means for some to teach that humanly produced righteousness could be meritorious. Nevertheless, he does expect
his own teaching and preaching to accomplish much toward training
people in true righteousness and faith. Indeed, he believes that without
proper instruction (meaning instruction like his own) people would do
works of righteousness in vain.

> We must bring forth the voice of the law that men may be made
> to fear and come to a knowledge of their sins and so be converted
> to repentance and a better life. But we must not stop with that, for
> that would only amount to wounding and not binding up, smit-
> ing and not healing, killing and not making alive, leading down
> into hell and not bringing back again, humbling and not exalting.
> Therefore we must also preach the word of grace and the promise
> of forgiveness by which faith is taught and aroused. Without this
> word of grace the works of the law, contrition, penitence, and all
> the rest are done and taught in vain.[67]

With regard to practices that constitute what it means to be the
church in the world for Luther, Hütter enumerates several categorical
means by which a Christian may be marked off as a distinct creature
from the world: proclamation of God's word and its reception in faith,
confession, and deed; baptism; Eucharist; office of the keys; ordination/
offices; prayer/doxology/catechesis; way of the cross/discipleship.[68] By

66. Ibid.

67. Luther, "Freedom of a Christian," 616.

68. Hütter, "Church as Public," 354–55. Hütter adds a few of his own marks of what
distinguishes a church as uniquely "public" in its own right. His intention is to demonstrate that Luther believed it was not only dogma but also practices that marked off the
"public" nature of the church. Hütter's primary project is to demonstrate (in the modern context more so than in Luther's) that the church must be understood as "public"

advocating such practices as a way of marking off the distinct "public" nature of the church, Luther does not seem to have abandoned the usefulness of action as epistemologically valuable.

Luther struggles with this issue somewhat when it comes to the issue of instructing children. He devoutly wishes for Scripture to be taught to young people so that they might learn to correctly handle it. Still, he must acknowledge that it is only through the Holy Spirit that correct understanding of Scripture, and any other form of correct living, can be found. Thus correct teaching, in this case the teaching of Greek and Hebrew, becomes the medium through which the Holy Spirit might appropriately prepare young people to learn Scripture well.

> Although the Gospel came and still comes to us through the Holy Spirit alone, we cannot deny that it came through the medium of languages, was spread abroad by that means, and must be preserved by the same means.
> . . . In proportion then as we value the Gospel, let us zealously hold to the languages.[69]

Obviously someone would need to teach people to read Greek and Hebrew, and read it well, so that proper interpretation, from Luther's perspective, could continue. This is at least one way in which Luther's understanding of church seems to parallel, or at least shadow, Aristotle's polis. Training and teaching are not the problem. People constantly need to be taught and shown the "right way." The problem happens when this teaching becomes an end in itself, leading to the belief that the teaching and learning can themselves serve sufficiently to ground a person's justification before God. This seems to be Luther's objection to Aristotle's *Ethics*, via the Scholastics. However, this also seems to be a caricature of Aristotle, even in spite of his paganism. Aristotle desired formation of character as much as Luther. Luther is, rightly, defensive over the issue of works' contributing to or being preparatory for justification. However,

---

in contradistinction to the secular "public," rather than deriving its constitutive marks from either succumbing to modernity (Adolph von Harnack) or opposing it (Erik Peterson). Both options leave the church finally defined in yet modernistic terms.

69. Luther, "To the Councilman of All Cities in Germany that They Establish and Maintain Christian Schools," 715–16. One may question the spiritual aspirations of Luther in this writing, since his primary goal could be interpreted as the welfare of the German nation. Nevertheless this particular instruction is for the welfare of the gospel for future generations.

in sanctification Luther seems open to making use of the external in character formation. It seems that the distinction between the two contexts in which external works are said to contribute (justification and sanctification) is sometimes blurred. Perhaps Luther wasn't as far from Aristotle, at least in sanctification, as he may have thought.

Luther's kingdoms become instructive once again here. He acknowledges that the way in which God directs each of the "realms" under his authority (though there are no kingdoms outside his authority) is by differing means. "In the secular rule it is the sword and the fist, in the spiritual it is the Word and the mouth, in the angelic it is reason and sense."[70] What is interesting about this passage is how Luther later defines the direction of the Word. It is not merely the text of Scripture. The kingdom of the spirit, or the church, is ruled by more than just the words of Scripture, though certainly they are paramount and foundational. Luther explains: "By the Word I understand all that pertains to the spiritual rule, such as spiritual gifts, 1 Cor. 12:5, Eph. 4:11, Rom. 12:6f., and the sacraments and the like."[71] Luther was by no means opposed to the use of many of the schooling aspects of the church when it came to rightly directing the church toward its proper end. These were the means by which he understood God to be directing the church, but at the same time, they also included human activity. Indeed, as Hagen notes, it is "the spiritual kingdom, being the kingdom of the right hand ... [that] God rules through the church."[72]

One other note seems pertinent before leaving our discussion of Luther. As mentioned above with regard to free will, Luther does not, indeed he could not, advocate some sort of autonomous, humanistic individualism. One was committed to either God or the Devil. Nevertheless, a question still remains whether an inherent spiritual individualism of sorts exists within Luther. If the Holy Spirit deals with believers directly, and believers are all (each and every one of them) priests,[73] then does a real sense of community still remain on which Luther can build an ecclesiology?

70. Luther, "Lectures on Zechariah—1527," 172.
71. Ibid.
72. Hagen, "Luther's Doctrine of the Two Kingdoms," 115.
73. E.g., see Luther's "Freedom of a Christian," 606–7.

Luther believes he can still have a functioning ecclesiology of sorts, but his answer is not terribly satisfying. Luther believes that each person is responsible to watch out for the best interests of others. In his view, "A man does not live for himself alone in this mortal body to work for it alone, but he lives also for all men on earth; rather, he lives only for others and not for himself."[74] By becoming servants of one another and looking first to the interests of others before their own (Phil 2:1–5), believers can thus become what Christ desires of them in the world. As Luther states,

> Hence, as our heavenly Father has in Christ freely come to our aid, we also ought freely to help our neighbor through our body and its works, and each one should become as it were a Christ to the other that we may be Christs to one another and Christ may be the same in all, that is, that we may be truly Christians.[75]

Thus the believer does not live for his or her own sake. Instead the welfare of others is the paramount concern that drives how believers function in community. This is directly the result of the life the believer has in Christ, for "Where the gospel is preached, communities of love are created."[76] Indeed, one cannot be a Christian without living first for others.

> We conclude, therefore, that a Christian lives not in himself, but in Christ and in his neighbor. Otherwise he is not a Christian. He lives in Christ through faith, in his neighbor through love. By faith he is caught up beyond himself into God. By love he descends beneath himself into his neighbor. Yet he always remains in God and in his love . . .[77]

The problem that arises with this Christian ethic, if it can be called such, is that one is left with some doubt about how to do it. How does one ascend to God and descend to his neighbor? Luther's answer would likely be to say that this occurs through the Holy Spirit. In Luther's context, this answer might have been sufficient, given that he lived in a community that valued training, and that likely could hardly conceive of any other way to instruct people to listen to the Spirit. Luther could

74. Ibid., 616.
75. Ibid., 619–20.
76. Steinmetz, *Luther in Context*, 121.
77. Luther, "Freedom of a Christian," 623.

act as a "father" and train those under him. But he does not, indeed he likely could not, identify his ecclesiology with the workings of the community. Likely, Luther lived in a community, perhaps even a culture, in which moral apprenticeship was the overarching tendency. However, by merely presupposing that the community would exist in which training would take place, Luther has inadvertently left his ecclesiology open to the whims of post-Enlightenment readers' individualism. By making spiritual formation the direct result of immediate contact with the Holy Spirit in his invisible form (by this I mean *not mediated* through other humans in whom he resides), and by assuming that a community of moral training would be the context in which this encounter with the Spirit would typically be discussed, Luther has set the stage for ecclesiology to become merely the collection of individuals, each responsible for his or her own participation, and each participating as he or she see fit (i.e., as the Spirit directs). Had Luther foreseen such a situation, it is likely that his teachings would have taken a different tone. Nevertheless, others later latched onto the ideas of individual freedom and spirituality, and wed them to an individualized pneumatology that is more primary than ecclesiology. Luther would undoubtedly be dismayed at such a turn.

Conclusion

In chapters 1, 2, and 3 above, we reviewed Hauerwas's critique of system as a tool for those engaging in what he would term a more liberal strategy of theological investigation. Hauerwas rightly identifies systematics as primarily concerned with discovering and justifying universal truth claims. Such justification is based on the rationality of theological knowledge. In other words, such knowledge is available to any rational creature and could only be counted as knowledge when divorced from any particularistic viewpoint. Consequently, knowledge that claims an attachment to history, including to the history of Jesus, is deemed too contingent to be considered true. Hauerwas has demonstrated, by discussing Kant and others, that such a view of universal knowledge needs to be understood as a product of certain historical circumstances; understanding the notion of universal knowledge as itself contingent on history makes such a notion as universal knowledge self-contradictory. Hauerwas argues that what is needed is an epistemology that takes history into account—an epistemology open to the kind of claims theologians make about the relationship of knowledge to action, and to the claim of Jesus to be the Truth.

Chapter 4 set out to display Hauerwas's alternative to systematic knowledge. Here he provides the reader with a fairly "thick" depiction of what a narrative epistemology would look like and how it would function in theology. By discussing Barth, and placing Barth against the backdrop of Aquinas and Aristotle, we were able to see that Hauerwas's narrative epistemology reverses the Enlightenment primacy given to thought over action. In Hauerwas's reading of the Enlightenment, thought, or theoretical knowledge, was given the high ground with regard to what constituted knowledge, with action deriving from the principles of knowledge provided by thought. In contrast to this, Hauerwas sees action as primary in a narrative epistemology. Aristotle, as assimilated into Christian theology through Aquinas, was particularly helpful here. Aristotle rightly understood that moral training, which, by and large, is theology for Hauerwas, requires the kind of practice that only apprenticeship affords. Therefore, the knowledge gained in apprenticeship derives not from thought but from the actions themselves. The impact of such an epistemological shift for Hauerwas is that now theology must be understood through the lens of the narrative, or formative, community, which is the church. Ecclesiology, then, takes on an epistemological role in any claims the church might make regarding knowledge and truth. Instead of being discovered in a historical vacuum, truth is now centered, as is theologically appropriate, on the person of Jesus. For the church to know truth, it must likewise be truthful to his story. In other words, one of the more important elements the church bears in demonstrating its veracity is its faithfulness to the life of Jesus.

Chapter 5 fleshed out the way in which the church demonstrates this faithfulness through its witness to the world of the lordship of Jesus. Here the full impact of Hauerwas's needed ecclesiology is seen. As the historical community of faith, the church submits itself to the headship of Jesus. This is not knowledge exclusive to the church, since the whole world is subject to his rule. The church's goal is to live his lordship in such a way as to call the world to acknowledge its place before him as subject to him as well. The message of the church is not a message of bowing before a malevolent dictator. On the contrary, it is a call for all to participate in the loving relationship that marks the very heart of the

Godhead itself. This notion of being drawn into participation in God is the way in which the church is raised to be more than itself. It is not a mere human community. It is a community that strives to be the very body of Christ.

It is on this point of the church being a divine community that we discovered Hauerwas' most serious problem. While he makes an effort to provide the human community of the church with a divine connection through the sacraments, this remains a rather sporadic and mystical connection. It was seen that Hauerwas would be far better served to ground the connection in a robust doctrine of the Holy Spirit. This would give him the means to overcome the anthropological reductionism into which he seems to lapse. At the same time, pneumatology would provide him with greater warrant for making the claim to divine participation by the church. The church is finally made the body of Christ only through the Spirit.

In the face of many decades, at least, of emphasis on the supernatural working of the Spirit in the lives of individuals, the final chapters of this study provide a concerted theological effort toward a more precisely scriptural portrayal of the ministry of the Holy Spirit in the natural or human community of the church. The Spirit works primarily in the community of faith, and only secondarily in the individual. This does not dismiss individual participation in the activity of the Spirit. Instead, recognition of the corporate working of the Spirit brings needed humility to claims of the Spirit's presence in the lives of individuals. Training, or in Aristotelian language, apprenticeship, becomes the way in which people are invited into the community of worship. Ecclesiology is the proper context in which to place any discussion of the work of the Spirit (i.e., the connection between the human and the divine), since it is to the *head of the church—Jesus—*that the Spirit directs all people within the church. Just as the deity of the Son has often eclipsed his humanity, so the supernatural work of the Spirit seems to have entirely covered his place in the natural working of the community of the church. While not denying the supernatural elements of the Spirit's ministry, this study has shown that the more primary locus of the Spirit's work is found in the activity of the church being church. This is perhaps the most obvious connection between the work of Hauerwas and the original discussions of the Holy Spirit offered in these chapters. Hauerwas has endeavored to demonstrate the primacy of churchly activities in his epistemological efforts. Chapters 6 and 7 offer a depiction of the Spirit working in the midst of the people of the church. As they, themselves, work to be church, their faithfulness to living the gospel lifts what might otherwise be considered common activities to the level of primary or foundational acts. Being church is the primary work of Christians. By developing more thoroughly scriptural meditations on the Spirit, being church may also become the primary work of theology. Further, it is only in development of ecclesiology in the context of pneumatological participation of the church in God that theology can be regarded once again as primarily for the church.

Our last chapters attempted to reconcile such notions with some of the more dearly held doctrines of Protestantism. Luther's understanding of the priesthood of the believer and of the role of the church were examined from the perspective of his beliefs regarding the indwelling of the Spirit and how the community of the church functions in regard to training its members. Luther was by no means opposed to a form of discipleship resembling Aristotelian apprenticeship, even though he bore great disdain for the Aristotelianism he had been taught, and that was used to defend certain Roman doctrines. In the end, Luther's understanding of the community of the church and of the function of the Spirit within it don't seem far distant from what has been presented in this study. Though Luther may have certainly wished to emphasize specific issues regarding the role of the church and Spirit in justification, his understanding of sanctification seems open to the scriptural interpretation that we have taken above. In the least, it would seem he would not be opposed to it.

The question of the role of theology for the church has not been addressed in direct fashion in any of the chapters above. However, the answer should be plain to the reader at this point. Theology is not merely a body of information or a listing of facts for anyone to read and understand as they would the facts of any other science. Certainly the listing of our beliefs about God is critical, and the creeds and statements of belief serve a tremendous purpose, but their purpose is skewed if left at the level of information. The more primary purpose is for preserving unity of the faith, and training believers in the life of Jesus. Discipleship, or the conforming of one's life to the life of Jesus, is woefully thin if we all simply agree about statements on a page. Instead we must push deeper to use theology as a tool in the church for shaping and molding the character of believers. Once again, action takes center stage, but the acts are never ends in themselves. Just as it is biblically inappropriate to hold to a works justification, so too it would be inappropriate to hold to a works sanctification. The actions we perform in enacting the life of Jesus in the church today serve to conform *us* to his image, not to conform our deeds to his image. The distinction is critical, and points us toward a model of sanctification rich in character development. When others "see your good works and glorify your Father who is in heaven" (Matt 5:16), they are seeing a man or woman who *is* like Jesus, not merely one who acts like Jesus. It is in the doing that we can become, but without becoming, what we do or say is finally meaningless!

Bibliography

Works by Stanley Hauerwas

Hauerwas, Stanley. *After Christendom? How the Church Is to Behave If Freedom, Justice, and a Christian Nation Are Bad Ideas.* Nashville: Abingdon, 1991.

———. *Against the Nations: War and Survival in a Liberal Society.* Minneapolis: Winston, 1985.

———. *A Better Hope: Resources for a Church Confronting Capitalism, Democracy, and Postmodernity.* Grand Rapids: Brazos, 2000.

———. *Character and the Christian Life: A Study in Theological Ethics.* San Antonio: Trinity University Press, 1975.

———. *Christian Existence Today: Essays on Church, World, and Living in Between.* Durham: Labyrinth, 1988.

———. *A Community of Character: Toward a Constructive Christian Social Ethic.* Notre Dame: University of Notre Dame Press, 1981.

———. *Dispatches from the Front: Theological Engagements with the Secular.* Durham: Duke University Press, 1994.

———. *God, Medicine, and Suffering.* Grand Rapids: Eerdmans, 1990.

———. *In Good Company: The Church as Polis.* Notre Dame: University of Notre Dame Press, 1995.

———. *Matthew.* Brazos Theological Commentary on the Bible. Grand Rapids: Brazos, 2006.

———. "On Keeping Theological Ethics Theological." In *Revisions: Changing Perspectives in Moral Philosophy*, edited by Stanley Hauerwas and Alasdair MacIntyre, 16–42. Notre Dame: University of Notre Dame Press, 1983.

———. "On Learning Simplicity in an Ambiguous Age: A Response to Hunsinger." *Katallagete* 10 (1987) 43–46.

———. *Prayers Plainly Spoken.* Downers Grove: InterVarsity, 1999.

———. *Sanctify Them in the Truth: Holiness Exemplified.* Nashville: Abingdon, 1998.

———. *Should War Be Eliminated? Philosophical and Theological Investigations.* Père Marquette Theology Lecture: 1984. Milwaukee: Marquette University Press, 1984.

———. "Storytelling: A Response to 'Mennonites on Hauerwas.'" *The Conrad Grebel Review* 13 (1995) 166–73.

———. *Suffering Presence: Theological Reflections on Medicine, the Mentally Handicapped, and the Church.* Notre Dame: University of Notre Dame Press, 1986.

————. "The Church's One Foundation is Jesus Christ Her Lord; Or, In a World Without Foundations: All We Have is the Church." In *Theology Without Foundations: Religious Practice and the Future of Theological Truth*. Nashville: Abingdon, 1994.

————. *The Moral Value of the Family*. Notre Dame: University of Notre Dame Press, 1978.

————. *The Peaceable Kingdom*. Notre Dame: University of Notre Dame Press, 1983.

————. "The Sanctified Body: Why Perfection Does Not Require a 'Self.'" In *Embodied Holiness*, edited by Samuel M. Powell and Michael E. Lodahl, 19–38. Downers Grove: InterVarsity, 1999.

————. *Truthfulness and Tragedy: Further Investigations in Christian Ethics*. Notre Dame: University of Notre Dame Press, 1977.

————. *Unleashing the Scripture: Freeing the Bible from Captivity to America*. Nashville: Abingdon, 1993.

————. *Vision and Virtue: Essays in Christian Ethical Reflection*. Notre Dame: University of Notre Dame Press, 1974.

————. "Where Would I Be Without Friends?" In *Faithfulness and Fortitude: In Conversation with the Theological Ethics of Stanley Hauerwas*, edited by Mark Thiessen Nation and Samuel Wells, 312–32. Edinburgh: T. & T. Clark, 2000.

————. "Why the Truth Demands Truthfulness: An Imperious Engagement with Hartt." *Journal of the American Academy of Religion* 52 (1984) 141–47.

————. *Wilderness Wanderings: Probing Twentieth-Century Theology and Philosophy*. Boulder: Westview, 1997.

————. *With the Grain of the Universe: The Church's Witness and Natural Theology*. Grand Rapids: Brazos, 2001.

Hauerwas, Stanley, with Michael Baxter. "The Kingship of Christ: Why Freedom of 'Belief' Is Not Enough." In *In Good Company: The Church as Polis*, 199–216. Notre Dame: University of Notre Dame Press, 1995.

Hauerwas, Stanley, with John Berkman. "A Trinitarian Theology of the Chief End of All Flesh." In *In Good Company: The Church as Polis*, 185–98. Notre Dame: University of Notre Dame Press, 1995.

Hauerwas, Stanley, and Charles Pinches. *Christians Among the Virtues: Theological Conversations with Ancient and Modern Ethics*. Notre Dame: University of Notre Dame Press, 1997.

Hauerwas, Stanley, and David Burrell. "From System to Story: An Alternative Pattern for Rationality in Ethics." In *Why Narrative? Readings in Narrative Theology*, edited by Stanley Hauerwas and L. Gregory Jones, 158–90. Eugene, OR: Wipf & Stock, 1997.

Hauerwas, Stanley, and L. Gregory Jones, editors. *Why Narrative? Readings in Narrative Theology*. Eugene, OR: Wipf & Stock, 1997.

Hauerwas, Stanley, Nancey Murphy, and Mark Nation, editors. *Theology Without Foundations: Religious Practice and the Future of Theological Truth*. Nashville: Abingdon, 1994.

Hauerwas, Stanley, and Charles Pinches. *Christians among the Virtues: Theological Conversations with Ancient and Modern Ethics*. Notre Dame: University of Notre Dame Press, 1997.

Hauerwas, Stanley, and William H. Willimon. *Resident Aliens: Life in the Christian Colony.* Nashville: Abingdon, 1989.

——. *The Truth About God: The Ten Commandments in Christian Life.* Nashville: Abingdon, 1999.

——. *Where Resident Aliens Live.* Nashville: Abingdon, 1996.

Other Works Cited

Albrecht, Gloria H. "Myself and Other Characters: A Feminist Liberationist Critique of Hauerwas's Ethics of Christian Character." In *The Annual of the Society of Christian Ethics* (1992) 97–114.

Alexander, Donald L., editor. *Christian Spirituality: Five Views of Sanctification.* Downers Grove: InterVarsity, 1988.

Aquinas, Thomas. *Summa Theologiae.* 5 vols. Translated by the Fathers of the English Dominican Province. Westminster, MD: Christian Classics, 1948.

——. *On Nature and Grace: Selections from the* Summa Theologica *of Thomas Aquinas.* Translated and edited by A. M. Fairweather. Library of Christian Classics 11. Philadelphia: Westminster, 1954.

Aristotle. *The Nicomachean Ethics.* Translated by Martin Ostwald. Indianapolis: Bobbs-Merrill, 1962.

——. *The Nicomachean Ethics.* Translated by J. E. C. Welldon. Buffalo: Prometheus, 1987.

Barrett, C. K. *The Gospel according to St. John: An Introduction with Commentary and Notes on the Greek Text.* London: SPCK, 1958.

Barth, Karl. *Church Dogmatics.* Vol. 2, *The Doctrine of God*, Part 2. Translated by T. H. L. Parker, Harold Knight, W. B. Johnson, and J. L. M. Haire. Edinburgh: T. & T. Clark, 1957.

——. *Church Dogmatics.* Vol. 4, *The Doctrine of Reconciliation*, Part 1. Translated by G. W. Bromiley. Edited by G. W. Bromiley and T. F. Torrance. Edinburgh: T. & T. Clark, 1956.

——. *Church Dogmatics.* Vol. 4, *The Doctrine of Reconciliation*, Part 2. Translated by G.W. Bromiley. Edited by G. W. Bromiley and T. F. Torrance. Edinburgh: T. & T. Clark, 1958.

——. *Church Dogmatics.* Vol. 4, *The Doctrine of Reconciliation*, Part 3, 2. Translated by G. W. Bromiley. Edited by G. W. Bromiley and T. F. Torrance. Edinburgh: T. & T. Clark, 1962.

——. *Dogmatics in Outline.* Translated by G. T. Thomson. New York: Harper and Row, 1959.

——. *The Christian Life: Lecture Fragments.* Translated by Geoffrey Bromiley. Grand Rapids: Eerdmans, 1981.

——. *The Humanity of God.* Richmond: John Knox, 1960.

——. "The Strange New World within the Bible." In *The Word of God and the Word of Man*, translated by Douglas Horton, 28–50. Harper Torchbooks. New York: Harper, 1957.

——. *The Theology of Schleiermacher.* Edited by Dietrich Ritschl. Translated by Geoffrey Bromiley. Grand Rapids: Eerdmans, 1982.

————. *Theology and Church: Shorter Writings, 1920–1928*. Translated by Louise Smith. New York: Harper and Row, 1962.

Basil, Saint. *On the Holy Spirit*. Translated with an introduction by David Anderson. Crestwood: St. Vladimir's Seminary Press, 1980.

Bauer, Walter, et al., editors. *A Greek English Lexicon of the New Testament*. 2nd edition. Chicago: University of Chicago Press, 1979.

Beasley-Murray, George R. *John*. Word Biblical Themes. Dallas: Word, 1989.

Beem, Christopher. "American Liberalism and the Christian Church: Stanley Hauerwas vs. Martin Luther King Jr." *Journal of Religious Ethics* 23 (1995) 119–33.

Berkhof, Hendrikus. *The Doctrine of the Holy Spirit*. Annie Kinkead Warfield Lectures, 1963–1964. Richmond: John Knox, 1964.

Bloesch, Donald G. *The Holy Spirit: Works and Gifts*. Downers Grove: InterVarsity, 2000.

Brennan, Geoffrey. "Stanley Hauerwas and the Critique of Secular Liberalism: A Report on St. Mark's Seminar." *St. Mark's Review* 141 (1990) 2–4.

Bruce, F. F. *The Epistle to the Galatians: A Commentary on the Greek Text*. NIGTC. Grand Rapids: Eerdmans, 1982.

Buckley, James J. "A Field of Living Fire: Karl Barth on the Spirit and the Church." *Modern Theology* 10 (1994) 81–102.

Buckley, Michael J. *At the Origins of Modern Atheism*. New Haven: Yale University Press, 1987.

Bultmann, Rudolph. *Theology of the New Testament*. Volume 2. Translated by Kendrick Grobel. New York: Scribner's, 1955.

Calvin, John. *Institutes of the Christian Religion*. Edited by John T. McNeill. Translated by Ford Lewis Battles. 2 vols. Philadelphia: Westminster, 1960.

Carlson, Arnold E. "Luther and the Doctrine of the Holy Spirit." *Lutheran Quarterly* 11 (1959) 135–46.

Carson, D. A. *Becoming Conversant with the Emergent Church: Understanding a Movement and Its Implications*. Grand Rapids: Zondervan, 2005.

Clayton, Philip. "In Whom We Have Our Being: Philosophical Resources for the Doctrine of the Spirit." In *Advents of the Spirit: Introduction to the Current Study of Pneumatology*, edited by Bradford Hinze, and D. Lyle Dabney, 171–205. Marquette Studies in Theology 30. Milwaukee: Marquette University Press, 2001.

Comstock, Gary. "Truth or Meaning: Ricoeur versus Frei on Biblical Narrative." *The Journal of Religion* 66 (1986) 117–40.

Dabney, D. Lyle. *Die Kenosis des Geistes: Kontinuität zwischen Shöpfung und Erlösung im Werk des Heiligen Geistes*. Neukirchen-Vluyn: Neukirchener Verlag, 1997.

————. "Starting with the Spirit: Why the Last Should Now be First." In *Starting with the Spirit*, edited by Gordon Preece and Stephen Pickard, 3–27. Task of Theology Today II Series. Adelaide, Australia: Australian Theological Forum, 2001.

Dempf, Alois. *Sacrum Imperium*. 2nd edition. Darmstadt: Wissenschaftliche Buchgemeinschaft, 1954.

Descartes, René. *Meditations on First Philosophy*. 3rd edition. Translated by Donald A. Cress. Indianapolis: Hackett, 1993.

Dickason, Fred. *Demon Possession and the Christian: A New Perspective*. Chicago: Moody, 1987.

Dulles, Avery. "The Spiritual Community of Man: The Church according to Saint Thomas." In *Calgary Aquinas Studies*, edited by Anthony Parel, 125–53. Toronto: Pontifical Institute of Mediaeval Studies, 1978.

Dunn, James D. G. *The Epistles to the Colossians and to Philemon: A Commentary on the Greek Text.* NIGTC. Grand Rapids: Eerdmans, 1996.

Ellingworth, Paul. *The Epistle to the Hebrews: A Commentary on the Greek Text.* NIGTC. Grand Rapids: Eerdmans, 1993.

Erickson, Millard J. *Christian Theology.* Grand Rapids: Baker, 1983.

Fee, Gordon D. *The First Epistle to the Corinthians.* NICNT. Grand Rapids: Eerdmans, 1987.

Femiano, S. "The Holy Spirit in Luther's Commentary on Galatians." *Canadian Journal of Theology* 8 (1962) 43–48.

Frei, Hans. "An Afterword: Eberhard Busch's Biography of Karl Barth." In *Karl Barth in Re-View,* edited by Martin Rumscheidt, 95–116. Pittsburgh Theological Monograph Series. Pittsburgh: Pickwick, 1981.

Fung, Ronald Y. K. *The Epistle to the Galatians.* NICNT. Grand Rapids: Eermans, 1988.

Gee, Donald. "The Gifts and Fruit of the Spirit." *Paraclete* 21 (1987) 21–26.

George, A. Raymond. "The Holy Spirit Transforms the Human Community into the Kingdom of God." *One in Christ* 16 (1980) 214–24.

Gerber, Leslie E. "The Virtuous Terrorist: Stanley Hauerwas and *The Crying Game.*" *Cross Currents* 43 (1993) 230–34.

Grosheide, F. W. *A Commentary on the First Epistle to the Corinthians.* NICNT. Grand Rapids: Eerdmans, 1953.

Gustafson, James M. "A Response to Critics." *Journal of Religious Ethics* 13 (1985) 185–209.

———. *Ethics from a Theocentric Perspective.* Vol. 1, *Theology and Ethics.* Chicago: University of Chicago Press, 1981.

———. "The Sectarian Temptation: Reflection on Theology, the Church, and the University." *Proceedings of Catholic Theological Society* 40 (1985) 83–94.

Hagen, Kenneth. "Luther's Doctrine of the Two Kingdoms." *Reformation and Revival Journal* 7 (1998) 103–27.

Hartt, Julian. "Theological Investments in Story: Some Comments on Recent Developments and Some Proposals." *JAAR* 52 (1984) 117–30.

———. "Reply to Crites and Hauerwas." *JAAR* 52 (1984) 149–56.

Healy, Nicholas. "The Logic of Karl Barth's Ecclesiology: Analysis, Assessment, and Proposed Modifications." *MT* 10 (1994) 253–70.

Heide, Gale. "The Nascent Noeticism of Narrative Theology: An Examination of the Relationship between Narrative and Metaphysics in Nicholas Lash." *Modern Theology* 12 (1996 459–81.

———. *This Is My Father's World.* Eugene, OR: Wipf & Stock, 1998.

———. *Timeless Truth in the Hands of History: A Short History of System in Theology.* Eugene, OR: Pickwick, forthcoming in 2009.

Henry, Carl F. H. *God, Revelation and Authority.* Vol. 5, *God Who Stands and Stays.* Waco: Word, 1983.

———. "Has the West a Future?" *Viewpoint* 3 (1999) 12–16.

Hinze, Bradford E. "Releasing the Power of the Spirit in a Trinitarian Theology." In *Advents of the Spirit: An Introduction to the Current Study of Pneumatology*, edited by Bradford E. Hinze and D. Lyle Dabney, 345–80. Marquette Studies in Theology 30. Milwaukee: Marquette University Press, 2001.

Hodge, Charles. *Systematic Theology*. Vol. 1. New York: Scribner, 1872.

Hoekema, Anthony A. *Created in God's Image*. Grand Rapids: Eerdmans, 1986.

Holland, Scott. "Mennonites on Hauerwas; Hauerwas on Mennonites." *Conrad Grebel Review* 13 (1995) 142–51.

―――. "The Problems and Prospects of a 'Sectarian Ethic': A Critique of the Hauerwas Reading of the Jesus Story." *Conrad Grebel Review* 10 (1992) 157–68.

Holmer, Paul L. "Christianity and the Truth." *LQ* 9 (1957) 33–41.

―――. *Making Christian Sense*. Spirituality and the Christian Life. Philadelphia: Westminster, 1984.

―――. *Theology and the Scientific Study of Religion*. Minneapolis: T. S. Denison, 1961.

Horton, Stanley M. "The Pentecostal Perspective." In *Five Views on Sanctification*, 103–35. Counterpoints. Grand Rapids: Academie, 1987.

Howe, Leroy T. "Holy Spirit and Holy Church." *Saint Luke's Journal of Theology* 22 (1978) 43–57.

Huebner, Harry. "Within the Limits of Story Alone?" *Conrad Grebel Review* 13 (1995) 161.

Hume, David. *An Enquiry Concerning Human Understanding and Other Essays*. Edited by Ernest C. Mossner. New York: Washington Square, 1963.

Hunsinger, George. *Disruptive Grace: Studies in the Theology of Karl Barth*. Grand Rapids: Eerdmans, 2000.

Hütter, Reinhard. *Evangelische Ethic als Kirchliches Zeugnis: Interpretation zu Schlusselfragen theologischer Ethik in der Gegenwart*. Erlander, Germany: Neukerchener, 1993.

―――. *Suffering Divine Things: Theology as Church Practice*. Grand Rapids: Eerdmans, 1997.

―――. "The Church as Public: Dogma, Practice and the Holy Spirit." *Pro Ecclesia* 3 (1994) 334–61.

Janz, Denis R. *Luther and Late Medieval Thomism: A Study in Theological Anthropology*. Waterloo: Wilfrid Laurier University Press, 1983.

Jenson, Robert W. "Hauerwas Examined." Review of *After Christendom?*, by Stanley Hauerwas. *First Things* 25 (1992) 49–51.

―――. "The Hauerwas Project." *Modern Theology* 8 (1992) 285–95.

―――. "You Wonder Where the Spirit Went." *Pro Ecclesia* 2 (1993) 296–304.

Kant, Immanuel. *Foundations of the Metaphysics of Morals*. Translated with an introduction by Lewis White Beck. 2nd edition. New York: Macmillan, 1959.

―――. *Religion within the Limits of Reason Alone*. Translated with an introduction by Theodore M. Greene and Hoyt H. Hudson. New York: Harper, 1960.

―――. "What Is Enlightenment?" In *Foundations of the Metaphysics of Morals*, translated with an introduction by Lewis White Beck, 85–92. 2nd edition. New York: Macmillan, 1959.

Keck, David. *Forgetting Whose We Are: Alzheimer's Disease and the Love of God*. Nashville: Abingdon, 1996.

Keen, Craig. "The Human Person as Intercessory Prayer." In *Embodied Holiness: Toward a Corporate Theology of Spiritual Growth*, edited by Samuel M. Powell and Michael E. Lodahl, 39–61. Downers Grove: InterVarsity, 1999.

Kerr, Fergus. *Theology after Wittgenstein.* Oxford: Blackwell, 1986.

King, Rachel Hadley. *The Omission of the Holy Spirit from Reinhold Niebuhr's Theology.* New York: Philosophical Library, 1964.

Kirkham, Richard L. *Theories of Truth: A Critical Introduction.* Cambridge: MIT Press, 1992.

Kleutgen, Joseph. *Institutiones theologica.* 1 Ratisbon, 1881.

Kohlberg, Lawrence. "Education for Justice: A Modern Statement of the Platonic View." In *Moral Education: Five Lectures*, by James M. Gustafson et al., with an introduction by Nancy F. Sizer and Theodore R. Sizer, 57–83. Cambridge, MA: Harvard University Press, 1970.

Kroeker, P. Travis. "The Peaceable Creation: Hauerwas and the Mennonites." *Conrad Grebel Review* 13 (1995) 136–41.

Ladd, George Eldon. *A Theology of the New Testament.* Grand Rapids: Eerdmans, 1974.

Lammers, Stephen E. "On Stanley Hauerwas: Theology, Medical Ethics, and the Church." *Second Opinion* 8 (1988) 128–42.

Lane, William L. *The Gospel of Mark.* NICNT. Grand Rapids: Eerdmans, 1975.

Lash, Nicholas. "Among Strangers and Friends: Thinking of God in Our Current Confusion." In *Finding God in All Things: Essays in Honor of Michael J. Buckley*, edited by Michael J. Himes and Stephen J. Pope, 53–67. New York: Crossroad, 1996.

——. *The Beginning and the End of 'Religion'.* Teape Lectures. Cambridge: Cambridge University Press, 1996.

——. *Believing Three Ways in One God: A Reading of the Apostles' Creed.* Notre Dame: University of Notre Dame Press, 1993.

——. *Theology on the Way to Emmaus.* London: SCM, 1986.

Lauritzen, Paul. "Is Narrative Really a Panacea? The Use of 'Narrative' in the Work of Metz and Hauerwas." *Journal of Religion* 67 (1987) 322–39.

Lindbeck, George. *The Nature of Doctrine.* Philadelphia: Westminster, 1984.

Lindstrom, Harold. *Wesley and Sanctification.* Nashville: Abingdon, 1946.

Lortz, Joseph. *Die Reformation in Deutschland.* Two volumes. 4th edition. Freiburg: Herder, 1962.

Louden, Robert B. *Kant's Impure Ethics: From Rational Beings to Human Beings.* New York: Oxford University Press, 2000.

Löwith, Karl. "History and Christianity." In *Reinhold Niebuhr: His Religious, Social, and Political Thought*, edited by Charles Kegley and Robert Bretall, 281–90. New York: Macmillan, 1956.

Luther, Martin. *D. Martin Luther's Werke: Kritische Gesamtausgabe.* Volume 2. Weimar, 1883.

——. "Disputation against Scholastic Theology." In *Martin Luther's Basic Theological Writings*, edited by Timothy F. Lull, 13–20. Minneapolis: Fortress, 1989.

——. *Lectures on Galatians, Chapters 1–6 (1519).* Luther's Works 27:151–410. Edited by Jaroslav Pelikan. St. Louis: Concordia, 1964.

————. *Lectures on Galatians, Chapters 5–6 (1535)*. Luther's Works 27:1–150. Edited by Jaroslav Pelikan. St. Louis: Concordia, 1964.

————. *Lectures on Genesis Chapters 15–20*. Luther's Works 3. Translated by George V. Schick. Edited by Jaroslav Pelikan. St. Louis: Concordia, 1968.

————. *Lectures on Romans*. Luther's Works 25. Translated by Jacob A. O. Preus. Edited by Jaroslav Pelikan. St. Louis: Concordia, 1972.

————. *Lectures on Titus*. Luther's Works 29:4–90. Edited by Jaroslav Pelikan. St. Louis: Concordia, 1968.

————. *Lectures on Zechariah (1527)*. Luther's Works 20. Translated by Walther M. Miller. Edited by Jaroslav Pelikan. St. Louis: Concordia, 1973.

————. *Luther's Works*. Edited by Jaroslav Pelikan, H. T. Lehmann, et al. 55 vols. St. Louis: Concordia, 1955–1986.

————. *Sermons on the Gospel of St. John. Luther's Works*, Vol. 24. Edited by Jarolsav Pelikan. St. Louis: Concordia, 1961.

————. "The Bondage of the Will." In *Martin Luther's Basic Theological Writings*, edited by Timothy F. Lull, 165–96. Minneapolis: Fortress, 1989.

————. "The Freedom of a Christian." In *Martin Luther's Basic Theological Writings*, edited by Timothy F. Lull, 386–411. Minneapolis: Fortress, 1989.

————. "To the Councilman of All Cities in Germany that They Establish and Maintain Christian Schools." In *Martin Luther's Basic Theological Writings*, edited by Timothy F. Lull, 460–78. Minneapolis: Fortress, 1989.

MacIntyre, Alasdair C. *After Virtue: A Study in Moral Theory*. 2nd edition. Notre Dame: University of Notre Dame Press, 1984.

————. *First Principles, Final Ends and Contemporary Philosophical Issues*. Aquinas Lecture: 1990. Milwaukee: Marquette University Press, 1990.

————. *Whose Justice? Which Rationality?* Notre Dame: University of Notre Dame Press, 1988.

Mangina, Joseph. "Bearing the Marks of Jesus: The Church in the Economy of Salvation in Barth and Hauerwas." *SJT* 52 (1999) 269–305.

Marshall, Bruce. *Trinity and Truth*. Cambridge Studies in Christian Doctrine 3. Cambridge: Cambridge University Press, 2000.

Martin, Dale B. *The Corinthian Body*. New Haven: Yale University Press, 1995.

McClendon, James William, Jr. *Doctrine*. Vol. 2, *Systematic Theology*. Nashville: Abingdon, 1994.

McClendon, James William, Jr., and James M. Smith. *Convictions: Defusing Religious Relativism*. Rev. edition. Valley Forge: Trinity, 1994.

McDonnell, Killian. "Communion, Ecclesiology, and Baptism in the Spirit: Tertullian and the Early Church." *TS* 49 (1988) 671–93.

McLaren, Brian D. *A New Kind of Christian: A Tale of Two Friends on a Spiritual Journey*. San Francisco: Jossey-Bass, 2001.

McQuilkin, J. Robertson. "The Keswick Perspective." In *Five Views on Sanctification* , 149–83. Counterpoints. Grand Rapids: Academie, 1987.

Michaelis, Wilhelm. "mimeomai, mimhthj, summimhthj." *TDNT* 4: 659–74. Edited by Gerhard Kittel. Grand Rapids: Eerdmans, 1967.

Milbank, John. "Enclaves, or Where Is the Church?" *New Blackfriars* 73 (1992) 341–52.

Moltmann, Jürgen. *The Spirit of Life: A Universal Affirmation.* Translated by Margaret Kohl. London: SCM, 1992.

Morris, Leon. *The Gospel according to John.* Revised edition. NICNT. Grand Rapids: Eerdmans, 1995.

Mott, Stephen Charles. *Biblical Ethics and Social Change.* New York: Oxford University Press, 1982.

Mühlen, Heribert *Una Mystica Persona: Die Kirche als das Mysterium der Heilsgeschichtlichen Identität des Heiligen Geistes in Christus und den Christen: Eine Person in Vielen Personen.* 3rd edition. Munich: Ferdinand Schöningh, 1968.

Muray, Leslie. "Confessional Postmodernism and the Process-Relational Vision." *Process Studies* 18 (1989) 83–94.

Murdoch, Iris. "The Sublime and the Good." *Chicago Review* 13 (1959) 42–55.

Nation, Mark Thiessen, and Samuel Wells. *Faithfulness and Fortitude: In Conversation with the Theological Ethics of Stanley Hauerwas.* Edinburgh: T. & T. Clark, 2000.

Nolland, John. *Luke 1—9:20.* WBC. Dallas: Word, 1989.

Novak, David. *The Election of Israel: The Idea of the Chosen People.* Cambridge: Cambridge University Press, 1995.

Oberman, Heiko A. *Luther: Man between God and the Devil.* Translated by Eileen Walliser-Schwarzbart. New York: Image, 1992.

Olson, Roger. "Wolfhart Pannenberg's Doctrine of the Trinity." *SJT* 43 (1990) 175–206.

O'Neill, J. C. "The Holy Spirit and the Human Spirit in Galatians: Galatians 5:17." *ETL* 71 (1995) 107–20.

Pannenberg, Wolfhart. *An Introduction to Systematic Theology.* Grand Rapids: Eerdmans, 1991.

————. *Anthropology in Theological Perspective.* Translated by Matthew J. O'Connell. Philadelphia: Westminster, 1985.

————. *Jesus, God and Man.* Translated by Lewis L. Wilkins and Duane A. Priebe. 2nd edition. Philadelphia: Westminster, 1968.

————. *Systematic Theology.* Volume 1. Translated by Geoffrey Bromiley. Grand Rapids: Eerdmans, 1991.

————. *Systematic Theology.* Volume 3. Translated by Geoffrey W. Bromiley. Grand Rapids: Eerdmans, 1998.

Placher, William. *The Domestication of Transcendence: How Modern Thinking about God Went Wrong.* Louisville: Westminster John Knox, 1996.

Preece, Gordon, and Stephen Pickard, editors. *Starting with the Spirit.* Task of Theology Today. Adelaide, Australia: Australian Theological Forum, 2001.

Prenter, Regin. *Spiritus Creator.* Translated by John M. Jensen. Philadelphia: Muhlenberg, 1953. Reprint, Eugene, OR: Wipf & Stock, 2001.

Prior, A. N. "Correspondence Theory of Truth." In *Encyclopedia of Philosophy,* 2:223–32. New York: Macmillan, 1967.

Quinn, Philip "Is Athens Revived Jerusalem Denied?" *AsTJ* 45 (1990) 49–57.

Quirk, Michael "Beyond Sectarianism?" *ThTo* 44 (1987). Pages 78-86.

Ramsey, Paul. *Basic Christian Ethics.* New York: Scribner's, 1950.

Rasmusson, Arne. *The Church as Polis: From Political Theology to Theological Politics as Exemplified by Jürgen Moltmann and Stanley Hauerwas.* Notre Dame: University of Notre Dame Press, 1995.

Ridderbos, Herman. *Paul: An Outline of His Theology.* Translated by John Richard De Witt. Grand Rapids: Eerdmans, 1975.

Roberts, Tyler T. "Theology and the Ascetic Imperative: Narrative and Renunciation in Taylor and Hauerwas." *MT* 9 (1993) 181–200.

Robertson, Archibald, and Alfred Plummer. *A Critical and Exegetical Commentary on the First Epistle of St. Paul to the Corinthians.* ICC. Edinburgh: T. & T. Clark, 1911.

Robertson, A. T. *Word Pictures in the New Testament.* Volume 5. Nashville: Broadman, 1

Runia, Klaas. "The Holy Spirit and the Church." *Evangelical Review of Theology* 9 (1985) 304–22.

Saucy, Mark. "Evangelicals, Catholics, and Orthodox Together: Is the Church the Extension of the Incarnation?" *JETS* 43 (2000)193–212.

Sauter, Gerhard. "Shifts in Karl Barth's Thought: The Current Debate between Right- and Left- Wing Barthians." Unpublished paper presented at the Barth symposium. State University of New York–Buffalo, 1986.

Schleiermacher, Friedrich. *The Christian Faith.* Translated by H. R. Mackintosh and J. S. Stewart. Edinburgh: T. & T. Clark, 1928.

Schmoller, Otto. *The Epistle of Paul to the Galatians.* Lange's Commentary on the Holy Scriptures 5 (no. 1) of the New Testament. Translated by C. C. Starbuck. Grand Rapids: Zondervan, 1960.

Scofield, C. I. "Personal Relationships and the Work of the Indwelling Spirit." *Fundamentalist Journal* 2 (1983) 40–41, 51.

Smith, R. Scott. *Truth and the New Kind of Christian.* Wheaton: Crossway, 2005.

Smith, Timothy L. "Thomas Aquinas's *De Deo*: Setting the Record Straight on His Theological Method." *Sapientia* 53 (1998) 119–54.

Song, Robert. *Christianity and Liberal Society.* Oxford Studies in Theological Ethics. Oxford: Clarendon, 1997.

Spinoza, Benedict. *A Theologico-Political Treatise.* Translated by R. H. M. Elwes. New York: Dover, 1951.

Steinmetz, David C. *Luther in Context.* Bloomington: Indiana University Press, 1986.

Stiver, Dan R. *The Philosophy of Religious Language: Sign, Symbol and Story.* Cambridge, MA: Blackwell, 1996.

Stout, Jeffery. *The Flight from Authority: Religion, Morality, and the Quest for Autonomy.* Revisions. Notre Dame: Notre Dame University Press, 1981.

Sykes, Stephen. *The Identity of Christianity: Theologians and the Essence of Christianity from Schleiermacher to Barth.* Philadelphia: Fortress, 1984.

Tasker, R. V. G. *The Gospel according to St. John.* TNTC. Grand Rapids: Eerdmans, 1992.

Tenney, Merrill. *John: The Gospel of Belief: An Analytic Study of the Text.* Grand Rapids: Eerdmans, 1976.

Tillich, Paul. *Systematic Theology.* Volume 3, *Life and the Spirit: History and the Kingdom of God.* London: Nisbet, 1964.

Tracy, David. *On Naming the Present: Reflections on God, Hermeneutics, and Church.* Concilium series. Maryknoll: Orbis, 1994.

Webster, John. *Barth's Ethics of Reconciliation.* Cambridge: Cambridge University Press, 1995.

Weisheipl, James A. *Friar Thomas D'Aquino: His Life, Thought and Works*, with corrigenda and addenda. Washington DC: Catholic University of America Press, 1983.

Wells, Samuel. *Transforming Fate into Destiny: The Theological Ethics of Stanley Hauerwas.* Reprint, Eugene, OR: Cascade, 1998.

Weston, William J. "The Invisible Church: The Missing Element in Hauerwas' *A Community of Character.*" *JRelS* 13 (1987) 95–105.

Whitmore, Todd D. "Beyond Liberalism and Communitarianism in Christian Ethics: A Critique of Stanley Hauerwas." In *The Annual of the Society of Christian Ethics.* Washington, DC: Georgetown University Press, 1989. Pages 207-25.

Williams, Bernard. "Rationalism," In *Encyclopedia of Philosophy*, 7:69–75. New York: Macmillan, 1967.

Wilson, Jonathan R. "From Theology of Culture to Theological Ethics: The Hartt-Hauerwas Connection." *Journal of Religious Ethics* 23 (1995) 149–64.

Winn, Albert Curry. "The Holy Spirit and the Christian Life." *Int* 33 (1979) 47–57.

Winward, Stephen F. *Fruit of the Spirit.* Grand Rapids: Eerdmans, 1981.

Wittgenstein, Ludwig. *Philosophical Investigations.* New York: Macmillan, 1953.

Wood, A. Skevington. "Spirit and Spirituality in Luther." *EvQ* 61 (1989) 311–33.

Wood, Allen. *Kant's Ethical Thought.* Modern European Philosophy. Cambridge: Cambridge University Press, 1999.

Wright, John H. "The Church: Community of the Holy Spirit." *TS* 48 (1987) 25–44.

Yoder, John Howard. *Body Politics: Five Practices of the Christian Community before the Watching World.* Nashville: Discipleship Resources, 1992.

———. *The Priestly Kingdom: Social Ethics as Gospel.* Notre Dame: University of Notre Dame Press, 1984.

Zizioulas, John D. *Being as Communion: Studies in Personhood and the Church.* Crestwood, NY: St. Vladimir's Seminary Press, 1985.

Other Works Consulted

Audi, Robert. *Action, Intention, and Reason.* Ithaca: Cornell University Press, 1993.

Barth, Karl. *Evangelical Theology.* Grand Rapids: Eerdmans, 1963.

Bernstein, Richard. *Beyond Objectivism and Relativism.* Philadelphia: University of Pennsylvania Press, 1991.

Dulles, Avery. *Models of Revelation.* Maryknoll: Orbis, 1983.

———. *The Craft of Theology: From Symbol to System.* New York: Crossroad, 1992.

Fackre, Gabriel. *The Christian Story.* 3d edition. Grand Rapids: Eerdmans, 1996.

Fowl, Stephen, E. and L. Gregory Jones, *Reading in Communion.* Grand Rapids: Eerdmans, 1991.

Frei, Hans. *Types of Christian Theology.* Edited by George Hunsinger and William C. Placher. New Haven: Yale University Press, 1992.

Harder, Lydia. "Dialogue with Hauerwas." *The Conrad Grebel Review.* 13 (1995) 152–56.

Harris, James F. *Against Relativism: A Philosophical Defense of Method*. LaSalle, IL: Open Court, 1992.

Hinze, Bradford E. *Narrating History, Developing Doctrine*. Atlanta: Scholars, 1993.

Kasper, Walter. *The God of Jesus Christ*. Translated by Matthew J. O'Connell New York: Crossroad, 1984.

Kaufman, Gordon. *The Theological Imagination: Constructing the Concept of God*. Philadelphia: Westminster, 1981.

Lewis, Paul. "Polanyian Reflections on Embodiment, the Human Genome Initiative and Theological Anthropology." *Tradition and Discovery* 22 (1996–97) 5–14.

Lints, Richard. "The Postpositivist Choice: Tracy or Lindbeck?" *JAAR* 56 (1993) 655–77.

Lonergan, Bernard, J. *Method in Theology*. Toronto: University of Toronto Press, 1971.

Louth, Andrew. *Discerning the Mystery: An Essay on the Nature of Theology*. Oxford: Clarendon, 1983.

MacIntyre, Alasdair C. *Three Rival Versions of Moral Enquiry: Encyclopaedia, Genealogy, and Tradition*. Gifford Lectures 1998. Notre Dame: University of Notre Dame Press, 1990.

McGrath, Alister E. *The Genesis of Doctrine: A Study in the Foundations of Doctrinal Criticism*. Cambridge: Blackwell, 1990.

———. *A Passion for Truth: The Intellectual Coherence of Evangelicalism*. Downers Grove: InterVarsity, 1996.

———. "The End of Enlightenment: Post-Modern or Post-Secular?" In *The Debate on Modernity*, edited by Claude Geffre and Jean-Pierre Jossua, 39–48. London: SCM, 1992. Milbank, John. *Theology and Social Theory*. Signposts in Theology. Cambridge, MA: Blackwell, 1991.

Moltmann, Jürgen. *The Trinity and the Kingdom: The Doctrine of God*. Translated by Margaret Kohl. San Francisco: Harper and Row, 1981.

Oden, Thomas C. *Systematic Theology*. Volume 3, *Life in the Spirit*. San Francisco: HarperSanFrancisco, 1992.

Ollenberger, Ben C. "Stanley Hauerwas and Mennonites: Insulated Entities?" *Conrad Grebel Review* 13 (1995) 162–65.

Pannenberg, Wolfhart. *Theology and the Philosophy of Science*. Translated by Francis McDonagh. Philadelphia: Westminster, 1976.

Patterson, Robert W. "To Tango or Tangle?" *Christianity Today* (January 6, 1997) 50–52. Phillips, Timothy R., and Dennis L. Okholm, editors. *The Nature of Confession: Evangelicals and Postliberals in Conversation*. Downers Grove: InterVarsity, 1996.

Placher, William C. "Postliberal Theology." In *The Modern Theologians: An Introduction to Theology in the Twentieth Century*, edited by David Ford, 2:115–28. New York: Blackwell, 1989.

Putnam, Hilary. *The Many Faces of Realism*. Paul Carus lectures: 16th ser. LaSalle, IL: Open Court, 1987.

Scalise, Charles J. *From Scripture to Theology: A Canonical Journey into Hermeneutics*. Downers Grove: InterVarsity, 1996.

Stell, Stephen L. "Hermeneutics in Theology and the Theology of Hermeneutics." *JAAR* 56 (1993) 679–703.

Thieman, Ronald. *Revelation and Theology: The Gospel as Narrated Promise*. Notre Dame: University of Notre Dame Press, 1985.

Van Huyssteen, Wentzel. *Theology and the Justification of Faith: Constructing Theories in Systematic Theology*. Grand Rapids: Eerdmans, 1989.

Yoder, John Howard. *The Politics of Jesus*. Grand Rapids: Eerdmans, 1972.

Name Index

Subject Index

Academic xv, 1, 18, 24, 30, 34, 37,
    53n., 73, 81, 93, 207
ad hoc xxii, 17, 43, 52
America 24, 31, 32n., 35n., 37n., 52,
    78n., 99, 105, 162n., 166n.,
    237n.
Anthropodicy65n., 86n.
anthropology xivn., xvii–xviii, xx,
    xxv, 4–5, 8–9, 11, 13, 28,
    41n., 46–47, 53n., 54, 56–58,
    67–69, 71n., 76, 79, 82, 91n.,
    101n., 110, 113, 125n., 137,
    138n., 142n., 143, 145–46,
    148, 150, 157, 182n., 185,
    188, 193, 205, 209n., 225, 257
anti–foundationalist (-ism) 3n., 49,
    125, 185
apprentice (-ship) xxviii, 76, 98,
    102, 109–10, 114, 118,
    150, 201–02, 205–08, 215,
    219–21, 227–28, 230, 269,
    274–77
Arminian 137n., 156n., 157n.
Autonomy xxiii, 4–5, 56, 58–60,
    63–65, 86, 156, 187, 202,
    251n., 256, 260
Baptism 1, 46n., 107, 124, 134,
    140n., 155n., 215n., 226, 230,
    245, 254, 271,
Barmen Declaration 82
bifurcation 90, 159
Catholic (Roman Catholic) 20n.,
    31, 61n., 100, 128n., 147,
    155n., 156n., 157n., 167–68,
    186n., 245, 248n., 251–52,
    253, 265,

Chiliast 247–48
Christology 7–8, 11, 38n., 87, 88n.,
    146, 153, 158, 228, 237
Coherence xix, xxiii–xxiv, 7, 24,
    44–46, 74, 110, 112,
Conscience 168, 190, 192, 197n.,
    200n., 259, 265
Corporate 108n., 136, 162n., 174,
    176, 178, 181n., 183, 189,
    193, 195–96, 198, 204, 207,
    232, 244–45, 276
correspondence theory of truth
    xiii–xiv, xix, xxiii, 5n., 24,
    110, 112, 113n., 124n.,
deconstruct 15n., 17, 23, 73
democratic 21, 33n., 56, 59, 64, 67,
    101n., 102, 105, 166, 201n.,
    225
demon 66, 172–74, 182, 250,
    259–60
Devil 246, 250, 254, 260–61, 273
Diet of Worms 256
disciple (-ship) xviii, 11n., 62, 77,
    87, 102, 106, 109, 175, 184,
    201, 210–11, 215, 220–21,
    271, 277–78
dualism 68, 181, 191
eschatology 11, 82–85, 87, 146n.,
    184
eschaton xxi, xxvi, 41, 70, 135n.,
    146n., 184n., 189, 221
Emergent (church) xvii–xviii, xix,
    91,
Enthusiast 267

Scripture Index